Philosophy, Literature, and the Dissolution of the Subject

STUDIES IN SOCIAL SCIENCES, PHILOSOPHY AND HISTORY OF IDEAS

Edited by Andrzej Rychard

Advisory Board

Joanna Kurczewska,
Institute of Philosophy and Sociology, Polish Academy of Sciences
Henryk Domański,
Institute of Philosophy and Sociology, Polish Academy of Sciences
Szymon Wróbel,
Artes Liberales College, University of Warsaw

VOLUME 6

Zeynep Talay-Turner

Philosophy, Literature, and the Dissolution of the Subject

Nietzsche, Musil, Atay

Bibliographic Information published by the Deutsche Nationalbibliothek
The Deutsche Nationalbibliothek lists this publication in
the Deutsche Nationalbibliografie; detailed bibliographic data is
available in the internet at http://dnb.d-nb.de.

This Publication was financially supported
by the Central European Educational Foundation, Warsaw.

Library of Congress Cataloging-in-Publication Data
Talay-Turner, Zeynep, 1979- author.
 Philosophy, literature, and the dissolution of the subject : Nietzsche, Musil, Atay / Zeynep Talay-Turner.
   pages cm -- (Studies in social sciences, philosophy and history of ideas, ISSN 2196-0151 ; volume 6)
 Includes bibliographical references and index.
 ISBN 978-3-631-65168-1 (print) -- ISBN 978-3-653-04501-7 (e-book) 1. Nietzsche, Friedrich Wilhelm, 1844-1900. 2. Self (Philosophy) 3. Literature--Philosophy. 4. Ethics. 5. Musil, Robert, 1880-1942--Criticism and interpretation. 6. Atay, Oguz--Criticism and interpretation. I. Title.
 B3317.T35 2014
 126--dc23
                            2014033099

ISSN 2196-0151
ISBN 978-3-631-65168-1 (Print)
E-ISBN 978-3-653-04501-7 (E-Book)
DOI 10.3726/ 978-3-653-04501-7

© Peter Lang GmbH
Internationaler Verlag der Wissenschaften
Frankfurt am Main 2014
All rights reserved.

Peter Lang Edition is an Imprint of Peter Lang GmbH.
Peter Lang – Frankfurt am Main · Bern · Bruxelles · New York ·
Oxford · Warszawa · Wien

All parts of this publication are protected by copyright. Any
utilization outside the strict limits of the copyright law, without
the permission of the publisher, is forbidden and liable to
prosecution. This applies in particular to reproductions,
translations, microfilming, and storage and processing in
electronic retrieval systems.

This publication has been peer reviewed.

www.peterlang.com

Acknowledgements

This book would not have been possible without the help and support of several people who contributed in the writing process.

First of all I am heartily grateful to Agata Bielik-Robson for introducing me to a new understanding of philosophy in general and Nietzsche, Musil and Blumenberg in particular.

I also would like to thank my parents Yusuf and Gulden Talay and my brother Goker Talay who always supported me wherever I was.

Finally Charles Turner: thank you for your incredible support and patience. I would not have been able to complete this book without your support.

Table of Contents

Introduction 9

Chapter I: Nietzsche on the Self and Morality 25
I.i.   Introduction 25
I.ii. The Self and the Christian Morality 27
I.iii. Nietzsche's Critique of Kant 32
I.iv. Nietzsche and Spinoza: Free will and Freedom 45
I.v.   Conclusion 59

Chapter II: Nietzsche's Remedy 61
II.i.   Introduction 61
II.ii. Nietzsche and Stoicism; The Care of the Self; A Modest Egoism 61
II.iii. The Sovereign Individual; *Amor Fati*; Eternal Return 70
II.iv. Conclusion 79

Chapter III: Intermediate Reflections; Philosophy and Literature 81

Chapter IV: Musil on Epistemology, Culture and the Self 93
IV.i.   Introduction 93
IV.ii. The Reception of Nietzsche in the German-speaking
        World and *Lebensphilosophie* 95
IV.iii. The Epistemological Background: Cause-effect 99
IV.iv. The Critique of Rationality; The Sense of Possibility 111
IV.v.   Culture and the Individual 118
IV.vi. Conclusion 131

Chapter V: Musil on Ethics 133
V.i.   Introduction 133
V.ii. Subjectivity, Free Will, Responsibility 133
V.iii. Essayism 139
V.iv. Ulrich's Company of Women 151
V.v.   'The Other Condition' and Ethics 153
V.vi. Conclusion: Ulrich Returns to the Parallel Campaign 168

Chapter VI: Intermediate Reflections II:
    Metaphor, Irony and Simile 171

Chapter VII: Atay on History and Authority.. 181
VII.i. Introduction 181
VII.ii. History: 'Yesterday, Today, Tomorrow' 184
VII.iii. 'Words, words, words': Excess of Words 195
VII.iv. Fathers and Sons: Authority and Bureaucracy 203
VII.v. Comedy, Irony and the Subject 208
VII.vi. Conclusion 213

Chapter VIII: Atay on the Self 215
VIII.i. Introduction 215
VIII.ii. The Self 215
VIII.iii. The Double 222
VIII.iv. Intertextuality and the 'Dissolution of the Subject' 227
VIII.v. The Originality Paradox 237
VIII.vi. Originality: The Act of Reading 251
VIII.vii. Conclusion 255

Conclusion 256

Bibliography 263

Index 277

Introduction

To the question 'what is self?' philosophers give a variety of answers. Some claim that such a thing does not exist at all, while others say the opposite and attempt to give us an account of the self by grounding it in God, spirit, substance, nature or brain, or body, or some combinations of these. Some turn to antiquity, claiming that we could understand things better if only we could establish a continuity between concepts at different times. In other words, they argue that when the ancients asked questions similar to today's, like 'what is the fundamental truth of human nature?' or 'what defines the identity of an individual?' they were, in fact, dealing with the one and the same sort of problem.

Whether such continuity – between the conception of the self in antiquity and in modern philosophical thought – exists or not extends the scope of this book, and despite the fact that our contemporary ideas about self stem from Descartes, it is well known that Greek philosophy is a rich source for philosophers and that they often find themselves in a constant dialogue with the Greeks (Nietzsche). So, I will give a synopsis of the conceptions of the self in different eras before we turn to modern conceptions of the self, and, correspondingly, its ethical ramifications.

Richard Sorabji claims that there is such a thing as self and that there was in the ancient Greek world. He says that *autos* ('same', emphatic 'himself') and the reflexive *heautos* ('himself') often come close.[1] Aristotle describes a friend as another self, *allos autos*. In *Republic* (IX, 589a-b), Plato uses the word *anthropos* ('human being') which denotes something closer to 'self' or 'person'.[2] The 'self' in the ancient philosophers is seldom identical with the soul, being sometimes connected with only one aspect of it, sometimes with the body, sometimes with the whole person. For Plato, the true self is reason or intellect. Michel Foucault famously argued that the 'care of the self' was a fundamental attitude throughout Greek, Hellenistic and Roman culture. Socrates, for instance, is always associated with the notion of 'caring for oneself'. The notion of the 'care of the self' was important for Plato, as well as for Epicureans, Cynics and Stoics. It is also found

---

1   Richard Sorabji, *Self: Ancient and Modern Insights about Individuality, Life, and Death* (Oxford: Clarendon, 2006), p. 32.
2   Pauliina Remes and Juha Sihvola, Introduction in *Ancient Philosophy of the Self*, ed. Pauliina Remes, Juha Sihvola (London: Springer, 2008), p. 5.

in Christianity, as a positive principle.[3] In fact the problem of what a self is may go back as far as Homer.

In Homeric society every individual has a given role and status within a well-defined system of roles and statuses. Kinship and the household are the key structures. In such a society a man knows who he is by knowing his role in these structures and through this he also knows what he owes and what is owed to him. There is no distinction between 'ought' and 'owe' in Greek (*dein*) and in Anglo-Saxon (*ahte*), and in Icelandic the word 'skyldr' ties together 'ought' and 'is kin to'.[4] Eduard Frankel wrote of Homeric man that

> a man and his actions become identical, and he makes himself completely and adequately comprehended in them; he has no hidden depths...In [the epics] factual report of what men do and say, everything that men are, is expressed, because they are no more than what they do and say and suffer.[5]

To judge a man therefore is to judge his actions. In other words, morality and social structure are in fact one and the same in heroic society. Thus, the assumption that some modern moral philosophers take to be essential characteristic of human selfhood, that is to say, the capacity to detach oneself from any particular standpoint, to step backwards and judge things from the outside, is just what the self of the heroic age lacks. There is no outside position to which to withdraw without becoming a stranger, or alien. There is no difference between trying to withdraw yourself from a given position and trying to make yourself disappear, in other words, wanting your own death.[6]

The virtues of Homeric society were different from those of Athens. For the Athenian man the question of the relationship between being a good citizen and being a good man becomes central. Then the virtues have their place within the social context of the city state and to be a good man is equal to being a good citizen. The virtues, for Plato, for instance, are not merely compatible with each other but the presence of each requires the presence of all. The assumption behind this thesis is that there is a cosmic order which 'dictates the place of each virtue in a total harmonious scheme of human life.'[7]

---

3   Michel Foucault, *The Hermeneutics of the Subject* (New York: Palgrave Macmillan, 2005), pp. 8-10.
4   Alasdair MacIntyre, *After Virtue: A Study in Moral Theory* (London: Duckworth, 1981), p. 115.
5   Quoted in MacIntyre, *After Virtue*, p. 115.
6   MacIntyre, *After Virtue*, p. 118-119.
7   MacIntyre, *After Virtue*, p. 133.

In the Platonist thesis concerning the unity of the virtues the idea of the mastery of the self through reason becomes central. To be master of oneself is to have the higher part of the soul (reason) rule over the lower part (desire). Only a rational person can attain the unity of the virtues. The idea of the unity of the virtues appears in Aristotle as well. Like Plato, Aristotle sees the exercise of the virtues as not *a* means to the end of the good for man. What constitutes the good for man is a complete human life lived at its best, and the exercise of the virtues is a central part of such a life, rather than a mere preparatory exercise to secure it.[8] According to Aristotle, what makes an object the kind of object that it is is what it does, in other words, its function, or characteristics. In this view, to be unified is to be teleologically organized. Correspondingly, a good action for Aristotle is the one conducted at the right time, in the right way, towards the right object, and with the right aim. That is to say, it is one that embodies the right principle. In *Nicomachean Ethics* there is a threefold structure: 1-human-nature-as-it-happens-to-be; 2-human-nature-as-it-could-be-if-it-realised-its-telos; 3- the precepts of ethics as the means for the transition from one to the other. There is a fundamental contrast between the first two and this is why we need the third one, namely, ethics which enables men to understand how they make the transition from former to the latter.

> Ethics therefore on this view presupposes some account of potentiality and act, some account of the essence of man as a rational animal and above all some account of the human *telos*. The precepts which enjoin the various virtues and prohibit the vices which are their counterparts instruct us how to move from potentiality to act, how to realise our true nature and to reach our true end.[9]

Our desires and emotions are educated by the use of such precepts, and it is reason which shows us what our true end is and how we can reach it. Thus, Aristotle's view is teleological.

Despite this resemblance between Plato and Aristotle, Sorabji, focusing on the on the Stoic theory of four *personae*, shows how ancient philosophy exhibits a large variety of discussions of self and selfhood. For Stoics, moral decision-making presupposed an understanding of one's individual character and position in the world:

> And this difference of natures has such force that sometimes one man ought to commit suicide, while another *in the same situation* (in *eadem causa*, only in some mss) ought not. For was Marcus Cato in a different situation (*alia in causa*) from the others who surrendered to Caesar in Africa? But perhaps with the others it would have been attributed to moral failure if they had killed themselves, because their lives had been less austere

---

8   MacIntyre, *After Virtue*, p. 140
9   MacIntyre, *After Virtue*, p. 50

and their habits more easy-going. Since nature had conferred on Cato an incredible gravity, and he had strengthened it by unceasing consistency, and had always persisted in his resolved purpose, it was right for him to die rather than to look on the face of a tyrant.[10]

By focusing on the importance of the unique individual of Cato, Sorabji underlines the contrast with the idea of moral obligation found in a modern philosopher such as Kant. While Kant sees moral obligation as applying universally, Cicero claims that Cato's suicide was morally right only for him. Sorabji says: 'It was unique to Cato that suicide was the right course, because his character was unique among those defeated here. The interest here is not only in the individual but in an individual whose character in the situation was unique.'[11] Cicero appeals to a theory of persona which goes back to the Stoic philosopher Panaetius. It is a view about what you must take into consideration while making decisions about what it is right to do. So the Kantian idea that you must consider the fact that you are a rational being is not enough. According to Panaetius, one needs to make decisions in the light of one's individual persona as well, that is: 'of the position you have been born into, the choices you have made, and what fortune has brought you.'[12] Personae are of course constituted partly by our roles like fatherhood or motherhood and so it is true that many of these roles are common to many people; nevertheless, there are characteristics that are not shared.[13]

Even though there are different views about whether the use of the word 'self' among the ancients is similar to uses of it today, at least it seems that there are basic assumptions about the ancient philosophy of the self on which many commentators agree:

1. In ancient philosophy the problem of self was usually discussed within metaphysics and ontology.
2. The Notion of selfhood is not construed as a domain of epistemological certainty, unlike Cartesian selfhood.

---

10   Quoted in Richard Sorabji, 'Greaco-Roman Varieties of Self', in *Ancient Philosophy of the Self*, p. 31
11   Sorabji, 'Greaco-Roman Varieties of Self', p. 31
12   Sorabji, *Self: Ancient and Modern*, p. 158
13   Sorabji, *Self: Ancient and Modern*, p. 158. In fact, Kant comments on Cato's suicide in his *Lectures on Ethics* but very briefly and he talks about suicide as a point about the legitimacy of the suicide not as a general point about decisions: 'It must certainly be admitted that in a case such as this, where suicide is a virtue, appearances are in its favour. But this is the only example which has given the world the opportunity of defending suicide.' Quoted in Sotabji, *Self: Ancient and Modern*, p. 171

3. Until Plotinus and Augustine, selves were regarded as parts of the objective world, and not addressed as aspects of individual experience.
4. Problems of self were approached within a teleological framework.
5. Ethical and political arguments, especially Plato's and Aristotle's, influenced the ways in which the problem of selfhood was discussed.[14]

All these basic assumptions will be addressed at various points, but for now the last assumption is crucial. Firstly, the idea that the concept of the self is inseparable from ethics is a recurring theme of this book; secondly, I shall suggest that our modern notion of the self is related to a particular sense of inwardness, one in which some sort of opposition between the inner/outer or inside/outside seems unavoidable. We tend to think that our thoughts, feelings and desires are 'within' us while the objects exist in the outer world. Taylor writes: 'We are creatures with inner depths; with partly unexplored and dark interiors. We all feel the force of Conrad's image in *Heart of Darkness.*'[15]

Even if, as Taylor suggests, the modern notion of the self is unthinkable without Plato's idea of the rational self, it was Augustine who stressed the opposition between the inner and outer man. The inner is the soul, whereas the outer is the bodily things, including our senses and even the memory storage. The road from the lower to the higher (and to the God) goes though our attending to ourselves as inner. This is very different from Plato's idea of finding out about 'the highest principle by looking at the domain of objects which it organises, that is, the field of the Ideas. In other words, Augustine shifts the focus from the domain of objects to be known to the activity of knowing, to the first-person stand point. Here the idea of self-knowledge or our search for our inner self is at the same time our search for God. Augustine's turn to the inner self was a turn to radical reflexivity, a method which will be taken up Descartes. However, Descartes gave a radical direction to the inner man of Augustine, placing the sources of morality, too, within us.[16]

It should be noted here even though Descartes is Augustinian in his method of radical reflexivity, it is a method that enables him to move from the first person experience into an objectified, impersonal stand-point. We have to objectify the world and our bodies in order to stand back and withdraw from them so that we

---

14 For Further discussion see Paulina Remes. Juha Sihlova, *Ancient Philosohy of the Self*, pp. 2-5.
15 Charles Taylor, *Sources of the Self: The Making of the Modern Identity* (Cambridge: Athenaeum Press, 1994), p. 111.
16 Taylor, *Sources of the Self*, pp. 127-158.

can have a clear and distinct idea about the objects in the outer world, in other words, 'to come to see them mechanistically and functionally, in the same way that uninvolved external observer would.'[17]

Descartes' rational self or 'the disengaged reason' is quite different from Plato's idea of self-mastery through reason, for in Plato one can realise his/her true nature 'as a supersensible soul' only when one turns 'towards the supersensible, eternal, immutable things. This turning will no doubt include my seeing and understanding the thing which surround me as participating in the Ideas which give them being.'[18] This is quite different from Descartes' mechanistic world according to which the universe is a mechanical clockwork system of bodies in motion.

Thus far this brief synopsis of the route from Plato's unified self to Descartes' method of radical reflexivity via Augustine may suggest a continuous tradition of thought and a stable background for the modern notion of the self. In contrast, Michel Foucault turns to the Greeks, not in order to emphasise continuity, nor in order to see the Greeks as an attractive alternative, but to defamilirize the taken-for-granted notions of the self, selfhood and subjectivity that are involved in our discussions of ethics. Foucault's work raises the question of methods of ethics.

We referred briefly to Kant. One criticism of ethical theories of the Kantian sort is that they are too abstract to be able to speak about particular human beings who lead particular lives. This is one way of formulating the old debate about universality and particularity.

In *The Republic* Plato announced that there was a long-standing antagonism between poetry and philosophy.[19] While literature shows us patterns of excellence in such a way that we are drawn towards their imitation, these patterns of excellence are themselves susceptible to judgment. If this is so, the problem arises of whether they are really patterns of excellence. If, having been brought up in a culture where our selves are also shaped through the values and literature of that culture, we can stand back and question whether their claim to be patterns of excellence is justified, then according to Plato, we need to refer to other standards that are beyond all cultural values and, accordingly, beyond literature. In other words, we need a timeless and unchangeable transcendent ground. This, for Plato, can be found in the Forms. Literature is mimesis, or imitation, and secondary to the real world, and the real world is itself an imperfect imitation of the transcendent ground, of the forms. So literature is removed from the transcendent ground by two degrees. In

---

17 Taylor, *Sources of the Self*, p. 145
18 Taylor, *Sources of the Self*, p. 145
19 Plato, *The Republic* (Cambridge: Cambridge University Press, 2000), 607b, p. 329.

Plato's account, such a ground can only be found in the realm of Being, as opposed to the world of coming into being and passing away, the world of Becoming.[20]

Such a notion of a transcendent ground has been influential throughout the history of philosophy. For some philosophers we can access this ground by means of reason, for others we can do so only through faith. Kant, though, undermined this philosophical position to some extent, and this break continues with, for example, Nietzsche. Nietzsche proposes a life not seen in terms of a submission to a moral obligation which is grasped as the most familiar experience of the common man and as the uncanniest of all experiences (Kant), but as a constant process of self-formation, of affirmation of one's own experiences and actions. At the centre of Nietzsche's mature work is an attack on modes of thought, such as Platonism, which posit a dualism between a true world outside the order of time, and an apparent world of change, becoming and mere semblance.

The debate about binary oppositions like Being and Becoming, the unitary self and the 'self' regarded as constant becoming also leads to a discussion between the language of philosophy and of literature. As we have seen, Plato regards literature as an imitation of the real world, so it can never provide a timeless transcendent measure; being a product of culture, which is itself to be judged, literature is also open to interpretation, to change. However, this is precisely why Nietzsche appreciates literature.[21] Nietzsche says that the discovery of our true life can be made through the creation of a work of art and this view captures his belief that one should 'become what one is.' Indeed, literature and art provided models of how to understand the world:

> ...we should learn from artists while being wiser than they are in other matters. For with them this subtle power usually comes to an end where art ends and life begins; but we want to be the poets of our life – first of all in the smallest, most everyday matters.[22]

---

20   Michael Weston, *Philosophy, Literature and the Human Good* (London; New York: Routledge, 2001), p. xi.
21   Nietzsche was not alone in his attempt to bring philosophy closer to literature. This was the main objective of some Romantics as well. For instance Schlegel claims that poetry and philosophy should be made one and that 'transcendental poetry' is still in a state of becoming. The distinguishing feature of humanity, for Schlegel, is that we can make our life a poem. Every individual 'bears within him his own poetry which must and should remain his own as surely as he is himself, as surely as there is anything original to him.' Friedrich von Schlegel, *Dialogue on Poetry and Literary Aphorisms,* trans. E. Behler and R. Struc Pennsylvania: Pennsylvania University Press, 1968), p. 54.
22   Friedrich Nietzsche, *The Gay Science*, trans. Walter Kaufmann (New York: Vintage, 1974), 299, p. 240. Hereafter *GS*.

Nietzsche has been very influential in his attempt to relate literature and philosophy. Following Nietzsche's critique of western metaphysics and the concept of unitary self, many contemporary thinkers claim that the language of philosophy which tends to conceptualize and generalize cannot be a good source for addressing the problems of human conduct, especially ethics. As a result of this they turn to literary works. For both Iris Murdoch and Martha Nussbaum, for instance, there is a general question of how we should live which is the concern of both philosophy and literature. The question is both empirical and practical. It is empirical because we don't have access to a transcendent standpoint, and practical since we must be able to experience it. Only literature can show in detail how we should conduct our lives. Murdoch claims that good art shows us not only the illusory unity of the self but also its real disunity. Post-Nietzschean philosophers like Derrida, Bataille and Blanchot claim that literature becomes the place where the fascination of dissolution can operate on our discontinuous selves. Similarly, D.Z. Philips claims that moral change is not progress, but coming to a new perspective on one's life, and that when we accept this we will be able to reinterpret the ethical value of the unity of a life in terms of becoming rather than eternity. In that sense, to engage with literature is to contemplate the possibilities and the impossibilities of sense for us.[23]

There are many other philosophers of ethics who subscribe to a form of inquiry which places literature at its centre. However, although one of the common features of the philosophers mentioned above is that they see in literature a richer account of the nature of ethical experience and of the idea of the self as becoming, they still tend to see literary works as a source of 'illustrations' of basically philosophical points. I try to avoid this, and to see literature as an activity that has its own claims to make. My aim is not only to discuss Nietzsche's critique of the constitution of the modern self and its ethical contents, but also to explore the ways in which this Nietzschean theme appears in literature. I will focus in particular on Nietzschean motifs in the writings of Robert Musil (1880-1940) and Oğuz Atay (1934-1977).

In order to do this I will focus on one aspect of this clearly large topic: the dissolution of the subject and its ethical content. Such ideas are found in Nietzsche's treatment of the self which, in turn, is strongly related to his notion of freedom, but they are also worked out and extended in the writings of Robert Musil and Oğuz Atay, both of whom were inspired by Nietzsche. I will ask three main questions.

---

23   Weston, *Philosophy, Literature*, pp. xvi-xix.

Firstly, if the self is an 'illusion', how can we still talk about ethical issues like promising and responsibility? In *On The Genealogy of Morality* Nietzsche tries to establish a connection between guilt, debt (*Schuld*), responsibility, punishment, conscience and the memory of punishment. This connection is quite speculative and also brief. But Musil explores these connections at great length through various transgressive characters who appear in his writings, in particular Moosbrugger, Törless and Ulrich, the central protagonist of Musil's master work *The Man without Qualities*, who throws off or ignores debts to the past or to tradition, and seeks to shape a future for himself. Musil's work is often an ironic commentary on such efforts.

Secondly, if there is not a unitary self, in other words, if the self is in a state of becoming, what kind of future can we create for ourselves and for others? Nietzschean ethics rests primarily on a 'relationship with oneself', but here I want to add that Musil's art enables him to explore ethical experiences while problematising the Nietzschean self and, correspondingly, Nietzschean ethics. Seen in these terms, the first two parts of *The Man without Qualities* are an experimental examination of Nietzschean ethics, while part three is an exploration of different modes of participation with the world and others. This difference is paralleled by a difference between monologic and dialogic presentation of the main characters.

Thirdly, Atay takes up Nietzsche's idea that 'the doer behind the deed' is a fiction in order to experiment with the idea of a life of pure imitation; if the doer is a fiction then can one become anyone by imitating the deeds of others? In *The Disconnected* the subjecthood of the main characters gives way to a state in which each of them is everyone and no-one, in which neither self-oriented nor other-oriented ethics seems to apply. Atay's subjects suffer from radical groundlessness, and as such the novel contains a problematisation of the Cartesian account of the subject, which regards the subject as a fixed identity and which assumes a human essence.

Here I should emphasise that I maintain a distinction between the 'subject' and the 'self'. Nietzsche's, Musil's and Atay's critique/problematisation of the 'subject' is directed against the Cartesian subject, the subject being the knower of the known (subject-object separation, 'the disengaged reason'). However, my main argument is that the idea of the dissolution of the subject was regarded by all of them as an opening toward a new discussion of the 'self'. Neither Nietzsche's nor Musil's anti-Cartesian thrust is directed so much against substance, or against the 'inner' self, as against the subject regarded as a defence mechanism. Against what?

17

With Hans Blumenberg we can say 'the absolutism of reality'. Blumenberg uses this phrase in the course of an argument whose centre is the claim that 'man came close to not having control of the conditions of his existence and, what is more important, believed that he simply lacked control of them.'[24] For Blumenberg, man is a limited being with limited resources and can survive only if he puts some distance between himself and the external world, which otherwise may overwhelm him. Overcoming the absolutism of reality is a function of many forms of human cognition: myths, stories, metaphors, religion, philosophy, science and technology. These may be seen as a defence mechanism, as a means of self-preservation for a vulnerable creature. The work of Nietzsche and Musil is of interest here because both appear to experiment with the idea of a defenceless self. Defencelessness can take several forms, but broadly speaking we may say that Nietzsche is in the tradition of the Participatory Self (joining the stream of reality-nature, becoming one with fate, blurring the distinction between outside and inside: a very Greek concept of the self in fact), while Musil is in the tradition of the Transcendental Self (withdrawing into its own reality, existing differently as a matrix of potentialities). There is, however, a third position, which we may call simply ambivalence. And that is one that I will associate with Oğuz Atay, who while rejecting the Cartesian self, does not seem to suggest any remedy. This is partly because of Atay's use of language, which more radically than Musil's, is hard to reconcile with a familiar philosophy of the 'self'.

The book is organised along the following lines. I begin with a brief overview of Nietzsche's position. According to Nietzsche, Descartes' formulation of the thinking 'I' and his formulation of the *a priori* belief in the 'I' as a substance is based upon a mistake. Descartes argues that 'if there is a thought there must be a thinker' and that consequently the existence of the 'I' is certain. Substance is given an *a priori* status and it is conceived as something beyond experience. Thinking, which is the basic ground of existence, is inseparable from the 'I', so that the 'I' can be found with certainty in its act of thinking. In the *Second Meditation*, Descartes states: 'I am a thinking thing, which is real, which truly exists.'[25] Nietzsche criticises the Cartesian account of the nature of 'I' which gives priority to the 'thinking act' of the knower over what is known; he also rejects the term *true existence*, principally because such an ontology is merely a projection of language:

---

24 Hans Blumenberg, *The Legitimacy of the Modern Age,* trans. Robert Wallace (Cambridge; Massachusetts; London: MIT Press, 1983), pp. 3-4.
25 Rene Descartes, *Meditations on the First Philosophy*, trans. John Cottingham (Cambridge: Cambridge University Press, 1986), p. 18.

[Language] everywhere sees a doer and doing;...it believes in the ego, in the ego as being, in the ego as substance, and it projects this faith in the ego substance upon all things – only thereby does it first *create* the concept of 'thing'...the concept of being follows and is derivative of, the concept of ego.[26]

In *On the Genealogy of Morals*, Nietzsche writes: 'there is no such substratum; there is no "being" behind the deed, its effect and what becomes of it; "the doer" is invented as an after-thought, – the doing is everything.'[27] The subject is a mere fiction or an addition; it becomes merely a product of the conceptual structure of philological, psychological, ontological and epistemological frameworks. Correspondingly, Nietzsche rejects the idea that the self has an idealized unity and an identity.

The basic problem that Nietzsche sees as following from this is 'how one becomes what one is', that is to say, becomes a creative individual who wills his/her will. This is not obviously an ethical question but – despite the *Übermensch* – in Nietzsche's hands it is. But ethics here does not primarily rest on our relation with others, but on our relation with ourselves, on the art of self-mastery and self-governance. Becoming what one is means being engaged in a constant process of affirmation of one's own experiences and actions; of enlarging the capacity for assuming responsibility for oneself; this Nietzsche calls 'freedom'. Moreover, his critique of the constitution of modern subjectivity is inseparable from his critique of the bourgeois-Christian subjectivity of his era.

In *Daybreak* Nietzsche draws our attention to the tension between culture and the individual, yet his understanding of the 'dissolution of the subject' in his criticism of culture is also the positive definition of the overman. The elements of the 'dissolution of the subject' – of the Ego, of form – which constitute the key to Nietzsche's work as criticism of culture are not pure symptoms of decadence. While it is true that Nietzsche regards culture as a tyranny against nature, he also believes that there is a selective object of culture which functions as forming a man capable of making use of the future, a free and powerful individual who is active. Nietzsche does not simply reject culture; nor does he suggest going back to nature: 'any custom is better than no custom.'[28] He criticizes a particular culture, the bourgeois-Christian culture in which the (Cartesian) subject is the centre of

---

26 Friedrich Nietzsche, *Twilight of the Idols*, in *The Portable Nietzsche*, trans. Walter Kaufmann, (London: Chatto&Windus, 1971), 'Reason in Philosophy', 5.
27 Friedrich Nietzsche, *On the Genealogy of Morality*, ed. Keith Ansell-Pearson (Cambridge: Cambridge University Press, 2002), I:13, p. 28. Hereafter *GM*.
28 Friedrich Nietzsche, *Daybreak: Thoughts on the Prejudices of Morality*, trans. R. J. Hollingdale (Cambridge: Cambridge University Press, 1997), I:16, p. 15.

meaning, an *agential self* who can be separated from its actions (Kant), and in which the chief purpose is to tame the 'human animal' and to give birth to a rational human being who has freedom of the will. For this freedom means the ability to subjugate oneself to a universal moral law.

This era is also one that lacks true philosophers, free spirits who can transform the culture, who will revalue values. The overman is not coming in an unknown future, she is precisely the individual without a centre, or, to anticipate the discussion in Part II, the individual without qualities. Gianni Vattimo insists that 'dissolution is what positively characterizes the overman.'[29] Nietzsche's overman is the result of liberating our potentialities for life from the restrictive concepts of man or human essence.

The 'dissolution of the subject', of the Ego or 'form', is an important theme of early twentieth century avant-garde literature, and it is no accident that Vattimo refers to Robert Musil as an example. Musil, born in Klagenfurt in 1880, is one of the great figures in German literature and one of the most remarkable in the history of the modern novel.[30] His major work *The Man without Qualities* was begun early in the nineteen-twenties, and the first volume was published in 1930. Although Musil died before he could finish the novel, it is one of the longest in literature.

The Man without Qualities is set in Vienna in 1913, and presents the pains and conflicts of the individuals and the degenerated morality of the bourgeois order through the eyes of its central character, the 32-year-old Ulrich. A synopsis of the novel is made difficult not only by its length and complexity, but also by the fact that the 'action' does not take place so much in the conduct of the characters or through events, but within the minds of the protagonists, so that we read of their emotions, the conflicts between their thoughts and behaviour, and their relations to each other, especially to *The Man without Qualities* – Ulrich – himself. I will focus on one central aspect of this complex web of representations of subjective reality in the novel: the 'dissolution of the subject' as a condition of becoming a 'man without qualities'. By means of this focus, I will also attempt to explore Musil's critique of the social order of his era since, like Nietzsche's, his critique of the constitution of modern subjectivity is inseparable from his critique of the culture and morality of his era.

---

29   Gianni Vattimo, *Dialogue with Nietzsche*, trans. William McCuaig (New York: Columbia University Press, 2006), p. 160.
30   Ernst Kaiser, and Eithne Wilkins, foreword in *The Man without Qualities* by Robert Musil trans. by Ernst Kaiser and Eithne Wilkins (London: Picador, 1982), p. viii.

Like Nietzsche, Musil criticizes the Cartesian conception of the self and he 'experiments' with the notion of the infinite possibilities of existence, which demands the 'dissolution of the subject'. The positive meaning of the 'dissolution of the subject' and the corresponding understanding of the subject in the process of 'becoming' is also encountered in Musil, however, it should be noted that Musil is also critical of Nietzsche's suggestion of a new understanding of morality, what he calls 'a trying morality'. In addition, what makes Musil different is that he realizes his critique through literature rather than through a poetic style of philosophy.

The protagonist Ulrich rejects the morality of his era, seeks ways of creating his own values and wishes to experience his individual freedom. At one point he proposes the idea of living 'hypothetically'; one who does so 'suspects that the given order of things is not as solid as it pretends to be; no thing, no self, no form, no principle is safe, everything is undergoing an invisible but ceaseless transformation, the unsettled holds more of the future than the settled, and the present is nothing but a hypothesis that has not yet been surmounted.'[31] Ulrich refuses to become the professor he might have been, refuses to take sides or indeed 'be' anything. His neutrality is embodied in the fact that his surname is never mentioned.[32] Such a person wishes to free himself/herself from the world in which the rules are ready-made. Ulrich appreciates an experimental life which enables one to be open to new experiences, to the 'possibilities of life'. A conversation between his friends Walter and Clarisse points this out:

> 'He is a man without qualities.'
> 'What is that?' Clarisse asked, with a little laugh.
> 'Nothing. That is the point- it is nothing!...You cannot guess at any profession from what he looks like, and yet he does not look like a man who has no profession, either.......Nothing is stable for him. Everything is fluctuating, a part of a whole, among innumerable wholes that are presumably part of a super-whole, which, however, he does not know the slightest thing about. So every one of his answers is a part-answer, every one of his feelings only a point of view, and whatever a thing is, it

---

31   Vattimo, *Dialogue*, p. 269
32   Kafka is well known for not giving the names or the full names of the characters. For instance, Joseph K., the protagonist of *The Trial*; *A Country Doctor* (short story); *A Hunger Artist* (short story) etc. In fact, Kafka was not the first who used this devise. We encounter it in the novellas of Heinrich von Kleist (1777-1811). For instance in *The Marquise of O* (1808) the Marquise of O was a daughter of a Colonel G. who was in charge in the citadel of the town M. Kafka was an admirer of Kleist. See Heinrich von Kleist, *The Marquis of O—: and Other Stories* (London: Penguin, 1978).

does not matter to him what it is, it is only some accompanying 'way in which it is', some addition or other, that matters to him.'[33]

The influence of Nietzsche on Musil is undeniable. Emer Herity suggests that 'An indication of Nietzsche's significance for Musil is given by the fact that only Goethe's name occurs more often than Nietzsche's in Musil's collected works, where references to the philosopher span a period of more than forty years and the full name is often abbreviated to 'N', a habit which suggests familiarity.'[34] Musil declared it 'Schicksal: Daß ich Nietzsche gerade mit achtzehn Jahren zum ersten Male in die Hand bekam. Gerade nach meinem Austritt vom Militär. Gerade im so und so vielten Entwicklungsjahr.'[35]

Nietzsche's significance for writers and thinkers was not limited to the German speaking world, nor even to European intellectual life. Just as Vattimo refers to Musil as an important yet oddly isolated figure in the twentieth-century avant-garde literature, so does Berna Moran refer to the Turkish writer Oğuz Atay.

According to Moran, *The Disconnected*, written in 1968 (published in 1971), was written in an atmosphere in which realist novels which aim to enlighten and inform people were respected and 'formalism and individualism were counted among aesthetic crimes.'[36] Considering the general atmosphere and the trends in Turkish literature of this era *The Disconnected* can be regarded as an avant-garde novel for 1970s in terms of its style and its subject, which handles the inner conflicts of individuals. As Moran says, *The Disconnected* is a novel 'which has turned its back on the realism of the 19th century, with one foot in modernism and the other in post-modernism.'[37] As Part II will suggest, Musil's novel, written half a century earlier, might be said to have one foot in modernism and one in realism.

Atay's subjects, like some of Musil's, suffer from groundlessness.[38] *The Disconnected* begins with the protagonist Turgut receiving the news that his friend Selim has committed suicide and left a letter for Turgut behind him. The death of

---

33 Robert Musil, *The Man without Qualities*, trans. Sophie Wilkins and Burton Pike (London: Picador, 1995), pp. 62-63.
34 Emer Herity, 'Robert Musil and Nietzsche', *The Modern Language Review*, Vol. 86, No. 4 (Oct., 1991), p. 911.
35 Herity, 'Musil and Nietzsche,' p. 911
36 Yıldız Ecevit, *"Ben Buradayım....": Oğuz Atay'ın Biyografik ve Kurmaca Dünyası* (İstanbul: İletişim Yayınları, 2005), p. 235.
37 Berna Moran, *Türk Romanına Eleştirel Bir Bakış* (İstanbul: İletişim Yayınları, 1992), V:2, p. 199.
38 Suna Ertuğrul, 'Belated Modernity and Modernity as Belatedness in *Tutunamayanlar*', *The South Atlantic Quarterly* 102, No. 2/3 (Spring/Summer 2003), pp. 629-645.

Selim and this letter shatter the everyday order in which silence and acceptance are dominant and lead Turgut to question his own situation. We encounter the protagonist Selim as impersonal, freed from fixed identities and fixed ideas. He is in a position of lack and imitation, in other words, of non-position, which provokes the question of human essence and identity. This groundlessness has led Selim to a constant search for identity, which has turned out to be a search for something which is not there. Throughout the novel the reader follows Turgut's becoming disconnected by following the traces of Selim. In other words, Turgut learns how to be in a position of lack and imitation by imitating Selim. The 'dissolution of the subject' is an important theme in *The Disconnected*; but it has different consequences from those that face *The Man without Qualities*.

Like Musil's Ulrich, Selim and Turgut are constantly questioning the artificiality of the social order and of the identities reproduced by it. Both reject it, yet, both seek ways of experiencing their individual freedom within it. In *The Disconnected*, the critique of the modern project that grounds meaning in the unity of the subject and human essence and the critique of the bourgeois order is also a commentary on Turkey in the 1960s, as is Musil's novel on Austria in 1913.

In the first three chapters I focus on Nietzsche's critique of the concept of the 'self' in the context of western metaphysics. Nietzsche claims that the constitution of the modern concept of the 'self' is inseparable from the context of culture, particularly bourgeois-Christian culture – morality – of his era. However, before the discussion of this, I present Nietzsche's critique of the distinctions between subject-object and cause-effect, since this provides the theoretical foundation for the modern conception of the 'self' which is followed by a dialogue of Nietzsche with both Kant and Spinoza both of whom Nietzsche admired but also criticised. However, I investigate the relationship between Nietzsche and these philosophers not to compare or contrast them but because for both Kant and Spinoza the concepts of the self and freedom are inseparable; as this is a recurring theme in Nietzsche's philosophy it is helpful to read him through Spinoza and Kant, who Nietzsche appreciated more than moralists of emotions such as Schopenhauer and Ree.

In the fourth and fifth chapters I focus on one central aspect of the complex web of representations of subjective reality in Musil's writings: the relationship between the 'dissolution of the subject', becoming a 'man without qualities', and ethics. Musil's ethics is mainly concerned with the experience of reality in the modern era, and I reflect on the role of time in his writing, in particular his account of how to turn an orientation to the present into a positive resource. Central to this is his idea of essayism, as a way of writing but also as a way of living.

In the last two chapters I focus on *The Disconnected*. Atay's Selim and Turgut, like Ulrich, reject the existing order of society, yet unlike Ulrich, they never appear to be in control of the processes of exploration that they undertake. Ulrich's search is a kind of experiment and he, as a trained scientist, knows it to be an experiment from which he may withdraw; Selim and Turgut are involved in something that, once begun, seems difficult to stop, except by means of suicide (Selim) or escape/withdrawal (Turgut).

The two novels were written in different times and different places, and so it is no surprise that, although they may have themes in common – the critique of the constitution of the modern 'self' and the 'dissolution of the subject', the creation of values and individual freedom – they are handled differently. While Ulrich does, to a certain extent, manage to live his life hypothetically, Selim and Turgut cannot realize that aim in their society. The cultural and historical differences that might have influenced the attitudes of the characters cannot be explored here. Instead, I attempt to explore both Atay's and Musil's critique of the modern conception of the subject, in other words what it means to be a 'man without qualities' or to be 'disconnected'.

Chapter I: Nietzsche on the Self and Morality

I.i. Introduction

One of the central questions, if not the central question, of Nietzsche's thought was the question of the decadence of modern man and the remedies for it. In searching for such remedies Nietzsche finds himself in dialogue with many philosophers, both ancient and modern. While Nietzsche claims that we can still learn things from the ancients his main addressees are modern philosophers – especially philosophers of morality – who, intentionally or unintentionally, have contributed to the decadence/decline of modern man. Its roots lie in the Christian morality – or slave morality – which Nietzsche sees as the morality of compassion or unegoism, but also in the philosophies of those – such as Paul Ree and Schopenhauer – whom he at one time admired.

Nietzsche's attacks on this morality may mislead us into thinking that his goal was an amoral one. In contrast, I will argue that his goal was not only not amoral but in fact to develop an ethics. Whether we call it self-cultivation or self-affirmation or self-mastery or even self-governance, Nietzsche attempts to replace traditional morality with an ethics, albeit one that primarily rests upon our relationship with ourselves rather than with others.[39] In *Daybreak* he says:

> It goes without saying that I do not deny – unless I am a fool – that many actions called immoral ought to be avoided and resisted, or that many called moral ought to be done and encouraged – but I think the one should be encouraged and the other avoided *for other reasons than hitherto*. We have to *learn to think differently* – in order at last, perhaps very late on, to attain even more: *to feel differently*.[40]

From what should we think and even feel differently? From the moralities that are based on unegoism or compassion, that is to say, from the philosophies of Schopenhauer and Paul Ree among others: 'it is the very essence of the emotion of pity that it strips away from the suffering of others whatever is distinctively

---

39 Here I keep the difference between ethics and moral. By origin the difference between two terms is that between Latin and Greek, each relating to a word meaning disposition or custom. One difference is that Latin moral is more to do with social expectation, Greek more individual. See Bernard Williams, *Ethics and the Limits of Philosophy* (London: Fontana, 1985), p. 6.
40 Nietzsche, *Daybreak* II:103, p. 60

personal.'[41] In *Daybreak*, for instance, he claims that the moral philosophy of Schopenhauer, John Stuart Mill and others is nothing but an echo of Christian morality. If useful social actions like empathy and sympathy and pity are regarded as moral actions, this is a general effect of Christianity on European sensibilities. This is rather explicit in Schopenhauer's understanding of compassion, 'the great mystery of ethics.'[42] In *The Will to Power* Nietzsche says that compassion 'must first be habitually sifted by reason; otherwise it is just as dangerous as any other affect.'[43]

At least here, Nietzsche praises Kantian morality (reason) over the philosophies of compassion, for Kant stands outside this trend by making autonomy the focus of his moral philosophy rather than focusing on sympathetic affects. Kantian autonomy presupposes that we are rational agents and our reason tells us what is consistent with duty and what is inconsistent. Through our awareness of categorical obligation we can resist the pull of desire. Where Nietzsche differs from Kant is that in Kant duty must always be a burden rather than a joyful inclination.[44] For Nietzsche whatever I do or whatever happens to me, whether it is suffering or doing something out of duty, should not be something against life; rather life is thoroughly to be affirmed. Kant also challenged established conceptions of morality as obedience by conceptions of morality as self-governance. This is Kant's moral egalitarianism.[45] Nietzsche neither rejects morality nor abandons the idea of self-governance. But his project is to reconsider and re-evaluate taken-for-granted values, for which we need to know the conditions under which these values have emerged and developed. As opposed to Kantian moral autonomy which is independent of the psychological truths about human beings, Nietzsche suggests a more modest task: our moral therapy

---

41   Nietzsche, *GS* 338, p. 269.
42   Arthur Schopenhauer, *On the Basis of Morality*, trans. E.F.J. Payne (Oxford: Berghahn, 1995), p. 144.
43   Friedrich Nietzsche, *The Will to Power*, ed. Walter Kaufmann (New York: Vintage, 1968), 928, p. 490. Hereafter *WP*.
44   Nietzsche, *Daybreak* IV:339, p. 163
45   John Skorupski, 'Morality as Self-Governance: Has it a Future?', *Utilitas*, Vol. 16, No: 2, 2004. Here I mean self-governance in the Kantian sense, that is to say, the capacity to give a law to oneself. However, this definition of self-governance is not exhaustive, and indeed it may not have to involve the idea of law at all. Variations on the theme of self-governance can be found in the work of numerous thinkers from St. Paul to Foucault.

is to be directed at the particular drives and capacities of individuals.[46] And Nietzsche attempts to replace traditional morality with an ethics which primarily rests on our relationship with ourselves rather than with others, which he sometimes calls self-affirmation or self-mastery or self-governance. And this understanding of ethics requires the dissolution of the subject, whether that subject is Cartesian or Kantian.

As we will see, Nietzsche's notion of the self is strongly related to his idea of the Eternal return, and in this respect he is much closer to Spinoza than Kant. It might even have been Spinoza himself who prompted the idea of eternal return, since Nietzsche seems to have discovered it only a few days after his discovery, in the summer of 1881, that Spinoza was his precursor.[47] Nietzsche claims that Spinoza is closest to him on the issues of the denial of the freedom of the will, teleology, the moral world order, the unegoistic and evil, though less close on time, culture, and science.

This chapter investigates Nietzsche's notion of the self, and its relationship with his understanding of ethics, reason, freedom of the will, and teleology. It is divided into three sections: (I.ii) Nietzsche's own account of the self in the context of his critique of slave morality, in particular Christian morality; (I.iii) his dialogue with Kant; (I.iv) his dialogue with Spinoza.

I.ii. The Self and the Christian Morality

I.ii.a. Subject-object and cause-effect

Nietzsche draws attention to prevailing ideas about the 'unity' of the 'agent' and the assessment of the moral value of action. Central to these is an attitude that sees the unity and consciousness of the person as being essential to the value-oriented agent, an agent who makes rational choices. The moral value of action is, accordingly, determined from the standpoint of a self who is a conscious rational agent, where 'conscious' and 'rational' mean: capable of acting in accordance with a table of moral values. Nietzsche rejects this view, and with it the entire framework in which the moral, religious and philosophical aspects of the constitution of the self are mutually implicated.

---

46   Keith Ansell-Pearson, 'Beyond Compassion: On Nietzsche's Moral Therapy in *Dawn*', *Continental Philosophy Review*, 2011, p. 23.
47   Keith Ansell-Pearson, *How to Read Nietzsche* (London: Granta, 2005), p. 20.

Nietzsche's target is what he perceives to be a general belief that our activity in the world can be separated into operations of the 'self' as 'subject', and the world as 'object'. Underlying these distinctions is the belief in an *I* that does something, *has* something and *has* a quality. Nietzsche believes that this distinction between subject and object is simply the projection of the subject–predicate relationship that characterizes the grammar of our language onto the structure of the world: 'One infers here according to the grammatical habit: "thinking is an activity, every activity requires an agent..."'[48]

Nietzsche argues that the projection of the distinction between subject and predicate onto the world is a product of the error that the 'will' is something that produces effects.[49] From the perspective of the subject it is believed that in every event there is an aim that is regarded as its cause. This cause-effect pattern can be found in the framework of the Cartesian tradition. Descartes argues that 'if there is a thought there must be a thinker' and consequently, the existence of the 'I' is certain. Substance is given an *a priori* status and it is conceived as something beyond experience. Thinking, which is the basic ground of existence, is inseparable from the 'I', so that the 'I' can be found with certainty in its act of thinking. In the *Second Meditation*, Descartes states: 'I am a thinking thing, which is real, which truly exists.'[50] In the Cartesian method of doubt the belief in subjective introspection leads to the belief in 'thinking'. Correspondingly, the same causal relationship is transferred to the interpretation of every action within the model of the distinction of doer and deed. All deeds are caused by a doer.

In *The Will to Power*, Nietzsche claims that human beings have a need for causality such as this; finding a cause for an event stabilizes experience, replacing something changing and indefinite with something unchanging and predictable. Yet rather than being a search for the circumstances on which the emergence of an experience or an event depends, this tendency to establish a cause and effect relationship is nothing but a way of giving meaning to the present. There are two psychological tendencies that lead human beings to impose a cause-effect formula on or seek a cause-effect relation in events. The first is a belief in the subject as doer, as the causal agent performing deeds:

> That which gives the extraordinary firmness to our belief in causality is not the great habit of seeing one occurrence following another but our inability to interpret events

---

48 Friedrich Nietzsche, *Beyond Good and Evil*, trans. Walter Kaufmann (New York: Vintage, 1966), 17, p. 24. Hereafter *BGE*.
49 Nietzsche, *Twilight*, 'Reason in Philosophy', 5
50 Descartes, *Meditations*, p. 18

otherwise than as events caused by intentions. It is belief in living and thinking as the only effective force – in will, in intention – it is belief that every event is a deed, that every deed presupposes a doer, it is belief in the 'subject.'[51]

The second is the desire to familiarize experience and overcome anxiety and danger:

> The supposed instinct for causality is only fear of the unfamiliar and the attempt to discover something familiar in it – a search not for causes, but for the familiar and the attempt to discover something familiar in it.[52]

Taken together, the need to believe in the existence of a subject, and the need to render events familiar, express nothing more than a desire for the self-preservation of the human being and for the preservation of the existing order. Moreover, the '*calculability of an event* does not reside in the fact that a rule is adhered to, or that a necessity is obeyed, or that a law of causality has been projected by us into every event: it resides in the *recurrence of "identical cases."*'[53] Nietzsche attempts to disrupt the division of subject and object by exposing what drives philosophers to make this division in the first place:

> In order for a particular species to maintain itself and increase its power, its conception of reality must comprehend enough of the calculable and constant for it to base a scheme of behaviour on it. The utility of preservation – not some abstract, theoretical need not to be deceived – stands as the motive behind the development of the organs of knowledge- they develop in such a way that their observations suffice for our preservation. In other words: the measure of desire for knowledge depends upon the measure to which will to power grows in a species: a species grasps a certain amount of reality in order to become master of it, in order to press into service.[54]

From the perspective of the subject the explanation of an event goes through two steps: First 'through mental images of the event that precede it (aims); secondly: though mental images that succeed it (the mathematical-physical explanation).'[55] Therefore, we assume that in every event there is an aim that is interpreted as the *cause* of that event. In other words, we seek a doer in every event. The concepts such as the thing as effective, the subject as doer, the will as something that produces effects are all inherent in the concept of 'cause', and lead to the creation of the 'effective subject', or the self of Western rationality and metaphysics who is

---

51 Nietzsche, *WP* 550, p. 295
52 Nietzsche, *WP* 551, p. 297
53 Nietzsche, *WP* 551, p. 297
54 Nietzsche, *WP* 480, pp. 266-267
55 Nietzsche, *WP* 562, p. 303

'agential' and has 'reason' and 'free will'. Cause and effect are transformed into other distinctions such as doer and deed, agent and action.

This mistake about causality is not only an epistemological one. The modern notion of the self is comprehended by the concept of the subject (having an idealized unity underlying all its attributes) and of substance (as an entity with an ontological privilege). But the constitution of the 'agential self' is also a question of morality.

I.ii.b. The self and morality

In Nietzsche's discussion of morality the interpretation of the self contained within the Christian tradition plays a prominent role, not least because Christian morality is so central to western morality. According to Nietzsche, the standards of evaluation in Christian morality are such as to impose an *unconditioned ought* and the *universality of the law of reason* which apply to all human beings. This is coupled with the idea that only free human action, action performed with the freedom of the will, can have moral value. Considering these assumptions the actions of human beings are evaluated as 'good' or 'evil' depending on human choices. As a result the agent is regarded responsible for his or her choices. As a whole, this kind of morality applies to a free, rational human being: a *moral agent*.

The Christian hypothesis proposes a rational man as moral agent who has freedom to act according to the rules of reason. It imposes a 'divine order' independent of human conditions. Concepts such as virtue, duty, and 'the good-in-itself' are posited as the highest concepts.

> This type of men *needs* to believe in an unbiased 'subject' with freedom of choice, because he has an instinct of self-preservation and self-affirmation in which every lie is sanctified.[56]

Such a system of morality creates an order whose rules are held to be universally applicable.

But here Nietzsche goes much further, for he says that Christian morality is merely the product of a *need for order* that is innate in men 'inasmuch as at all times, as long as there have been human beings, there have also been herds of men (clans, communities, tribes, peoples, states, churches) and always a great many people who obeyed, compared with the small number of those commanding.'[57]

---

56 Nietzsche, *GM* I:13, p. 29
57 Nietzsche, *BGE* 199, p. 110

The type of man who needs to be given orders, and who obeys them, is not simply the Christian – he is the slave. And the triumph of slave morality is the invention of the subject.

Even though the criticism of Christian morality is a recurring theme in Nietzsche's philosophy, it is especially so in *On the Genealogy of Morality*. The second essay of *GM* entitled '"Guilt", "Bad Conscience" and related matters' gives an historical account of the production of the 'sovereign individuals', those people who are able to act autonomously, to make and keep promises. The essay on the 'Master and Slave Morality' is a history of the practical interests presupposed by the idea of the subject. In the essay on the 'Ascetic Ideal' he seeks to expose the auto-destructive character of the attempts to legislate moral rules from the point of view of a disembodied God.

I.ii.c. The inseparability of the subject and the deed

Despite his famous statement in *GM* I:13 'the doer is a mere fiction' and 'the doing is everything', Nietzsche does not simply deny that there is a subject of the deed, rather he is claiming that it is not separate from the activity, it is in the deed, in other words, you are what you do. What Nietzsche suggests seems to be a quite different relationship between the self and the deed than a cause and effect relationship which regards the subject as the cause of the deed and which is based on the belief that will is something that produces effects.

Understanding the difference between such an expressivist notion of action and an intentionalist or causal account is important because it helps us to understand how we can still talk about actions in Nietzsche when it can appear that he denies any sort of agency. According to Robert Pippin, Nietzsche:

> ...is not denying that strength 'expresses itself' in acts of strength. He is in fact asserting just that, that there is such an expression, and so appears to be relying on a notion of expression, rather than intentional causality, to understand how the doer is in the deed.[58]

Pippin claims that this expressivist notion of action owes much to Hegel. Consider this: 'The true being of a man is rather his deed; in this the individual is actual...'[59]

---

58 Robert B. Pippin, 'Agent and Deed in Nietzsche's Genealogy of Morals', in *A companion to Nietzsche*, ed. Keith Ansell-Pearson (Oxford: Blackwell, 2006), p. 379.
59 Quoted in Robert B. Pippin, 'Lightning and Flash, Agent and Deed', in *Nietzsche's On the Genealogy of Morals*, ed. Christa Davis Acampora (Oxford: Rowman Littlefield, 2006), pp. 131-145

or this: 'whatever it is that the individual does, and whatever happens to him, that he has done himself, and he *is* that himself.'[60] This similarity turns on what Pippin calls a *nonseparability* thesis about intention and action, and correspondingly a *nonisolatability* claim.

According to the first one, intention-formation and articulation are always being transformed. I may start a project thinking that my intention is X, but gradually I come to understand that this was not my real intention, so that it must have been Y and so on. That is to say: 'my subjective construal at any time before or during the deed has no privileged authority. The deed *alone* can "show" one who one is.'[61]

According to the second thesis or *nonisolatability* thesis, on the other hand, the conditions under which one would regard an intention as justifying an action have to be taken into consideration as well, and this draws our attention not only to the character of the person but also to the community or tradition of which he or she is a part.

This anti-Cartesian account of the self focuses on a continuing expression of the subject through her deeds. A contemporary Kantian scholar Christine Korsgaard claims that the idea of the inseparability of the subject and the deed lies at the heart of Kantian morality as well. She also argues that it is only Kantian philosophy that can provide a true basis for morality, self-governance, and self-constitution.[62] Against this, Nietzsche's *amor fati* suggests a vision of the human being that is clearly distinct from Kantian autonomy, in particular from any Kantian orientation of conduct in terms of the moral law. Nevertheless, I suggest here that many of Nietzsche's formulations of the meaning of selfhood, ethics, and freedom do presuppose a dialogue with Kant, one for which Kant provided much of the vocabulary.

I.iii. Nietzsche's Critique of Kant

I.iii.a. Morality as self-governance: Kant

In *The Invention of Autonomy*, Jerry Schneewind argues that during the seventeenth and eighteenth centuries established conceptions of morality as obedience were challenged and eventually replaced by conceptions of morality as self-governance.

---

60 Georg Wilhelm Friedrich Hegel, *Phenomenology of Spirit*, trans. A.V. Miller (Oxford: Oxford University Press, 1977), 404, p. 242.
61 Pippin, 'Lightning and Flash, Agent and Deed', p. 139
62 Christine M. Korsgaard, *Self-Constitution: Agency, Identity and Integrity* (Cambridge: Cambridge University Press, 2009)

There are two components in the morality of obedience of the seventeenth century. On the one hand, we are: 'required to show deference and gratitude as we obey our Creator's commands, which cover morality as well as religious worship.' The other component concerns human moral abilities:

> Most people are unable to think well enough to give themselves adequate moral guidance; most people are also too weak-willed and too strongly driven by their desires and passions to behave decently without credible threats of punishment for transgression and promises of reward for compliance. The majority, therefore, must defer to the exceptional few whom God has enabled to understand, follow, and teach his moral orders.[63]

In contrast to this, morality as self-governance focuses on the belief that we all 'have an equal ability to see ourselves what morality calls for and are in principle equally able to move ourselves to act accordingly' regardless of threats or rewards from others.[64] These views, Schneewind adds, have been so widely accepted that most philosophy starts by assuming them. Not only in philosophy but even in daily life we assume that people are capable of understanding and equally competent as moral agents. This assumption is the radical difference between the moral views of the seventeenth century and those of the eighteenth century. Such a transition from morality as obedience to the morality as self-governance made a crucial contribution to the western liberal vision, which, in turn, helped to establish a new relationship between the individual and society.[65]

Schneewind allocates the last few chapters to Kant's efforts to find a satisfactory *a priori* ground for morality as self-governance. Kant's solution is the invention of autonomy. It is an 'invention' in Schneewind's words, not a discovery, because, as Skorupski suggests, Schneewind 'does not believe, as Kant believes, that we can be thought to have transcendental freedom as 'members of a noumenal realm.'[66] As Schneewind says:

> Kantian autonomy presupposes that we are rational agents whose transcendental freedom takes us out of the domain of natural causation. ...Through it each person has a compass that enables 'common human reason' to tell what is consistent with duty and what is inconsistent. Our moral capacities are made known to each of us by the fact of reason, our awareness of categorical obligation that we can respect against

---

63 Jerome B. Schneewind, *The Invention of Morality: a History of Modern Moral Philosophy* (Cambridge: Cambridge University Press, 1997), p. 509.
64 Schneewind, *The Invention of Morality*, p. 4
65 Schneewind, *The Invention of Morality*, pp. 5-6
66 Skorupski, 'Morality as Self-Governance', p. 134

the pull of desire. Because they are anchored in our transcendental freedom, we cannot lose them, no matter how corrupt we become. Kant sees his theory as the only way to defend the conviction Rousseau gave him of the importance of honouring the common moral understanding.[67]

Morality as self-governance has been an influential idea. However, according to Skorupski a decline in the attraction of transcendental idealism should lead us to ask whether we can still maintain the moral egalitarianism and the idea of self-governance that Kant was committed to and, correspondingly, whether conceptions of morality have a future.[68] Before we inquire into the philosophy of Kant I would like to turn to the relationship between the Enlightenment project and morality, for according to some philosophers the problems of moral theory emerge as the product of the Enlightenment project itself.

I.iii.b. Enlightenment project: Failure or success?

The Enlightenment philosophers of the eighteenth century were loyal to the authority of reason and to the assumption that reason could justify everything: morality, religion and the state. But by the end of the eighteenth century these assumptions were thrown into question; in particular, it seemed that the more science and philosophy advanced the less room was there for the authority of Bible.[69]

This tension between reason and faith was already seen in the mid eighteenth century by Hume. At the close of the first book of the *Treatise of Human Nature* Hume sees a conflict between reason and faith which led to the sceptical conclusion that the only thing he knew was his own passing impressions, and that there is no empirical justification for the assumption that there are necessary connections between events. Correspondingly, while questioning the idea that there is harmony between reason and nature Hume claims that if we examined our sense impressions we find only accidentally repeated sequences which are the product of our imagination and habits of association.[70] Hume's skeptical conclusions are rather important since, as Frederick Beiser suggests, 'it was in the revival of Hume's skepticism at the end of the eighteenth century that we find the first glimmering of a problem which was to

---

67 Schneewind, *The Invention of Morality*, p. 515
68 Skorupski, 'Morality as Self-Governance', p. 135
69 Frederick C. Beiser, *The Fate of Reason: German Philosophy from Kant to Fichte* (Cambridge; Mass.: Harvard University Press, 1987), pp. 1-2.
70 Beiser, *The Fate of Reason*, pp. 3, 11

haunt philosophy toward the close of the nineteenth century: nihilism.'[71] And it was Kant's mission in the First *Kritik* to oppose Humean scepticism and to rescue faith in reason and science. In the 'Transzendental Deduktion' and 'Zweite Analogie', Kant argues that the principle of causality 'is a necessary condition ascribing objectivity to experience, of distinguishing between the subjective order of perceptions and the objective order of events themselves. This objectivity is not given to us, however, it is created by us'; in other words, 'this principle applies to experience only because our *a priori* activity has made experience conform to it.'[72]

However, for some thinkers of his time Kant's defence of the idea that there is harmony between reason and nature was a failure since it showed that this supposed harmony held only for appearances, not things-in-themselves. Johann Georg Hamann, the father of the *Sturm und Drang* movement, was one of them. Hamann argues that reason is: not autonomous but governed by the subconscious; cannot grasp the particular or explain life; inseparable from language; not universal but relative to a culture.[73] He regards Kant as a Platonist who hypostasises a self-sufficient noumenal realm, while he is an Aristotelian who believes that reason resides in things. We need a critique of language, too, which is the source of every confusion; Kant, in fact, is just another victim of a very old error, the belief that thought precedes language.[74]

In the idea that reason exists only in language and that language is nothing other than the custom and conventions, Hamann anticipates Nietzsche, who a hundred years later will claim that the distinction between subject and object is simply the projection of the subject–predicate relationship that characterizes the grammar of our language onto the structure of the world. Unlike Hamann, however, Nietzsche will not find a remedy in faith, which appears to make him partly a late representative of the eighteenth century idea of morality as self-governance but also the herald of the post-enlightenment critique of morality.

According to Alasdair MacIntyre, Nietzsche and Kant are part of the same problem, two aspects of the same enlightenment project, one that was bound to fail.[75] Key to this failure is that Kant – along with Hume, Diderot, Smith, Kierkegaard and others – rejects any teleological view of human nature:

---

71 Beiser, *The Fate of Reason*, pp. 3-4. It was Friedrich Heinrich Jacobi who introduced the term nihilism into modern philosophy.
72 Beiser, *The Fate of Reason*, pp. 11-12
73 Beiser, *The Fate of Reason*, p. 18
74 Beiser, *The Fate of Reason*, p. 40
75 Alasdair MacIntyre, *After Virtue: A Study in Moral Theory* (London: Duckworth, 1981), p. 50.

the individual moral agent, freed from the hierarchy and teleology, conceives of himself and is conceived by the moral philosophers as sovereign in his moral authority. On the other hand, the inherited, if partially transformed rules of morality have to be found some new status, deprived as they have been of their older teleological character and their even more ancient categorical character as expressions of an ultimately divine law.[76]

The failure of Enlightenment project – to provide a true basis for morality or a guide for conduct – was most clearly seen by Nietzsche; but however much he appeared to uphold ancient aristocratic virtues, Nietzsche simply replaced the fictions of Enlightenment individualism with a set of individualist fictions of his own.[77]

MacIntyre's solution to the problem is to draw the reader's attention to the Aristotelian understanding of action. The Enlightenment project was a failure, a consequence of the mistaken rejection of the Aristotelian tradition in the first place. He says:

> Unless there is a telos which transcendens the limited goods of practices by constituting the good of a whole human life, the good of a human life conceived as a unity, it will both be the case that a subversive arbitrariness will invade the moral life and that we shall be unable to specify the context of certain virtues adequately. These two considerations are reinforced by a third: that there is at least one virtue recognised by the tradition which cannot be specified at all except with reference of the wholeness of the human life.[78]

MacIntyre believes that this conception of a whole human life is absent from the thought of practically all modern philosophers of morality. Either there is a fragmentary conception of that life or wholeness is theorised but in purely individualistic terms. For MacIntyre, the concept of a whole human life cannot be divorced from a broader tradition of practices. That is what is meant by communitarianism.

In his confrontation with Enlightenment morality, MacIntyre could not avoid the work of either Kant or Nietzsche. In the next section I suggest that, contrary to MacIntyre, that is a good reason to examine their relationship, and to see the differences between them as more significant than their roles in a single story of enlightenment failure.

---

76   MacIntyre, *After Virtue*, p. 60
77   MacIntyre, *After Virtue*, p. 122
78   MacIntyre, *After Virtue*, p. 189

I.iii.c. Nietzsche's critique of Kant: Free will

In *Groundwork* Kant defines free will as a rational causality which can be efficient without being determined by alien causes (4:446).[79] Alien causes include our desires and inclinations, and a non-rational being which does not have a free will is determined solely by these causes. Since freedom is a property of the will and only a rational being that has the capacity to act in accordance with reason has a free will, it follows that it is only a rational being that can have freedom. What is the ground of free will? Free will must be self-determining, and since it is a causality it must act according to some law. Kant says: 'Since the concept of causality brings with it that of laws in accordance with which,...something else, namely an effect, must be posited, so freedom...is not for that reason lawless but must instead be a causality in accordance with immutable laws but of a special kind' (4:446). Now, if the will is free, then no principle can be ascribed to it from outside, and so Kant concludes that the freedom of the will must be autonomous, that is to say, have its own law. But then the question arises of where this law comes from. Kant's answer is this: the will is a law itself which 'indicates only the principle, to act on no other maxim than that which can also have as object itself as a universal law' (4:446); this is the formula of the categorical imperative, and also the principle of morality.

In *The Critique of Practical Reason*, Kant argues that the moral law is to be accepted as an ultimate fact of experience. As rational creatures we find ourselves commanded by a moral imperative. Moral obligation is on the one hand the most familiar experience of the common man, while on the other it is the uncanniest of experiences. Obligation is both insistent and inescapable. In that sense, moral obligation is a task that we are called to that distinguishes it from every determination of desire that issues from self-love. Through the experience of obligation, we are called to the 'intelligible' or 'noumenal' order. The moral law must be expressed as a categorical imperative since it commands us unconditionally. At the same time, in the decision to obey or disobey we discover the possibility of our freedom. Autonomous individuals act as both 'sovereigns' and 'subjects' if they obey the very law that they promulgate to themselves. The autonomous will does not submit to anything beyond itself. The heteronomous will, on the other hand, is a will that allows itself to be governed by some external principle, and cannot serve as the proper basis for morality; morality presupposes autonomy. To see this we must look at how a free will deliberates.

---

79 Immanuel Kant, *Groundwork of the Metaphysics of Morals* (Cambridge: Cambridge University Press, 1998), p. 52.

According to Kant, inclinations are grounded in what he calls 'incentives'. When the incentive of the object is pleasant, then the inclination says: it would be pleasant to bring about this particular end by acting in this particular way. Now, if pleasure were law to you, in other words, if your will were heteronomous, then you would act to get this pleasurable End without thinking twice. However, if you are autonomous, nothing external can be a law to you. Then the question you should ask is different: whether I take this to be my law. In other words, the question is whether the maxim passes the categorical imperative test. The categorical imperative is therefore the law of a free will.

Nietzsche comments on Kant's autonomy in *The Gay Science:*

> What? You admire the categorical imperative within you? The 'firmness' of your so-called moral judgment? This 'unconditional' feeling that 'here everyone must judge as I do'? Rather admire your *selfishness* at this point. And the blindness, pettiness, and frugality of your selfishness. For it is selfish to experience one's own judgment as a universal law; and this selfishness is blind, petty and frugal because it betrays that you have not discovered yourself nor created for yourself an ideal of your own, your very own- for that could never be somebody else's and much less that of all, all![80]

One way of putting this is to say that Kant appreciates self-governance (sovereignty) and makes it the focus of his philosophical project, but on the other, betrays it by conflating it with the simple fulfilment of our rational nature. Kant destroys self-governance by imprisoning the individual through the rule of an impersonal law, while, at same time, he overestimates our rational nature. However, to say that Nietzsche simply denies that agents act rationally and consciously as a result of which they can be held responsible is to ignore the particular evaluation of free will. As Thomas Bailey claims, Nietzsche's 'venomous rejection of morality is directed at those forms of evaluation which demand that an agent radically differ from what he already is or, even, from what he naturally could be...or that man transcend his natural existence in the name of "a higher world."'[81] Nietzsche is critical of the notion of free will that he equates with *causa sui*. His non-metaphysical naturalism, on the other hand, offers a positive compatibilist alternative to the notion of the will that he rejects and argues that willing is a much more complicated phenomenon than the traditional way of thinking believes.[82]

---

80 Nietzsche, *GS* 335, p. 265.
81 Thomas Bailey, '"The Animal that may Promise": Nietzsche on the Will, Naturalism, and Duty', *Pli*, Coventry: Warwick University Press, 11, 2001, p. 108.
82 Nietzsche, *BGE* 19, p. 25

Firstly, Nietzsche insists that mental events, including those involving willing, are physiological. In *GM* he writes:

> that 'sinfulness' in man is not a fact, but rather the interpretation of a fact, namely a physiological upset....even 'psychic suffering' does not seem to be a fact at all, but simply an interpretation (causal interpretation) of facts that could not be formulated exactly up till now.

In *BGE* he discusses his understanding of willing. Firstly, in all willing there is a plurality of sensations and a muscular tension 'towards' something and 'away' from something else, namely the sensation of the condition we leave and the sensation of the condition towards which we go. Thus, feelings are to be recognized as an ingredient of will. Secondly, in every act of will there is commanding thought which cannot be separated from the 'willing'. Thirdly, 'will is not only a complex of sensation and thinking, but it is above all an *affect*: and specifically the affect of the command.'[83] So, the will is 'above all an *affect*' and more specifically, an affect arising from the relation between the commanding and obeying. Now, in all willing 'we are at the same time the obeying and the commanding parties', and as the obeying party we know the 'sensations of constraints, impulsion, pressure, resistance, and motion which usually begin immediately after the act of willing.' But we generally disregard this and deceive ourselves by means of synthetic concept 'I' which 'has become attached to the act of willing – to such a degree that he who wills believes sincerely that willing *suffices* for action.' Nietzsche writes: '"Freedom of the will" – is the expression for the complex state of delight of the person exercising volition, who commands and at the same time identifies himself with the executor of the order – who, as such, also enjoys the triumph over obstacles but thinks within himself that it was really his will itself which overcame them.'[84]

Nietzsche also expresses this idea via the language of forces. Whenever there are relationships between forces, and those forces are unequal, a body is constituted. This body may be chemical, biological, social or political. The dominant forces are known as the *active* the dominated forces are known as *reactive*.[85] Not only this, we may speak of the reason of the body – as opposed to that of the soul or the mind defended by the 'despisers of the body'.[86]

---

83   Nietzsche, *BGE* 19. p. 25
84   Nietzsche, *BGE* 19, p. 26
85   Gilles Deleuze, *Nietzsche and Philosophy*, trans. Hugh Tomlinson (London: Athlone Press, 1983), p. 40.
86   *Gay Science*, 357; *Will to Power* 524; *Thus Spoke Zarathustra*, 'On the Despisers of the Body'.

> The body is a great reason, a manifold with one sense, a war and a peace, a herd and a herdsman.
>
> A tool of the body is your small reason too, my brother, which you call 'spirit', a small tool and toy of your great reason.
>
> ...
>
> Behind your thoughts and feelings, my brother, stands a mighty commander, an unknown wise man – his name is Self. In your body he dwells, he is your body.[87]

A detailed exploration of the principle of active and reactive forces is beyond the scope of this book, yet we can briefly conclude that in Nietzsche's self there is a kind of combat, only it is not a combat between passion and reason. In a more Spinozistic approach,[88] Nietzsche says that what you are is what your body is, or what your body can do. Despite his famous statement in *GM* I:13 'the doer is a mere fiction' and 'the deed is everything', Nietzsche does not simply deny that there is a subject of the deed, rather he is claiming that it is not separate from the activity, in other words, it is in the deed. What Nietzsche suggests seems to be a quite different relationship between self and the deed than a cause and effect relationship in which the subject is the cause of the deed. This positive conception of the free will, then, involves acting fully within one's character, and accepting oneself for what one is and affirming oneself as a whole.

Now, recall Pippin's *nonseparability* thesis and a *nonisolatability* claim which he attributes to Nietzsche. According to the former intention-formation and articulation are always being transformed. That is to say, the deed alone has the privileged authority over my subjective construal since it is only the deed than can show who one is.[89] According to the latter the conditions under which one would regard an intention as justifying an action have to be taken into consideration, and this, in turn, draws our attention not only to the character of the person but also to the community in which he lives or to the tradition. The most notable representative of this view is perhaps MacIntyre, for whom the concept of an intention is unintelligible apart from the concept of the unity of a human life, which, in turn, is unintelligible apart from the concept of a tradition. This mutual implication of intention, biography and tradition was, according to him, central to the classical

---

87   Friedrich Nietzsche, *Thus Spoke Zarathustra*, trans. Graham Parkes (Oxford: University of Oxford Press, 2005), I:4, 'On the Despisers of the Body'
88   Nietzsche himself points out the similarity between his (earlier) thought and Spinoza's, remarking to Overbeck in a postcard, 'I have a *precursor*, and what a precursor!' Quoted in Yirmiyahu Yovel, *Spinoza and Other Heretics* (Oxford: Princeton University Press, 1992), Vol. II, p. 105.
89   Pippin, 'Lightning and Flash, Agent and Deed', p. 139

Athenian age; but for MacIntyre, modern moral philosophers have severed this relationship, seeing the essential characteristic of human selfhood in the capacity to detach oneself from any particular standpoint, to step backwards and judge things from the outside.[90] In fact, Nietzsche would agree with MacIntyre, as long as this community is not decadent. However, Nietzsche asks: how is it possible to affirm life in a society in which self-denial is demanded (Christian morality), how one can become a creative individual who wills his/her own will, how one can be his/her own master?

Nietzsche's anti-Cartesian, anti-Christian account of the self focuses on a continuing expression of the subject through her deeds; for example, happiness (*eudaimonia*) can/must be available to us within this world, not in another reality which can be attained only through self-renunciation. In fact, in his understanding of willing Nietzsche owes a lot to Stoic materialism. According to the Stoics, the emotions are cognitive, i.e. they are evaluative judgments whose objects are external goods on which we have no control. Similarly, Nietzsche claims that feelings are the product of beliefs and judgments.[91] In *Daybreak* 35 Nietzsche writes:

> 'Trust your feelings!' – But feelings are nothing final or original; behind feelings there stand judgments and evaluations which we inherit in the form of feelings (inclinations, aversions). The inspiration born of a feeling is the grandchild of a judgment – and often of a false judgment.[92]

Like the Stoics Nietzsche claims that 'by freeing ourselves of such evaluations we prevent ourselves from adding to our suffering or setbacks the agonising thought that what we are suffering is an evil of injustice.'[93] In other words, Nietzsche claims that an external event cannot be inherently good or bad, or in Stoic terms external events are *indifferent*, it is we who assert value judgments.

As a genealogist, Nietzsche appeals to etymological evidence in order to indicate how, in different languages, the words that are used to indicate 'good' are derived from the words that express the self-affirmation of the Master, how the noble gives himself names which show superiority.[94] For instance, the Latin word *bonus* derives from *duonus*, meaning 'man of war', while *malus* derives from *melas* which is the name for the common man as 'the dark coloured one.' Moreover,

---

90 MacIntyre, *After Virtue*, pp. 118-119
91 On Nietzsche and Stoics see Michael Ure, 'Nietzsche's Free Spirit Trilogy and Stoic Therapy', *Journal of Nietzsche Studies*, 38, (2009).
92 Nietzsche, *Daybreak*, I: 35, p. 25
93 Ure, 'Nietzsche's Free Spirit', p. 68
94 Nietzsche, *GM* I:5

the German *gut* means 'godlike' or the man 'of godlike race' which is identical with the popular (originally noble), name of the Goths.[95] By multiplying these examples, Nietzsche attempts to show that 'noble', 'aristocratic' is the basic concept from which 'good' in the sense of spiritually noble developed.

He asserts that the discrimination of moral values has originated either amongst the powerful – the rulers – or amongst the ruled – the slaves. The master's being conscious of the difference between him and the ruled results in a feeling of joy, whereas for the ruled this consciousness of distinction results in pessimism. The Attic culture of tragedy, for instance, represents the true nobility of culture since it expresses the controlled powers of life within the unifying context of Apollo and Dionysus whereas the triumph of Christianity represents the vengeance of the slave.

> The noble type of man experiences *itself* as determining values; it does not need approval; it judges, 'what is harmful to me is harmful in itself'; it knows itself to be that which accords honor to things; it is *value-creating*. Everything it knows as part of itself it honors: such a morality is self-glorification.[96]

In contrast to the psychology of the noble type, in slave morality we find the pessimistic type of man, who looks at the virtues of the powerful with *ressentiment*. The slave and the master differ in nature: 'the man of *ressentiment* needs to conceive of a non-ego, then to oppose himself to this non-ego in order finally to posit himself as self.'[97] The slaves, the weak people 'are just weak; it is good to do nothing *for which we are not strong enough.*'[98] The oppressed says:

> Let us be different from evil people, let us be good! And a good person is anyone who does not rape, does not harm anyone, who does not attack, does not retaliate, who leaves the taking of revenge to God, who keeps hidden as we do, avoids all evil and asks little from life in general, like us who are patient, humble and upright.[99]

In the mouths of slaves, values are still created; but the point of departure is positing the other as evil. From the point of view of the slave, the evil one is the one who acts, whereas the good one is the one who holds himself back from doing evil, but effectively from acting. Here we must recall Nietzsche's claims about causality and the doer-deed distinction, because the further point is that the evil one is the one who acts in spite of the fact that he could have acted otherwise. The

---

95   Nietzsche, *GM* I:5
96   Nietzsche, *BGE* 260, p. 205
97   Deleuze, *Nietzsche and Philosophy*, p. 121
98   Nietzsche, *GM* I:13, p. 29
99   Nietzsche, *GM* I:13, p. 29

slave attributes the actions of the evil one to choice. The emergence of slave morality is the product of experiencing himself as subject to command, as powerless. This experience expresses itself as *ressentiment* because the slave accounts for his suffering in terms of 'free will' and bad conscience: he could have acted otherwise. The slave seeks a guilty agent for his powerlessness and in the mouth of the slave this guilty agent is the noble one.

In fact, Nietzsche is close to Kant in saying that we can never know exactly what are our motives are, and that we may believe we perform an action out of respect for the moral law but in fact it may have been performed out of self-love. A bad person, for Kant, is governed by the principle of self-love which is conceived as a kind of *egoism* expressed in acting on maxims oriented to the pursuit of their own happiness. Self-love, for Kant, is 'opposed to *morality* as a threat, a challenge, a danger' and it is an opposition, says David Owen, 'whose stakes are intensified by Kant's acknowledgement that self-love is an ineliminable feature of finite desiring (hence happiness-seeking) in creatures such as human beings and, consequently, that one can never be sure that actions complying with one moral duties are solely motivated by respect for the moral law.' Self-love cannot provide an objective basis for morality. In the section on 'Egoism' in *Anthropology from a Pragmatic Point of View*, Kant says:

> ... the moral egoist limits all purposes to himself; as a eudaemonist, he concentrates the highest motives of his will merely on profit and his own happiness, but not on the concept of duty. Because every other person has a different concept of what he counts as happiness, it is exactly egoism which causes him to have no touchstone of a genuine concept of duty which truly must be a universally valid principle. All eudaemonists are consequently egoists.[100]

However, if self-love is the threat and an enemy of morality for Kant, it is something that should be praised for Nietzsche. Self-affirmation or self-love is at the centre of Nietzsche's ethics, an understanding of ethics which cannot find in reason a ground for morality, and which sees ethics as resting primarily on a relationship with ourselves. What sort of self?

One attempt to develop an understanding of selfhood that departs from Kant can be derived from phenomenology. David Thompson, for instance, drawing on Merleau-Ponty, suggests that the unity of an action and the unity of an agent are inseparable, but starts from the body and its abilities rather than reason.

---

100 Quoted in David Owen, 'Autonomy, Self-Respect and Self-Love: Nietzsche on Ethical Agency,' in *Nietzsche on Freedom and Autonomy*, ed. Ken Gemes and Simon May (Oxford: Oxford University Press, 2009), p. 220.

Merleau-Ponty's 'lived body', for instance, unlike the body of physics, is not an object to be perceived; rather it is the one that perceives.[101] If Kant's categories are the conditions for objects in a physical world, the perceiving body, for Merleau-Ponty, is the condition for objects; the acting body is the condition for actions. In that sense, body-perceiver (body-subject) and body-agent are one and the same thing. The potentialities of perception are motor capacities of the body: 'The lived body is as much a unity of action as of perception; indeed, the unity of perception, properly understood, *is* a unity of action.'[102] Lived body's unity is an ongoing task to be accomplished. The constitution of both the body and its world originate in the same process, and this is what Merleau-Ponty calls being-in-the-world. Unification of the deed and the self happens on the bodily level and the self/action structure is constituted by being-in-the-world rather not by being 'synthesized' by some disembodied, intellectual being. It is not some explicit law or principle, like the categorical imperative.[103]

So far so good. But what is Thompson's alternative? His account is naturalistic, if the idea of a culturally constructed narrative self is unarguably the currently accepted way of attributing responsibility, this is not because it satisfies a need laid down by an abstract ideal or principle, but because it is simply the latest stage of an evolutionary process, one that does not cease to operate once that stage has been reached. Thompson thinks, for instance, that if we do make a distinction between people to whom we do and people to whom we do not attribute responsibility, it is grounded in a sense of their bodily capacity; so we do not attribute responsibility to someone with Alzheimer's disease, because their capacity for narrative unity is simply broken.

If Thompson is right in claiming that philosophers who overestimate reason fall into intellectualism,[104] then his naturalistic account overestimates the body, or even assumes a separation between mind and body, another dichotomy that Nietzsche attempts to overcome. According to Nietzsche this separation is an illusion, as are those others that constrain our thinking: subject and object, 'free

---

101 David Thompson, 'Body as the Unity of Action', 2011, p. 5. The article is available in Thompson's website: http://www.ucs.mun.ca/~davidt/bodyunityaction.pdf
102 Thompson, 'Body as the Unity of Action', p. 6
103 Thompson, 'Body as the Unity of Action', p. 6
104 For instance Christian Wolff can be regarded an intellectualist 'who believes that there is no gap between recognizing an act as good and the act of willing it.' He believes that 'immoral behaviour is always the result of mistaken beliefs about goodness.' See Lucas Thorpe, 'The Point of Studying Ethics According to Kant', *The Journal of Value Inquiry*, 40 (2006), pp. 461-474.

will' and determinism etc. Nietzsche's rejection of this separation is rooted in the thought of Spinoza and in particular in Spinoza's physics of bodies. This involves both a preservation of the limits of bodies and a blurring of them.

I.iv. Nietzsche and Spinoza: Free will and Freedom

I.iv.a. Free will and determinism

The connection between Nietzsche and Spinoza has often been remarked on.[105] In fact, Nietzsche himself already pointed out the similarity between his (earlier) thought and Spinoza's, remarking to Overbeck in a postcard, 'I have a *precursor*, and what a precursor!' He goes on to say:

> Not only is his over-all tendency like mine – making knowledge the most powerful affect – but in five main points of his doctrine I recognize myself; this most unusual and loneliest thinker is closest to me in precisely these matters: he denies the freedom of the will, teleology, the moral world order, the unegoistic, and evil. Even though the divergences are admittedly tremendous, they are due more to the difference in time, culture, and science.[106]

Although here Nietzsche tends to downplay the differences between Spinoza and himself, later he becomes a radical critic of Spinoza. We can appreciate this if we call his formula for his philosophical affirmation: *Amor fati* – love of fate. He says: 'It simply comes back, it finally comes home to me – my own self.'[107] In *Spinoza and Other Heretics*, Yovel tells us that this formula, which was not used before Nietzsche, is, in fact, 'a polemical transformation of Spinoza's *amor dei intellectualis*, rejecting the primacy of the intellect and putting *fatum* in place of Spinoza's nature-God as the object of love.'[108] Although they seem to be two opposed approaches, these two formulae involve a kind of 'love of necessity'. However, while law of *ratio* is the basis for this necessity for Spinoza, indeterminate *fatum*, which cannot be explained through concepts and rational laws, has a crucial role

---

105 See, for example, Edwin Curley, *Behind the Geometrical Method: A Reading of Spinoza's Ethics* (Princeton, NJ: Princeton University Press, 1988), pp. 126-35; Gilles Deleuze, *Spinoza: Practical Philosophy*, trans. Robert Hurley (San Francisco: City Lights Books, 1988), pp. 17-29; and Yirmiyahu Yovel, *Spinoza and Other Heretics* (Princeton, NJ; Oxford: Princeton University Press, 1992), Vol.2, pp. 104-35.
106 Quoted in Yovel, *Spinoza*, p. 105
107 Nietzsche, *Zarathustra*, III:1, 'The Wanderer'
108 Yovel, *Spinoza*, p. 104

in Nietzsche's philosophy of affirmation. This divergence puts Nietzsche in a constant dispute with Spinoza, and, yet, as I suggest below, for both of them the 'love of necessity' is an important component of freedom.

In his postcard to Overbeck, Nietzsche cites the denial of freedom of the will as one of the similarities between himself and Spinoza. Yet what is freedom without freedom of the will?

In order to understand Spinoza's rejection of the freedom of the will, it is necessary to begin with his notion of God – Nature. In the Appendix to the first part of *Ethics*, he makes a list of God's properties:

> that he exists necessarily; that he is unique; that he is and acts from the necessity alone of his nature; that (and how) he is the free cause of all things; that all things are in God and so depend on him that without him they can neither be nor be conceived; and finally that all things are predetermined by God, not from freedom of the will *or* infinite absolute good pleasure, but from God's absolute nature, *or* infinite power.[109]

This amounts to a rejection of the idea of a transcendent God who created the world out of his will, and hence of the idea that God's nature could be different. We call things contingent 'only because of a defect of our knowledge' of the order of things.[110] To imagine that the order of things could be different would be to attribute another nature to God, which would be a rejection of the perfection of God.[111] God's freedom which is incompatible with 'absolute will', is in fact, a 'free cause', acting from the necessity of a nature which includes neither will nor intellect. In other words, Spinoza's God has no purpose and no interest in the actions of human beings.

The Appendix to Part I is crucial because it contains a transition from the nature of God to the nature of the human mind, and seeks to expose a prejudice about the freedom of human beings: 'That all men are born ignorant of the causes of things, and that they all want to seek their own advantage, and are conscious of this appetite.'[112] Thinking that they are conscious of their appetites, human beings think that they are free. However, according to Spinoza this belief in free will is an error. Spinoza illustrates the point through a thought experiment suggesting that when a stone is set in motion by an external cause, it will think that as far as it can it strives to continue to move:

---

109 Baruch Spinoza, *Ethics* (London: Penguin 1996), appendix.
110 Spinoza, *Ethics*, Ip33s1
111 Spinoza, *Ethics.*, Ip33s2
112 Spinoza, *Ethics.*, I, appendix

Of course since the stone is conscious only of its striving, and not at all indifferent, it will believe itself to be free, and to persevere in motion for no other cause than because it wills to. ......And this is that famous human freedom which everyone brags of having, and which consists only in this: that men are conscious of their appetites and ignorant of the causes by which they are determined.'[113]

Spinoza claims that men have a tendency to act on account of an end (recall Nietzsche's critique of the error of cause and effect). However, this is an imposition of man's own way of thinking on nature rather than an understanding of nature. This error arises out of man's searching nature for what is convenient for man's own use. Then he adds:

> And knowing that they had found these means, not provided them for themselves, they had reason to believe that there was someone else who had prepared those means for their use.[114]

He adds that the mind is embedded within the causal order of nature, 'In the mind there is no absolute, or free, will, but the mind is determined to will this or that by a cause which is also determined by another, and this again by another, and so to infinity.'[115] He explains this point by means of the following 'demonstration':

> The Mind is a certain and determinate mode of thinking and so cannot be a free cause of its own actions, *or* cannot have an absolute faculty of willing and not willing. Rather, it must be determined to willing this or that by a cause which is also determined by another, and this cause again by another, and so on.[116]

According to this will itself is just a part of a causal chain which is dependent on an infinite chain of circumstances. To desire this or that is not a choice but the outcome of a whole range of conditions. We encounter a similar approach in Nietzsche. For Nietzsche fate is nothing but a chain of events. To set man and fate over against one another is an error, for whenever we act we create our own events, determine our own fate. In 'The Wanderer and his Shadow'[117] will and fate are inseparable; every action is a fulfilment of fate. Even when we try to resist fate – which itself is an imaginary resistance – 'it is precisely fate that is here fulfilling

---

113 Quoted in Genevieve Lloyd, *Routledge Philosophy Guidebook to Spinoza and Ethics* (London; New York: Routledge, 1996), p. 46.
114 Spinoza, *Ethics*, I appendix
115 Spinoza, *Ethics.*, IIp48
116 Spinoza, *Ethics*, IIp48d
117 'The Wanderer and His Shadow' was published as an additional book to *Human, all too Human* in 1879.

itself.'[118] What Nietzsche means is that the agent can develop an internal power to increase its capacity to receive and interpret external events. This is what *Amor fati* is about.

Although Spinoza uses the concepts like 'substance', 'attribute' and 'mode', he transforms them into the terms of his own thought. For instance, in *Ethics* he transforms the idea of Cartesian God which was presented as a substance in a unique sense independent of all other beings, into the idea of God as a unique substance of which all other things are modifications. According to Descartes there are two kinds of substances: 1- thinking substance, or soul, or mind; 2- extended substance. Then Descartes divides the former into two: 1a- Infinite thinking substance (God); 1b- Finite thinking substance (mind or soul). Spinoza rejects both of Descartes' distinctions: there is only one substance and it is infinite. More importantly this substance is neither thinking nor extended. Whereas for Descartes, thought and matter are two different kinds of substances, for Spinoza they are attributes of God. The Cartesian thinking substance becomes the mind of God, and Spinoza's determinism and his notion of an immanent God – Nature – are strongly related to his notion of the 'self'.

Like Spinoza, Nietzsche rejects the idea of the 'self' as an idealized unity. He criticises 'idealism' for ignoring the claim of the body and neglecting the impact of psychological and physiological factors upon our apprehension of the world. As we have seen, Nietzsche writes: 'There is no such substratum; there is no "being" behind the deed, its effect and what becomes of it; "the doer" is invented as an after-thought, the doing is everything.'[119]

In this respect Nietzsche's rejection of the freedom of the will and, correspondingly, of the idea of a unique 'self', accords with that of Spinoza. However, there is a crucial difference because Nietzsche in addition rejects any sort of 'substance', be it Descartes' or Spinoza's. In *The Gay Science* he writes:

> In order that the concept of substance could originate – which is indispensable for logic although in the strictest sense nothing real corresponds to it – it was likewise necessary that for a long time one did not see nor perceive the changes in things. The beings that did not see so precisely had an advantage over those that saw everything 'in flux.'[120]

Yovel thinks that this may be directed at Spinoza even though Spinoza's name is not mentioned: 'Nietzsche's critique of 'logic' and rationalist postulates centres

---

118 Friedrich Nietzsche, *Human, all too Human*, trans. Hollingdale (Cambridge: Cambridge University Press, 1986), p. 325. Hereafter *HH*.
119 Nietzsche, *GM* I:13, p. 28
120 Nietzsche, *GS* 111, p. 171

around the concept of self-identical 'things', which is also the basis for the category of substance – Spinoza's major concept.'[121] He adds, 'the myth of the will, or the subject as agent, also underlies the concept of substance itself. On several occasions Nietzsche analyses the concept of substance as a consequence of concept of the subject, not the reverse.'[122] Nietzsche does not mean that Spinoza supports the idea of the subject – this would be unjust – only that he did not go far enough and face the indeterminate *fatum* which implies the lack of *any* order and rational ground. Spinoza's insistence on 'substance' is 'nothing more than a desire for the self-preservation of the human being and for the preservation of the existing order.'

In another passage Nietzsche makes his critique more explicit, this time referring to Spinoza directly:

> The wish to preserve oneself is the symptom of a condition of distress, of a limitation of the really fundamental instinct of life which aims at *the expansion of power* and, wishing for that, frequently risks and even sacrifices self-preservation. It should be considered symptomatic when some philosophers – for example Spinoza who was consumptive – considered the instinct of self-preservation decisive and *had* to see it that way; for they were individuals in conditions of distress.[123]

This raises a question about Nietzsche's alternative to this 'defensive' concept of the self. In discussing this problem we will see that the difference between Nietzsche and Spinoza concerns more than their views about substance and subject. It hinges on the understanding of the relationship between the individual and time. The Nietzschean remedy for the decline of modern man will involve a new relationship between the individual and his past, present and future. It is this relationship with time that marks the difference between Nietzsche's understanding of freedom and selfhood and Spinoza's.

I.iv.b. The individual and time

To understand what Spinoza means by freedom we should inquire into his notion of selfhood – body – and its relation to culture. Of course one may wonder what the borders of a 'self' are if there is no distinction between body and mind as there is in Descartes, according to whom the 'self' can be separated from its own body along with the rest of the world. However, Spinoza suggests a physics of bodies

---

121 Yovel, *Spinoza*, p. 119
122 Yovel, *Spinoza.*, p. 120
123 Nietzsche, *GS* 349, pp. 291-292

– be they social or physical – which involves both a preservation of the limits of bodies and a blurring of them.

> The human mind does not know the human body itself, nor does it know that it exists, except through ideas of affections by which the body is affected.[124]
>
> The mind does not know itself, except insofar as it perceives the ideas of the affections of the body.[125]

These propositions suggest that the mind knows itself only through the particular ideas deriving from its relations to its body, and correspondingly to other bodies. The mind as the idea of the body has a past in which it was affected by other bodies since it strives to imagine things that enhance the body's power of acting,[126] yet 'when the mind imagines those things that diminish or restrain the body's power of acting, it strives, as far as it can, to recollect things which exclude their existence.'[127] These imaginations are associated with affects from the past. However, the 'self' is also an actually existing body moving towards the future. While the mind tries to protect its unity as a temporal and spatial being, it is also open to new possibilities by being open to new interactions with other bodies which leave traces on the body as well as in the mind. In that sense, this constant struggle of bodies to articulate themselves in a whole of which they are part, blurs the borders between them. Such a relationship with time and with other spatial bodies leaves no room for a fixed identity. In this temporal aspect, in its capacity for imagination and memory, lies the mind's instability, since numerous different traces of the past on different bodies will create different reactions to present events.[128] Moreover, even the same mind – body – will react differently at different times. This means we have no control over our imagination or our recollection of things. Spinoza shows this in the following way: 'If the human body has once been affected by two bodies at once, then afterwards, when the mind imagines one of them, it will immediately recollect the other also.'[129]

According to Spinoza mind and body are the same thing and the physical forces that affect the body affect the mind as well. Now, we find a similar approach in Nietzsche. In *Thus Spoke Zarathustra* he writes: 'Behind your thoughts and feelings,

---

124 Spinoza, *Ethics*, IIp19
125 Spinoza, *Ethics*, IIp23
126 Spinoza, *Ethics*, IIIp12
127 Spinoza, *Ethics*, IIIp13
128 Spinoza, *Ethics*, IIIp51
129 Spinoza, *Ethics*, III14d

my brother, stands a mighty commander, an unknown wise man – his name is Self. In your body he dwells, he is your body.'[130] Keith Ansell-Pearson draws our attention to the similarity between Nietzsche and Spinoza in their understandings of the body:

> Bodies do not evolve by establishing closed or fixed boundaries between themselves, between an inside and an outside; if this were the case nothing could, in fact, evolve. This means that a body does not have an identity that is fixed once and for all, but is essentially informed by a plastic and adaptive power, one capable of profound change. Such change takes place through processes of assimilation and incorporation.[131]

Both the English word 'incorporation', and the German word used by Nietzsche, *Einverleibung*, literally mean a taking into the body.

So far this Spinozist 'self' does not seem to be very different from the Nietzschean 'self'. However, the difference between them lies in the fact that for Spinoza, imagination is also a precondition for reason, and reason is a precondition for freedom. This is what Nietzsche rejects.

As we have seen the mind – body – is a part of a whole, meaning Nature or God: 'it is impossible that a man should not be part of Nature, and that he should be able to undergo no changes except those which can be understood through his own nature alone, and of which he is the adequate cause.'[132]

Now, there is a crucial link between this account of time – imagination and memory – and freedom. As long as the mind conceives things 'from the dictate of reason', not from the imagination, 'it is affected in the same way, whether the idea is of a future or a past thing, or of a present one' since 'whatever the mind conceives under the guidance of reason, it conceives under the same species of eternity, or necessity.'[133] In the following Scholium, Spinoza claims that once the mind is affected in the same way by the idea of a present, or future or past thing as a result of conceiving the things 'from the dictate of reason', it 'would want the good it conceived as future just as it wants the good it conceives as present. Hence, it would necessarily neglect a lesser present good for a greater future one, and what would be good in the present, but the cause of some future ill, it would not want at all.' This suggests that once we know the reason of an event which makes us sad, for example, we will know how to avoid sadness in the future, and thus be freed from enslavement by our passions. Such knowledge also increases

---

130 Nietzsche, *Zarathustra*, I:4, 'On the Despisers of the Body'
131 Ansell-Pearson, *Nietzsche*, p. 46
132 Spinoza, *Ethics*, IVp4
133 Spinoza, *Ethics*, IVp62d

the individual's sense of responsibility since the more I understand the reasons for my actions, the greater is my ability to choose what I will do in the future.

This is an important moment in Spinoza's ethics, and he seems to share this view of the future with Nietzsche, who also sees the future as something that can be 'created'. However, Nietzsche himself claimed that one of the main divergences between him and Spinoza lies in their accounts of time. Why should that be?

In order to understand Nietzsche's critique of Spinoza's philosophy of time we should concentrate on what he says about remembering, promising and forgetting. In 'On the Uses and Disadvantages of History for Life'[134] he makes a distinction between animals and human beings in terms of different relationships with time, and asks how it was possible for an animal to become an animal able to make promises. He repeats the question in *GM*: 'To breed an animal with the prerogative to *promise* – is that not precisely the paradoxical task which nature has set herself with regard to humankind?' The task is paradoxical because animals, as *a historical* beings, are content with a passive forgetfulness, and thus basically happy, and do not have to bear the burden of living with a past, present and future. This burden is exemplified by the fact that human forgetfulness is not *vis inertiae*, but rather a process where our experiences are digested; its purpose is to 'shut the doors and windows of consciousness for a while.'[135] Producing a being with the capacity to make promises requires a counter-device to the active force of forgetting:

> ...it is the *will's memory*: so that a world of strange new things, circumstances and even acts of will may be placed quite safely in between the original 'I will', 'I shall do' and the actual discharge of the will, its act, without breaking this long chain of the will.[136]

Nietzsche celebrates the active force of forgetting and warns about the costs of countering it: 'it is impossible to live happily without forgetting.' This requires knowledge of the plastic power of a human being as well as of a culture 'to transform and incorporate into oneself what is past and foreign, to heal wounds, to replace what has been lost, to recreate broken moulds.'[137] In that sense, memory is not a mere recollection of events, it is also strongly related to our emotional life. Objects, things, people can remind us of what is already forgotten and what we wish to forget. This means that we do not have control over our memories, that it

---

134   Friedrich Nietzsche, *Untimely Meditations* (Cambridge: Cambridge University Press, 1986), pp. 57-125, II Hereafter *UM*.
135   Nietzsche, *GM* II:1, p. 38
136   Nietzsche, *GM* II:1, p. 39
137   Nietzsche, *UM* II.

has an existence independent of the will. As Marcel Proust shows, any accidental encounter with a smell, or a taste can remind us of our past.

Up to this point it does not seem that there is a significant divergence between Spinoza and Nietzsche on the question of time and the idea that we should relieve ourselves from past events and create our own futures. After all, it might have been Spinoza himself who prompted the idea of eternal recurrence, which Nietzsche seems to have discovered only a few days after his discovery that Spinoza was his precursor (summer of 1881).[138] However, later Nietzsche becomes a critic of Spinoza. Why should this be?

As we have seen, Nietzsche himself appreciates Spinoza's rejection of free will. He even accepts that Spinoza, like him, attempts to introduce a notion of selfhood similar to his own. However, this was not more than an attempt since, as Yovel emphasizes, the concept of substance is, in fact, a consequence of the concept of subject. Can such illusory concepts as substance and subject be removed? They can, but only on one condition: that God is dead!

In the *GM*, he refers to a moment in Spinoza's life when he 'turned his attention to the question of what actually remained for him, himself, of that famous *morsus conscientiae*.' Nietzsche recalls that Spinoza's God is free, that is, that he is not a God who 'operates everything *sub ratione boni*' since that 'would mean that God is subject to fate.'[139] In line with this, Spinoza says that what is left of this bite of conscience is 'the opposite of gladness', a mere sadness that things did not turn out as one expected. Now, Nietzsche says that this means that 'The world for Spinoza had returned to that state of innocence in which it had lain before the invention of bad conscience…For millennia wrongdoers overtaken by punishment have felt *no different than Spinoza* with regard to their "offence,"'[140] saying in effect that the crimes for which they were punished were a mistake, perhaps even an accident. Such an unchristian attitude would have as its consequences the need to learn from one's mistakes rather than to be bitten by conscience; it would be a situation in which the individual was capable of self-improvement, but it would not entail the need for moral improvement. One's own crimes would be akin to 'illness, misfortune or death', but nothing more.

However, despite Spinoza's appearing to endorse this non-Christian approach to ethics – my past misdemeanours were an unavoidable misfortune that I may seek to avoid in the future, but not evidence of my sinfulness – Nietzsche still

---

138 Ansell-Pearson, *Nietzsche*, p. 20
139 Nietzsche, *GM* II:15, p. 60
140 Nietzsche, *GM* II:15, p. 60

sees this as an approach to ethics in which the individual is trapped by or tied to the past. In Spinoza's determinism, then, although sadness at what was expressed in the deed is not the Christian's guilt, it functions in much the same way, implying just as strongly that 'it happened' rather than 'I willed it.' Spinoza's individual is just as much in thrall to his or her memory as anyone else. Moreover, it is still a subject, maybe not a Cartesian subject, but a subject who suffers from the idea of 'I could have been someone else', a feeling of guilt at not being other than what one is.

Active forgetting, however, is precisely one of the characteristics that Nietzsche attributes to his ideal human being (sometimes he calls him/her the sovereign individual, sometimes the overhuman) who has power over himself and his fate. He knows that he does not have power over 'it was': but active forgetting means the absence of guilt. In *Zarathustra* Nietzsche had praised forgetting: 'Innocence the child is and forgetting, a beginning anew, a play, a self-propelling wheel, a first movement, a sacred Yea-saying.'[141] What Nietzsche suggests is a new relationship with time: through active forgetting – appropriate incorporation – we can redeem the present from the past which brings the power to create our own futures. This is what Nietzsche means by recreating 'it was' into a 'thus I willed it.'

However, for Nietzsche's part this would be missing Spinoza's point since, according to Spinoza, as long as we live under the guidance of reason we never suffer from not having been someone else. But as we will see, Nietzsche rejects this Spinozistic notion of reason.

I.iv.c. *Reason and culture*

As we have seen, according to Spinoza once the mind is affected in the same way by the idea of a present, or future or past thing as a result of conceiving the things 'from the dictate of reason', it 'would want the good it conceived as future just as it wants the good it conceives as present.' Reason, for Spinoza, is intimately connected with *conatus* which is the desire to persevere our being. 'Each thing' says Spinoza 'as far as it can by its own power, strives to persevere in its being.'[142] Reason is the faculty commonly set over against natural drives towards self-preservation. In Spinoza's ethics instead of striving for things because we judge them as good 'we judge something to be good because we strive for it, will it, want it, and desire

---

141 Nietzsche, *Zarathustra*, I:1, 'On the Three Transformations'
142 Spinoza, *Ethics*, IIIpVI

it.'[143] However, it should be noted that Spinoza does not say that we should suppress our passions – that would be impossible – rather by accepting their necessity and understanding their operations, we can become free. And Spinoza adds 'the essence of reason is nothing but our mind, insofar as it understands clearly and distinctly.'[144] By saying 'Insofar as the mind understands all things as necessary, it has a greater power over the effects or is less acted on by them',[145] he means that as we come to understand the actual causes of our emotions, we decrease the power of the emotions over us and we also exert the power of our intellect.

For Nietzsche this 'faith in reason' is another illusion:

> Gradually, man has become a fantastic animal that has to fulfil one more condition of existence than any other animal: man *has* to believe, to know from time to time *why* he exists; his race cannot flourish without a periodic trust in life – without faith in reason.[146]

Further in *GS*, Nietzsche refers to Spinoza: 'The meaning of knowing. – *Non ridere, non lugere, neque detestari, sed intelliegere*! says Spinoza[147] as simply and sublimely as is his wont.'[148] Nietzsche, however, claims that we suppose that *intelligere* stands opposed to the instincts, whereas it is 'nothing but a *certain behaviour of the instincts toward one another.*'[149] The gap between the two philosophers widens when Spinoza moves to another line of argument: the desire to preserve ourselves leads us to the desire to live with others in a state of harmony and agreement. Co-operation with others in society enhances our rational nature and elevates us to freedom. Two people working together, for instance, produce more power than a single individual. In that sense, the first human being Adam, was the least free man since he did not have any interaction with anyone.

> To man, then, there is nothing more useful than man. Man, I say, can wish for nothing more helpful to the preservation of his being than that all should so agree in all things that the minds and bodies of all would compose, as it were, one Mind and one Body; that all should strive together, as far as they can, to preserve their being; and that all, together, should seek for themselves the common advantage of all.[150]

---

143 Spinoza, *Ethics*, IIIp9s
144 Spinoza, *Ethics*, IV26d
145 Spinoza, *Ethics*, Vp6
146 Nietzsche, *GS* 1, p. 75
147 'Not laugh, not to lament, nor to detest, but to understand.'
148 Nietzsche, *GS* 333, p. 261
149 Nietzsche, *GS* 333, p. 261
150 Spinoza, *Ethics*, IVp18s

'From this', he concludes that 'men who are governed by reason – that is men who, from the guidance of reason, seek their own advantage – want nothing for themselves that they do not desire for other men. Hence they are just, honest, and honourable.'[151] In his *Bodies, Masses, Power*, Montag summarises Spinoza's account of parallelism of the mind and body and its relation to freedom through the following formulae: 'there can be no liberation of the mind without the liberation of the body' and 'there can be no liberation of the individual without collective liberation.'[152] Recalling Spinoza's *amor dei intellectualis* and his insistence on determinism, this means only those who can understand the causes of events can reach freedom as long as they live in a society where there is the possibility of being affected by other spatial bodies infinitely.

This implies that there is neither altruism nor selfishness in nature. This is also related to Spinoza's dynamic character of striving for self-preservation which Nietzsche attacks. For some commentators the phrase 'striving for self-preservation' necessarily leads to egoism since if the nature of individuals is alike, there is a gap between self-seeking and seeking the good of others, and such a gap does not bring collaboration but only conflict.[153] Against this, Lloyd states that:

> What we find in Spinoza is a reconceptualising of the relations between individuals. Spinoza's point is not that an individual – identifiable independently of its relations with others – necessarily pursues its own interests rather than theirs. It is rather that what it is to be an individual is to be both determined to act through the mediation of other modes and likewise to determine others.[154]

Nietzsche would see such a harmonious society as utopian. What is his alternative?

There is no opposition between nature and culture in Spinoza, whereas there is in Nietzsche. In fact he even regards the activity of culture as a 'tyranny against

---

151 Spinoza, *Ethics*, IVpl8s
152 Warren Montag, *Bodies, Masses, Power* (London; New York: Verso, 2000), p. Xxi.
153 Lloyd, *Spinoza and Ethics*, p. 75. Lloyd refers to Jonathan Bennett's *A Study of Spinoza's Ethics* saying: 'Bennett is too restrictive, both in his interpretation of what is involved in Spinoza's equation of self-preservation and the actual existence of individuals, and in his presentation of Spinoza's ethic as a version of egoism. If to preserve one's being is necessarily to exert causal power on some modes, and also to be acted upon by others, the distinction between self and other becomes here something quite different from what we are accustomed to in models of incidental interaction between independently existing individuals.' See also Jonathan Bennett's *A Study of Spinoza's Ethics* (Cambridge: Cambridge University Press, 1984), pp. 231-253; 289-310.
154 Lloyd, *Spinoza and Ethics*, p. 75

nature'.[155] However, Nietzsche's account of nature and culture is more complicated than that: while it is true that he regards culture as a 'tyranny against nature', he also believes that there is a selective object of culture whose function is to form a man capable of promising and thus of making use of the future, a free and powerful man who is active. Moreover, he writes 'any custom is better than no custom.'[156] After all it is culture that produced Napoleon, Goethe, and even Nietzsche himself.

If Nietzsche does not simply reject culture, nor does he suggest going back to nature. He criticises a particular culture; bourgeois-Christian culture which regards the subject as the centre of meaning and which is inseparable from the Cartesian conception of the 'self', and a modern project whose aim is to tame the 'human animal' and to give birth to a certain type of modern subject: a rational human being who has freedom of the will, where this freedom means being able to subjugate oneself to a universal moral law. It also entails an *agential self* who can be separated from its actions.

In the famous section 'On the Three Metamorphoses', Nietzsche proposes a more dynamic relationship between the individual and culture, embodied in three moments, symbolized in turn by the figures of the camel, the lion, and the child. As the camel the individual incorporates tradition before he/she finds the strength to challenge it (as a lion); then, this act of negation is followed by the creation of a new perspective, the child. '*Destruction as the active destruction of the man who wants to perish and to be overcome* announces the creator.'[157] Nietzsche's ideal man, by contrast, is the one who will be able to say 'No' (forgetting) to tradition and who will create his/her own perspective. In opposition to the last man's need for self-preservation stands 'the man who wants to perish', the product of the selective function of culture. This man who wants to perish is able to say 'Thus I willed it', rather than 'it happened', in other words, she accepts her past as well her present for she accepts herself who is expressed in her deeds. This, however, does not mean that she does not take responsibility for whatever she did.

This tension between the individual and culture seems to be very different from Spinoza's ideal culture. Spinoza insists on the idea that the power of thought of the many is necessarily greater than that of the few; this goes against the argument that to let the multitude be engaged with the political matters creates nothing but chaos:

> For if, while the Romans are debating, Saguntum is lost: on the other hand, while a few are deciding everything in conformity with their own passions only, liberty and

---

155 Nietzsche, *BGE* 188, p. 100
156 Nietzsche, *Daybreak* I:16, p. 15
157 Deleuze, *Nietzsche and Philosophy*, pp. 177-178

the general good are lost. For men's natural abilities are too dull to see through everything at once; but by consulting, listening, and debating, they grow more acute, and while they are trying all means, they at last discover those which they want, which all approve, but no one would have thought of in the first instance.[158]

It seems that there is one 'truth', one ideal state which can be attained through 'consulting, listening and debating'. Regarding his determinism which claims that there is a perfect order in nature of which we are part, and his notion of reason, it is obvious that the most ideal state would be the most perfect one which can be achieved only through the 'guidance of reason'. As opposed to Spinoza's ideal harmonious society, Nietzsche claims that culture always demands self-denial: 'Self-overcoming is demanded, *not* on account of the useful consequences it may have for the individual, but so that the hegemony of custom, tradition, shall be made evident in despite of the private desires and advantages of the individual: the individual has to sacrifice himself – that is the commandment of the custom.'[159]

In the section entitled 'On self-overcoming' Nietzsche writes:

The living did I pursue; I followed the greatest and the smallest paths that I might understand its way.

With a hundredfold mirror I caught its look when its mouth was closed, that its eye might speak to me. And its eye did speak to me.

But wherever I found the living, there too I heard the speech about obedience. All that is living is something that obeys.

And this is the second thing: whoever cannot obey himself will be commanded. This is the way of the living.

But this is third thing that I heard: that commanding is harder than obeying. And not only because the commander bears the burden of all who obey, and this burden can easily crush him.[160]

Whatever lives also obeys, but not all who live command; those who cannot command themselves are fated to be commanded. At the same time, 'commanding is harder than obeying'. This means when an individual commands himself/herself he/she pays for this commanding since he/she must be ready to reject every fixed horizon – and every comfort or consolation! – that the existing order imposes.

---

158 Baruch Spinoza, *Tractatus Politicus*, trans. R. H. M. Elwes (New York: Dover Publications, 1951), chp. 9, para. 14.
159 Nietzsche, *Daybreak* I:9, p. 11
160 Nietzsche, *Zarathustra*, II:12, 'On Self-overcoming'

As opposed to Spinoza's freedom which can be attained only by those who can understand the causes of events as long as they live in a society where there is the possibility of being affected by the other spatial bodies infinitely, Nietzsche celebrates an ethics which does not primarily rest on our relation with the others, but on our relation with ourselves, on the art of self-mastery and self-governance. For Nietzsche 'Becoming what one is' means being engaged in a constantly continuing process of affirmation of one's own self; of enlarging the capacity for the responsibility for oneself. This for Nietzsche is freedom.

I.v. Conclusion

I argued that Nietzsche praised Kantian morality (reason) over the philosophies of compassion, i.e. the philosophies of Ree and Schopenhauer. Rather than focusing on sympathetic affects Kant makes autonomy the focus of his moral philosophy. However, Nietzsche is critical of the Kantian assumption that human beings are rational agents and that our reason tells us what is consistent with duty and what is not. It seems that Nietzsche sees Spinoza as much closer to his notion of the self and ethics than Kant, especially on the issues of the denial of the freedom of the will, teleology, the moral world order, the unegoistic and evil. However, like Kant, Spinoza assumes that we can attain a good life only through our capacity to use reason. Both Kantian autonomy and Spinozistic morality underestimate the psychological truths about human beings, and so Nietzsche suggests a more modest task: our moral therapy is to be directed at the particular drives and capacities of individuals. In the next chapter I will explore Nietzsche's remedy.

Chapter II: Nietzsche's Remedy

II.i. Introduction

This chapter is devoted to Nietzsche's remedy for the decline of modern man. It centres on the idea of a 'trying' or experimental morality; this in turn is related to the idea of philosophy as an art of living. This latter is a Stoic idea and so in the first section (II. ii) I give a synopsis of Nietzsche's relationship with Stoic ethics. In the second section (II.iii) I focus on the sovereign individual as it appears in *Genealogy* (1887), a book that Nietzsche wrote in his so-called later period, some five years after *The Gay Science* in which we encounter the thoughts of *amor fati* and eternal return.

II.ii. Nietzsche and Stoicism; The Care of the Self; A Modest Egoism

In formulating his own conception of philosophy as an art of living Nietzsche is indebted to Stoicism. Especially during his so-called 'Free Spirit Trilogy' period (*Human, all too Human, Daybreak*, and *The Gay Science*) he refers to the Stoics numerous times, adopting a form of Stoic therapy in *Daybreak* (1881). Although *The Gay Science* (1882) contains a critique of Stoic therapy and also of Stoic cosmology, he can no less avoid a dialogue with the Stoics than he can with Spinoza. In this section I will not give a detailed account of Stoic philosophy, but rather focus on Stoic ethics, central to which are ideas of self-mastery and the care of the self.

We saw in the last chapter that Nietzsche detected a root of the decline of modern man in Christian – or slave – morality, and that he characterised this as a morality of compassion or unegoism. He found a robust assault on this morality in the philosophy of the Stoics.

The Stoics start with the Socratic idea of virtue: virtue is absolutely necessary for *eudaimonia*. However, they go further, claiming first that virtue is not only necessary for happiness, but is identical with it, and develop a notion of the good person which they equate with that of the self-commanding person. A good person is free in so far as he/she is not a slave of external events. Finally Stoics claim that all emotions, not only pity but also fear, grief, anger, envy and the like, are based on evaluative judgments.[161]

---

161 Martha Nussbaum, 'Pity and Mercy: Nietzsche's Stoicism', in *Nietzsche, Genealogy and Morality: Essays on Nietzsche's Genealogy of Morals,* ed. Richard Schacht (Berkeley; London: University of California Press, 1994), p. 146.

To start with the last point, it is in *Daybreak* where we encounter a sustained discussion of pity, along with several references to Stoics like Epictetus. According to Nietzsche, pity or compassion – the sort to be found in the moral philosophy of Schopenhauer, John Stuart Mill, and Christian morality which sees empathy and sympathy as moral actions – is an acknowledgment of weakness not only in the pitied but also in the pitier, and in that respect it is not altruistic but rather egoistic:

> 'No longer to think of oneself.' – Let us reflect seriously upon this question: why do we leap after someone who has fallen into the water on front of us, even though we feel no kind of affection for him? Out of pity: at that moment we are thinking only of the other person – thus says thoughtlessness…The truth is: in the feeling of pity – I mean in that which usually and misleadingly called pity – we are, to be sure, not consciously thinking of ourselves, but are doing so *very strongly unconsciously*…An accident which happens to another offends us: it would make us aware of our impotence, and perhaps of our cowardice, if we did not go to assist him.[162]

Nietzsche offers an alternative, Stoic position:

> To view our own experiences with the eyes with which we are accustomed to view them when they are the experiences of others – this is very comforting and a medicine to be recommended. On the other hand, to view and imbibe the experiences of others *as if they were ours* – as is the demand of a philosophy of pity – this would destroy us, and in a very short time…Moreover, the former maxim is certainly *more in accord* with reason and the will to rationality, for we adjudge the value and meaning of an event more objectively when it happens to another than we do when it happens to us: the value for example, of a death, or a money-loss, or a slander.[163]

A second aspect of Stoic ethics is the notion of a good person as a self-commanding person. A good person is free because she is not a slave of external events. Nietzsche too suggests an understanding of ethics which does not primarily rest on our relation with others, but on our relation with ourselves, on the art of self-mastery and self-governance.

In fact, this sort of ethics was not only a distinctive feature of Stoic but of Greek and Roman thought, even of early Christian asceticism. According to Michel Foucault, the real difference between later Christian morality and Greek pagan morality is less a matter of 'interiority' than of forms of relationship with the self: 'Greeks did not battle the "other"; he crossed swords with himself.'[164] The point of

---

162 Nietzsche, *Daybreak*, II:133, p. 84
163 Nietzsche, *Daybreak* II: 137, p. 87
164 Michel Foucault, *A History of Sexuality: The Uses of Pleasure* (New York: Pantheon, 1986), p. 68.

this ascetic relationship with the self was not to eliminate desire, nor to diminish the intensity of pleasure; control, instead, was the issue. According to Foucault, 'this ascetic was not organized or conceived as a corpus of separate practices that would constitute a kind of specific art of the soul, with its techniques, procedures, and prescriptions. It was not distinct from the practice of virtue itself; it was the rehearsal that anticipated that practice.'[165] I shall dwell on the principle of the care of the self as we encounter it in Greek thought because it is central to much of Nietzsche's remedy for modern ills.

Foucault claims that for the Greeks, the precept of the 'care of the self' was 'one of the main principles of cities, one of the main rules for social and personal conduct and for the art of life.'[166] And this principle was associated with the Delphic principle 'Know yourself.' In other words, in the Greco-Roman culture knowledge of oneself could be realised as the consequence of the care of the self. This idea, Foucault argues, has become rather obscure for us because our philosophical tradition gave importance to one half of this ethical doctrine, to the Delphic principle 'Know yourself.'[167]

For the Stoics, for instance, taking care of the self was not an easy task: 'There is the care of the body to consider, health regiments, physical exercises without overexertion, the carefully measured satisfaction of needs. There are the meditations, the readings, the notes that one takes on books or on the conversations one has heard, notes that one reads again later, the recollection of truths one knows already but that need to be more fully adapted to one's own life.'[168] Moreover, care of the self is in close relation with medical thought and practice: 'the improvement, the perfecting of the soul that one seeks in philosophy…increasingly assumes a medical coloration.'[169] Foucault gives us several medical metaphors employed to emphasise the activities that are necessary for the care of the self. Epictetus, for instance, tells his pupils that they should see themselves above all not as students but as patients who had to be cured: 'You wish to learn syllogisms? You must first attend to your ulcers, and stay your flux, and arrive at peace in your mind.'[170] However, it should be noted that 'the focus of attention in these practices

---

165 Foucault, *Uses of Pleasure*, p. 77
166 Michel Foucault, 'Technologies of the Self', in *Ethics, Subjectivity and Truth*, ed. Paul Rabinow (New York: The New Press, 1997), p. 226.
167 Foucault, 'Technologies of the Self', p. 226
168 Michel Foucault, 'The Cultivation of the Self', in *History of Sexuality*, Vol 3 (New York: Vintage Books, 1986), p. 51.
169 Foucault, 'The Cultivation of the Self', p. 55
170 Quoted in Foucault, 'The Cultivation of the Self', p. 55

of the self is the point where the ills of the body and those of the soul can communicate with one another and exchange their distresses.'[171] This notion that physical forces that affect the body affect the mind as well is similar to that of Nietzsche. However, Nietzsche's own Stoicism is more complicated than this.

According to Nietzsche the self is a site on which the structuring and organising of our drives occurs. He claims that when 'we rely on introspection or self-consciousness to discover our motives and intentions we are involved in processes of selection and interpretation; that is, we do not simply retrieve so-called "mental facts" in such acts.'[172] Rather, we 'impose, form, organize, and categorize our inner experiences just as we do our outer experiences.'[173] What are these drives? Who/what organises them? Moreover, if we can never know what our real motives are then how is autonomy or self-mastery or self-governance possible? According to Ansell-Pearson, to the second question Nietzsche has a twofold answer:

(a) one practices the passion of knowledge, treating oneself as a site of experimental self-knowledge; (*Daybreak* and *The Gay Science*)
(b) one exercises an intellectual conscience, a superior form of conscience, or the conscience behind one's conscience (*The Gay Science*).[174]

In several places Nietzsche calls for a life which should be lived experimentally. In *Daybreak* he says: 'the best we can do in this *interregnum* is to be as far as possible our own *reges* and found little *experimental states*. We are experiments: let us also want to be them!'[175] Similarly in *The Gay Science* he says: 'I favour any *skepsis* to which I may reply: "Let us try it!" But I no longer wish to hear anything of all those things and questions that do not permit any experiment.'[176]

In a note from 1880, Nietzsche insists that the intellect has to sharpen itself in the struggle with various drives.[177] This idea sounds un-Nietzschean, sounds like Kant's elevation of reason or intellect. But it refers to a more Stoic notion, an ethics which claims that we should dissolve the emotions which are tied to external events, and that we can do this by shifting our evaluations about them, because feelings are the product of judgments and beliefs, which are not drives. This is

---

171 Foucault, 'The Cultivation of the Self', p. 56
172 Ansell-Pearson, 'Beyond Compassion', p. 7
173 Ansell-Pearson, 'Beyond Compassion', p. 7
174 Ansell-Pearson, 'Beyond Compassion', p. 17
175 Nietzsche, *Daybreak*, V:453, p. 191
176 Nietzsche, *GS* 51, p. 115
177 Ansell-Pearson, 'Beyond Compassion', p. 18

Nietzsche's position in *Daybreak*; however, in *The Gay Science* he goes further. There he still claims that feelings are a product of judgments and beliefs, but asks whether we see should not simply welcome or affirm our feelings, whether or not they promote pleasure or pain: 'Pleasure and displeasure were so tied together that whoever *wanted* to have as much as possible of one *must* also have as much as possible of the other – that whoever wanted to learn to "jubilate up to the heavens" would also have to be prepared for "depression unto death."'[178] Rather than intellect or reason, then, Nietzsche refers to what he calls 'intellectual conscience'.

Nietzsche claims that we always appeal to our conscience to understand whether whatever we did is right or wrong. But such an appeal is based on the belief that our conscience is infallible. In fact, any judgment we make has a prehistory in our drives, inclinations, likes and dislikes and experiences. For this reason we should ask the questions 'How did it originate there?' and 'What is it that impels me to listen to it?' There are a hundred ways in which we can listen to our conscience, but we often take this or that judgment for the voice of conscience and this 'may be due to the fact that you have never thought much about yourself and simply have accepted blindly that what you had been told ever since your childhood was right.'[179] If we had thought better, observed better, we would not call this 'duty' or 'conscience'. Here, Nietzsche – referring implicitly to Kant – claims that anyone who still concludes that 'in this case everybody would have to act like this' has not been taking steps towards self-knowledge. Otherwise he would know that

> every action that has ever been done was done in an altogether unique and irretrievable way, and that this will be equally true of every future action; that all regulations about actions relate only to their coarse exterior; that these regulations may lead to some semblance of sameness, *but really to some semblance...*; that our opinions about 'good' and 'noble' and 'great' can never be proved to be true by our actions because every action is unknowable.[180]

A strong intellectual conscience, then, will not be afraid to be suspicious about everything. It is not an easy task though since anyone calling for an intellectual conscience is 'as lonely in the most densely populated cities as if he were in a desert.'[181]

Nietzsche concludes the second book of *Daybreak* with the following sentences:

> But our counter-reckoning is that we shall restore to men their goodwill towards the actions decried as egoistic and restore to these actions their *value – we shall deprive*

---

178 Nietzsche, *GS* 12, p. 85
179 Nietzsche, *GS* 335, p. 264
180 Nietzsche, *GS* 335, p. 265
181 Nietzsche, *GS* 2, p. 76

them of their bad conscience! And since they have hitherto been by far the most frequent actions, and will continue to be so for all future time, we thus remove from the entire aspect of action and life its *evil appearance!* This is a very significant result! When man no longer regards himself as evil he ceases to be so![182]

For Ansell-Pearson it is clear that Nietzsche 'wishes to restore a good conscience to egoism and to encourage his readers to practice a care of self.'[183] He wishes to replace morality – morality of compassion, or unegoism – with the self-cultivation or the care of self. Anyone who flees from himself or hates himself is doing nothing but just rescuing himself from himself in others.[184] But it is precisely this:

> to flee from the ego, and to hate it, and to live in others and for others – that has hitherto, with as much thoughtlessness as self-confidence, been called *'unegoistic' and consequently 'good.'*[185]

Referring to one of Nietzsche's notes from 1881, Ansell-Pearson names such a call a modest ego: 'Stop feeling oneself as this phantastic ego!…Discover the errors of the ego!…Get beyond 'me' and 'you'! Learn to feel (*empfinden*) cosmically!'[186] What does Nietzsche mean by 'to feel cosmically'? In order to understand this we should return to Nietzsche's Stoicism.

John Sellars distinguishes between two ideal types of Stoicism: Human stoicism and Cosmic Stoicism. The former he associates with Lipsius and Seneca: 'The Human Stoic conceives the world as something external and hostile ['absolutism of reality']. His Stoicism consists of a heroic response to whatever this hostile world throws at him.'[187] Sellars further claims that Hegel's presentation of Stoicism in the *Phenomenology of Spirit* conforms to the image of the Human Stoic: the Stoic withdraws into himself, his consciousness because he has no control over the external events; correspondingly, the Stoic seeks mental freedom because he has no freedom in the outer world.

In contrast to this we have Cosmic Stoicism which Sellars associates with Marcus Aurelius and Epictetus. In Marcus, for instance, the self is an inner citadel and the principal motivation behind this, says Sellars, 'is a desire to overcome the boundary between the individual self and the Cosmos so that there is no longer any

---

182 Nietzsche, *Daybreak* II:148, pp. 93-94
183 Ansell-Pearson, 'Beyond Compassion', p. 19
184 Nietzsche, *Daybreak* V:516, p. 207
185 Nietzsche, *Daybreak* V:516, p. 207
186 Quoted in Ansell-Pearson, 'Beyond Compassion', p. 21
187 John Sellars, 'An Ethics of the Event', *Angelaki: Journal of the Theoretical Humanities*, 11:3, 2007, p. 164.

opposition between the two.'[188] We see such a concern with the self in Spinoza, according to whom God is the only truly free being and identified with Nature. For a Cosmic Stoic:

> Only the Cosmos as a whole has complete freedom. It always acts according to its own nature, never hindered by an external cause. From the perspective of the Cosmos, then, the distinction between internal and external causes falls away. This distinction is thus always only relative to the perspective of a particular finite mode of being. The philosophical task is to try – so far as it is possible – to attain a cosmic perspective from which the boundary between oneself and Nature is overcome.[189]

A true Stoic says Epictetus is 'a man who desires to be of one mind with God, and never to cast blame on God or man again.'[190] As opposed to this, for a Human Stoic like Seneca fate, the will of God, is conceived as something external to oneself.

In *Daybreak* 23 Nietzsche speculates that for many thousands of years people thought that things were animate, with a power to cause harm which made human beings feel impotent towards them; this was the origin of most superstitious practices and rituals: 'for one needed to secure oneself against things, just as against men and animals, by force, constraint, flattering, treaties, sacrifices.'[191] In other words, these superstitious practices and rituals functioned to turn the feeling of powerlessness or anxiety into a feeling of power. However, he further adds, this feeling of fear and impotence was so strong and continuous that 'the *feeling of power* has evolved to such a degree of *subtlety* that in this respect man is now a match for the most delicate balance. It has become his strongest propensity; the means discovered for creating this feeling almost constitute the history of culture.'[192] This 'speculation' reminds us of Blumenberg's account of the development of many forms of human cognition. As we said in the Introduction, Blumenberg claims man is a limited being with limited resources and can survive only if he puts some distance between himself and the external world, which otherwise may overwhelm him. Overcoming the absolutism of reality is a function of many forms of human cognition: myths, stories, metaphors, religion, philosophy, science and technology. As an observation about the history of human cognition this is something that Nietzsche might have agreed with; unlike Blumenberg, however, he is not always sanguine about it, nor does he seek to endorse it. The Human Stoicism

---

188 Sellars, 'An Ethics of the Event', p. 164
189 Sellars, 'An Ethics of the Event', p. 164
190 Quoted in Sellars, 'An Ethics of the Event', p. 164
191 Nietzsche, *Daybreak* I: 23, p. 19
192 Nietzsche, *Daybreak* I: 23, p. 19

according to which the world is something external and hostile ('absolutism of reality') gives way to a rival, more affirmative therapy, and a rejection of the Stoic distinction between what is within my power and what is not. For Epictetus, for instance, nature 'is to be understood as a purposefully designed rational *cosmos*. Correspondingly, the self is to be understood as a rational will that is able to comprehend the cosmos and master itself in suspending all impulses to interfere with the natural order.'[193] This rationality of the will and cosmos is what Nietzsche opposes; and his opposition becomes clearer in his later writings.

We know that Nietzsche read Epictetus and Seneca very carefully and one of his primary sources about Stoicism is Epictetus' *Handbook*.[194] As Michael Ure shows, Nietzsche adopts a sort of Human Stoicism in *Daybreak*, or a philosophical understanding based on Stoic therapy, whereas he adopts a sort of Cosmic Stoicism in the early 1880s – in *The Gay Science*, for instance. These two attitudes can be associated with what Nietzsche calls Mohammadian (*HH*, 'The Wanderer and Its Shadow' 61) and the Russian fatalism (*Ecce Homo*). Mohammadian fatalism opposes man and fate and puts them as two identities against each other whereas he sees the Russian fatalism as a remedy for resentment: 'accepting oneself as if fated, not wishing oneself "different."'[195] When Deleuze claims that Stoic ethics is a precursor to Nietzsche's *amor fati* he has in mind Cosmic Stoicism, a discussion which we will come in the following section.[196]

In the previous chapter I said that it might have been Spinoza who prompted the idea of eternal return, which Nietzsche seems to have discovered only a few days after his discovery that Spinoza was his precursor (summer of 1881), however, Spinoza himself adopts a Stoic immanent ontology (God=*Natura*). However, by saying this I don't mean that Nietzsche adopts Spinoza's Stoicism, after all Nietzsche's classical education focused particularly on Stoicism and among his first publications were three studies of Diogenes Laertius's *Lives of the Philosophers*.[197] And the Greek idea of the eternal return as a cosmological understanding of the universe was not unknown to Nietzsche.[198] In fact, many

---

193 R. O. Elveton, 'Nietzsche's Stoicism: The Depts are Inside', in *Nietzsche and Antiquity*, ed. Paul Bishop (Rochester, NY; Woodbridge, Suffolk: Camden House, 2004), p. 194.
194 Ure, 'Nietzsche's Free Spirit Trilogy', p. 69
195 Nietzsche, 'Why I am so wise,' *Ecce Homo*, 6
196 Gilles Deleuze, *The Logic of Sense*, trans. Mark Lester (London: Continuum, 2001), p. 172.
197 Nussbaum, 'Pity and Mercy', p. 139.
198 On the idea of the eternal return see Mircea Eliade, *The myth of the Eternal Return, or, Cosmos and History*, trans. Willard R. Trask (Princeton: Princeton University Press, 1971).

scholars knew the doctrine of eternal recurrence of Heraclitus and Empedocles, Plato and Aristotle, Eudemos and the Stoics, yet, what makes Nietzsche unique is his perceiving 'in it creative possibilities for the future, in opposition to a Christianity which is reduced to moral values.'[199] Nietzsche treats this problem at age 18 – twenty years before *Zarathustra* – in two papers called 'On Fate and History' (1862) and 'The Freedom of the Will and Fate' (1862), and ten years before 'On the Uses and Disadvantages of History for Life.' In these essays he asks: 'is the ultimate standard and the pattern of our existence the classical view of the world as an eternal cosmic, evolving in periodic cycles, or is it the Christian view of the world as a unique creation out of nothing, called forth by the omnipotence of a non-natural God? Is the ultimate being a divine cosmos, recurrent like a circle in itself, or a personal God, revealing himself not primarily in nature but in and to humanity under the sign of the cross?'[200] Twenty years later Nietzsche decides that 'it is the world which redeems our contingent existence, reintegrating the Christian ego into the order of cosmic necessity, i.e., into the Eternal recurrence of the same.'[201]

I said earlier that it is in *The Gay Science* Nietzsche is critical of Stoic therapy (Human Stoicism), and moves towards a Cosmic Stoicism, in the course of which he develops his own rival therapy. In *The Gay Science* we encounter *amor fati* and the eternal return, ideas that Nietzsche develops more in *Zarathustra* (1883-5) and *Genealogy* (1887), and also in the Book V of *The Gay Science* (1887).

---

199 Karl Löwith, *Meaning in History* (Chicago: Chicago University Press, 1949), p. 219.
200 Löwith, *Meaning*, p. 215.
201 Löwith, *Meaning*, pp. 215-216. However, Löwith further claims that Nietzsche does not realise that 'his contra *Christianos* was an exact replica in reverse of the *contra gentiles* of the Church Fathers. Not only the eternal recurrence which was discussed by Origen, Justin, and Augustine but all the general topics of Christian apologetics against pagan philosophers recur in Nietzsche's philosophy' (220). In other words, Nietzsche's *Antichrist* is nothing but a repetition of the old complaint about Christians' being brutal and crude, and thus the manifestation of a reactive attitude incompatible with Nietzsche's own philosophy. *Zarathustra*, both in terms of style and content, is a counter*gospel* and the eternal recurrence does not in fact overcome the Christian idea of progress and futurism. When in *GM* Nietzsche writes: 'This man of the future will redeem us, not just from the ideal held up till now, but also from.....nihilism..... this Antichrist and anti-nihilist, this conqueror of God...– *he must come one day*' (Nietzsche, *GM*, II:24, p. 71), Löwith might ask here whether this 'man of the future' is anything other than the Christian messiah.

II.iii. The Sovereign Individual; *Amor Fati*; Eternal Return

In the first chapter we introduced Nietzsche's critique of the modern self, of the subject-object relation, and we ended it with a reference to Christian morality in particular and slave morality in general. Nietzsche's uses a specific method, 'genealogy' in his analysis of morality, a method which is concerned with that 'which can be documented, which can actually be confirmed and has actually existed, in short, the whole, long, hard-to-decipher hieroglyphic script of man's moral past!'[202] Genealogy seeks for the various reasons of an event and relations of power rather than focusing on a cause-effect formula. However, Nietzsche is also – perhaps largely – preoccupied with another problem: the problem of 'higher humanity'. On its own the genealogy of morality is not enough. There is a larger question: 'how can we reverse the decline of modern culture?' Nietzsche uses different models in his discussions. Sometimes he frames his question in terms of master and slave moralities, sometimes in terms of the overhuman and the last man. Yet, the basic problem that he deals with is 'how one becomes what one is', that is to say, become a creative individual who wills his/her own will. In that sense, his philosophical strategy seems to be directed by a single goal: individual sovereignty or self-governance.[203]

Although he does not have an explicit theory of sovereignty, it is a theme that recurs in his writings. In the second essay of *GM*, he writes:

---

202 Nietzsche, *GM* preface 7, p. 8.
203 As a faithful follower of Nietzsche, Michel Foucault has a similar approach in his call for 'freedom' and a life lived as a 'scandal of truth'. In his analysis of the art of governance, Foucault turns to the Greek understanding of self and to Christian morality. He asks: how do subjects become active, how is the government of the self and others open to subjectifications? In antiquity, training to achieve self-governance was not different from the training necessary to govern others. Such training was not separate from the process of constituting oneself as a free person. On the other hand, in later Christianity, 'there was to be a differentiation between the exercises that enabled one to govern oneself and the learning of what was necessary in order to govern others; there was also to be a differentiation between the exercises themselves and the virtue, moderation and temperance for which they were meant to serve as training'. For Foucault, the real difference between later Christian morality and Greek pagan morality is not a matter of interiority; instead the difference resides in the forms of relationship with the self: 'the Greek did not battle the 'other'; he crossed swords with himself.' Michel Foucault, *The Uses of Pleasure* (New York: Pantheon, 1986), p. 77.

> Let us place ourselves, on the other hand, at the end of this immense process the tree actually bears fruit, where society and its morality of custom finally reveal what they were simply *the means to*: we then find the *sovereign individual* as the ripest fruit on its tree, like only to itself, having freed itself from the morality of custom, an autonomous, supra-ethical individual (because 'autonomous' and 'ethical' are mutually exclusive), in short, we find a man with his own, independent, enduring will, who *has the right to make a promise* – and has a proud consciousness quivering in every muscle of *what* he has finally achieved and incorporated, an actual awareness of power and freedom, a feeling that man in general has reached completion.[204]

According to this passage sovereignty is the product and outcome of a long process, but I will argue that at the same time it represents a new beginning and a new way of thinking associated with the affirmation of life. Nietzsche praises the sovereign individual as the master of 'free will' with power over himself and his fate. In that sense, the sovereign individual seems to be a candidate for Nietzsche's future ideal, the overhuman.

In *BGE* Nietzsche presents the following historical sequence: 1) a pre-moral *(vormoralische)* period in which the value or disvalue of an action was derived from its consequences 2) a moral period which shifts from assessing consequences to assessing 'intentions' and which involves the first attempts at self-knowledge. 3) a 'post-moral' *(aussermoralische)* period which is a threshold upon which we 'immoralists' stand and in which we believe that morality in the traditional sense, the morality of intentions, was a prejudice. With respect to the 'post-moral' period Nietzsche writes:

> The overcoming of morality, in a certain sense even the self-overcoming of morality –let this be the name for that long secret work which has been saved up for the finest and most honest, also the most malicious, consciences of today, as living touchstones of the soul.[205]

Today, we immoralists stand at the threshold.

As we have seen at the beginning of the second essay of *GM* Nietzsche introduces his striking figure the 'sovereign individual', claiming that finally 'the tree actually bears fruit, where society and its morality of custom finally reveal what they were simply *the means to*: we then find the *sovereign individual* as the ripest fruit on its tree.'[206] This seems to refer to the 'modern' era; but the 'end of the

---

204 Nietzsche, *GM* II:2, p. 40
205 Nietzsche, *BGE* 32, p. 45
206 Lawrence J. Hatab argues that the 'supra-moral' sovereign individual in *GM* is similar to the second stage since 'the German term is *übersittlich*, and *sittlich* can match what

process' may also be read as lying ahead of the present, so that the sovereign individual which 'must come one day' would be Nietzsche's ideal and 'man of future', the overhuman. Towards the end of *GM* he writes:

> This man of the future will redeem us, not just from the ideal held up till now, but also from those things *which will have to arise from it*, from the great nausea, the will to nothingness, from nihilism, that stroke of midday and of great decision which makes the will free again, which gives earth its purpose and man his hope again, this Antichrist and anti-nihilist, this conqueror of God and of nothingness – *he must come one day*...[207]

Besides, the second essay ends with the following passage:

> - But what am I saying? Enough! Enough! At this point just one thing is proper, silence: otherwise I shall be misappropriating something that belongs to another, younger man, one 'with more future', one stronger than me – something to which *Zarathustra* alone is entitled, *Zarathustra the Godless*...[208]

In this respect, although they are quite different in terms of style, *GM* and *Zarathustra* should be read as complementary texts. The *GM* attempts to redeem the present from past while the *Zarathustra* is future-oriented. Yet, the common issue that concerns Nietzsche in both is the 'art of living' which requires self-mastery, the imperative of sovereignty. The sovereign individual is the one who says: 'we are responsible to ourselves for our own existence; consequently we want to be the true helmsman of this existence and refuse to allow our existence to resemble a mindless act of chance.'[209] In that sense, since sovereignty is a matter of self-mastery and self-overcoming, giving it a didactic articulation would be to

---

the *BGE* passage calls pre-moral, and thus might be designated as 'ethical,' not moral. So the coming phenomenon forecast by Nietzsche in *BGE* is not something like the sovereign individual, who is supra-ethical in being rationally, or autonomously, moral; the coming sense of valuation is post-moral in being post-rational, post-autonomous, post-sovereign.' Moreover, Hatab claims that there is an ambiguity about the 'end of process' here and many commentators who take the sovereign individual as Nietzsche's ideal read the end as ahead of the present. On the other hand, Hatab suggests that a 'ripe fruit' is more likely something that has been actualized. Therefore, Hatab concludes that the sovereign individual cannot be Nietzsche's ideal and should not interpreted as the 'man of future,' Hatab, L.J. 'Breaking the Contract Theory: The Individual and the Law in Nietzsche's *Genealogy'*, in *Nietzsche, Power and Politics*, ed. Hermann W. Siemens and Vasti Roodt (Berlin; New York, 2008), pp 169-190.

207 Nietzsche, *GM* II:24, p. 71
208 Nietzsche, *GM* II:25, p. 71
209 Nietzsche, *UM* III:1

circumscribe it in advance. For instance, although Zarathustra can be regarded as an exemplar of the sovereign individual, he refuses to be followed and imitated: 'Now I bid you lose me and find yourselves; and only when you have all denied me will I return to you.'[210]

As we have seen, Nietzsche does not simply reject culture,[211] precisely because one of its products is the sovereign individual. However, this product is not a product in the sense of a final stage. Nietzsche uses a number of metaphors to express this idea. In *GM* man is a path and a bridge.[212] In *Zarathustra* we read:

> The human is a rope, fastened between beast and overman – a rope over an abyss.
>
> A dangerous across, a dangerous on-the-way, a dangerous looking-back, a dangerous shuddering and standing still.
>
> What is great in the human is that it is a bridge and not a goal: what can be loved in the human is that it is a *going-over* and a *going under*.[213]

According to Nietzsche, the human is a rope between beast – inhuman – and overhuman. Yet he does not claim that there is a linear progress in history and that the stage of overhuman is inevitable outcome of this development. Nor does he claim that the overhuman is a period or stage; rather it is a way of thinking, a new beginning which requires the imperative of sovereignty.

In the second essay of *The Untimely Meditations*, Nietzsche claims that animals are *ahistorical* beings that live upon a passive forgetfulness which is the fundamental reason for their happiness. Moreover, he claims that promising relies upon some kind of power: remembering. Promising depends upon a labour and its enhancement appeared through a developmental process in which a counteracting forgetting was diminished. However, although Nietzsche offers an account of how remembering accomplished its victory over forgetting in the course of human development, he does not simply suggest turning back to an inhuman or pre-human stage. How could he when, as we have seen, there is no developmental schema at work?

As we have seen, forgetfulness is an active ability to suppress 'which takes place with our physical consumption of food, our so-called ingestion.' Prehuman or inhuman means forgetting anything outside the present moment. With *mnemotechniques*, on the other hand, the human animal learned how to promise

---

210 Nietzsche, *Zarathustra*, I:22, 'On the Bestowing Virtue'
211 As we have seen in *Daybreak* 16 Nietzsche writes: 'Any custom is better than no custom.'
212 Nietzsche, *GM* II:16
213 Nietzsche, *Zarathustra*, prologue 4

and remember. Just as the slave – the human – invented bad conscience in order to hurt itself through inventing a holy God, he also became a prisoner of his own past, a past that imprisons through the faculty of memory. This faculty – the suppression of active forgetting – makes the human will to hold onto the 'it was', and teaches him that he cannot change the past. In other words, he cannot will backwards.

Active forgetting, however, is precisely one of the characteristics that Nietzsche attributes to the sovereign individual who has power over himself and his fate. He knows that he does not have power over 'it was': but active forgetting means the absence of guilt and bad conscience. In *Zarathustra* Nietzsche had praised forgetting: 'Innocence the child is and forgetting, a beginning anew, a play, a self-propelling wheel, a first movement, a sacred Yea-saying.'[214] What Nietzsche suggests is a new relationship with time: through active forgetting – appropriate incorporation – we can redeem the present from the past which brings the power to create our own futures. There is an intimate connection between these ideas and Nietzsche's thought of the eternal return, a thought which emerges first time in his notes from summer, 1881:

> We have to put the past – our past and that of all humanity – on the scales and *also* outweigh it – no! This piece of human history will and must repeat itself eternally; we can leave that out of account we have no influence over it.[215]

Here Nietzsche talks about the redemption of the past not only at the individual level but also at the social level. To start with the latter, Nietzsche's most extended discussion of history occurs in his 'On the Uses and Disadvantages of History for Life.' He claims that history pertains to humanity in three respects: as a being who acts and strives; as a being who preserves and reveres; and as a being who suffers and seeks deliverance. Correspondingly, he distinguishes between three different species of history: the monumental, the antiquarian and the critical.[216] The monumental entails an attempt to emulate the past, the antiquarian an attempt to preserve the past, and the critical an attempt to redeem the present from the past. Every nation requires a certain kind of knowledge of the past, but this knowledge, according to Nietzsche, is worthwhile only as long as it is in the service of life. At the beginning of the essay he writes: 'We need it, [history] that is to say, for the

---

214 Nietzsche, *Zarathustra*, I:1, 'On the Three Transformations'
215 Nietzsche, 'Notes from 1881', in *The Nietzsche Reader*, ed. Keith Ansell-Pearson and Duncan Large (Oxford: Blackwell, 2006), p. 239.
216 Nietzsche, *UM* II

sake of life and action, not so as to turn comfortably away from life and action.....
We want to serve history only to the extent that history serves life...'[217]

What does Nietzsche suggest then? Instead of focusing on past events, Nietzsche proposes an interpretation of history which will redeem the past in order to be open to the future; this requires us to be partially 'unhistorical', when necessary to partially forget: *'the unhistorical and the historical are necessary in equal measure for the health of an individual, of a people and of a culture.'*[218] He seems to suggest a combination of these two species, that is to say, past moments must be focused on as long as they serve life, as long as they inspire men for the great events. In fact, even though he suggests the unhistorical and the historical equally, in the concluding passage of the essay he is favour of the suprahistorical and the unhistorical, for the 'malady of history' can be cured only by administering an antidote to the historical. What he means by the suprahistorical is 'the art and power of *forgetting* and of enclosing oneself within a bounded *horizon*' and by the unhistorical 'the powers which lead the eye away from becoming towards that which bestows upon existence the character of the eternal and the stable, towards *art* and *religion.'*[219] Nietzsche does not tell us how this would succeed; however, what he is clear about is what kind of person the genuine 'historian' should be, namely, one who is capable of creative interpretation:

> To sum up: history is written by the experienced and superior man. He who has not experienced greater and more exalted things than others will not know how to interpret the great and exalted things of the past. When the past speaks it always speaks as an oracle: only if you are an architect of the future and know the present will you understand it.[220]

Nietzsche is not very clear about what this combination of the unhistorical and the suprahistorical should look like; his point, however, is that modern historians cannot redeem themselves from their dependence on modern conceptions and from their hidden motives. For instance, they construed Thucydides as an historian and correspondingly regarded the Greeks as 'historically minded'. For Nietzsche, on the other hand, the Greeks managed to find the balance between the historical and unhistorical. When he calls the Greeks unhistorical,[221] Nietzsche does not mean that the Greeks do not possess any consciousness of the past, for this

---

217 Nietzsche, *UM* II, p. 59
218 Nietzsche, *UM* II, p. 63
219 Nietzsche, *UM* II, p. 120
220 Nietzsche, *UM* II, p. 94
221 Nietzsche, *UM* II

would be saying that they are inhuman; they did not allow their past to mummify their present, to dominate their culture. This is why he says: 'when Zeus created Achilleus, Helen and Homer, he was shortsighted and he failed to understand the human race. The actual result was not the annihilation of mankind, but the birth of Greek culture.'[222] In other words, it is quite telling that Greeks perceive their pasts through a possible fiction: the *Iliad*. They do not perceive their past only from the standpoint of success; moreover, their failure does not become a catastrophe. In fact in *The Birth of Tragedy* he welcomes myths and fictions claiming that it would be more difficult to face reality without myths, as long that is as we should not accept them as facts or truths.[223] In fact Nietzsche's position is not very different from that of Hans Blumenberg who devoted hundreds of pages to the function of mythic thought. 'Stories are told', according to Hans Blumenberg, 'in order to kill something. In the most harmless, but not the least important case: to kill time. In another and more serious case: to kill fear.'[224] Mythic thought functions as a compensation to reduce the anxiety of the helpless ego and transform it into a more bearable fear.[225]

Another point that Nietzsche emphasises explicitly in his essay is the particular conceptions of history that he is attacking.[226] He calls his meditations 'untimely' or 'thoughts out of season' because he attacks the orthodoxies of the nineteenth century philosophies of history.

The first conception of history that he criticises is found in eschatological theories according to which history has a goal: Hegel belongs to this trend and it is Hegel who tyrannized the individual by making history the supreme power of the universe. The second one is the scientific conception of history whose leading figure was Leopold von Ranke who claimed that a disciplined empiricism would recreate the past as it really happened. In fact such an attitude was not uncommon

---

222 Quoted in Neville Morley, '"Unhistorical Greeks": Myth, History, and the Uses of Antiquity', in *Nietzsche and Antiquity*, ed. Paul Bishop (New York: Camden House, 2004), p. 21.
223 See Morley, '"Unhistorical Greeks": Myth, History, and the Uses of Antiquity'
224 Hans Blumenberg, *Work on Myth* (Cambridge; London: MIT Press, 1985), p. 34.
225 Blumenberg, *Myth*, p. 4-5
226 There are several ideas about what sort of combination can contribute to genuine historiography. See Keith Ansell-Pearson, *The Nietzsche Reader*, ed. Keith Ansell-Pearson and Duncan Large (Oxford: Blackwell, 2006); Peter Berkowitz, *Ethics of an Immoralist* (Cambridge; London: Harvard University Press, 1995); Lee Congdon, 'Nietzsche, Heidegger, and History', *Journal of European Studies* 3 (1973), pp. 211-217.

in the nineteenth century Germany, for the second half of this century was the period of turning from idealism to positivism.[227] Nietzsche strongly rejects this as well, for such a reconstruction of the past can mummify things as a result of which we can live in the past rather than appreciating the present.

The redemption of the present is a theme which gets more clarification in his *Zarathustra*, which was published between the years 1883-85. Here, Nietzsche's understanding of ethics – an ethics based on the relationship with ourselves rather than with others – becomes clearer as well.

Zarathustra is 'a seer, a willer, a creator, a future itself and a bridge to the future.' When Zarathustra turns to the past he always sees the same thing: 'fragments and limbs and dreadful chances – but no men.' As a redeemer of the present, Zarathustra's ability lies in the fact that he can 'compose into one and bring together what is fragment and riddle and dreadful chance'. In other words, he can redeem the past and transform every 'It was' into an 'thus I willed it.'[228] This redemption is related to Nietzsche's thought of the eternal return.

Nietzsche's 'doctrine' of the eternal return is central to his account of the 'self'. It originates from the conception of the world and life as a whole in which things are endlessly repeated in a circular course: 'In every now, Being begins; around every here rolls the ball of there. The centre is everywhere. Crooked is the path of eternity.'[229] The assumption of this theory is that everything that has already happened in the universe, is happening now, and will happen in the future. This means that the world exists in such a way that it becomes and passes away but it never ceases doing so.[230] This idea of eternal return is opposed to the idea of linear time, or to any teleological view of human nature, but it is also not a theory of eternal order. On the contrary, it is a critique of the idea that there is a state of equilibrium in the world. Nietzsche says that if universe had a state of equilibrium, if becoming had a final state, it would already have been attained.

From our perspective, the idea of the eternal return is important, not so much as a cosmological understanding of the universe, but as Nietzsche's understanding of the self, and correspondingly, ethics. Saying this I am not underestimating the idea of eternal return as a cosmological understanding, after all in 1880-1881 when Nietzsche developed the ideas of the eternal return and *amor fati* he was deeply engaged with Stoics like Epictetus (*Handbook*) and Marcus Aurelius

---

227 Congdon, 'Nietzsche, Heidegger', p. 212.
228 Nietzsche, *Zarathustra*, II:20, 'On Redemption'
229 Nietzsche, *Zarathustra*, III:13, 'The Convalescent'
230 Nietzsche, *WP* 1066, p. 549

(*Meditations*).[231] In *The Gay Science* (1882), however, Nietzsche attempts to free himself from his Stoic notion of *amor fati* and the Greek thought of the eternal return, and instead, develops his own rival therapy which is based on affirmation of life, of ourselves including our weaknesses. It might be claimed that his thought of *amor fati* and eternal return is nothing but a repeat of Stoic vision and Greek thought; however, I claim that it may be so only if we regard the eternal return just as a cosmic understanding. In his later writings like *Zarathustra* and especially in *Genealogy* Nietzsche puts emphasis on the ethical dimension to the thought of eternal return. And to repeat what Löwith said, Nietzsche saw in the idea of eternal return 'creative possibilities for the future, in opposition to a Christianity which is reduced to moral values.'[232]

It is this experience of the eternal return that cannot be incorporated by pre-human, inhuman since they don't have faculty of memory, nor can it be incorporated by humans since its memory – bad conscience – suspends active forgetting. Unlike the inhuman, Zarathustra has a memory-faculty through which he can transcend the present moment, yet, unlike the human he can also employ this faculty to transcend the past.[233] This does not mean that Zarathustra is capable of changing the past, but that he has the power to say that what he has already done is the product of his willing, and that he will want it again if it happens to him in the future. Thus, instead of 'it was', he says: 'But thus I will it! Thus, I shall will it!' In other words, we encounter a new centre of organisation of the self in Nietzsche: the sovereign centre of the will intensified in the vision of eternal return. As Ansell-Pearson emphasises 'becoming is inconceivable without memory, including a techniques of memory, in which the product always exceeds the law of production (as in the example of Nietzsche's sovereign individual in which the "tree" of the social straitjacket – the morality of the custom – gives rise to a "fruit" that enjoys the supra-ethical power of living beyond.)'[234]

As opposed to priestly appropriation of bad conscience which turns the will against the individual, Zarathustra's conscience enables him to keep promises to his future self,[235] to affirm what he/she is and what he/she will be. Thus, Nietzsche's

---

231 Ure, 'Nietzsche's Free Spirit', p. 73
232 Karl Löwith, *Meaning in History* (Chicago: Chicago University Press, 1949), p. 219.
233 Paul S. Loeb, 'Finding the *Übermensch* in Nietzsche's *Genealogy of Morality*', in *Nietzsche's On the Genealogy of Morals*, ed. Acampora, pp. 163-177.
234 Keith Ansell-Pearson, *Viroid Life: Perspectives on Nietzsche and the Transhuman Condition* (London; New York: Routledge, 1997), p. 24.
235 Nietzsche, *GS* 335, 270

own account of will which should be understood from the perspective of eternal return does not depend upon the *causa sui* theory of 'free will' nor is there any conflict between the qualities – promising, responsibility – that he appreciates and those of which he himself is critical (i.e. Kantian notion of promising and responsibility which assumes a rational agent). 'Becoming what one is' means being engaged in a constantly continuing process of affirmation of one's own experiences and actions; of enlarging the capacity for assuming responsibility for oneself. This for Nietzsche is 'freedom'.[236] The eternal return implies this ability to want one's own life and the whole world as they are. Nietzsche says: 'My formula for greatness in a human being is *amor fati*'[237] because 'it finally comes home to me – my own self.'[238]

Nietzsche experiments, then, with the idea of a self that is defenceless but also fearless. The first condition of this experiment is the dissolution of the subject. Only then can we be both experimenters and subjects of our experiments, experiments done for the sake of 'true' or 'deeper' self. Nietzsche's self can be called the Participatory Self (joining the stream of reality-nature, becoming one with fate, blurring the distinction between outside and inside), however, becoming one with fate here is not only to be understood as a cosmological process, but as: 'accepting oneself as if fated, not wishing oneself "different."'[239] Whenever we act we create our own events, in other words, we determine our own fate, every action is a fulfilment of fate. Nietzsche repeats with Epictetus: 'Do not seek events to happen as you want, but want events as they happen, and your life will flow well.'[240] The Stoic affirmation, then, 'hinges on both elevating the limited, partial self toward a universal Whole, so that individual frustrations and obstacles disappear, and identifying one's will with universal Reason or providence.'[241] In Nietzsche, however, it is Reality ('absolutism of reality') that the fearless self should attempt to become one with.

II.iv. Conclusion

Nietzsche says at one point that the discovery of our true life can be made through the creation of a work of art; he says 'we want to be the poets of our life', a view

---

236 Nietzsche, *Twilight,* 'Skirmishes of an Untimely Man', 38
237 Nietzsche, 'Why I am so wise', *Ecce Homo,* 10
238 Nietzsche, *Zarathustra,* III:1, 'The Wanderer'
239 Nietzsche, 'Why I am so wise', *Ecce Homo,* 6
240 Quoted in Ure, 'Nietzsche's Free Spirit Trilogy', p. 75
241 Ure,'Nietzsche's Free Spirit Trilogy', p. 75

that captures his belief that one should 'become what one is.' It implies, though it does not follow through the idea, that literature and art might provide models of how to understand the world.

A common theme in the nineteenth and twentieth century philosophy has been the idea of the limits of philosophy, of what philosophy cannot say or grasp by means of concepts. If these limits exist, the question arises of what lies beyond them, and of how this can be expressed. The early Wittgenstein believed that whatever it was could not be expressed in language and should be met with silence, while Hans Blumenberg argued that beyond the limits of conceptuality lies not silence but metaphor, metaphor that then acts as a source at which conceptuality replenishes itself. For philosophers of religion, beyond conceptuality lies revelation. One conclusion that might be drawn from this is that there are some things that philosophy cannot express, but that might be expressed – or pointed to, gestured at – by other modes of world-orientation. Parts II and III of this book will explore the claims of literature to be one of those modes. In order to get there, however, we need to say something about Nietzsche's own style, or styles, in which the boundaries between philosophy and other modes of expression are loosened.

Chapter III: Intermediate Reflections; Philosophy and Literature

We have suggested that there is a complicated relationship between the concepts of fate and free will, and that to set man and fate over against each other is to posit a false dichotomy, or one that closes off too many important questions.[242] Such positing may be seen as the product of linguistic and semantic 'fictions'. As early as 1862 in 'Freedom of Will and Fate'[243] Nietzsche writes:

> We find that people believing in fate are distinguished by force and strength of will; whereas men and women who, according to an inverted comprehension of Christian tenets, let things happen (since 'God will make everything turn out alright') allow themselves, in a degrading manner, to be presided over by circumstances.[244]

For Nietzsche fate is nothing but a chain of events. Whenever we act we create our own events, in other words, we determine our own fate. And this is what *amor fati* is about.

In *The Gay Science amor fati* is the art of being a Yes-Sayer[245] to life, to ourselves, in other words, it is the ability to "give style' to one's character', to be poets of our lives[246] which is a rare art. It cannot be realised by everyone simply because it requires an absolute honesty about oneself, an acceptance of the strengths and weaknesses of one's own nature and the fitting of 'them into an artistic plan until every one of them appears as art and reason and even the weaknesses delight the eye.'[247] Those who are not satisfied with themselves and those who see in their inclinations nothing but sickness and evil are unjust towards their nature,[248] and, are dangerous because continually ready for revenge.

When the eternal return is presented for the first time, it is as the absolute affirmation of life. Nietzsche writes:

> You will find again every pain and pleasure and every friend and enemy and every hope and every error and every leaf of grass and every shaft of sunlight, the whole nexus of all things. This ring, in which you are a tiny grain, shines again and again.[249]

---

242 Nietzsche, *HH,* p. 325
243 Nietzsche, 'Freedom of Will and Fate', in *The Nietzsche Reader.*
244 Nietzsche, 'Freedom of Will and Fate', in *The Nietzsche Reader*, p. 16
245 Nietzsche, *GS* 276, p. 223
246 Nietzsche, *GS* 299, p. 240
247 Nietzsche, *GS* 290, p. 232
248 Nietzsche, *GS* 294, p. 236
249 Nietzsche, 'Notes from 1881', in *The Nietzsche Reader*, p. 240.

Nietzsche calls the thought of eternal return the 'new *heavy weight*': 'The question in everything that you want to do: "is it the case that I want to do it countless times?"'[250]

This absolute affirmation of our life requires, first of all, the dissolution of the subject, and an understanding of everything as becoming:

> To deny ourselves as individuals, to look into the world through as *many* as possible, *to live* in drives and activities *so as* to create eyes for ourselves, *temporarily* abandoning ourselves to life so as to rest our eye on it temporarily afterwards.[251]

Deleuze identifies the thought of the eternal return with the problematisation of the past and affirmation of future.[252] For Deleuze, the future can radically change the temporal modalities of the past and the present. In his *Deleuze and Guattari's Philosophy of History* Jay Lampert argues that:

> groundlessness constitutes the future. If it were not de-grounded, disentangled from its contexts, disinvested from the pleasures it provided, rendered free for new interpretations, the omni-contemporaneous past would be a frozen instant... Since the past contains the *totality* of possible events, there is no time beyond it to serve as the ground of events; by definition, totalities, and only totalities are ungrounded. The past is a totality; totalities are ungrounded; ungrounded events exist *only* as future possibilities.[253]

In other words, the past does not have an independent temporal horizon. The fact that there is no such transcendent temporal horizon means all past events exist as ungrounded and can, therefore, be reinterpreted or re-enacted eminently. This is why, for instance, we don't remember childhood events continuously, but only after an adult event triggers them.[254]

It is important for the reflections in this chapter that Deleuze and others resort to literature in order to prosecute their philosophical case: 'Proust's work is not oriented to the past and the discoveries of memory, but to the future and the progress of an apprenticeship.'[255] It is becoming other than what we are, 'becoming' an Egyptologist whose life is devoted to a task of constant learning how to

---

250 Nietzsche, 'Notes from 1881', in *The Nietzsche Reader*, p. 239
251 Nietzsche, 'Notes from 1881', in *The Nietzsche Reader*, p. 239
252 Gilles Deleuze, *Difference and Repetition*, pp. 141-142
253 Jay Lampert, *Deleuze and Guattari's Philosophy of History* (London: Continuum, 2006), p. 56
254 Lampert, *Deleuze and Guattari*, p. 57
255 Gilles Deleuze, *Proust and Signs*, trans. Richard Howard (Minnesota: University of Minnesota Press, 2000) p. 26.

read signs and of interpretation and creation.[256] Deleuze emphasises that in Proust memory and creation are two aspects of the same production – that is interpreting and deciphering are the 'process of production itself.' With a similar approach, Girard maintains that, Proust 'discards the classical method of transposition in the novel.' Marcel the writer and the narrator is in a constant transformation through the remembrance of the past and in the end 'The hero... will become a novelist.'[257] Through writing the writer becomes other than he is. However, Girard continues, recapturing the past is 'to welcome a truth which most men spend their lives trying to escape, to recognize that one has always copied Others in order to seem original in their eyes and in one's own.'[258]

Thus, only a groundless subject can be a redeemer of the past (active forgetting) and create his own future. Pierre Klossowski, like Deleuze, claims that the thought of the eternal return of the same, 'came to Nietzsche as an *abrupt awakening* in the midst of a *Stimmung*, a certain tonality of the soul.'[259] This *Stimmung* emerged as a thought only gradually, however, 'it preserved the character of a revelation – as a sudden unveiling.'[260] Klossowski, then, asks: 'How can a tonality of the soul, as *Stimmung*, become a thought, and how can the highest feeling, – the *höchste Gefühl* – namely, the Eternal return become the supreme thought?'[261]

According to Klossowski, the tonality of the soul is a fluctuation of intensity and the intensity must see itself as an object in order to become a thought, and to interpret itself. Now, the point is the intensity has no meaning apart from being intensity. Then the question arises: how can a meaning be constituted in the intensity? 'Precisely' says Klossowski, 'by turning back to itself even in a new fluctuation! By turning back on itself, by repeating and, as it were, imitating itself, it becomes a sign.'[262] In other words, through repetition a tonality of the soul becomes ossified, that is to say, becomes a sign, something as communicable in a public sphere.[263] According to Klossowski, this is why the early versions of the presentation of the thought of the eternal return (in 1881 notes and in *The Gay*

---

256 Deleuze, *Proust*, pp. 90-92.
257 René Girard, *Deceit, Desire, and the Novel: Self and Other in Literary Structure*, trans. Yvonne Freccero (Baltimore; London: John Hopkins University Press, 1976), p. 302.
258 Girard, *Deceit, Desire*, p. 38
259 Pierre Klossowski, *Nietzsche and the Vicious Circle*, trans. Daniel W. Smith (University of Chicago, 1997), p. 56.
260 Klossowski, *Vicious Circle*, p. 56
261 Klossowski, *Vicious Circle*, p. 60
262 Klossowski, *Vicious Circle*, p. 60
263 Klossowski, *Vicious Circle*, p. 62

Science) is quite different from how we encounter it in *Zarathustra*. In its early versions, the thought is articulated in a way that it becomes a communicable sign, but this also meant the loss of the original *Stimmung*. Such a loss necessitated a new style, namely the poetic and even prophetic style of *Zarathustra*. Or as Ian James claims, 'in trying to speak of an experience which is radically unspeakable or to translate into thought that which cannot be thought, Nietzsche's writing can only ever be a form of parody.'[264] Klossowski and James both seem to see the emergence of the idea of the eternal return as a call rather than an attitude and thought that Nietzsche developed over the course of time. It may be better, however, to put aside this interpretation and focus on the change in the style that the thought itself has brought about.

Nietzsche was aware of theories of parody from Hobbes through Kant, Schiller, and Goethe to Schopenhauer. It is a practice that can be traced back to the early Greek rhapsodists. The word parody is a combination of Greek *para* (meaning parallel, alongside) and *ode* (meaning song). So, parody literally means 'beside song.' The first parodies were sung beside the original ones delivered by the rhapsodists but inverted the original songs while still offering some epic harmonies. For instance, in *The Battle of the Frogs and Mice*, one of the surviving examples, frogs and mice substitute for Achaians and Trojans.[265] Kiremidjian defines parody as following: 'A parody is a kind of literary mimicry which retains the form or stylistic character of the primary work, but substitutes alien subject matter or content.'[266] How does the parodist work?

> The parodist proceeds by imitating as closely as he can the formal conventions of the work being parodied in matters of style, diction, meter, rhythm, vocabulary, and the countless other elements subsumed under the word form. But at the same time he substitutes subject matter, or content, or in an Aristotelian context actions or objects which are entirely alien to that form. He thus establishes a jarring incongruity between form and content.[267]

So it is quite possible that Nietzsche the philologist was also quite aware of the early versions of parody whose function was the problematisation of an issue. But like Goethe, Nietzsche, also conceives parody in aesthetic terms. In fact, an aphorism in *Human, All too Human* sees parody as the basis of all art:

---

264 James, *Pierre Klossowski*, p. 95
265 Kiremidjian, 'The Aesthetics of Parody', p. 232-233
266 G. D. Kiremidjian, 'The Aesthetics of Parody', *The Journal of Aesthetics and Art Criticism*, Vol. 28, No. 2 (Winter, 1969), p. 232.
267 Kiremidjian, 'The Aesthetics of Parody', p. 232

> *Affection of scientificality on the part of artists:* – Schiller believed, like other German artists, that if one possesses spirit one is free to *improvise with the pen* on all kinds of difficult subjects. And now his prose essays lie there – in every respect a model of how not to tackle scientific questions of aesthetics and morals –.... The temptation to which the artist so readily and so comprehensively succumbs for once to enter fields barred expressly to *him* and to put a word in with regard to *science*.... this temptation draws the artist so far as to show all the world what it has no reason to see at all, namely that his thinking-room looks narrow and in disorder – and why not? He does not live in it! – that the storecupboards of his knowledge are in part empty, in part filled with a medley of junk – and why not? This state of things is at bottom not at all ill-suited to the artist-child...and of this too he truly has no cause to be ashamed! – on the other hand, he often displays no little art in *imitating* all the blunders, bad habits and bogus scholarliness to be found in the scientific guild, in the belief that those things belong, if not to the heart of the matter, at any rate to its outward appearance; and this, precisely, is what is comical about such artists' writing: without wishing to, the artist here, nonetheless does what it is his office to do – to *parody* the scientific and inartistic nature, for a parodistic posture is the only posture he ought to adopt towards science, insofar, that is, he remains an artist and only an artist.[268]

Here parody is a mode of expression of an artist. 'The artist', says Gilman 'as creator functions parodically in relationship to all rigorous structuring.'[269] Although in this passage Nietzsche seems to be making a claim about the limits of the artist's competence – he knows little about scientific matters – his virtue is that he mistrusts and avoids any kind of systematisation, be it in the natural sciences or anywhere else.[270] Parody mocks such systematisation and with it the idea of fixed structures. In the revised edition of *The Gay Science* – a book which starts and ends with Nietzsche's poems – Nietzsche makes this point more explicit:

> But if anyone could, he would surely pardon more than a little foolishness, exuberance, and 'gay science' – for example, the handful of songs in which a poet makes fun of all poets in a way that may be hard to forgive. Alas, it is not only the poets and their beautiful 'lyrical sentiments' on whom the resurrected author has to vent his sarcasm: who knows what victim he is looking for, what monster of material for parody will soon attract him? '*Incipit tragoedia*' we read at the end of this awesomely aweless book. Beware! Something downright wicked and malicious is announced here: *incipit parodia*, no doubt.

---

268 Nietzsche, *HH*, p. 340
269 Sander L. Gilman, *Nietzschean Parody: an Introduction to Reading Nietzsche* (Aurora, Colo.: Davies Group, 2001), p. 21.
270 Nietzsche, *Twilight*, 'Maxims and Arrows', 26

It should be noted that 'The Tragedy Begins' (*Incipit tragoedia*) is the title of *GS* 342 which is the last aphorism of book IV and the text of this aphorism is, in fact, the beginning of *Zarathustra*. At that point Kaufmann draws our attention to the idea that *Zarathustra* 'is something of a parody.'[271] In a letter to Malwida von Meysenburg in 1883 Nietzsche refers to *Zarathustra*:

> It is a wonderful story: I have challenged all religions and written a new 'sacred book!' And in all seriousness, it is as serious as any other book, even though it accepts laughter into religion.[272]

Nietzsche's parodic style as an artistic mode of expression which can be used as a weapon against the fixed structures is most readily discerned in his poems. For instance, as early as 1858, Nietzsche writes a poem which is a parody of a traditional German Christmas hymn which can be found both in Lutheran and Catholic churches. Nietzsche's poem goes like this:

> Es ist ein Röslein entsprossen
> In holder Maienzeit
> Von Blättlein zart umschlossen
> Gleich einem Sterbekleid
> Doch als die rauhen Lüfte
> Das Röslein angerüht
> Und als die zarten Düfte
> Sturm und Wind entführt[273]

The original hymn goes as following:

> Es ist ein Ros entsprungen
> Aus einer Wurzel zart,
> Als uns die alten sungen,
> Von Jesse kam die Art,
> Und hat uns ein Blümlein bracht
> Mitten im kalten Winter
> Wol zu der halben Nacht[274]

---

271 Kaufmann, introduction in *The Gay Science*, p. 33
272 Quoted in Horst Hutter, *Shaping the Future: Nietzsche's New Regime of the Soul and Its Ascetic Practices* (New York; Oxford: Lexington Books, 2006), p. 119.
273 A roselet has bloomed / in pure may tide / encompassed by tender leaves / like a shroud / Yet as the rough winds / touch the rose / and as the mild breezes / are captured by storm and wind. Quoted in Gilman, *Nietzschean Parody*, p. 17. Quoted in Gilman, *Nietzschean Parody*, p. 17.
274 A rose has sprung / out of a tender root / As the ancients sang to us / it came from Jesse / and brought us a flowerlet / midst in the cold winter / in the middle of the night. Quoted in Gilman, *Nietzschean Parody*, p. 17

Gilman argues that Nietzsche adapts 'the *carpe diem* motif from Goethe's 'Heideröslein' ['Heather Rose']' to secularise the original poem. In other words, through the master's style Nietzsche's parody becomes 'the interplay between the model and the copy, between the existing order and new ordering.'[275] As Horst Hutter quite rightly observes, in his attempt to overcome the Western metaphysical tradition, namely, the philosophies or teachings of Socrates, Plato and Jesus, Nietzsche adopts a writing style which makes sense 'if one sees them as motivated by mimetic rivalry with these cultural icons, the "idols" of the Christian West.'[276] Hutter further adds that Nietzsche 'wishes to displace them from their positions, and in doing this he imitates them in the very manner in which he adopts to attack them.'[277]

In fact, Nietzsche's understanding of parody is not only an aesthetical phenomenon but also it is related to his understanding of history as well as his notion of the self. According to Nietzsche, 'the repetitive nature of history generates an endless series of parodies.'[278] In *Beyond Good and Evil*, Nietzsche writes:

> ....we are the first age that has truly studied 'costumes' – I mean those of moralities, articles of faith, tastes in the arts, and religions – prepared like no previous age for a carnival in the grand style, for the laughter and high spirits of the most spiritual revelry, for the transcendental heights of the highest nonsense and Aristophanean derision of the world. Perhaps this is where we shall still discover the realm of our *invention,* that realm in which we, too, can still be original, say, as parodists of world history and God's buffoons – perhaps, even if nothing else today has any future, our *laughter* may yet have a future.[279]

Here, Nietzsche seems to say that modern man cannot make history anymore, that he lacks any sort of originality. All he can do is parody past events. But why would this be such a bad thing? Nietzsche, in fact, opposes the idea of progress and of making history as the great or highest achievement of humanity: 'The European of today is of far less value than the European of the Renaissance.'[280]

If parody is one way of opposing progress, another is aphorism:

> Of all that is written I love only that which one writes with one's own blood.
> ....

---

275 Gilman, *Nietzschean Parody*, p. 39
276 Hutter, *Shaping the Future*, p. 113
277 Hutter, *Shaping the Future*, p. 113
278 Gilman, *Nietzschean Parody*, p. 33
279 Nietzsche, *BGE* 223, p. 150
280 Friedrich Nietzsche, *The Anti-Christ*, trans. R. J. Hollingdale (London: Penguin, 1968), 4, p. 116.

Whoever writes in blood and aphorisms does not want to be read, but rather to be learnt by heart.

In the mountains the shortest way is from summit to summit; but for that you must have long legs. Aphorisms should be summits: and those to whom they are addressed should be tall and lofty.[281]

It is not just that the content in his aphorisms is repeated constantly, but it is also that through aphorisms Nietzsche avoids any kind of conceptualisation. His aphorisms, full of references to different philosophers from different eras as well as to Nietzsche himself, amount to a sort of incompleteness. They are open-ended and invite the reader in to a creative experience of reading. Since anything that is covered comprehensively would mean conceptualisation and hence ossification, Nietzsche believes that the aphorism – and sometimes essayism – would be the best way of communicating his thoughts to his reader. Recall Zarathustra's attempt to redeem the past for the sake of present – or of life – and to become the creator of his life, or recall Nietzsche's call for the genuine 'historian' who is capable of creative interpretation: through a creative reading which requires absolute participation and attention, the reader can/should forget the taken-for-granted values – her past – that are imposed on her. The incompleteness of Nietzsche's aphorisms and essays is meant to suggest to the reader a future full of possibilities, a future that will be fulfilled in the act of reading. In this respect, just as there is no doer behind the deed, so the writing style is not a vehicle with which to express thoughts that are already there.

According to Klossowski, the Sils-Maria ecstasy – the high tonality of the soul – 'was no longer Nietzsche's alone' but had to be '*mimed* by Zarathustra's *bombastic gesticulations.*'[282] Klossowski claims that the Sils-Maria *Stimmung* was transformed into a sign language: a language that is used by the stage actors to mime and parody their subject. As the Swiss writer Max Frisch says 'writing is not communication with the readers, not even communication with oneself, but communication with the inexpressible.' The paradox of writing lies in this: 'the more exactly one succeeds in expressing oneself, the more clearly appears the inexpresssible force, that is to say the reality, that oppresses and moves the writer.'[283]

This is why Zarathustra does not and cannot teach his doctrine; he is the redeemer of the past but when it comes to the thought of the Eternal return, he is hesitant to teach it to his disciples, not because he does not want to but simply

---

281 Nietzsche, *Zarathustra*, I:7, 'On Reading and Writing'
282 Klossowski, *Vicious Circle*, p. 100
283 Max Frisch, *I'm not Stiller*, trans. Michael Bullock (London: Penguin, 1982), p. 289

because he cannot. This is why he says: 'Now I bid you lose me and find yourselves; and only when you have all denied me will I return to you.'[284]

However, Nietzsche could not have remained silent about his experience either, not only because he thought he had gone mad and had to turn his experience into a thought (Klossowski) but also for someone who attempts to find a remedy to the decline of mankind silence would mean violence. Moreover he had to write since this was his responsibility to the future. As Frisch says: 'We possess language in order to become mute. He who is silent is not mute'[285] Nietzsche makes this point clear in a letter to Lou-Salome:

> One should only speak where one is not permitted to remain silent, and only speak of that which one has overcome – everything else is babble, 'literature', a lack of self-control. My writings only speak of my overcomings: I am in them with everything that has become to me, *ego ipsissimus*, yes, even if a prouder expression is permitted, *ego ipsissimum*.[286]

Here Nietzsche means that through his writing he overcomes himself, he becomes other than he is. It is only through writing that he could observe himself in such a close way. Writing does not merely mean communicating but it also means thinking better, self-observing. Writing means reading the self. Moreover, through writing Nietzsche could deconstruct the traditional ways of thinking and writing – through parody – and could be read by those who can participate in the act of thinking through the act of reading. This was Nietzsche's task: responsibility to the future. He makes this point quite clear in *Human, all too Human*: '*Writing and the desire for victory.* – Writing ought always to advertise a victory – an overcoming of *oneself* which has to be communicated for the benefit of others.'[287]

The mission of the free spirit as a writer – philosopher or poet – should be future oriented:

> *The poet as signpost to the future.* – That poetic power available to men of today which is not used up in the depiction of life ought to be dedicated, not so much to the representation of the contemporary world or to the reanimation and imaginative reconstruction of the past, but to signposting the future: – not, though, as if the poet could, like a fabulous economist, figuratively anticipate the kind of conditions nations and societies would prosper better under and how they could then be brought about. What he will do, rather, is emulate the artists if earlier times of the gods and

---

284 Nietzsche, *Zarathustra*, I:22, 'On the Bestowing Virtue'
285 Frisch, *I'm not Stiller*, p. 289
286 Quoted in Hutter, *Shaping the Future*, p. 110
287 Nietzsche, *HH*, p. 248

imaginatively develop a fair image of man; he will scent out those cases in which, in the midst of our modern world and reality and without any artificial withdrawal from or warding off of this world, the great and beautiful soul is still possible, still able to embody itself in the harmonious and well-proportioned and thus acquire visibility, duration and status of a model, and in so doing through the excitation of envy and emulation help to create the future.[288]

The language of *Zarathustra* is an experiment which is consistent with Nietzsche's understanding of life and the self. As we have seen, Nietzsche calls for a life which should be lived like experiments. In *Daybreak* he says: 'the best we can do in this *interregnum* is to be as far as possible our own *reges* and found little *experimental states*. We are experiments: let us also want to be them!'[289] Or in *The Gay Science* he says: 'I favour any *skepsis* to which I may reply: 'Let us try it!' But I no longer wish to hear anything of all those things and questions that do not permit any experiment.'[290] In another passage from *The Gay Science:*

> But we, we others who thirst after reason, are determined to scrutinize our experiences as severely as a scientific experiment – hour after hour, day after day. We ourselves wish to be our experiments and guinea pigs.[291]

Now, the term 'Versucher' has the double meaning of 'experimenter' and 'tempter'. To be a *Versucher* requires the ability to create: 'Every creator is at once someone who tempts others and who *experiments on (tempts) himself and others* in order to create something that *does not yet exist*: a set of forces capable of *acting upon* and *modifying that which exists.*'[292] However, creation is also 'to break the gregarious habits' and then 'to *do violence* to what exists.'[293] A change in values requires a change in the creators of values. Zarathustra is a creator who seeks companions, not corpses or herds or believers because the creator seeks fellow-creators, those who inscribe new values on new tables.[294] This was Nietzsche's attempt: to be a creator of a thought, and accordingly, of a distinctive way of writing which meant a break with traditional philosophy and writing styles.

It is enduring habits that secure harmony in a social order. And this is what education is about: 'one tries to condition an individual by various attractions and

---

288 Nietzsche, *HH*, p. 235
289 Nietzsche, *Daybreak* V:453, p. 191
290 Nietzsche, *GS* 51, p. 115
291 Nietzsche, *GS* 319, p. 253
292 Klossowski, *Vicious Circle*, p. 127
293 Klossowski, *Vicious Circle*, p. 129
294 Nietzsche, *Zarathustra*, prologue 9

advantages to adopt a way of thinking and behaving' and then it becomes a habit, instinct and passion which 'will dominate him *to his own ultimate advantage* but "for the general good."'[295] '*Enduring* habits I hate,'[296] says Nietzsche. Once we are trapped in enduring habits which the social order imposes on us – 'for example, owing to an official position, constant association with the same people a permanent domicile, or a unique good health'[297] – we cannot easily leave the security that is provided by the repetition of the enduring habits. The more we are trapped in this illusory security the less we are close to ourselves, and, in turn, the less we are open to the possibility of the 'elevated moods' or of an experience like Sils-Maria.[298] Living experimentally means living without relying on any truths, living in uncertainties. It is becoming one with fate.

As we have seen, Nietzsche is pre-occupied with the question of how we can reverse the decline of modern culture, how we can reach a higher humanity. For him we can make things beautiful and desirable for us even when they are not in themselves.[299] About this we could learn something from physicians and but even more from artists who 'are really continually trying to bring off such inventions and feats.'[300] Thus, Nietzsche is not pessimistic about the future of humanity, on the contrary, it is the modern man – or a version of the modern man, the sovereign individual – who represents a new beginning and a new way of thinking associated with the affirmation of life. Zarathustra says: 'Verily a site of convalescence shall the earth yet become! And already a new fragrance wafts about it, bringing health – and a new hope!'[301] But this still raises the question of how.

Nietzsche attempts to transform the 'elevated moods' – i.e. his Sils-Maria *Stimmung* – into life. It may be the case that 'most people simply do not believe in elevated moods' and that 'to be a human being with one elevated feeling' might be a dream and a 'delightful possibility' for most people. Nevertheless, Nietzsche says, 'history might one day give birth to such people.'[302]

> What has so far entered our souls only now and then as an exception that made us shudder, might perhaps be the usual state for these future souls: a perpetual movement

---

295 Nietzsche, *GS* 21, p. 93
296 Nietzsche, *GS* 295, p. 237
297 Nietzsche, *GS* 295, p. 237
298 Nietzsche, *GS* 288, p. 231
299 Nietzsche, *GS* 299, p. 239
300 Nietzsche, *GS* 299, p. 239
301 Nietzsche, *Zarathustra*, I:22, 'On the Bestowing Virtue'
302 Nietzsche, *GS* 288, p. 231

between high and low, the feeling of high and low, a continual ascent as on stairs and at the same time a sense of resting on clouds.[303]

In *Testaments Betrayed*, Milan Kundera argues that Nietzsche's refusal of systematic thought has a crucial consequence: Nietzsche brings philosophy nearer to the novel. Through Nietzsche's writing, Kundera continues, 'the barriers between the various philosophical disciplines which have kept the real world from being seen in its full range, are fallen, and from then on everything human can become the object of a philosopher's thought.'[304] Just as Kundera refers to Nietzsche as a philosopher who brings philosophy nearer to novel by making everything human the subject of philosophy which, in turn, necessitates a new way of writing, so does he refer to Robert Musil as a novelist who brought the novel closer to philosophy.[305] Moreover, like Nietzsche Musil brings together the ethical and the aesthetical through his art.

Musil's literature's ethical function – his essayism – lies in its being 'a complex medium of meaning-production through which humans are given to test thorny moral issues and experiment with new solutions.'[306] Like Nietzsche, Musil's suggests the recognition of a new understanding of morality, what he calls 'a trying morality'. I will employ this term when 'trying' to understand the idea of possibility as it is discussed in Musil. This idea of possibility is not an intertextual matter for the interpreter to notice. Musil describes Ulrich as a man of possibility on many occasions and he does so because of his own engagement with Nietzsche's ideas, ideas about ethics, about how a live should be lived. Moreover, like Nietzsche, Musil believed that in order to get at those ideas, or make them live on the page, it was necessary to break with the dominant versions of novel writing in contemporary Europe.

---

303 Nietzsche, *GS* 288, p. 231
304 Milan Kundera, *Testaments Betrayed*, trans. Linda Asher (London: Faber and Faber, 1995), p. 175.
305 Kundera, *Testaments*, p. 176
306 Patrizia McBride, *The Void of Ethics: Robert Musil and the Experience of Modernity* (Illinois: Northwestern University Press, 2006), p. 101.

Chapter IV: Musil on Epistemology, Culture and the Self

IV.i. Introduction

The Man without Qualities is set in Vienna in 1913, and presents the pains and conflicts of individuals through the eyes of its central character, the 32-year-old Ulrich. A synopsis of the novel is made difficult not only by its length and complexity, but also by the fact that the 'action' does not take place so much in the conduct of the characters as within the minds of the protagonists, so that we read of their emotions and the conflicts between their thoughts and behaviour, as well as of their relations to each other. The novel contains many characters, just as one might find in a realist novel, but the experimental or avant-garde character of Musil's work consists in the fact that the action and the characters have been selected to emphasize that, behind the order that seems to be working when seen from the outside, nothing works properly, and the resulting corruption generates individuals who have little or no 'reality' to hold on to.

Perhaps the most prominent recurring event or action is the symbolic project called the Parallel Campaign. In response to the celebration marking the jubilee of German Emperor Wilhelm II's thirtieth year upon the throne, and partly in response to the German celebrations of the one hundredth anniversary of the defeat of Napoleon at Leipzig in 1813, a project has been announced to celebrate the seventieth jubilee of the Austrian Emperor. The problem is that the Habsburg Empire, which in the novel is referred to as *Kakanien*, is exhausted and decaying.[307] Musil describes in an ironic way how the characters in the novel gather around the Parallel Campaign, and how the individuals of a country which lacks a central willpower try to generate a purpose and a leading idea in order to provide social cohesion. The hero of the novel, Ulrich, is able to see the absurdity of this, but also the social decadence that it represents.

A second set of events is the case of Moosbrugger, a worker who has brutally murdered a prostitute in one of Vienna's parks; like the Parallel Campaign, it is a way of revealing the degenerate character of the Austrian legal system and of

---

307 Kakanien is a play on words that takes the semi-official phrase '*Kaiserlich und Königlich*' (imperial and magisterial) and turns it into a means of satire. The first part of 'Kakanien' is 'kaka', which in Italian and also in Turkish means 'shit' or 'rubbish.' Musil may also have had in mind 'kakistocracy', rule by the worst.

bourgeois morality in general; when Moosbrugger appears for the first time in the novel, his case is described as 'finally something interesting for a change';[308] his case is much in the news and fascinates many people. In contrast to the other characters – especially Ulrich – Moosbrugger's appearance is described in detail. Here Musil emphasizes the exhausted character of legality and morality, writing that Moosbrugger's face is 'blessed by God with every sign of goodness',[309] and that most people are unable to match this honest and innocent face with the horrible crime he is accused of. This incompatibility prevents both the reporters and the psychiatrists from displaying a clear position and decision. According to some psychiatrists, the murderer that should be regarded as a normal person should be held responsible for the murder he has committed, while according to some, due to his mental state he should not be arrested but should be treated as a medical case. Ulrich is not interested in the Moosbrugger case because he wants to prove him right or to assist justice; what he is really interested in is how such an event brings people together and why it is that people show an interest in this case that they never show towards their neighbours.

Part three of the novel is an attempt to think about morality and the world via a treatment of love. Ulrich has a sister Agathe, whom he hasn't seen for years. Their relationship is the focus of a third theme: how to undergo a different kind of participation in the world, one which is beyond any cultural and ideological grounds. As David Luft puts it, 'they enter into a relationship of intimacy and trust which is otherwise entirely presuppositionless and open to risk.'[310] This experience amounts to, or would amount to, the rejection of any conventional morality based upon the regulating of feelings.

I discuss these themes in more detail in the next chapter. Before doing so, it is necessary to establish what kind of writer and thinker Musil was, and in particular to understand the background – philosophical and literary – to his approach to the self as it appears in *The Man without Qualities*. First (IV.ii) I discuss the reception of Nietzsche in the German-speaking world and *Lebensphilosophie*; I (IV.iii) give a synoptic account of Musil's epistemology and its relationship with contemporary debates in the natural and social sciences; his critique of rationality and the idea of sense of possibility is addressed; in a final section (IV.iv) I discuss his understanding of culture and his role as a writer in a modern society.

---

308 Robert Musil, *The Man without Qualities*, trans. Sophie Wilkins and Burton Pike (London: Picador, 1995), p. 68. Hereafter *MwQ*.
309 Musil, *MwQ*, p. 67.
310 David Luft, *Robert Musil and the Crisis of European Culture 1880-1942* (Berkeley; Los Angeles; London: University of California Press, 1984), p. 250.

IV.ii. The Reception of Nietzsche in the German-speaking World and *Lebensphilosophie*

In the 1890s Nietzsche's writings began to appear in literary and experimental journals in Germany such as *Die Gesellschaft*. Nietzsche became 'a prominent part of the German avant-garde's conceptual armoury.'[311] For expressionists, for instance, Nietzschean philosophy was liberating since it suggested that metaphysical 'truth' and objective reality are little more than constraining illusions. Kurt Pinthus, the German writer and journalist, and the editor of the expressionist anthology *Menschheitsdämmerung* wrote: 'Reality is not outside us but rather in us...All the great ideas of mankind did not engender themselves through the force of facts, not through the demands of reality, but rather immediately out of the self-creative, future-directed spirit of man.'[312] In his plays, the Austrian expressionist playwright Arnolt Bronnen, illustrates 'the brutalisations of the expressionist Nietzsche nexus.'[313] In *Parricide*, (*Vatermord*, 1922), for instance, a young boy kills his father, dismisses his mother. The only motive behind his deed is 'the vitalist freedom the act itself endows.'[314] This motive was a leitmotif of many expressionists who were inspired by Nietzsche.

Another German expressionist poet, novelist and essayist, Gottfried Benn, claimed that 'Nietzsche demonstrated the error of assuming that humans had an intrinsic or metaphysical content. There was, indeed, no such thing as the "person" – there were only symptoms.'[315] Benn emphasised that Nietzsche abolished the content and the substance in favour of expression. He also, perhaps more than any other expressionist, held onto the idea of the death of God, claiming that 'the transcendence of nihilism meant ridding oneself of the torment of modern self-consciousness, induced by humanity's rift with nature. This meant a return to the preconscious, pre-logical, primal and inert state.'[316]

Other Nietzsche-inspired influential literary people of the time were the poet Stefan George (1868 – 1933) and his circle, which included Friedrich Gundolf, Ernst Kantorowicz, and Ludwig Klages. They took much of their

---

311 Steven E. Aschheim, *The Nietzsche Legacy in Germany 1890 – 1990* (Berkeley; London: University of California Press, 1994), p. 53.
312 Quoted in Aschheim, *The Nietzsche Legacy*, p. 65
313 Aschheim, *The Nietzsche Legacy*, p. 68
314 Aschheim, *The Nietzsche Legacy*, p. 68
315 Aschheim, *The Nietzsche Legacy*, p. 65
316 Aschheim, *The Nietzsche Legacy*, pp. 68-69

anti-scientific approach and aesthetic vitalism from Nietzsche. According to George and his followers the cosmic dimensions of life could not be apprehended through scientific knowledge, but only through aesthetic and poetic sensibilities. In that they were similar to Romantics, and like the Romantics they claimed to be apolitical, even hostile to politics. However, their critique of scientific knowledge and their claim that the transformation of society towards a higher culture and superior type of man – *Übermensch* – could be possible only through aesthetics was political in a broader sense. 'The circle encompassed people ranging from a future leader of the German resistance to Nazism, Count von Stauffenberg, to anti-Semites like Ludwig Klages; Jews like Ernst Kantorowicz, Gundolf and Wolfskehl; and those like Ernst Bertram who were attracted to Nazism.'[317]

While Bertram turned Nietzsche into a 'nation-saving prophetic myth', Pannwitz saw *Übermensch* as 'cosmic man…the synthesis of all human types…the crystalline representative of the cosmos.'[318] Similarly Alfred Schuler and Ludwig Klages developed a cosmic and mythic vision of Nietzsche, a vision which was accompanied by anti-Semitism. Schuler and Klages were members of an esoteric Gnostic group known as Cosmics. In their reading of Nietzsche neither Schuler nor Klages gave any room to individualism and to the self. Klages' category of 'elemental ecstasy', for instance, came directly from *The Birth of Tragedy*, which Klages saw as a text which sought to penetrate 'though the limits of "individuation" into the life of the elements.'[319] As Karl Polanyi says, for Klages 'Nietzsche was the philosopher of the Orgiastic; the rest was no good' and he adds: 'The "rest" means Zarathustra, Titanic Individualism, the Superman.'[320] What mattered for Klages was the Dionysian realm. In order to emphasise this he made a distinction between the *Seele* (soul) and *Geist* (mind), the former being the life-affirming (Dionysian realm), the latter life-destroying (Socratic rationalism). In Klages' hands Nietzsche's notion of the self – the will to power – was the agent of an aggressive mind that cut people off from their natural roots, from their cosmic unity.[321] Life, according to Klages, 'arose out of a fundamental division of body and soul, a rupture and a lost unity of cosmological principles, an erotic nearness

---

317   Aschheim, *The Nietzsche Legacy*, p. 76
318   Quoted in Aschheim, *The Nietzsche Legacy*, p. 77
319   Quoted in Aschheim, *The Nietzsche Legacy*, p. 80
320   Karl Polanyi, 'The Essence of Fascism', in *Christianity and the Social Revolution*, ed. John Lewis, and Donald K. Kitchin (New York: Charles Scribner's Sons, 1936).
321   Aschheim, *The Nietzsche Legacy*, pp. 80-81

(*Nähe*) to nothingness that cannot be surpassed.'[322] In other words, Klages' vitalism or *Lebensphilosophie* was, as Lukács put 'an open combat against reason and culture.'[323] Lukács even sees Klages as the one who is responsible for the fascicization of *Lebensphilosophie*.[324] In fact, Lukács names Klages, along with Heidegger and Bergson, a founder of modern vitalism.[325]

Long associated with Nazism, *Lebensphilosophie* lost its influence and only recently re-emerged thanks partly to scientific developments and partly to reinterpretations of Nietzsche and Bergson by philosophers like Agamben, Deleuze and Foucault. Of course, we did not have to wait until the 1980s for a new reading of Nietzsche: in the 1920s Klages' irrationalist, cosmic approach already had its opponents: Musil was one of them.

Even though *Lebensphilosophie* can be traced back to an opposition between being (Parmenides) and becoming (life as a flux; Heraclitus),[326] it emerged in the nineteenth century as a reaction against the rise of positivism, putting emphasis on a life as it is lived from the inside. The first journal dedicated to *Lebensphilosophie*, in fact, was established as early as the 1790s, and by the 1830s a few books started to emerge like Friedrich Schlegel's *Vorlesungen über die Philosophie des Lebens* (Lectures on the philosophy of life, 1827), in which Schlegel criticised the systematic philosophy of the day. Romantics like Friedrich Heinrich Jacobi or Novalis can be considered contributors to a philosophy devoted to critical self-cultivation. After the romantics it was Nietzsche and Dilthey that put emphasis on

---

[322] Nitzan Lebovic, 'The Beauty and Terror of Lebensphilosophie: Ludwig Klages, Walter Benjamin, and Alfred Baeumler', *South Central Review*, Vol. 23, No. 1, Spring 2006, p. 25.
[323] Lebovic, 'The Beauty and Terror of Lebensphilosophie', p. 27
[324] Lebovic, 'The Beauty and Terror of Lebensphilosophie', p. 27
[325] Lebovic, 'The Beauty and Terror of Lebensphilosophie', p. 27
[326] According to Heraclitus everything is in a state of flux. However, he does not simply say that everything changes or everything is in motion, instead there is unity in diversity. He stresses that it is the tension of the opposites which is essential to the unity of the One, or in other words, there is Being as Becoming, or Identity as Difference. According to this understanding Being itself is the thing which\who is always in a state of change, of becoming. The tension between the opposites creates endless becoming but its becoming is its Being. As opposed to Heraclitus, Parmenides claims that there is only Being, the One, that the concept of Becoming is just an illusion. Being, Reality and the Thought is the very same thing and there is only 'it is' and this 'it is' cannot not be. In this sense, there is no nothing. The thing that I talk about and think of is the very same thing otherwise I would not be able to think and talk about it.

wholeness above all, and on the importance of an internal relationship between philosophy and life.[327]

It is not easy to summarise the distinctive characteristics of *Lebensphilosophie*, since different philosophers emphasised different aspects of life and its relationship with philosophy. Thus, I will focus on those who were directly influenced by Nietzsche in one way or another. As Scott Lash observes there are three important generations of modern vitalists: 'There is a generation of 1840–45, i.e. Nietzsche and Gabriel Tarde; the generation of 1860, Bergson and Simmel; and the generation of 1925–33, Gilles Deleuze, Foucault and Antonio Negri. Lash adds: 'There seem to be two vitalist genealogies. One connects Tarde to Bergson and Deleuze, and the other runs from Nietzsche through Simmel to Foucault. The Bergsonian tradition focuses on perception and sensation while the Nietzschean tradition focuses on power.'[328]

Even though, as we saw, vitalism, or a form of Nietzsche's vitalism, became a means for the rise of anti-Semitism, vitalism or *Lebensphilosophie* did not disappear. The currency of vitalism, says Lash, re-emerged 'in the context of changes in the science, with the rise of uncertainty and complexity.' *Lebensphilosophie* is still valid since 'the notion of life has always favoured an idea of becoming over one of being, of movement over stasis, of action over structure, of flow and flux.'[329] Life for the philosophers of life is understood in its opposition to mechanism (Descartes): in mechanism there is an external causation, in which patterns or movements are determined.

Whether Musil can be regarded as a philosopher of life in the sense of *Lebensphilosophie* is debatable. Like many philosophers of his time he is critical of modern science, of the commitment to causal determinism in which things happen according to the principle of sufficient reason; at the same time he is also critical of the direction Nietzschean vitalism took. To the question 'Is life to dominate knowledge and science, or is knowledge to dominate life?' Nietzsche's answer is clear: life is the higher, the dominating force. For the expressionist vitalist this meant an irrational, anti-intellectual Nietzsche. This vitalism was totally different from its French counterpart, from, for instance, Henri Bergson's élan vital according to which the distinction between the unconscious flow of life and ossifying intellect was key. The (rational) faculty of memory was missing in the *Lebensphilosophie* of people like Klages, Schuler, George etc. Musil strongly opposes

---

327 Lebovic, 'The Beauty and Terror of Lebensphilosophie', pp. 25-26
328 Scott Lash, 'Life (Vitalism)', *Theory, Culture & Society*, 23: 323, (2006), p. 323.
329 Scott Lash, 'Life (Vitalism)', p. 324

these cosmic-orgiastic readings of Nietzsche as well as the opposition between intellect and soul, or life and science etc.

IV.iii. The Epistemological Background: Cause-effect

It is noteworthy that the biography of Ulrich, the man without qualities, shows a close similarity to that of Musil the author. Musil had already completed his studies in mechanical engineering when, at the age of twenty-three, he started to study philosophy at the Friedrich-Wilhems University in Berlin. He finished his graduate studies in 1908 with a doctoral thesis on Ernst Mach under the supervision of Carl Stumpf, who was a friend and also teacher of Husserl. His dissertation was a critique of Machean epistemology which, while rejecting the law of causality, claims that our knowledge is based only on sensations.

Even though his dissertation was on Mach, and he studied experimental psychology, as we know from his diaries Musil had always been more interested in ethics than psychology.[330] In the end, it was not as a student but as the author of *The Man without Qualities* that Musil committed himself to his main interest. But before we see how he pursued it, we should focus on the debates that were taking place in both the natural and social sciences at the end of the nineteenth century and the beginning of the twentieth century, particularly in the German-speaking world, debates that form the background to many passages in the novel.

The German physicist Gustav Theodor Fechner (1801-87) had undertaken psychological experiments in order to prove that, contra Descartes, mind and body are not two separate entities but two different images of the same entity. As we have seen, some two centuries earlier Spinoza had already made this claim. However, what makes Fechner different from his precursors who claimed the same thing is the fact that he attempted to base his argument on a scientific method. He developed a method which enabled him to infer psychic sensation by measuring physiological stimuli. In other words, 'he introduced a functional equation for calculating the threshold at which a sensory stimulus becomes a conscious sensation.'[331] Fechner called this theory 'psychophysics' and hoped that one day it would be possible to give an empirical account of the interconnection of mind and

---

330 Robert Musil, *Diaries* (New York: Basic Books, 1998), p. 442
331 Thomas Sebastian, *The Intersection of Science and Literature in Musil's The Man without Qualities* (New York: Camden House, 2005), p. 12.

body. Fechner affirms the basic ideas of Hume in his rejection of cause-and-effect, and hoped to put an end to this debate.[332]

Our aim is not to give a detailed account of Fechner's thinking but to emphasize that Musil was aware of these debates. His thesis adviser was Carl Stump (1848-1936) who had a major role in making psychology a discipline in its own right and who also combined descriptive with experimental psychology. He did his major research on audio perception and as a result of his studies he came to the conclusion that a distinction is to be made between affect and what he called *Gefühlsempfindungen* (emotional sensations). Sensations like toothache or tickling are accompanied by the latter and are simply sensations of pleasure or displeasure. They can be localised since one can point out where the pain is. Affective states, such as joy, anger, fear or hope, are different because they contain a cognitive (evaluative) element, and originate in some sort of judgment (Nietzsche).[333]

Musil, however, did not write his dissertation on crucial debates that were dominant at the time in experimental psychology but on Mach who radicalised psychophysics by claiming that psychology and physics start from the same point, namely, from sensations. According to Mach we are only aware of sensations: science does not explain nature but only describes it. In relation to this idea Mach claims that there are no causal laws: 'Science cannot ferret out hidden forces, for it proposes only "functional" diagrams, or charts of relationships.'[334] Since the world is in flux, complete knowledge of it is impossible. There are no substances and causalities, there is no centre that would allow one to posit a structured whole. In his *Analysis of Sensations*, Mach writes:

> Colours, sounds, temperatures, pressures, spaces, times, and so forth, are connected with one another in manifold ways; and with them are associated dispositions of

---

332 Sebastian, *Science and Literature*, pp. 12-13. Fechner's psychophysics influenced figures such as Wilhelm Wundt (1832-1920) and Emil Kraepelin (1856-1926) in experimental psychology but also political economists. Max Weber, for instance, sought to apply Kraepelin's work in the study of industrial labour. On this see Wolfgang Schluchter 'Psychophysics and Culture', in *The Cambridge Companion to Weber*, ed. Stephen P. Turner (Cambridge: Cambridge University Press, 2000), pp. 59-82. As we have seen Nietzsche was also interested in psychophysics. However, especially in *Ecce Homo* Nietzsche takes its claims further: 'How to nourish yourself so as to attain your maximum of strength, of *virtue* in the Renaissance style—of moraline free virtue?' Friedrich Nietzsche, *Ecce Homo* (London: Penguin, 1979), p. 52. Nietzsche's formulation here is an interesting amalgam of Fechner and Feuerbach.
333 Sebastian, *Science and Literature*, p. 14
334 Allen Thiher, *Understanding Robert Musil* (Columbia: South Carolina Press, 2009), p. 35

mind, feelings and volition. Out of this fabric, that which is relatively more fixed and permanent stands prominently forth, engraves itself on the memory, and expresses itself in language. Relatively greater permanency is exhibited, first, by certain complexes of colours, sounds, pressures, and so forth, functionally connected in time and space, which therefore receive special names, and are called bodies. Absolutely permanent such complexes are not.[335]

Mach agrees with Hume in rejecting the Cartesian cogito on the grounds that there is no empirical evidence for its existence. Hume writes: 'when I enter most intimately into what I call *myself*, I always stumble on some particular perception or other, of heat or cold, light or shade, love or hatred, pain or pleasure. I never can catch *myself* at any time without a perception, and never can observe anything but perception'.[336] As Sebastian rightly points out, the first chapter of *The Man without Qualities* presents this Humean or Machean idea of stream of sensations:

> Hundreds of noises wove themselves into a wiry texture of sound with barbs protruding here and there, smart edges running along it and subsiding again, with clear notes splintering off and dissipating.[337]

Mach says that he abandoned Kant's 'thing-in-itself' after he discovered that 'on a bright summer day in the open air, the world with my ego suddenly appeared to me as one coherent mass of sensations, only more strongly coherent in the ego.'[338] He rejects the Kantian distinction between the phenomenon and noumenon, claiming that there is no foundation for believing in any *a priori* conditions. There is no clear boundary between pre-scientific everyday experience and the theoretical constructions of modern science, an idea which makes him come to the conclusion that only sensations are reality.[339] He also claims that time and space are relations built up out of experience, in other words, that there are not two worlds, one in motion and one at rest (Being and Becoming).

While endangering philosophical concepts like space and time by claiming that they have accidental, historical and psychological content, Mach also claims that

---

335 Quoted in Sebastian, *Science and Literature*, p. 23
336 David Hume, *A Treatise of Human Nature* (Oxford: Clarendon, 1978), p. 252. It is noteworthy that Musil was attacked by his contemporaries for being too intellectual for a novelist, and Hume was criticised for being too literary for a philosopher. See Dagmar Barnouw, 'Skepticism as a Literary Mode: David Hume and Robert Musil', *Comparative Literature*, Vol. 93, No. 5, (Dec., 1978), pp. 852-870.
337 Musil, *MwQ*, p. 3
338 Quoted in Sebastian, *Science and Literature*, p. 25
339 Leszek Kołakowski, *Positivist Philosophy* (Harmondsworth: Penguin, 1972), p. 142.

the individual, like many other elements, is merely a relatively stable complex of sensational elements:[340]

> The ego must be given up. It is partly the perception of this fact, partly the fear of it, that has given rise to the many extravagances of pessimism and optimism, and to numerous religious, ascetic, and philosophical absurdities.[341]

What is essential to the causal connection exists only in abstraction. Mach's aim was to overcome the dichotomy between mind and body, between subject and object. Like Nietzsche, he claims that it is language which posits an intentional agency, the dualism of subject and object which is inherent in the philosophies of Descartes and Kant.

Nevertheless, in his dissertation Musil is critical of Mach's epistemology: 'individual precepts only have meaning when placed in a total gestalt.'[342] Musil is also skeptical towards Mach's rejection of cause-effect relationship. He cites the following passage from Mach:

> There is neither cause nor effect in nature. Nature is there only once. The recurrence of like cases in which A is always connected with B, i.e., of what is essential to the causal connection, exists only in the abstraction which we perform for the purpose of reducing facts.[343]

We saw that Nietzsche had already given a psychological explanation of man's belief in logical concepts:

> Supposing there were no self-identical 'A', such as is presupposed by every proposition of logic (and of mathematics), and the 'A' were already mere appearance, the logic would have a merely apparent world as its condition. In fact, we believe in this proposition under the influence of ceaseless experience which seems to confirm it. The 'thing' – that is the real substratum of 'A'; *our belief in things* is the precondition of our belief in logic. The 'A' of logic is, like the atom, a reconstruction of the thing – If we do not grasp this, but make of logic a criterion of true being, we are on the way to positing as realities all those hypostases: substance, attribute, object, subject, action, etc.; that is, to conceiving a metaphysical world, that is a 'real world' (- this, however, is the apparent world once more -)[344]

---

340 Luft, *Crisis*, pp. 81-82
341 Quoted in Luft, *Crisis*, p. 82
342 Thiher, *Understanding*, p. 34
343 Robert Musil, *On Mach's Theories* (Washington: The Catholic University of America Press, 1982), p. 44-45.
344 Nietzsche, *WP* 516, p. 279.

Nietzsche's point is that even though science and logic presuppose the existence of substance, attribute, and so on, we should never forget that they are hypostases, not realities. Similarly, Mach claims that we should not even use these terms and that, in fact, science does not and cannot offer an explanation of the world ('Nature is there only once').

Musil questions Hume's and Mach's claim that the law of causality is a mere fiction and that laws are merely functional descriptions of relations holding among sense data. In this respect he is closer to empirical realism or to Kant who claims that there is 'thing-in-itself', albeit that we cannot know it. In other words, Musil the scientist does not want to give up the sense of certainty. However, Musil the author – or the protagonist Ulrich – who started to write his novel some thirteen years after the dissertation, seems to be more Machean or at least more experimental, and not only for the obvious reason that a novel is not a philosophical treatise. The young novelist Musil was not yet ready to reject Newtonian physics. It may be that Törless' search for a unity between the outer and the inner can be read with a psychological and psychoanalytical approach,[345] but it is also a longing for a metaphysical ground, in a Kantian or Schopenhauerian way, for an 'in-itself-ness' of things, something existing outside of time and space, a transcendental self. Just as we saw Nietzsche grappling with Kantian ideas about autonomy, duty and the moral law, so the young novelist Musil was having his own battles with the Kantian transcendental self. What is that?

Any understanding of Kant's notion of the self requires a closer look at the second edition version of the Transcendental Deduction in the first *Critique*.[346] Kant starts with the assumption that we somehow have empirical knowledge – experience (*Erfahrung*), an idea which does not make Kant different from his predecessors in the epistemological tradition including Descartes and Hume. However, Kant further claims that experience requires not only empirical concepts but also *a priori* concepts, and he gives us a list of these concepts, i.e. categories. Then he introduces Transcendental Deduction to demonstrate the legitimacy of these categories. In fact, Transcendental Deduction does not focus on the categories in particular but is more concerned 'with establishing the *Form*

---

345 For psychological and psychoanalysis readings of *Törless* see Karl Corino, *Robert Musil, Eine Biographie*, (Reinbek: Rowohlt, 2003); Tim Mehigan, *The Critical Response to Robert Musil's The Man without Qualities*, New York: Camden House, 2003).

346 Immanuel Kant, *The Critique of Pure Reason*, trans. Paul Guyer and Allen W. Wood (Cambridge: Cambridge University Press, 1998). Hereafter *CPR*.

des Denkens, the general structure of experience into which the categories will fit.'[347] And this is where the transcendental unity of apperception, the 'I think' appears.

Kant makes a distinction between empirical self-consciousness and transcendental self-consciousness.[348] The former refers to consciousness of oneself and one's psychological states in inner sense (we will come to the latter later):

> ..how the I that I think is to differ from the I that intuits itself...and yet be identical with the latter as the same subject, how therefore I can say that *I* as intelligence a *thinking* subject cognize myself as an object that is *thought*, insofar as I am also given to myself intuition, only, like other phenomena, not as I am for the understanding but as I appear to myself.[349]

He insists that it is the empirical self-consciousness which is an intuition of self, it is the self as an object of perception. Here the self can become an object of knowledge, being subject to the categories, and accordingly it is not a thing in itself or *a priori* but an appearance.[350] Empirical self-consciousness then takes the form of a subject-object relationship. The self is part of the world; hence there is a part-whole relationship between the world and the empirical self. It is the empirical self which distinguishes me from others; it is the individual self which has a history, and personality.[351] It is not transcendental, i.e. it is not the condition of the possibility of experience.

In the synthetic original unity of apperception, on the other hand, Kant says 'I am conscious of myself not as I appear to myself, nor as I am in myself, but only that I am. This representation is a thinking, not an intuiting.'[352] Thus the proposition 'I think' is a judgment concerning 'mere apperception' of myself as the one who is thinking. The 'I think' must accompany all representations. It is the condition that guarantees the unity of my experiences since one cannot think without presupposing a subject. However, the 'I' is not my concrete or biographical self, rather it is an 'impersonal', transcendental self. It is nobody's self.[353] Kant says that transcendental self-consciousness 'is a bare consciousness (*ein blosses*

---

347 David Carr, *The Paradox of Subjectivity: the Self in the tRanscendental Tradition* (Oxford: Oxford University Press, 1999), p. 62.
348 Kant, *CPR*, B152
349 Kant, *CPR*, B155
350 Kant, *CPR*, B155
351 Carr, *The Paradox of Subjectivity*, p. 50
352 Kant, *CPR*, B157
353 Sebastian, *Science and Literature*, pp. 27-28

Bewusstsein) that accompanies all concepts.'[354] In other words, the transcendental unity of apperception is not conceptual, it does not refer to something empirical in nature.

So far so good. However, the question is whether Kant actually says that there are two selves. The answer is a simple no, for the empirical self and transcendental self are two descriptions of ourselves, or as Carr puts it 'we are conscious of our selves under two descriptions; and we are not in a position to decide between them.'[355] What is crucial here is that Kant's account of the transcendental self is ineffable, it is beyond any subject-object duality because when something is effable we can express it through language, in other words, there has to be a distinction between subject and object. The distinction of subject-object in the mind becomes the distinction of subject-predicate in the language and such a distinction is the necessary condition for any judgment. In that sense, the empirical self, being an object of thought, is effable. The transcendental unity of self consciousness, on the other hand, can be neither an object, nor a subject. It cannot be an object because it grounds all concepts *a priori*. It cannot be a subject because then it would require an object. We may conclude that the necessary condition for anything to be effable or repeated (Musil) is the subject-object duality. In that sense, the transcendental unity of consciousness is ineffable. Consider this passage from *Törless:*

> He felt as though torn between two worlds: one was the solid everyday world of respectable citizens, in which all that went on was well regulated and rational, and which he knew from home, and the other was a world of adventure, full of darkness, mystery, blood, and undreamt-of surprises. It seemed then as though one excluded the other.[356]

It is clear that Musil had Kant and Schopenhauer in his mind in passages like this in Törless. Schopenhauer begins *The World as Will and Representation*[357] by declaring that the world is a representation which means as knowing objects what we know is just perception; we do not know what the sun is but our eyes see it and our hands feel it. In other words, whatever we encounter in the world is our representation of it. However, there is another dimension of the world as will (or in Kantian terms 'thing-in-itself') which is outside space, time and causality. In his

---

354 Kant, *CPR*, A346/B404
355 Carr, *The paradox of Subjectivity*, p. 65
356 Robert Musil, *Young Törless*, trans. Eithne Wilkins and Ernst Kaiser (New York: Pantheon, 1964), p. 50.
357 Arthur Schopenhauer, *The World as Will and Representation* (New York: Dover Publications, 1969). Hereafter *TWWR*.

metaphysics the body is a key element:[358] we are aware of our body in two ways: we perceive it as an object of space and time; we perceive it from within, as an item of self-conscious experience. To demonstrate this, for instance, if I am writing with a pen and attend to my hand, I perceive it as an object existing in space and time; however, if I suddenly focus on my consciousness of the act of writing, I become aware of the resistance of the pen and feel the pressure as it moves up and down on the paper. In this state of mind I discover my body as will.[359] Now, it seems that Törless is experiencing the world and his body at the threshold between these two different states and longing for access to this world beyond our experience.[360]

We may conclude that Musil, the author of *Törless* is, in fact, more in the tradition of transcendental self (Kant), the self withdrawing into its own reality. Like Nietzsche he experiments with defenselessness and fearlessness, with the idea of dissolution of the subject for the sake of a new, a 'deeper' self. However, unlike Nietzsche, Musil is more sceptical about the idea of the self's joining the stream of Reality, of becoming one with fate. Musil the author of *The Man without Qualities*, however, seems to be more sceptical about both Schopenhauer and Kant and to be more ready to experiment with new ways of explaining the phenomenon – especially in the realm of Ethics – in other words, he asks whether it is possible to live at all if we give up causality. However, to say that Musil advocates Nietzschean self more in *The Man without Qualities* would be an hasty conclusion, for Musil, in fact, is rather critical of Nietzschean, participatory self. He might still be in the tradition of the transcendental self, but he also questions the transcendental self of Kant as something outside of time and space.

Musil's scepticism about the transcendental self of Kant and Schopenhauer leads him experiment with probability theory. We can follow his experiment with this thought through following the chains of thought of Ulrich. For instance, according to Ulrich, it is repetition which underlies all rationalisation. Scientific knowledge presupposes the repetition of the same:

> Science is possible only where situations repeat themselves...We'd have no way of understanding or judging anything if things flitted past us only once. Anything that has to be valid and have a name must be repeatable, it must be represented by

---

358 Schopenhauer, *TWWR* 18
359 David E. Cartwright, *Historical Dictionary of Schopenhauer's Philosophy* (Oxford: Scarecrow Press, 2005), p. xlix.
360 For Musil's reception of Schopenhauer see Kelly Coble, 'Positivism and Inwardness: Schopenhauer's Legacy in Robert Musil's *The Man Without Qualities*', *The European Legacy*, 2006, 11:2, pp. 139-153.

many specimens, and if you have never seen the moon before, you'd think it was a flashlight.[361]

Or somewhere else Ulrich says:

> In a vortex of events that never repeat themselves, we could obviously never formulate the profound insights that A equals A, or that greater is not the lesser, but would be living in a kind of dream, a condition abhorred by every thinker.[362]

This means that it is not only in the realm of scientific knowledge that repetition is the ultimate principle: 'if our acts were unrepeatable, then there would be nothing to be expected of us, and a morality that could not tell people what was expected of them would be no fun at all.'[363] The quality of repetitiveness adheres also to money, indeed it reaches its highest degree in money: 'As long as it keeps its value, it carves up all the world's pleasures into those little building blocks of purchasing power that can then be combined into whatever one pleases.'[364] This echoes Georg Simmel's analysis of money in social life: 'Money is concerned only with what is common to all, i.e., with the exchange value which reduces all quality and individuality to a purely quantitative level.'[365] Science, money, morality: the coherence and meaning of each depends upon repeatability.

It is against this background that Musil gives his chapters titles like 'Bank Director Leo Fischel and The Principle of Insufficient Cause', which refers to Leibniz's 'Principle of Sufficient Reason'.[366] Here Ulrich tells his banker friend, whose world is one that depends upon the certainties provided by repeatable events, that 'in our real, I mean our personal, lives and in our public-historical lives, everything

---

361 Musil, *MwQ*, p. 409
362 Musil, *MwQ*, p. 552
363 Musil, *MwQ*, p. 553
364 Musil, *MwQ*, p. 553
365 Georg Simmel, 'The Metropolis and Mental Life', in *On Individuality and Social Forms* (Chicago and London: The University of Chicago Press, 1971), p. 326.
366 In fact the theory can be traced back to Plato. In *Timaeus* while he is criticizing the cosmology of his predecessors who attempted to explain the element of the universe through one of the four elements, namely water, air, fire or earth, Plato claims that something changing cannot be an element of the universe since it belongs to the sensual world. Plato argues that nothing changes or becomes without a cause, so there must be an unchanging Being or Cause of the universe. This Plato calls Demiurge. See *Timaeus, and Critias* (Harmondsworth: Penguin, 1971). In Aristotle it is the 'unmoved mover' which is the primary cause of the universe. See Aristotle, *Metaphysics* (New York: Columbia University Press, 1952), Book XII.

that happens happens for no good or sufficient reason.'[367] At another time Ulrich tells General Stumm that theology cannot become an empirical science, since, God 'was seen only once, at the Creation, before there were any trained observers around.'[368] Here, once again, Ulrich claims that without repetition of the same no scientific observation is possible. In Leibniz's world, on the other hand, all beings are absolutely determined by the will of God, meaning that, there are only singularities and that there cannot be two entities alike. Nothing in the world could be imagined to exist by mere chance. In Leibniz God knows the best of all possible worlds[369] (in Schopenhauer's pessimistic philosophy it is the worst possible world we are living in); in Ulrich's understanding, by contrast, God knows all possible worlds, yet, does not really know which one is the best.[370] We read that Ulrich thought in this way even when he was a child, that once he has written a school essay on the theme of love of country; unlike his schoolmates he has written that anyone who really loves his country cannot think that his country is the best in the world. He adds to this statement a second one: 'God Himself probably preferred to speak of His world in the subjunctive of possibility…, for God creates the world and thinks while He is at it that it could just as well be done differently.'[371]

The idea that this world is just one of many possible ones, that god might be bored or disappointed with his own creation, has a parallel in the idea of the self as possibility, one that will be central to Musilian ethics. Musil's rejection of a Cartesian notion of the self follows a similar trajectory to Nietzsche's. Recall Descartes' ontological proof of God. Descartes states that the idea I have of a being more perfect than my own (God) must necessarily have been given to me by a being who is indeed more perfect than me, namely God. All the attributes of God (infinite, eternal, immutable, independent, supremely intelligent, supremely powerful) are such that, Descartes says, 'the more carefully I concentrate on them the less possible it seems that they could have originated from me alone.'[372] From this it follows that from the simple fact that I exist, and have in me the idea of a supremely perfect being God's existence is proven.[373] Descartes starts from the thinking I because, he claims, we have a clear and distinct knowledge of an effect before having a

---

367 Musil, *MwQ*, p. 140
368 Musil, *MwQ*, p. 409
369 Gottfried W. Leibniz, *Discourse on Metaphysics and Related Writings* (Manchester: Manchester University Press, 1988), Discourses 1-16; p. 97.
370 Musil, *MwQ*, p. 14
371 Musil, *MwQ*, p. 14
372 Descartes, *Meditations*, p. 31
373 Descartes, *Meditations*, pp. 24-37

clear and distinct knowledge of its cause. For instance, I know that I exist before knowing why I exist. This is exactly where Spinoza criticises Descartes. Spinoza starts from God; from the Cause claiming that it is not enough to show how effects depend on causes, but one must go beyond this and show how true knowledge of an effect itself depends on knowing its cause.[374]

In fact, in his method Spinoza is Aristotelian. In *Metaphysics*, Aristotle tells us that science should deal with that which is primary, and on which the other things depend, and in virtue of which they get their names. This primary thing is 'substance'; metaphysics as a science should be concerned with 'substance' since all things are either substances or the attributes of substances. This 'substance' which is the cause of everything is eternal and immovable rather than subject to change. Other sciences like mathematics and physics are theoretical, yet, it is not clear whether their objects are separable from matter or not. The knowledge of 'substance' also belongs to a theoretical science, yet, it should be prior to both mathematics and physics. The science of this immovable substance must be the first philosophy, and universal.[375] Aristotle does not just say that knowledge must discover causes; it must, in Deleuze's words, 'reach the cause on which the effect depends; he said that an effect is not known, except to the extent that its cause is already, and better known.'[376] And this thesis is what Spinoza takes up from Aristotle. But why was it that important to start from the Cause, God? Because, according to Spinoza 'to know by causes is the only way to know essence.'

Leibniz's criticism of Descartes is quite similar to that of Spinoza's: even though clarity and distinctness allow us to recognize an object, they never give us true knowledge of the object. They may tell us something about the external qualities of the object but cannot tell anything about the essence of the same object. In other words, they do not say anything about the cause which explains why the thing is what it is. Both Spinoza and Leibniz are searching for a *sufficient reason,* something which is lacking throughout Cartesianism. This search makes them both discover 'the expressive content of ideas' and 'their explicative form.'[377] In other words, for both Spinoza and Leibniz the word 'expression' becomes a vital concept in their philosophy: God manifests (or expresses) itself in all our ideas and behaviours. Or consider this: 'By God I understand a being absolutely infinite, that

---

374 Gilles Deleuze, *Expressionism in Philosophy: Spinoza* (New York: Zone Books, 1990), p. 157.
375 Aristotle, *Metaphysics*, Book IV
376 Deleuze, *Expressionism*, p. 157
377 Deleuze, *Expressionism*, p. 154

is, a substance consisting of an infinity of attributes, of which each one *expresses* an eternal and infinite essence.'[378]

Now one of the claims of this book is that not only Cartesianism but this expressive notion of the self is questioned throughout *The Man without Qualities*. The man without qualities or without particularities does not have any essence or substance to be expressed in any way. It cannot be a singularity or particularity in the Leibnizian sense since there is nothing that is distinctive or particular about him. In his notes Musil says his essential particularity is that he is nothing in particular.[379] The force and tension of the novel derives partly from the fact that, one the basis of his background – his family, education, and social environment – one might have expected a man like Ulrich precisely to be striving to be a man of substance, even a 'great man', recognized as such through his deeds. In fact, by the time he is twenty-two he has begun three careers: as a mathematician, a soldier and an engineer. Each of these was an attempt by 'a man of possibility' – which we all are to an extent – to become 'a man of reality'. None of these has provided a ground for him and each has rapidly become meaningless. In addition, just as he fails to commit himself to any profession, so he fails to become a passionate supporter of any particular idea. The point however is that it is just this failure to be a mathematician, a soldier or an engineer that can be seen as a condition for self-development; he realizes that to construct one's identity through universal values and beliefs – which might well have lost their validity – or to behave according to the more circumscribed ethical codes of particular professions, makes people indifferent to their potentialities. In other words, the problem of the division of labour which beset German thought from Goethe to Weber, was not to be overcome by reference to an all-embracing idea of humanity based upon Kantian or other 'universal' principles.

The Man without Qualities contains many passages that describe, or attempt to describe, the internal workings of Ulrich's mind. However, as I said earlier, Musil does not focus exclusively on this, and the first part of the novel introduces a series of characters many of whom have a position in life, a career, as well as characters

---

378 Spinoza, *Ethics* (London: Penguin 1996), Id6. Schopenhauer the atheist and the philosopher of the will explains the principle of sufficient reason without referring to the existence of God. In fact the principle of sufficient reason was subject to Schopenhauer's doctoral thesis (1813). In the thesis Schopenhauer claims that there are four ways in which something relates to a ground or reason: causal explanations; empirical observation; mathematical explanations; the explanations of action. See Schopenhauer, *On the Fourfold Root of the Principle of Sufficient Reason* (New York: Cosimo, 2007).

379 Maurice Blanchot, *The Book to Come* (Stanford: Stanford University Press, 2003), p. 137.

who are committed to their own ideas. What makes Ulrich different is his detachment. At first this is presented by means of a contrast with these characters. The world of professions and social positions is represented by Count Leinsdorf, an Austrian civil servant and the co-ordinator of the Parallel Campaign, Count Tuzzi, at whose house the meetings of the campaign are held, Ulrich's father and his brother-in-law Hagauer, both legal scholars, the simple-minded General Stumm von Bordwehr, the Austrian imperial army's representative at the meetings of the campaign, the bank director Leo Fischel, and the domestic servants Rachel and Soliman. The world of ideas is represented by the young radical Hans Sepp and his friend Gerda, daughter of Fischel, Count Tuzzi's wife Diotima (Ulrich's cousin), and by Ulrich's friends Walter and Clarisse. Ulrich's conversations with Walter and Clarisse – who is described among other things as a reader of Nietzsche – are an important way of presenting his view of the world. Ulrich, eventually, being a man of intellect more than of anything else, starts questioning the order of bourgeois life and of taken-for-granted moral values. However, unlike many people from his era he does not praise reason over feeling or vice-versa. Musil depicts an era which lost its faith in the nineteenth century's emphasis on reason. In that sense, Musil, like Nietzsche, questions the value of scientific knowledge. He also, again like Nietzsche, questions the moral values of his era. However, he is not anti-rationalist or amoral. The attitude of Ulrich, the man without qualities, is one of ambivalence: scientific rationality can be criticized from the point of view of morality, and that morality may be criticized from the point of view of science, and Ulrich so to speak occupies the space from which both critiques are possible without at first seeking to transcend them.

IV.iv. The Critique of Rationality; The Sense of Possibility

In one pivotal chapter, Musil reflects on the 'peculiar predilection of scientific thinking for mechanical, statistical, and physical explanations that have, as it were, the heart cut out of them':

> The scientific mind sees kindness only as a special form of egotism; brings emotions into line with glandular secretions; notes that eight or nine tenths of a human being consists of water; explains our celebrated moral freedom as an automatic mental by –product of free trade; reduces beauty to good digestion and the proper distribution of fatty tissue; graphs the annual statistical curves of births and suicides to show that our most intimate personal decisions are programmed behaviour; sees a connection between ecstasy and mental disease; equates the anus and the mouth as the rectal

and the oral openings at either end of the same tube – such ideas, which expose the trick, as it were, behind the magic of human illusions, can always count on a kind of prejudice in their favour as being impeccably scientific.[380]

Scientific rationality in this sense is both disillusioning and dehumanizing. It replaces the living texture of experience with a skeleton of 'causes', 'drives', 'impulses', and the like.

In fact, the late eighteenth century German speaking world was marked with the debate between, on the one hand, the advocates of reason, on the other hand people like Hamann and Jacobi who questioned the authority of reason. The early German Romantics – like Novalis and Schlegel – claimed that it was because of the absolute authority that was given to reason that people lost their feelings for nature, bonds with the community and finally their faith in religion.[381]

Ulrich's – the man without qualities' – reaction to all this is one of ambivalence. He is enough of a romantic not to be an advocate of the idea of progress, but nor can he give up on the values that Enlightenment promised. Like Kant, Musil believes that 'Enlightenment is mankind's exit from its self-incurred immaturity.'[382] In fact, this is the paradox of the Enlightenment: As Jeffrey Alexander argues 'on the one hand, there is the disillusionment and an existential despair that psychological maturity and cultural integrity cannot be sustained. On the other hand, there is real evidence of the increasing autonomy and strength of the individual.'[383]

---

380 Musil, *MwQ*, pp. 327-328
381 It should be noted that the young romantics did not find remedy in irrationalism. They appreciated the critical power of reason. They even claimed that we had to take criticism to its limits. A critical reason is also self-conscious, that is to say, it is aware of its limits. The question, then, is 'How is it possible to restore unity with nature and the community without forfeiting the freedom that comes from criticism?' They found the remedy in art, in aestheticism. It is the artist who can transcend rational criticism. See Frederick Beiser, *The Early Political Writings of the German Romantics* (Cambridge: Cambridge University Press, 1996), pp. xvi-xvii.
382 Immanuel Kant, 'An Answer to the Question: What is Enlightenment?' in *What is Enlightenment?,* ed. James Schmidt (Berkeley; Los Angeles; London: University of California Press, 1996).
383 Jeffrey Alexander, "The Dialectic of Individuation and Domination: Weber's Rationalization Theory and Beyond", in *Max Weber, Rationality and Modernity,* ed. Sam Whimster and Scott Lash (London: Allen and Unwin, 1987), p. 187. This paradox forms Max Weber's sociology as well. Weber appreciates rationalization in the sense that it gives opportunity for liberation, however, he also states that modern people are also being governed and dominated by institutions that are man-made. While Weber agrees with Nietzsche in ignoring the 'fact that science – that is, the techniques of

Ulrich's principle of insufficient reason expresses the indeterminacy of the world once it is believed that there is no such thing as a 'supreme cause' or any real purpose in the world, and it also says that the world is ruled by mere chance. In Ulrich's world everything could have been otherwise or could be not at all. A demonstration of this point occurs in the very first chapter of the novel.

After giving us a description of a metropolis where 'dark clusters of pedestrians formed cloudlike strings' and 'hundreds of noises wove themselves into a wiry texture of sound with barbs protruding here and there', the narrator tells us of a scene in which a couple witnesses an accident in which a man is hit by a truck; as he lies on the pavement, and before an ambulance arrives, a crowd gathers 'like bees clustering around the entrance to their hive.'[384] The couple discuss the accident. The lady feels disturbed by its sudden violence, but her male companion then explains to her that such trucks have a braking-distance that is too long. The lady has no idea what a braking-distance is, nor does she care to understand it, however, this technical expression calms her down by establishes a distance between her and a disturbing reality. Musil's description of this chaotic city life reminds us of Georg Simmel's metropolitan type which 'creates a protective organ for itself against the profound disruption with which the fluctuations and discontinuities of the external milieu threaten it.'[385] The metropolitan type does not and cannot act in an emotional way, there is no room for feelings in the chaotic structure of metropolis life, rather, Simmel argues, the metropolitan type reacts rationally. So does Musil's couple. Coming close enough to see the victim, the lady has 'a queasy feeling

---

    mastering life based on science – has been celebrated with naïve optimism as the way to *happiness*' he is even more critical of the modern anti-scientific prophets in the Germany of his time. Modern rationality – of science, of organization and so on – is here to stay. Max Weber, 'Science as a Vocation' in *Max Weber's 'Science as a Vocation'* eds. Peter Lassman, Irving Velody and Herminio Martins (London: Unwin Hyman, 1989) p. 17. As he says in *Economy and Society*, 'bureaucracy is in the process of creating the iron cage of the future which man, like the fellahs of ancient Egypt, will one day be helplessly forced to obey.' Quoted in Ralph Schroeder, "Personality and 'Inner Distance': The Conception of the Individual in Max Weber's Sociology', *History of the Human Sciences* 4 (1991): 69. Similarly in 'Science as a Vocation' he states that 'there are in principle no *mysterious, incalculable* powers at work, but rather that one can in principle master everything through *calculation*. But that means the disenchantment of the world' (p. 13). Similarly, Musil, in a more indirect way, gives a similar message: we are living in a world in which even we ourselves became calculable, however, this does not mean that we should appreciate feelings over reason or vice-versa.

384 Musil, *MwQ*, p. 4
385 Simmel, 'Metropolis', p. 326

in the pit of her stomach.'[386] Though she feels irresolute and helpless, thanks to the gentleman's rational explanation her confrontation with death does not shatter her. Order is maintained.

But Musil is telling us about something more than our desire to put things in order, to make unfamiliar familiar, even, paradoxically, through a technical language which is foreign to us. The gentleman's explanation gives the technical reason for the accident; if these trucks had a better braking system, the accident could have been avoided. But it does not tell us why it had to happen to this particular person rather than another; the cause-effect explanation is only a partial or relative explanation of the event, which remains otherwise contingent.

Perhaps sensing the unease that such contingency arouses – why didn't this happen to me? – at this point the gentleman starts to give some statistics: 'According to American statistics, one hundred ninety thousand people are killed there every year by cars and four hundred fifty thousand are injured.'[387] The point here is that in statistics there is not 'this particular' or 'that particular' person, there are no singularities but only generalisations, averages. We should reflect here on the paradoxical relationship between causal laws and statistical regularities.

Causal laws may or may not be said to 'govern' events in the natural world, but causal mechanisms do require that events that display cause and effect relationships are repeatable, that they have a sameness to them: if we say that water will boil when heated to 100 degrees centigrade we assume that each time we heat a pan of water to that temperature it will boil, and we assume that we can demonstrate this with a unique pan of water. On the other hand, if we repeated this demonstration we would never say that each repetition was a random event.

Now, the lorry hitting the pedestrian is precisely a random, contingent event, and one is tempted to say that it is a singularity. When the gentleman calms the woman by means of statistics, he does after all refer to a large number of cases, each of which was unique to the individuals who were affected. However, by the end of the nineteenth century, where there were such statistics there was also the science of probability. And the science of probability proposes a set of 'laws' which operate according to averages, trends, likelihoods and so on. And these averages, trends and likelihoods are abstracted from any particular case. Based on the statistics, the gentleman could have told the woman what the probability was of her being hit by a lorry. But in a real sense he would not be telling her anything about her own experience. He would be telling her about the possibility of anyone,

---

386 Musil, *MwQ*, p. 5
387 Musil, *MwQ*, p. 5

of the average person, being hit by the lorry. And the average person does not exist, cannot be individuated. The law of averages does not apply to any individual case, whereas causal laws must apply to all individual cases. This is also why the idea of probability is compatible with the idea of randomness. In fact, it presupposes randomness. Musil establishes his interest in this apparently paradoxical fact in the first chapter of the novel and pursues it throughout. It is exemplified in Ulrich's discussion of 'the law of large numbers':

> One person may commit suicide for this reason and another for that reason, but when a great number is involved, then the accidental and the personal elements cancel each other out and what is left...but that is just it: what *is* left?....what is left is what each one of us as layman calls, simply, the average, which is a 'something' but nobody really knows exactly *what*.[388]

And yet, this not knowing exactly what is left over once a statistical average is established is interpreted by Musil not as a ground for nihilism, or a dead end, or as a link between functionalism and meaninglessness. On the contrary, precisely because the law of averages or probability presupposes randomness and contingency, the acceptance of a world governed by probability is the acceptance of a world in which the individual's biography is governed, in principle, by pure chance. The laws of probability only 'apply' for large numbers. But individuals only live once; it is only on the basis of large numbers of random events that statistics that mean anything can be compiled. Ulrich's reflections on this paradox therefore lead him to an emphasis on what he calls 'the sense of possibility'. As we shall see, Ulrich, the man of possibilities, in fact discovers a sort of freedom in the world governed by the 'law of probability', a freedom that enables him to see his life as an experiment.

Recall that in 'On the Uses and Disadvantages of History for Life', Nietzsche proposes an interpretation of history which will redeem the past in order to be open to the future. This, as we have seen, requires us to be partially 'unhistorical', when necessary to partially forget and to be partially historical for the health of an individual, of a people and of a culture. Now, even though this combination of

---

[388] Musil, *MwQ*, p. 532. It is worth noting, though, that Durkheim's *Suicide*, published in 1897, accepted the first part of this proposition, abstracting from the myriad 'reasons' for individual suicides and trying to account for variations in the rates of suicide, but didn't entirely accept the conclusion. On the basis of the averages he tried to construct a diagnosis of the pathologies of modernity. See Emile Durkheim, *Suicide* (London: Routledge, 2002). See also in Ian Hacking, *The Emergence of Probability* (Cambridge: Cambridge University Press, 2007).

these two 'species' is what Nietzsche suggests, in the concluding passage of that essay he seems to be in favour of the suprahistorical and the unhistorical, for the 'malady of history' can be cured only by administering an antidote to the historical. Similarly, in *The Man without Qualities* Ulrich seems to have a peculiar notion of history. One day on his way home in the streetcar some thoughts about history occur to Ulrich:

> A hundred years earlier they had sat in a mail coach with the same look on their faces, and a hundred years hence, whatever was going on, they would be sitting as new people in exactly the same way in their updated transport machines.[389]

Ulrich's observations here are of course partly a variation on remarks made by both Simmel and Benjamin on the effects of transportation on interpersonal relations: 'Interpersonal relationships in big cities are distinguished by a marked preponderance of the activity of the eye over the activity of the ear',[390] exemplified by the 'not pleasant experience' of sitting together in buses, trams and trains. The point here, however, is that Ulrich's suprahistorical viewpoint makes him reluctant to see technological progress as having such a significant impact: people in trains look at each other in the way they once did in mail coaches, and they will do so in the future. If this is modernity it is a fairly stable modernity.

However, 'a fairly stable modernity' is not what Ulrich's vision of history implies. It is supremely sensitive to change, but equally resistant to the idea of progress in history. And it is the absence of progress which makes it possible to say that people a hundred years ago and people a hundred years hence are 'the same' in some way:

> the course of history was therefore not that of a billiard ball – which once it is hit, takes a definite line – but resembles the movement of clouds, or the path of a man sauntering through the streets, turned aside by a shadow here, a crowd there, an unusual architectural outcrop, until at last he arrives at a place he never knew or meant to go to. The present is always like the last house of a town, which somehow no longer counts as a house in town. Each generation wonders 'Who am I, and what were my forebears?' It would make more sense to ask: 'Where am I?' and to assume that one's predecessors were not different in kind but merely in a different place; that would be a move in the right direction, he thought.[391]

---

389 Musil, *MwQ*, p. 391
390 Quoted in Walter Benjamin, *Charles Baudelaire: A Lyric Poet in the Era of High Capitalism* (London: Verso, 1983), p. 38.
391 Musil, *MwQ*, p. 392

Here, the sort of discussion of the relationship between the randomness of events and the sense of order provided by statistical probability is repeated in Ulrich's statement about historical experience, historical experience which is both historical and suprahistorical.

In a conversation with Clarisse and Walter Ulrich makes his point even more explicit by presenting 'them with his scheme for living the history of ideas instead of the history of the world.'[392]

> The difference, he said to begin with, would have less to do with what was happening than with the interpretation one gave it, with the purpose it was meant to serve, with the system of which the individual events were a part. The prevailing system was that of reality, and it was just like a bad play. It is not for nothing that we speak of a 'theatre of world events' – the same roles, complications and plots keep turning up in life.... Apart from the truly notable exceptions, the successful political molders of the world in particular have a lot in common with the hacks who write for the commercial theatre; the lively scenes they create bore us by their lack of ideas and novelty, but by the same token they lull us into that sleepy state of lowered resistance in which we acquiesce in everything that put before us. Seen in this light, history arises out of routine ideas, out of indifference to ideas, so that reality comes primarily of nothing being done for ideas. This might be briefly summed up, he claimed, by saying that we care too little what is happening and too much about to whom, when, and where is happening, so that it is not the essence of what happens that matters to us but only the plot; not the opening up of some new experience of life but only the pattern of what we already know, corresponding precisely to the difference between good plays and merely successful plays.[393]

In fact, like Nietzsche, Ulrich claims that history is full of numbers and 'big' names (monumental history), however, even though, for instance, 'a young man with an active mind, is 'sending out ideas in every direction', only 'those that find a resonance in his environment will be reflected back to him and consolidate, while all the other dispatches are scattered in space and lost!'[394] In other words 'in the course of time, commonplace and impersonal ideas are automatically reinforced while the unusual ideas fade away. So that almost everyone with a mechanical certainty is bound to become increasingly mediocre' and this according to Ulrich 'explains why, despite the thousandfold possibilities available to everyone, the average human being is in fact average.'[395] But does that mean that all human beings

---

392 Musil, *MwQ*, p. 395
393 Musil, *MwQ*, pp. 395-396
394 Musil, *MwQ*, p. 121
395 Musil, *MwQ*, p. 121

are average? Does it mean that it is impossible to do something extraordinary? As we have seen, the theory of probability implies that it is not impossible at all. That was what the discussion of randomness and contingency, and the paradox of freedom contained within the idea of probability, was all about.

However, that discussion was not much more than a preparation of the ground; 'freedom through probability' is not a very exciting slogan, nor will it take us very far into Musil's vision of freedom, individual possibility and ethics. For that we have to look elsewhere. One of the places we have to look is his understanding of culture and the individual.

IV.v. Culture and the Individual

In 1935 Musil gave a speech at the International Congress of Writers for the Defence of Culture in Paris. The congress was intended as the continuation of ideas and strategies that had been pursued by the Communist Party since the Congress of Soviet Writers in Moscow in 1934. The thematic areas included 'Cultural Heritage', 'Humanism', 'Nation and Culture', 'The Individual' and 'The Role of the Writer in the Society'.[396] The intention was 'to build bridges between the Communist and the bourgeois intelligentsia after Russia's entry into European politics.'[397] The day it opened, 10th May, witnessed the Nazi-organised book burning in Berlin.

Musil's speech may have been a disappointment for many who were present, for in contrast to the praise of collectivism which was the dominant attitude of the participants, Musil praised individualism: the moving force behind culture was always the creative individual.[398]

It would not be an exaggeration to say that most of *The Man without Qualities* is an attempt to make the individual creative and powerful in a way that might go beyond the statistical average. It is an attempt to show it is possible to be an

---

396 Klaus Amann, 'Robert Musil: Literature and Politics' in *A Companion to the Works of Robert Musil*, ed. Philip Payne, Graham Bartram, Galin Tihanov (New York: Camden House, 2007), p. 62.
397 Amann, *Companion*, p. 62
398 In fact, even in nineteen sixties and seventies there were still many scholars – like Ulrich Schelling (1968), Laermann (1970), and Bohme (1974) – who, adopted Lukács' understanding of realism and felt obliged to attack Musil for contributing to the moral and cultural decline by attacking the spirit of postwar collectivism along with the Habsburg state. Mehigan, *The Critical Response*, p. 12.

anti-average man. Among the draft phrases for the Paris Congress we find the following sentences:

> [The defence of culture does not mean much to me. What does, is the defence of the individual as its source.
> The individual must be creative, the community can only help him.
> We are a part of the whole that is dependent on politics but stands in opposition to it.][399]

He claims that:

> The empowered individual mind is the goal, and also the producer, of culture. The interaction of society and culture should ideally aim at the liberation of the empowered individual, who creates values that, perforce, must be generalised in society if society is to be transformed by them.[400]

Musil also defended the autonomy of art and the artist and claimed that the artist had to be independent from any ideology, from the political claims of the state or class or nation etc. He began his speech by claiming that culture was harmed not only by the enemies but also by the friends of culture, and in saying this Musil knew that the organisers of the Congress were among these friends. He also said that he wanted to speak unpolitically which meant that he was there as an author not as a supporter of any ideology which, again, was against the spirit of the Congress. Having made his position rather clear, namely, 'culture is not bound to any political form', he then attempted to answer the following questions: what is culture? How do cultures arise and vanish?[401] These were of course questions which had occupied Nietzsche.

In the concluding part of his speech he defined culture as something:

> transcending the boundaries of time and nation, which prohibited those 'die der Kultur dienen' (who serve culture) from completely identifying with 'dem Augenblickszustand ihrer nationalen Kultur' (the momentary state of their national culture.[402]

Musil's answer to the organisers of the Congress was clear: only political instruments are to be used against the totalitarianism of any ideology, whether it is extreme Right or Left. The unpolitical means, i.e. literature and art, are not to be used against any political formation. Perhaps Musil's approach can be compared to that of Milan Kundera. Kundera's characters in his novels are generally regarded as people who are engaged in a struggle to assert themselves against the suppression

---

399 Quoted in Amann, *Companion*, p. 70
400 Thiher, *Understanding*, p. 28
401 Amann, *Companion*, p. 70
402 Amann, *Companion*, p. 80

by the state.[403] However, Kundera strongly opposes this claim saying that his novels can be seen as political only by virtue of their being unpolitical. For instance, in response to the description of *The Joke* as 'a major indictment of Stalinism', he protested that it was a love story.[404]

Of course, the claim that *The Joke* is a love story is as exaggerated as the claim that it is an indictment of Stalinism. In the same way, Musil's assertion of a distinction between writing and politics, and his rejection of the idea of the political novel or the political mission of the writer, does not imply a purist vision of art for art's sake. Modernist in its experimentalism, *The Man without Qualities* is also realist in ways that are comparable with the nineteenth century novel. Nowhere is this clearer than in his depiction of character and the cultural context and milieu in which they act. Or fail to act.

Musil was so much a part of the culture he depicts that Maurice Blanchot described his work not only as ironical but also self-ironical. Musil himself is a man of Kakania, almost an aristocrat.[405] In depicting the atmosphere of *fin-de-siècle* Vienna, *The Man without Qualities* also offers a critique of bourgeois culture in general. This is not because Musil projects specifically Viennese experience onto modernity in general, but because Vienna itself was a kind of laboratory of modernity:

> Social and political movements as opposed as Nazism and German anti-semitism on one hand and Zionism on the other had their origins in Old Vienna, as did some of the central elements in modern Catholic social thought and the original adaptation of Marx, known as 'Austro-Marxism.'[406]

Musil comments on this atmosphere at an early stage in the novel:

> All in all, how many amazing things might be said about this vanished Kakania! Everything and every person in it, for instance, bore the label of *kaiserlich-königlich* (Imperial-Royal) or *kaiserlich* und *königlich* (Imperial *and* Royal), abbreviated as

---

403 This is claimed partly because of Kundera's political background. He was a supporter of the Czech Communist party in the aftermath of the Second World War. However, on the basis that Kundera's writings failed to conform to the model of 'Socialist Realism' Kundera was expelled from the party. When Warsaw Pact forces moved into Prague in August 1968 to suppress the Prague Spring, he was removed from his teaching post at the Prague Film School and his novels were banned. In 1975 Kundera left Czechoslovakia to live in France.
404 Robert Thomas, 'Milan Kundera and the Struggle of the Individual,' *Libertarian Alliance*, Cultural Notes, No.23, London, 1991.
405 Blanchot, *The Book to Come*, p. 136
406 Alan Janik and Toulman, Stephen, *Wittgenstein's Vienna* (New York: Simon and Schuster, 1973), p. 36.

'k.k.' or 'k.&k.', but to be sure which institutions and which persons to be designated by 'k.k.' and which by 'k.&k.' required the mastery of a secret science. On paper it was called the Austro-Hungarian Monarchy, but in conversation it was called Austria....Liberal in its constitution, it was administered clerically. The government was clerical, but everyday life was liberal. All citizens before the law were equal, but not everyone was a citizen.[407]

It was the 1848 upheaval which brought the eighteen-year old Franz Joseph to the throne. His rather long reign – sixty-eight years – created a kind of illusory stability within the Empire. Even though he seemed to introduce some liberal values like the introduction to the western part of monarchy of universal suffrage in 1907, this was, in fact, to protect the Emperor's control over the Army against those Hungarians who wanted to establish their own Army.[408] In fact, it was an era in which nothing could stop the increasing spirit of nationalism in the Empire, and, in fact, all over Europe. As Janik and Toulmin observe:

> After studying nineteenth-century Habsburg history, one can hardly deny the charm of Hegelian dialectic, as a mode of historical explanation; for in it one continually sees situations begetting their own opposites. The effort to introduce German in place of Latin, so as to streamline Imperial administration, begat Hungarian and Czech cultural nationalism by reaction, and this in due course developed into a political nationalism. Slav Nationalism in politics and economics in turn begat German economic and political nationalism; and this in turn begat anti-Semitism and a natural Jewish reaction.[409]

Vienna, above all, was a bourgeois society and Musil's cultural critique focuses on the values of this society. The third quarter of the nineteenth century was the Golden Age for the Viennese bourgeoisie. It was the period of industrial expansion, the *Gründerzeit* 'which created the material fortunes on which the next generation depended for leisure in which to cultivate arts.'[410]

Noteworthy here, and something that recalls Musil's claim about the distinction between art/literature and politics at the Paris Congress, is one of the main characters in *The Man without Qualities*, the German industrialist Paul Arnheim, who appears to unite material fortunes and the arts. And politics. At one and the same time Arnheim is attempting to buy oil fields in Galicia and participating actively in the doomed Parallel Campaign; in other words he is trying to bridge politics

---

407 Musil, *MwQ*, p. 29
408 Janik, *Wittgenstein*, p. 38
409 Janik, *Wittgenstein*, p. 39-40
410 Janik, *Wittgenstein*, p. 42

and culture, business and art. Arnheim is modelled partly on Walther Rathenau, the essayist and industrialist who became foreign minister in the first years of the Weimar Republic and was murdered in a right wing terrorist attack in 1922, and also on Werner Sombart, whom Musil met on the same day that he met Rathenau. Sombart and Rathenau knew each other and had common friends in the artistic environment of Berlin.[411]

Sombart, the author of *Der moderne Kapitalismus* (1902) saw the genesis of capitalism in self-interest and desire for profit. However, in his *The Jews and Modern Capitalism* (1911) a radical turning away from this position is rather explicit: in the latter book Sombart attempts to explain the economy as a phenomenon of culture rather than as the outcome of the interplay between supply and demand.[412] Similarly at one point the narrator of *The Man without Qualities* tells us that Arnheim:

> was notorious for quoting poets at board meetings, and for insisting that economy could not be separated from other human activities and could be dealt with only within the larger context of vital problems, national, intellectual, and even spiritual.[413]

The idea that 'economy could not be separated from other human activities' is more Sombart than Rathenau. As to the 'spiritual', it is clear that Musil refers to Rathenau's use of the 'soul' in his own writings:[414] 'Arnheim's pamphlets and books proclaimed nothing less than the merger of soul and economics, or of ideas and power.'[415]

Arnheim is in many ways Ulrich's great rival. Not in the sense that he is someone to be struggled against over the same resources, but in the sense that he represents a different way of approaching reality as such, a different attitude to experience, the belief that separate spheres of experience can be united. And Arnheim's implicit belief in synthesis, 'bridging' art and business, culture and politics, was by no means the only version of how to achieve unity. That there were several such versions, and movements that expressed them, was itself a response to the widely-perceived fragmentations brought about by industrialisation, and especially by the rapid industrialisation of Germany, Austria and Russia. As Stefan Jonsson observes:

---

411 Galin Tihanov, 'Robert Musil in the Garden of Conservatism', in *A Companion to the Works of Robert Musil*, ed. Philip Payne, Graham Bartram, Galin Tihanov (New York: Camden House, 2007), p. 133
412 Tihanov, *Companion*, p. 137
413 Musil, *MwQ*, p. 205
414 Musil, *MwQ*, p. 422
415 Musil, *MwQ*, p. 111

Once the development of industrialization and urbanization had gained momentum, however, the transformations that followed were felt to be all the more dramatic. Many were alarmed by the prospect of a future society in which economic quantification, scientific abstraction, and professional specialization would make it impossible for the individual to relate 'naturally' to the world and to fellow beings.[416]

One way in which Musil catches people's reaction to this transformation and to an unknown future is through his depiction of the participants of the Parallel Campaign (see above). These people gather around this project enthusiastically, perhaps, seeing it as a symbol of the Old Order, as something to hold onto. As we have seen, the Parallel Campaign creates a sort of illusory union among the members of the action. Musil's choice of such an 'action' is not coincidence. During the first quarter of the twentieth century, Austrians – not the Austro-Hungarian Empire citizens, but only the Austrian people – were more desperate than at any other time for a unity within the Empire. Intellectuals were meeting, discussing and writing about possible solutions. Just after the WW1, Musil, himself was among those intellectuals who believed a solution lay in an annexation with Germany.[417] Of course, this attitude changed for many after 1933. Within this environment some thinkers even found the remedy in mysticism, particularly, in the fourteenth century mystic and theologian Meister Eckhart's mysticism whose Christian-Neoplatonist metaphysics provided some ideas about the relationship between the state and the individual. In fact, the very title of the novel, *The Man without Qualities*, echoes the phrase 'áne eigenschaft' ('without qualities') which was used by Eckhart 'to designate the condition of being "empty and free" for a mystical union with God.'[418] Such a union requires one to become timeless and spaceless. He/she has to be free from any agency or subjectivity. However, while for Eckhart being without qualities means a mystical readiness to unite with God, in Musil it refers to Ulrich's wilful opposition to full or meaningful participation in his social and political environment.[419]

In fact, Musil's borrowing from Eckhart was not untypical of the time; Eckhart's mysticism was 'much on the minds of a range of German-language writers

---

416 Stefan Jonsson, *Subject without Nation: Robert Musil and the History of Modern Identity* (London: Duke University Press, 2000), p. 23.
417 This is basically what his 1919 essay entitled 'Anschluss with Germany' is about. See Robert Musil, 'Anschluss with Germany', in *Precision and Soul* (Chicago: University of Chicago Press, 1990). Hereafter *PS*.
418 William Crooke, *Mysticism as Modernity: Nationalism and The Irrational in Hermann Hesse, Robert Musil, and Max Frisch* (Oxford; New York: Peter Lang, 2008), p. 15.
419 Crooke, *Mysticism,* p. 78

and thinkers'[420] during the first decades of twentieth century. Two noteworthy ones from opposite ends of the political spectrum were Gustav Landauer, pacifist, internationalist and social anarchist, and Alfred Rosenberg: the 'philosophical *Führer* of Nazi intellectualism.'[421] Both thinkers 'saw in Eckhart's mystical rhetoric a means of unifying disparate populations, bringing isolated modern individuals into *unio mystica* with a specifically German collective.'[422]

Landauer, for instance, places nation above state: it is a true illusion that creates genuine unity, whereas state is bad, a false illusion that cannot transcend space and time:

> Landauer's mystic solution to state-produced disaffection re-imagined the individual's relationship to the nation as a *gottlose Mystik* ['God-less mysticism'] in which the desired object of the *unio mystica* is no longer God but the collective of other men and women existing in the cultural boundaries of a particular nation.[423]

Rosenberg's understanding or reading of Eckhart is not dissimilar to that of Landauer's. According to Rosenberg[424] only in an *eigenschaftslos* state free from time and space, can the desire for union with God be awakened. However, unlike Landauer, or even Eckhart, Rosenberg locates the mystical essence not 'in the giving up of the self…but rather in the act of inflating the ego with God so that God could be born into the soul.' This means:

> The isolated individual seeks oneness not with God but with this *Wesen* [essence], 'the new identity-creating force' that invited into or…ignited in the individuals' soul, creates a new *national* type. In a mystically compressed time-space that overcomes historical and geographical divisions, the German state would exist in the German knight, in the Prussian officer, the Baltic Hanser, in the German soldier and in the German farmer.'[425]

Thus, through a mystical unlearning of time and space, Rosenberg suggests a racial state type. Our referring to both opposite extreme examples is no coincidence. Landauer and Rosenberg, each in his own way, saw a kind of opportunity for a new formation of nation/state, for a new beginning. They both longed for a unity in society and found the remedy in a mystical union between the individual and

---

420 Crooke, *Mysticism*, p. 29
421 Crooke, *Mysticism*, p. 29
422 Crooke, *Mysticism*, p. 29
423 Crooke, *Mysticism*, p. 37
424 See Adolf Rosenberg, *Der Mythus des 20. Jahrhunderts: Eine Wertung der Seelich-geistigen Gestaltenkämpfe Unserer Zeit* (München: Hoheneichenverlag, 1934).
425 Crooke, *Mysticism*, p. 45

the state or the nation. Such a longing for unity, whether at individual level or national, was not an uncommon attitude among the German speaking *fin-de-siècle* intellectuals. However, what makes Musil distinctive among his contemporaries is the fact that for him such longing is in vain; there is no such thing as unity and moreover, it is no bad thing. For Ulrich the 'dissolution of the subject' that is a condition of becoming a 'man without qualities' is vital, not in order to be able to unite with God, but to be able to be open to one's potentialities, or even to be able to live as a matrix of potentialities.

Musil sees groundlessness and homelessness both at the social and individual levels as an inherent feature of modernity, and believes that any attempt to deny or avoid this would result in self-destruction or in Promethean over-ambition. The famous opening paragraph of *The Man without Qualities* is a crucial hint:

> A barometric low hung over the Atlantic. It moved eastward toward a high-pressure area over Russia without as yet showing any inclination to bypass this high in a northerly direction. The isotherms and isotheres were functioning as they should. The air temperature was appropriate relative to the annual mean temperature and to the aperiodic monthly fluctuations of the temperature. The rising and setting of the sun, the moon, the90 phases of the moon, of Venus, of the rings of Saturn, and many other significant phenomena were all in accordance with forecasts in the astronomical yearbooks. The water vapour in the air was at its maximal state of tension, while the humidity was minimal. In a word that characterizes the facts fairly accurately, even if it is a bit old-fashioned: It was a fine day in August 1913.

Here, the scientific and the everyday descriptions seem equally valid; the one is not superior to the other.

This opening chapter illustrates how neither the language of science – faith in reason that the Enlightenment promised – nor inadequate conventions of realism can capture the 'Machean flux of sensations in which everything – the people, their 'bourgeois identities, the name of the city – has become subjective and unreal.'[426]

Musil already articulated some of these ideas in an essay entitled 'German as a Symptom', dated 1923. He begins with a comparison between the intellectual of 1900 and of 1923. The *fin-de-siècle*, the prewar intellectual is distinguished by the belief in a better future, the postwar intellectual by escapism to the past: hope has given way to hopelessness. As Patrizia McBride puts it:

---

426 Malcolm Spencer, *In the Shadow of Empire: Austrian Experiences of Modernity in the writings of Musil, Roth and Bachmann* (Rochester, N.Y.: Camden House, 2008), p. 16.

The ideological confusions of the prewar years lay for Musil in the litany of ideological opposites that battled each other in the cultural arena – rationalism\irrationalism, Nietzschean elitism\socialism, materialism\idealism, humanism and racism, internationalism and nationalism. These highly polarized visions all shared one thing in common: a bold spirit of experimentation and a positive sense of future.[427]

This *fin-de-siècle* attitude was the result of 'a will to be different and to do things differently from the way people had done them in the past.'[428] Desire, will, hope were the concepts that characterized the prewar era. As opposed to this optimistic, even utopian understanding of future, the bloody war – the future that they were waiting for – created a pessimistic postwar intellectual who wished a return 'to some idealized, idyllic past and a more manageable rhythm of life.'[429] In other words, Austrians in search of unity and wholeness focused either on past or future. In both cases, though, the present was rejected. Karl Mannheim would develop a similar diagnosis in *Ideology and Utopia* (1929); he thought that political life was being pulled apart by conservatives who saw the present only from the perspective of the past (ideology) and by radicals who saw the present only from the perspective of a better future (utopia).[430]

The Man without Qualities takes place in the year 1913, one year preceding the war, and one may wonder why Musil chose it. Musil started to write the novel in 1924, and he died without completing it. Either he could not finish it or he never intended to do so. Either way, this seemed to symbolise the unfinishability of modernity. More importantly, he worked on it for almost twenty years, long enough to witness the divergence in the prewar and postwar attitudes. Even though the events take place in one year, in 1913, Musil was writing as an author, even as an outsider,[431] who distanced himself from both attitudes. He was neither nostalgic about a past that 'never existed' nor did he believe in a better future promised by revolutionaries.

---

427 Patrizia McBride, *The Void of Ethics: Robert Musil and the Experience of Modernity* (Illinois: Northwestern University Press, 2006), p. 78.
428 Musil, *PS*, p. 170
429 McBride, *The Void*, p. 87
430 Karl Mannheim, *Ideology and Utopia: An Introduction to the Sociology of Knowledge* (London: Routledge and Kegan Paul, 1966).
431 Musil never saw himself as an Austrian. About *The Man without Qualities* he said: 'I dedicated this novel to German youth. Now to the youth of today….but to the youth which will come in time and will have to begin precisely where we stopped before the war'. Quoted in Luft, *Crisis*, p. 160.

Having witnessed the war, authors like Joseph Roth (1894-1939) and Stefan Zweig (1881-1942),[432] were extremely pessimistic and even nostalgic.[433] While Roth's nostalgia (from the Greek, meaning 'return home' and 'pain') is present in all his works, he is also aware of the fact that 'the past he longs to return to has irrevocably vanished, and that those vestiges of it that still remain are about to be swept away by the new, anti-Semitic, fanatically German dictatorship.'[434] The past that he constructs in his novel *Radetzkymarsch*,[435] in fact, 'never existed except in the minds of those who seek escape from the condition of modernity.'[436] This kind of nostalgia, or a constant longing for a past that never existed, for Musil was a result of the gap between an idealized notion of the good life and the fact that people failed to realise it.

If as one possible response to the crisis of modernity there is nostalgia[437] at the other end of the spectrum there is escapism to the (or a) future. In some ways the Parallel Campaign, one of the recurring themes in *The Man without Qualities*, fuses nostalgia and future-oriented escapism.[438] Regarding the fact that the novel is set in Vienna in 1913, there are no nostalgic figures in the novel in Roth's sense. All the characters that gather around the Parallel Campaign are the representatives of those who believe in a better future, albeit a future which will never exist. How does the Parallel Campaign provide such an escapism? Simply through the fact that it provides a sense of illusory purpose.

---

432 Zweig committed suicide with his wife in 1942 after he finished his autobiographical novel *The World of Yesterday*.
433 For further discussion about nostalgia and Roth see Malcolm Spencer, *In the Shadow of Empire: Austrian Experiences of Modernity in the writings of Musil, Roth and Bachmann*.
434 Spencer, *Musil, Roth and Bachmann*, p. 7
435 *Radetzkymarsch* is a story about the decline and eventually fall of the Austro-Hungarian Empire through the stories of three generations of Trotta family. See Joseph Roth, *The Radetzky March* (London: Allen Lane, 1974).
436 Spencer, *Musil, Roth and Bachmann*, p. 7
437 Bryan Turner regards nostalgia as crucial product of modernization. See Bryan S. Turner, 'Periodization and Politics in the Postmodern' in *Theories of Modernity and Postmodernity*, ed. Bryan S. Turner (London; Newbury Park; New Delhi: Sage, 1990), p. 7.
438 Jeffrey Herf argues that Nazi ideology fused an orientation to the past with an orientation to the future as well, but in a far more explosive way, namely, by combining a belief in ultra modern technology with variousstrands of pre-modern religiosity. See Jeffrey Herf, *Reactionary Modernism* (Cambridge: Cambridge University Press, 1984).

The symbolic recurring event of the Parallel Campaign is partly a response to the German celebrations of the one hundredth anniversary of the defeat of Napoleon at Leipzig.[439] A project has been announced to celebrate the jubilee of the Austrian Emperor. The problem is that the Habsburg Empire is exhausted. Musil describes in an ironic way how the characters in the novel gather around the Parallel Campaign, trying to generate a central willpower for a country that does not have one, trying to generate a purpose and a leading idea in order to provide social cohesion. Ulrich is able to see the absurdity and social decadence that it represents.[440]

Ulrich learns about the Parallel Campaign from a letter he receives from his patriotic father, who explains that the Austrian Year will be the year of a great peace jubilee. The starting point of the Parallel Campaign, which is administered by Count Leinsdorf and the Head of the Department Tuzzi's beautiful wife Diotima, who is a cousin of Ulrich's, is that 'something must be done.' However, nobody knows what is to be done. According to the Count, this action will not only demonstrate Austria's peaceful approach to the world, but at the same time, it will prove the trust of the people in the Austrian-Hungarian Monarchy. Besides, Diotima claims that the true Austria was the whole world and 'the world would find no peace until its nations learned to live together on a higher plane, like the Austrians

---

439 The Battle of Leipzig (16-19 October 1813) was fought by the coalition armies of Russia, Prussia, Austria and Sweden against the French army of Napoleon. Napoleon was defeated and had to retreat into France.

440 Anna Wołkowicz claims that Parallel Campaign is based on The Forte Circle which existed from 1910-1915. It was begun by European intellectuals. Seeing the danger of coming war their aim was to build a supranational organisation. Among the members were Martin Buber, Walter Rathenau, Gustav Landauer, and Erich Gutkind (a German-Jewish philosopher of religion and science). The Easter meeting in 1914 in Potsdam lasted three days. It was attended by many intellectuals, mostly German: Frederik Van Eden, Henri Borel, Martin Buber, Gustav Landauer, Erich Gutkind, Florens Christian Rang, Poul Bjerre (Swedish psychoanalyst and writer) and Theodor Gustav Norlind (Swedish writer). Ironically enough the circle dissolved in 1915 as a result of some members' supporting the war and writing propaganda on behalf of their respective countries; the Parallel Campaign would dissolve with the shattering effect of reality. Wołkowicz, Anna. *Mystiker der Revolution: der utopische Diskurs um die Jahrhundertwende: Gustav Landauer, Frederik van Eeden, Erich Gutkind, Florens Christian Rang,Georg Lukács, Ernst Bloch.* Warszawa: Wydawnictwo Uniwersytetu Waszawskiego, 2007, pp. 53-63. See also Lou Marin, 'Can we save true dialogue in an Age of Mistrust? The encounter of Dag Hammarskjöld and Martin Buber,' *Critical Currents*, 8 (January 2010), pp. 45-47.

in their Fatherland.'[441] Contrary to the thesis that 'the will to peace of Austria shall be proven', the German nationalists regard this action as anti-German, and the Slav nationalists consider it as anti-Slavic. What is at stake here is the objective of identifying the purpose of being a whole multiethnic state, just as the idea of wholeness accompanies dominant ideas about selfhood. That search for wholeness was hopeless, since as Musil puts it, 'there is no longer a whole person confronting a whole world, but a human something floating in the universal stream of culture.' Almost all the characters in *The Man without Qualities* are seeking a kind of unity or wholeness through an illusionary ideology, or by committing themselves to some big ideas or ideals or purpose.

The exception is Ulrich, the man without qualities, who is quite aware of the fact that only through such an existence, an existence that requires the lack of any telos or transcendent values, can he be a 'man of possibilities' rather than a dreamer. This implies an optimistic understanding of reality, where reality, that is, present reality, is seen as a space of possibility, or rather a time of possibility, a larval period that is waiting to be shaped by a creative individual. This sort of ethical thinking finds its reflection in Ulrich's idea of essayism (of which more in the following chapter) which fulfils the idea of an ethics that does not rely on essential and transcendent meanings. Essayism, defined as the examining an event from diverging perspectives without attempting to reduce them to a common set of co-ordinates, epitomizes not only the characteristics of the antagonist Ulrich, namely being a man of possibilities, but also the open-ended movement of aesthetic imagination in the novel. Thus, even the novel's not being completed is compatible with Ulrich's project. In his *Legislators and Interpreters: On Modernity, Postmodernity and Intellectuals*, Bauman presents modernity as 'an essentially unfinished' but also unfinishable project, its open-endedness being seen 'as the paramount, perhaps defining, attribute.'[442]

Musil sees the experience of modernity, namely the feeling of homelessness, groundlessness, or lack of any centre, as an opportunity for a new way of existence. Of course, he describes essayism as a 'utopian' idea but by this he does not mean the sort of collective utopia that has been a feature of modern political thought for several centuries. Musil attempts to deconstruct this use of utopia by seeing it as something 'not realised yet' or as 'unrealised possibility' rather than as a 'Nowhereland' (from Greek '*ou*' (not) and '*topos*' (place)).

---

441 Musil, *MwQ* p. 185
442 Zygmunt Bauman, *Legislators and Interpreters: On Modernity, Postmodernity and Intellectuals* (Cambridge: Polity Press, 1987), pp. 115-116.

Ulrich is convinced that 'when one is placed in the dark, one should not begin to sing out of fear, like a child',[443] i.e. there is no escape from the self, in turn, from the present. Why not then consider the present as something that is full of possibilities and that would be conceived as a mould to be shaped? The chapter entitled 'If there is a sense of reality, there must also be a sense of possibility' is crucial here. Ulrich claims that whoever says that if there is a sense of reality, there must also be a sense of possibility does not say 'here this or that has happened, will happen, must happen; but he invents: Here this or that might, could, or ought to happen.'[444] If such a person is told that something is the way it is, he/she thinks that 'it could probably just as well be otherwise.' What does such an attitude bring us apart from uncertainties? This, in fact, is what Musil is after: only through the sense of possibility, or uncertainty, can we can 'invent':

> A possible experience or truth is not the same as an actual experience or truth minus its 'reality value' but has – according to its partisans – at least something quite divine about it, a fire, a soaring, a readiness to build and a conscious utopianism that does not shrink from reality but sees it as a project, something yet to be invented. After all the earth is not that old, was apparently never so ready as now to give birth to its full potential.

In the following paragraph he says:

> It is reality that awakens possibilities, and nothing would be more perverse to deny it. Even so, it will always be the same possibilities, in sum or on the average, that go on repeating themselves until a man comes along who does not value the actuality above the idea. It is he who first gives the new possibilities their meaning, their direction, and he awakens them....he, too, naturally has a sense of reality; but it is a sense of possible reality, and arrives at its goal much more slowly than most people's sense of their real possibilities.[445]

Musil sees mankind at the beginning of a project, in a time of passage, yet one that it does not yet understand, an idea which recalls Nietzsche's striking figure of the sovereign individual of *The Genealogy of Morality* who is the product of our modern era and who stands at the threshold of something he can only dimly perceive. As we have seen, Nietzsche describes him/her as: 'the ripest fruit on its tree, like only to itself, having freed itself from the morality of custom, an autonomous, supra-ethical individual.'[446]

---

443 Musil, *MwQ*, p. 232
444 Musil, *MwQ.*, p. 11
445 Musil, *MwQ.*, p. 11
446 Nietzsche, *GM* II:2, p. 40

I began this section with the discussion of Musil's notion of modernity, particularly the experience of modernity in Austria. Through Ulrich's chains of thought and his dialogues with the other characters in the novel, Musil shows us the hopeless quest for the wholeness of the individuals as well as for the unity of a society which lacks any sort of central power and even any national or racial identity. As opposed to these attempts, Musil invites us to consider the experience of the complexity of modernity as a new beginning and a new way of thinking associated with the affirmation of life. However, as we shall see, considering this 'new beginning' – both in Nietzsche[447] and Musil – in conventional linear terms or eschatologically and apocalyptically would be misguided.

Unlike many prewar and postwar intellectuals who 'nearly always sought' remedy 'regressively in turning away from the present', either by longing for a never existed past or by a belief in a social future, Musil finds it neither in the past or in the future – at least not in the future that is not related to the present. This recalls Foucault's account of Baudelaire in 'What is Enlightenment?'[448] According to Baudelaire, modernity is often characterized in terms of the discontinuity of time, in other words, a break with tradition, a feeling of novelty. It is the attitude 'that makes possible to grasp the 'heroic' aspect of the present moment' and 'it is the will to 'heroise' the present.' In the spirit of Nietzsche, Musil attempts to redeem the past for the sake of present, and he also attempts to create our own futures. Thus, he suggests a 'trying morality' which requires a new relationship with ourselves.

IV.vi. Conclusion

Ulrich adopts the formula 'it thinks' rather than Cartesian 'I think.' He insists that only through the rejection of such a fixed, illusionary subject, and of the idea of the identity of individual subject and collective essence can we see the positive meaning of the dissolution of the subject. The goal of Musil's art is the 'trying' or 'experimental morality' of the ethical person, the motivated human being who creates meaning out of himself. Ulrich thinks that only through such a change in

---

447 Some commentators conceive Nietzsche's overhuman in conventional linear terms as that which comes after humans, yet, this would be incompatible with the understanding of Eternal Return of the Same.
448 Michel Foucault, 'What is Enlightenment?', in *The Foucault Reader*, ed. Paul Rabinow (London: Penguin,1991), pp. 32-50.

attitude towards life and ourselves can we free ourselves from the rigid rules of conventional morality[449] which works as a control mechanism by judging the past constantly as self-justification or as regret. While rejecting conventional morality, Ulrich's ethics asks about the next step: 'Such a person would have to live without end and decision, yes, precisely without reality. And, nonetheless, it is so that it always depends only on the next step.'[450] Only a man without qualities could bear such a lack of a fixed and final form for morality and the world, and could transform the transition period into a new beginning, into a new relationship with the world, life and ourselves and others. However, this is not as easy as Musil the author suggests; one thing that makes it difficult is that it requires a new participation in the world.

Now, the application of such an attitude at the individual level would be to develop the ability and willingness to accept responsibility for everything we have done, since what we have done constitutes us. The 'self' is not something that must be discovered but created, and, correspondingly, we must be the creators of our future. This activity in Nietzsche's terms is the 'art of living'. Such a person must not be enchained in the past (nostalgia or conventional morality), nor should he escape to the future which may also mean procrastination. Or the most dangerous of all is Elias Canetti's eccentric and doomed scholar Kien in *Auto Da Fé* who epitomizes both escapisms: 'Let the present be the past and we shall not notice the bruises. The present is alone responsible for all pain. He longed for the future, because then there would be more past in the world.'[451]

All this requires a closer look at Musil's understanding of ethics, and a closer look at *The Man without Qualities*.

---

449 Here saying conventional morality I am referring to Christian morality or moralities based on compassion.
450 Musil, *MwQ* p. 170
451 Elias Canetti, *Auto da fé* (London: Picador, 1978), p. 145.

Chapter V: Musil on Ethics

V.i. Introduction

I said in the last chapter that Musil had declared himself more interested in ethics than in psychology (IV.ii). This may sound like a surprising statement in view of Musil's oft-noted psychological grasp. However, I will show that it is just this that makes Musil an ethical thinker – or writer – of the first rank. In the first section of this chapter (V.ii) I discuss the case of Moosbrugger the sex murderer, whose trial revolves around the question of accountability and raises issues about the constitution of the self, sanity and insanity, free will, and personal responsibility versus social determination. The main question in Moosbrugger's case is whether a compulsive serial killer should be held accountable for his crimes. Then, (V.iii) I investigate the relationship between ethics and essayism, both as a writing style and as a way of living. After giving a brief account of Ulrich's relationship with other women (V.iv), I focus on the relationship between Ulrich and his forgotten sister Agathe that is the heart of part three of the novel (V.v). The account of their relationship is an attempt to think about morality and the world via a treatment of love, and about how to undergo a different kind of participation in the world, beyond any cultural and ideological grounds.

V.ii. Subjectivity, Free Will, Responsibility

The case of the murderer Moosbrugger who brutally kills a prostitute in a park in Vienna is of interest to both rationalists – criminologists, psychiatrists, lawyers – and moralists, and Musil describes the faltering efforts of both of these groups to make sense of it. The moralist can see only a murder, the guilty subject (guilt and subjectivity were closely connected for Nietzsche) and the obvious punishment, the death penalty, which is in fact handed down; the psychiatrist argues from the standpoint of the natural sciences, claiming that human behaviour is determined, and thus issues like guilt and free will are not valid at all; the legal expert insists on holding on to the notion of intent, central to criminal law in the Austro-Hungarian empire; finally the chaplain focuses on the limits of human understanding in cases that only God can comprehend.

The incommensurability of these perspectives is illustrated by the fact that legal discourse cannot decide on sanity and insanity and must rely on the judgments of medical experts, while medical discourse sees the mind-body relationship in a scientific way without concerning itself with issues like free will or accountability. A conversation between a psychiatrist and a legal expert ends with the doctor proposing that only religion can offer universal standards. The undecidability of Moosbrugger's case reflects the impossibility of finding a superior standpoint or consensus.[452] Of course, at the trial, as at any trial, a decision has to be made; the incommensurability of standpoints cannot be the last word. The decision is not a matter of compromise or consensus, nor is it the product of the superior reasoning of one body of experts, but a reflection of a specific legal imperative. Musil's description of this, however, retains a sense of the incommensurability of points of view whose differences somehow have to be resolved, or rather denied:

> Law courts resemble wine cellars in which the wisdom of our forefathers lies in bottles. One opens them and could weep at how unpalatable the highest, the most effervescent, degree of the human striving for precision can be before it reaches perfection. And yet it seems to intoxicate the insufficiently seasoned mind. It is well known phenomenon that the angel of the medicine, if he has listened too long to lawyers' arguments, too often forgets his own mission. He then folds his wings with a clatter and conducts himself in court like a reserve angel of law.[453]

The sense that the experts are unable to arrive at a consensus over Moosbrugger, at a rational explanation for his conduct, is deepened by the fact that Moosbrugger himself gives an account of how he came to commit the murder to which he has confessed. Their failure does not surprise Ulrich, however, who learns about the case from the newspaper and becomes fascinated by it.

Moosbrugger was born as a poor devil, an orphaned shepherd boy in a hamlet, and a lonely shepherd during most of his life. He is described as someone whose abnormal upbringing had made him extremely shy towards women. This state later developed into an irrational fear which made him behave in a sadistic way towards prostitutes. Moosbrugger claims that he did not intend to kill the woman, and in addition to denying the accusations, he also rejects the dishonour of being labelled as a mentally retarded man. He drifted into it due to the doubtful behaviour of 'this woman's caricature' and he insists that instead of focusing on the murder as a concept, the conditions leading to this event should be considered. However, the judge tries to fit this event into the frame of previously witnessed

---

452 In fact, this tension between different experts is given in a more detailed way in an unpublished chapter of the novel. See Patrizia McBride, 'On the Utility of Art for Politics: Musil's "Armed Truce of Ideas"', *The German Quarterly*, Vol. 73, No. 4 (Autumn, 2000), p. 379.
453 Musil, *MwQ*, p. 263

murder cases and consequently asks the same questions asked previously many times. Moosbrugger's manner is that of a man openly challenging the system of law and proud of it. He does not deny what he has done; yet he regards his deeds as, and wants them to be understood as the mishaps of a philosophy of life. While in the judge's eyes he was the source of his actions, for Moosbrugger, 'they had perched on him like the birds that had flown in from somewhere or other.'[454] As he himself declares, he 'may have lacked only the education and opportunity to make something different out of this impulse, an angel of mass destruction or a great anarchist.'[455]

Ulrich believes that Moosbrugger is unique and fascinating because of his circumstances. It was they, not Moosbrugger's 'personality' or his 'subjectivity', that were unique. These circumstances might have been totally different and so he might have been a totally different person. Here Musil is not an advocate of determinism; claiming that 'the causes must lie in the circumstances'.[456] Instead, he saying something to Nietzsche's discussion of fate and free will. Recall that Nietzsche claims that fate is nothing but a chain of events, and that to set man and fate over against one another is an error; we create our own events each time we act. What Nietzsche means is that the agent can develop an internal power to increase its capacity to receive and interpret external events. Musil believes that circumstances are the conditions of subjectivity, but at the same time only conditions. In this connection he says that 'immoralists' such as Luther and Eckhart who were radical, and even revolutionary, in their understanding of Christianity, would not have been influenced by any taken-for-granted values, would have judged the case in a more profound manner, understood Moosbrugger, and set him free.

This takes us to the discussion of free will and subjectivity. The law often invokes the notion of free will to justify holding individuals responsible for their actions. In other words, responsibility is grounded in the agent's capacity to choose her actions freely. In her *Freedom within Reason*, Susan Wolf suggests that to be a responsible agent a person needs to satisfy three conditions. First she or he must have control over her behaviour; second he must be capable of being informed and governed by relevant considerations; and third, her 'control must be ultimate – her will must be determined by her self, and her self must not, in turn be determined

---

454 Musil, *MwQ* p. 75
455 Musil, *MwQ*, p. 71
456 Musil, *PS* p. 120

by anything external to it' which Wolf calls the 'condition of autonomy.'[457] As we have seen, in the Moosbrugger case the psychiatrists say that he cannot be held responsible, resting their idea on the assumption of a common set of permanent characteristics that excuses the person – failure to learn from experience, failure to follow a life plan – while the lawyers, representatives of justice, see Moosbrugger as just another murderer who must be responsible for his acts. Yet both claims suggest a continuous self whose deeds would be in harmony with the previous actions. In the free will paradigm the word 'continuous' refers to temporality, that is to say past, present and future actions must be in accordance with each other.

Musil's discussion of circumstances, on the other hand, questions the existence of fixed human characteristics from which normative consequences follow and the idea of a self-identical subject endowed with free will. Paradoxically, however, if there is one person in the novel who is in harmony with himself it is Moosbrugger. All the other characters in the novel, by contrast, including Ulrich, fail to find a balance between the inner and the outer – between the inner self and outer world, or reason and feeling, or id, ego and superego – and are teetering on the edge of crisis or sometimes even madness. This is why Ulrich cannot stop himself thinking: 'If mankind could dream as a whole, that dream would be Moosbrugger.'[458]

It goes without saying that this is not a comforting conclusion. And it raises the question of how to avoid mental crisis or madness without having to seek the sort of harmony that Moosbrugger exemplifies. This requires, first of all, a change in our understanding of the self. And Ulrich seems to suggest an alternative account of responsibility that views the self as constantly engaged in the process of defining the boundaries of its spatial, temporal, and social identity.

This notion of the self may once again be understandable against a Nietzschean background. When Nietzsche says 'there is no being behind the deed' he means the subject is a mere fiction or an addition; it becomes merely a product of the conceptual structure of philological, psychological, ontological and epistemological frameworks. In a note from 1905, Musil joins Nietzsche (and Ernst Mach) in his preference for the formulation 'it thinks' rather than the conventional Cartesian 'I think':

> The thought is not something that observes an inner event, but, rather, it is this inner event itself.

---

457 Susan Wolf, *Freedom within Reason* (New York; Oxford: Oxford University Press, 1990), p. 10.
458 Musil, *MwQ* p. 77

We do not reflect on something, but, rather, something thinks itself in us. The thought does not consist in the fact that we see something clearly, which has evolved itself in us, but, rather, that an inner development emerges into this bright region.[459]

Thus, in the spirit of Nietzsche, Musil argues that the need to believe in the existence of a subject expresses nothing more than a desire for the self-preservation of the human being and for the preservation of the existing order. He says: 'that which is incommunicable and, the encapsulation in the self, is what makes people need good and evil. Good and evil, duty and violation of duty, are forms in which the individual establishes an emotional balance between himself and the world.'[460]

> Even a sex-murderer is, in some cranny of his soul, full of inner hurt and hidden appeals; somehow the world is wronging him like a child, and he does not have the capacity to express this in any other way than the way he has found the works for him. In the criminal there is both a vulnerability and a resistance against the world, and both are present in every person who has a powerful moral destiny. Before we destroy such a person – however despicable he may be- we ought to accept and preserve what was resistance in him and was degraded by his vulnerability. And no one does morality more harm than those saints and scamps who, in tepid horror over the form of a phenomenon, refuse to touch it.[461]

Musil agrees with Nietzsche that the projection of the distinction between subject and predicate onto the world is a product of the Cartesian belief that the 'will' is something that produces effects, that all deeds are caused by a doer.[462]

The Moosbrugger case is the most explicit illustration of this understanding in *The Man without Qualities*. Here, in his constant references to the trial, instead of referring to the will of the subject, Musil emphasizes the complex interweaving of the factors that would create the particular circumstances that might have led to the crime. However, the important point is that this reference to circumstances is the opposite of determinism; on the contrary, Musil's discussion of the influence of circumstance is closely connected to the ideal of living essayistically. Later we will see that it is precisely through an embrace of circumstance rather than a denial of them that the individual may learn a new ethics rather than the acceptance of his social being.

As we have seen, an important influence on Musil here was Ernst Mach who argues that 'natural events are more complex than the notion of cause implies; that

---

459 Quoted in Luft, *The Crisis*, p. 60
460 Musil, *PS* p. 39
461 Musil, *PS* p. 39
462 Nietzsche, *Twilight*, 'Reason in Philosophy', 5.

individual events cannot be isolated from their complex network of relations; and that the temporal reversibility of laws makes nonsense of traditional formulations of causality.'[463] Thus he insists that we have to give up the traditional cause-effect formula in favour of functional relations 'that were simply abbreviations of observations and procedures.'[464] This scientifically refined concept of function had an impact on Musil's art and thought, and he adopted the notion of function developed within modern physics as a crucial key point for his ethical thinking. He transferred the theory of functions to the realm of ethics: 'Good appears not as a constant, but as a variable function.' With respect to this he says: 'people are not capable of changing laws; but they certainly can change situations in this sense, no matter how many immanent laws may have contributed to them.'[465] It should be noted here that Musil depicts an era which lost its faith in both reason and morality, but that the distinctiveness of Ulrich is that he is neither anti-rationalist nor amoral, but ambivalent.

In fact, Musil distinguishes between the moralist and the ethicist:

> The moralist adopts an existing corpus and arranges them in logical order. He does not add value to these values, rather he adds to them a system. Basic precepts, principles...are relationships, positions within the system.[466]

Ethik, on the other hand, belongs in a completely different order of experience:

> Typically different – namely different in terms of their type – are the ethicists. Names: Confucius, Lao-tse, Christ and Christianity, Nietzsche, the mystics, the essayists. [...] Their contribution to ethics is concerned not with the form but the material.
>
>   They have new ethical experiences.
>
>   They are other people.[467]

Now, recall the idea that the quality of repetitiveness which is the condition of the possibility of scientific research adheres to morality as well: 'if our acts were unrepeatable, then there would be nothing to be expected of us, and a morality that could not tell people what was expected of them would be no fun at all.'[468] In the realm of Ethics, on the other hand, there is no such thing as repetition. It is beyond any sort of conceptualisation.

---

463   Luft, *Crisis*, p. 84
464   Luft, *Crisis*, p. 84.
465   Musil, *PS,* p. 170
466   Musil, *Diaries* (New York: Basic Books, 1998), p. 312.
467   Musil, *Diaries*, p. 312
468   Musil, *MwQ*, p. 553

So far I have discussed Ulrich's attitude towards the judgments of both rationalists – criminologists, psychiatrists, lawyers – and moralists of Moosbrugger, and Musil describes the weak efforts of both of these groups to make sense of it. Ulric is skeptical about both attitudes, and he seems to have little faith in human progress. And indeed, Ulrich says: 'every step forward is also a step backward. Progress always exists in only one particular sense. And since there is no sense in our life as a whole, neither is there a thing as progress as a whole.'[469]

At the same time, this is an important passage. Although Ulrich does not believe in progress 'as a whole', he does believe that there is technical progress. In a chapter called 'The Ideal of the Three Treatises, or the Utopia of Exact Living', he writes that 'all the knowledge that has led our species from wearing animal skins to people flying, complete with proofs, would fill a handful of reference books, but a bookcase the size of the earth would not suffice to hold all the rest....'[470] 'All the rest' includes the history of moral and political philosophy, religious doctrines and so on, where there is no progress. This leads Ulrich to consider another idea: 'The thought suggests itself that we carry on our human business in a most irrational manner when we do not use those methods by which the exact sciences have forged ahead in such exemplary fashion.' This does not mean that moral questions would become technical questions, but that 'it would be a useful experiment to try to cut down to a minimum the moral expenditure (of whatever kind) that accompanies all our actions, to satisfy our selves with being moral only in those exceptional cases where it really counts, but otherwise not to think differently from the way we do about standardizing pencils or screws.'[471] This attitude would be a more protected one against the 'absolutism of reality', it would even be regarded as a defence mechanism. However, I will show later that this experimental attitude is not the only one possible, and that Ulrich's attitude takes him beyond this attempt to establish a division of labour between rationality and morality. We can understand this if we focus on a very important chapter that follows the chapter on exact living. Here Musil discusses the idea of essayism.

V.iii. Essayism

In the last chapter we referred to Arnheim, the man who appears to move effortlessly between the pursuit of profit and the writing of influential books, between,

---

469 Musil, *MwQ*, p. 528
470 Musil, *MwQ*, p. 265
471 Musil, *MwQ*, p. 265

as Ulrich puts it, capital and the intellect, industry and art. As we have seen Arnheim was modelled on Walther Rathenau, who Musil had met immediately before World War I. Elias Canetti reports that 'when Rathenau met Musil, the former put his arm over the latter's shoulder in a gesture that was perhaps intended to be friendly but also patronising.'[472]

Where all the other characters are Austrian, Arnheim is German, and in some ways a representative of Europe as a whole. Unlike Ulrich, Arnheim is the man with all qualities, and has something to say about everything: philosophy, art, economics, and the world. He is the man of action and he has accepted Goethe's 'Denken um zu tun, Tun um zu denken!'[473] as his motto, and his life seems a realization of this aphorism.[474] Arnheim seems able to unite and synthesize all contrasts, and is the perfect expression of intellectual unity for the participants of the Parallel Campaign. He can combine economics and soul, or ideas and power. In an era where the old economic and political methods and rationality are doubted, this approach of Arnheim creates an effect as if the expected messiah has arrived.

> His activity spread over terrestrial continents and continents of knowledge. He knew everything: philosophers, economics, music, the world, sports. He expressed himself fluently in five languages. The world's most famous artists were his friends, and he bought the art of tomorrow when it was still green on the vine, at prices that were not yet inflated. He was received as the Imperial Court and knew how to talk with workers. He owned a villa in the latest style, which appeared in photographs in all the publications on contemporary architecture, and also, somewhere in the sandiest wastes of Prussia, a ramshackle old castle that actually looked like the decomposed cradle of Prussian chauvinism.[475]

In other words, 'what all others are separately, Arnheim is rolled into one.'[476]

But Arnheim can only be such a figure by reducing the world's complexity through neatly outlined dichotomies such as feeling and mind, rational and irrational, socialism and capitalism, and then appearing to transcend them:

> ...despite all the modernity the world is here being carved up once again into heaven and hell, whereas it is *between* both, made of some kind of mixture; and it is precisely

---

472 Philip Payne, 'Introduction: The Symbiosis of Robert Musil's Life and Works' in *Companion*, p. 38.
473 Believe to act, act to believe. Trans. by the author.
474 Wilhelm Braun, 'The temptation of Ulrich: the problem of true and false unity in Musil's *Der Mann ohne Eigenschaften*', *The German Quarterly* 29, No. 1 (January 1956), pp. 29-37.
475 Musil, *MwQ* p. 204
476 Musil, *MwQ*, p. 201

such a mixture (which still needs much more study) of good and evil, sick and healthy, egoistic and self-sacrificing, that the questions of the earth blossom forth.[477]

Arnheim's gift lies in his alleged and illusionary success in synthesizing the dichotomies as well as living in total harmony with himself:

> The basic pattern of his success was everywhere the same: Surrounded by the magic aura of his wealth and the legend of his importance, he always had to deal with people who towered over him in their own fields but who liked him as an outsider with a surprising knowledge of their subject and were daunted by his personally representing a field between their world and other worlds of which they had no idea. So it had come to seem quire natural for him to appear in a world of specialists as whole man, and to have the effect of a harmonious entity.[478]

However, the problem is that this fiction of wholeness and self-mastery collapses when he develops strong feelings towards Ulrich's cousin beautiful Diotima, who administers the Parallel Campaign with Count Leinsdorf. He is divided between his ordinary experiences and this other realm of experience – love and the Other – which is more authentic and deep and which requires honesty and an openness to the other as well as to oneself.

Against this, however, Musil wants to say that this dividedness or the dissolution does not pose a problem, that the real problem resides in a denial of the compartmentalization of the self by fictional and insincere means. This idea of an illusory fixed point in which the world and of the self only apparently coincide is encountered throughout the novel:

> Such fixed points, where the centre of a person's equilibrium coincides with the world's centre of equilibrium, may be, for instance, a spittoon that can be shut with a simple latch;…not to mention a metaphysical theory of the motions of celestial bodies…[479]

Ulrich rejects the Cartesian subject in principle, and supports instead the notion of the infinite possibilities of existence, which demands the recognition of a new understanding of morality, what Nietzsche called 'a trying morality'. Rejecting the morality of his era, he seeks ways of creating his own values; a man without qualities, he puts forward the idea of living 'hypothetically.' Such a person 'suspects that the given order of things is not as solid as it pretends to be; no thing, no self, no form, no principle is safe, everything is undergoing an invisible but ceaseless

---

477 Musil, *PS*, p. 55
478 Musil, *MwQ*, p. 207
479 Musil, *MwQ*, p. 147

transformation, the unsettled holds more of the future than the settled, and the present is nothing but a hypothesis that has not yet been surmounted.'[480] Ulrich refuses to become a professor, he refuses to take sides or indeed 'be' anything. Such a person wishes to free himself/herself from the world in which the rules are ready-made. Ulrich appreciates an experimental life which enables one to be open to new experiences. As Ulrich's friend tells his wife Clarisse:

> 'He is a man without qualities.'
> 'What is that?' Clarisse asked, with a little laugh.
> 'Nothing. That is the point- it is nothing!...You cannot guess at any profession from what he looks like, and yet he does not look like a man who has no profession, either.......Nothing is stable for him. Everything is fluctuating, a part of a whole, among innumerable wholes that are presumably part of a super-whole, which, however, he does not know the slightest thing about. So every one of his answers is a part-answer, every one of his feelings only a point of view, and whatever a thing is, it does not matter to him what it is, it is only some accompanying 'way in which it is', some addition or other, that matters to him.'[481]

Later on, Ulrich replaces his expression 'living hypothetically' with 'essayism'. 'Essayism' usually refers to a style of writing; but Musil asks whether it might also be a way of living. This is indicated by the title of the chapter, which includes the phrase: 'the Utopian idea of essayism.' He believes that he can live a better life if that life takes the form of an essay, a series of approaches to a topic that lacks a unified, encompassing perspective, and so avoids the stasis of conceptuality. Musil's definition of the essay also says something about his strategy as a novelist.

> The translation of the word 'essay' as 'attempt', which is the generally accepted one, only approximately gives the most important allusion to the literary model. For an essay is not the provisional or incidental expression of a conviction that might on a more favourable occasion be elevated to the status of truth or that might just as easily be recognized as error...an essay is the unique and unalterable form that a man's inner life takes in a decisive thought. Nothing is more alien to it than that irresponsibility and semi-finishedness of mental images known as subjectivity; but neither are 'true' and 'false', 'wise' and unwise', terms that can be applied to such thoughts... and yet the essay is subject to laws that are no less strict for appearing to be delicate and ineffable. There have been more than a few of such essayists, masters of the inner hovering life, but there would be no point in naming them. Their domain lies between religion and knowledge, between example and doctrine, between *amor intellectualis*

---

480   Gianni Vattimo, *Dialogue with Nietzsche*, trans. William McCuaig (New York: Columbia University Press, 2006), p. 269.
481   Musil, *MwQ*, pp. 62-63

and poetry; they are saints with and without religion, and sometimes they are also simply men on an adventure who have gone astray.[482]

In the following paragraph Musil writes that the mountain of commentary on the work of such essayists tends not to produce anything worthwhile, and so I will mention only the important claim that 'essay' means 'attempt'. There is an important connection here with Nietzsche's 'trying morality'.

In fact, behind Ulrich's search, there is his attempt to bring back the appropriate relationship between precision and soul, intellect and passion as well as between good and evil. Already in his first novel *Young Törless* Musil emphasised this theme along with the idea of the 'dissolution of the subject'. His subject matter is the adolescent child, adolescence being a critical period in the development of the individual. Törless is neither a child, nor an adult. In this liminal realm the individual who is not yet an individual must confront the split between an ordinary experience and the moments of mystical illumination which cannot be translated into the language of ordinary life.

Ulrich too is in between stages of a life but unlike Törless seems to have no rites of passage to see him through to the next one. Hence his 'exploratory' attitude seems to be more one of uncertainty, but according to Ulrich it is more like the absence of established certainties. In that sense, he does not trust moral values since he believes that the value of a quality depends on its surrounding circumstances – the theory of function rather than cause-effect paradigm – and 'the significance of all moral events seemed to him to be the function of other events on which they depended.'[483]

> An open-ended system of relationships arises, in which independent meanings, such as are ascribed to actions and qualities by way of a rough first approximation in ordinary life, no longer exist at all. What is seemingly solid in this system becomes a porous pretext for many possible meanings; the event occurring becomes a symbol of something that perhaps may not be happening but makes itself felt through the symbol; and man as the quintessence of his possibilities, potential man, the unwritten poem of his existence, confronts man as recorded fact, as reality, as character.[484]

Ulrich does not believe that the pluralistic structure of the modern world, and also the pluralistic nature of the self, should be overcome. Quite to the contrary, he sees in it a new opportunity, a new 'trying morality', a yet unrecognized possibility. But not for progress: 'every step forward is also a step backward. Progress always

---

482 Musil, *MwQ*, p. 273
483 Musil, *MwQ*, p. 270
484 Musil, *MwQ*, p. 270

exists in only one particular sense. And since there is no sense in our life as a whole, neither is there a thing as progress as a whole.'[485]

Now, as we have seen, behind Ulrich's search for a life in the form of essayism, there is his attempt to bring back the appropriate relationship between precision and soul, mind and body, intellect and passion. Yet, how could this be possible? Musil believes that human existence unfolds within two distinct domains of experiences, within *ratioid* and *non-ratioid* as he calls them in order to avoid taken-for-granted categorizations of western thought. Scientific precision which attempts to relate the ideas to each other within a cause-effect structure and aims to reach generalizations and natural laws belongs to the realm of *ratioid*. This *ratioid* territory 'is characterized by a certain monotony of facts, by predominance of repetition, by a relative independence of facts from one another, so that they can usually be joined to previously formed groups of laws....'[486] However, the events, things and people which are experienced in the realm of *non-ratioid* are unique and cannot be conceptualized and generalized.[487] If the focus on regularities in the realm of *ratioid* makes it possible to create the illusion of stable coordinates and to establish the 'rules with exceptions',[488] this illusion becomes impossible in the realm of the *non-ratioid*. The realm of the *non-ratioid* is to do with the values and judgments, ethics and aesthetic experience. Thus, the *non-ratioid* is defined by a 'dominance of the exceptions over the rules.'[489] However, it should be noted that Musil does not attempt to associate each domain with one particular faculty, in other words, he does not claim that the intellect dominates the *ratioid* while the feeling the *non-ratioid*. As McBride puts it:

> ...he emphasizes the nature of the phenomena that make up the two domains, and that demands specific modes of observation. Some phenomena are easily grasped by means of the criteria of rational cognition, ordering and anticipating experience through abstraction and systematization. For others those criteria of observation do not yield much. These latter phenomena form the nonratioid realm.[490]

---

485 Musil, *MwQ*, p. 528
486 Musil, *PS*, p. 62
487 This distinction was addressed by many philosophers during these period particularly by Neo-Kantians such as Wilhelm Windleband and Heinrich Rickert. See Klaus Christian Köhnke, *The Rise of Neo-Kantianism: German Academic Philosophy between Idealism and Positivism* (Cambridge: Cambridge University Press, 1991).
488 Musil, *PS*, p. 63
489 Musil, *PS*, p. 63
490 McBride, *The Void*, p. 65

This distinction reminds us of the distinction that Henri Bergson made between two different ways of knowing a thing: the way of analysis and the way of intuition. By intuition, Bergson means the kind of intellectual sympathy 'by which one is transported into the interior of an object in order to coincide with what there is unique and consequently inexpressible in it.'[491] Analysis, on the contrary, 'is the operation which reduces the object to elements already known, that is, common to that object and to others.'[492] In other words, analysis is a way to understand something by comparing it with other things, and by putting something under universal concepts. The function of positive science is analysis, it works with symbols. Positive science makes comparisons between forms, reducing the more complex to the simple. Thanks to science intelligence gives us life's material operations; however, this is only perspectivism, it is relative knowledge, thus, it never gives us the thing as it is, it is always going 'all around life, taking from outside the greatest possible number of views of it, drawing it into itself instead of entering it.'[493] By contrast intuition leads us 'to the very inwardness of life',[494] as well as to the 'deeper' self, however, this requires a particular form of ethics, an idea that Musil shares, as we shall see.

Musil claims that ethical experience has also been regarded as something about which we can conform to a system of guidelines and universal laws through the dichotomies like just/unjust, good/evil etc. So far the major ethical or moral thinkers, even in their attempt to establish a universal system or thought, always became the advocates of one particular religion or principle: Hegel's ideal state which would create the necessary conditions for individual freedom was the Protestant Prussian state; Kant was influenced by Pietism;[495] Musil's contemporary Bergson (1859-1941) construes a particular religion, Christianity, as superior.[496] Musil does not draw our attention to a particular religion and claims that it is hard

---

491 Henri Bergson, *The Creative Mind: An Introduction to Metaphysics* (New York: Citadel, 1946), p. 161.
492 Bergson, *The Creative Mind*, pp. 161-162
493 Henri Bergson, *Creative Evolution*, trans. Arthur Mitchell (Lanham: University Press of America, 1983), p. 176.
494 Bergson, *Creative Evolution*, p. 176
495 In *Protestant Ethic* Weber notes that Kant was strongly influenced by Pietism and that 'many of his ideas are strongly connected to ideas of ascetic Protestantism.' Harvey Goldman, *Max Weber and Thomas Mann: Calling and the Shaping of the Self* (Berkeley; Los Angeles; London: University of California Press, 1988), p. 121.
496 Henri Bergson, *The Two Sources of Morality and Religion* (Indiana: University of Notre Dame Press, 2006), pp. 209-266.

to evaluate manslaughter, killing an adulterer, duels, and executions, through the basic commandment 'thou shall not kill', and if, he says, one attempts to find the unifying rational formula for all this, 'one will find that it resembles a sieve, in using which the holes are no less important than the solid mesh.'[497]

What makes Musil something of a rarity is his attempt to apply scientific thinking to realms outside it, such as ethics. How would this be possible? As McBride puts it:

> Exact thinking enables the observer to recognize that science and knowledge are embedded in the domain of a relative certainty, whereas questions of value, of meaning, of interpretation of experience fall into the domain of the unique and incommensurable and thus do not allow for certainty and unequivocal results. It follows that applying the rigor and precision of scientific thinking to the realm of ethics entails precisely the opposite of seeking to establish regularities and rules for moral conduct. It involves acknowledging the singular and utterly contingent character of ethical events, as well as attempting to account for them without effacing their singularity.[498]

This means, 'every ethical event, if it is a real experience, has 'sides'. On one side it is good, on the other it is evil, on a third something that cannot quite be established as being either good or evil.'[499] According to this, 'Good appears not as a constant, but as a variable function.....Morality is as unlikely to collapse because of this as mathematics is to die from the same number being the square of two different numbers.'[500] Essayism allows Ulrich to 'examine once again all inner possibilities, to invent them anew, and at last to carry over the virtues of an unprejudiced laboratory technique from natural science to morality.'[501]

Literature seems to be the most suitable means for the investigation of the particular events that make up ethical experience. Or rather, we should say that Musil was an essayist-novelist or philosophical essayist whose object remains the personal case. It is the form of essayism that enables the writer 'to cultivate a type of thinking whose "sentimental" quality points to a particular interplay between intellect and feeling.'[502] For Musil the essay 'is the strictest form attainable in an area where one can*not* work precisely.'[503] The question why Moosbrugger behaved in the way he did or whether Törless was right or wrong in his indifference to the

---

497 Musil, *PS*, p. 63
498 McBride, *The Void*, p. 69
499 Musil, *PS*, p. 114
500 Musil, *PS*, p. 114
501 Quoted in Luft, *Crisis*, p. 101
502 McBride, *The Void*, p. 72
503 Musil, *PS*, p. 48

torture and the rape of his friend can be discussed only in a genuine essay.[504] The essay lies between two areas: 'it takes its form and method from science, its matter from art':

> The essay seeks to establish an order. It presents not characters but a connection of thoughts, that is, a logical connection, and it proceeds from facts, like the natural sciences, to which essay imparts an order. Except that these facts are not generally observable, and also their connections are in many cases only a singularity. There is no total solution, but only a series of particular ones. But the essay does present evidence, and investigates.[505]

Thus, through the essayistic form, literature's task should be the investigation of experience which respects particular reasons underlying the motives of individuals. Then, the task of the writer is 'to discover ever new solutions, connections, constellations, variables, to set up prototypes of an order of events, appealing models of how one can be human, to *invent* the inner person.'[506]

The word 'to invent' is crucial since it is connected with Ulrich's understanding of Nietzschean ethics, namely an 'ethics of becoming'. What is crucial about the relationship between life in the form essayism and the philosophy of becoming is that whatever goal is involved, it must be immanent to the process of becoming, not something that defines becoming externally. As Nietzsche says in *Ecce Homo*: 'man is overcome at every moment.'[507] Nietzsche summed up this approach to life with the phrase 'so it happened, thus I willed it', meaning that one should accept responsibility for everything that happens to one since what we have done constitutes us.

Literature's – essayism's – ethical function, then, lies precisely in its being 'a complex medium of meaning-production through which humans are given to test thorny moral issues and experiment with new solutions.'[508] Here, however, we may suggest that Musil follows Kant more than Nietzsche in his notion of aesthetic experience as a special interplay between the intellect and the faculty of sensibility. Indeed, he makes his dept to Kant clear in an essay from 1925 entitled 'Toward a New Aesthetic: Observations on a Dramaturgy of Film.'[509] Here the

---

504 Musil, *PS*, p. 49
505 Musil, *PS*, p. 49
506 Musil, *PS*, p. 64
507 Friedrich Nietzsche, *Ecce Homo*, trans. R. J. Hollingdale (Harmonsworth, Middlesex: Penguin, 1979), p. 107.
508 McBride, *The Void*, p. 101
509 Musil, *PS*, pp. 193-208

idea of essayism as a mediation between two realms is interpreted as the momentary touching of incommensurable states of mind – *ratioid* and *non-ratioid* – in the individual. This idea recalls Kant's image of art as a bridge connecting two incommensurable realms in the *Critique of Judgment*.[510] Through the basic characteristics of being the man without qualities compatible with his writing form, Musil attempts to transform aesthetical illuminations into life: 'the decisive factor is the ethical condition into which they transform us and how long they affect afterwards....since my youth I looked upon the aesthetic as the ethical.'[511] In that sense, literature for Musil is not detached from life 'but rather a human activity whose function and social impact appear different in every age and culture.'[512] This idea, as McBride puts it, 'prompted Musil to advance his own alternative model of literature as a "moral laboratory" in which new analysis and partial overviews are tested on singular moral cases.'[513] Art's function, then, lies in its ability to make us gain new perspectives on the world as a result of its capacity to disrupt ordinary experience. Art is 'a "disturbance" in which the elements of reality are reconstituted as an unreal whole that usurps the value of reality.'[514] In other words, unlike the advocates of Expressionism – or the critics of reason – according to whom there is a dichotomy between soul and reason, Musil claims that there is a constant interplay between these two realms – *ratioid* and *nonratioid* – or that they are even allies, however Musil describes this interaction by introducing a crucial temporal dimension, implying that what we call the experience of reality is not something in which reality is assimilated all at once:

> There are beautiful poems that few people understand at first glance; on the contrary, at first one understands nothing at all aside from details; only later does the sense 'begin to dawn'...at the moment of comprehension there is a mixing together, perceived sensuous form, and emotional excitement; afterward the experience is in part conceptually assimilated and fixed, and in part leaves behind a vague, usually unconscious deposit, which in some later situation in life can suddenly revive.[515]

In the previous chapter I said that Törless' search for a unity between the outer and the inner can be read as a longing for a metaphysical ground, in a Kantian or Schopenhauerian way, for 'in-itself-ness' of things, something existing outside

---

510 On this see McBride, *The Void*, pp. 97-128
511 Quoted in Luft, *Crisis*, p. 46
512 Quoted in McBride, *The Void*, p. 100
513 McBride, *The Void*, p. 100
514 Musil, *PS*, p. 196
515 Musil, *PS*, p. 204

of time and space, i.e. for a transcendental self. However, one important point on which Musil is sceptical about Kant is the idea that we cannot have absolute knowledge about certain things, including the self. Perhaps in that Musil is closer to Bergson than to Kant. In *Time and Free Will* Bergson suggests that we can actually have access to the things themselves, including the self, or the fundamental or deeper self, as Bergson calls it.

Bergson starts his description of the self with a theory of time, claiming that an original temporality is suppressed by a more vulgar conception of time, which belongs to clocks and calendars, and 'can be compared to spatiality, since every duration is interpreted through the model of geometric extension that things in the world possess.'[516] As opposed to this we have immanent time (time as lived from within); it is this time which is the interiority of self. Time, for Bergson, is 'a kind of *Gestalt* that produces the emergence of a self-transcendence out of an inner organization or pre-reflective duration'[517] (recall Musil's critique of Mach). Time here is duration: duration of mental acts, experiences as well as thoughts and sensations. Pure duration, Bergson says, 'is the form which the succession of our conscious states assumes when our ego lets itself live, when it refrains from separating its present states from its former states.'[518] Bergson defines pure duration as 'a mutual penetration, an interconnexion and organisations of elements, each one of which represents the whole, and cannot be distinguished or isolated from it except by abstract thought.'[519] That is to say, the states of consciousness are not objectified or separated from each other by space. This account of duration, he adds, would be given by a being who was ever the same and ever changing.'[520]

Bergson's time is 'pure consciousness'. Or duration is consciousness which is an organic totality or unity which is affected by every new element. I said that pure duration is organisations of elements, thus every new element means a reorganisation, and this in turn means the sense of the past alters due to the new development in the present. But what does it mean to remain ever the same and ever changing? The duration remains the same because it 'is pure reorganisation [*Gestalt*] of the organic whole of states of consciousness towards future.'[521] However, time

---

516 Roland Breeur, 'Bergson's and Sartre's Account of the Self in Relation to the Transcendental Ego', *International Journal of Philosophical Studies*, 9:2 (2001), p. 179.
517 Breeur, 'Bergson's and Sartre's Account of the Self', p. 179
518 Bergson, Henri Bergson, *Time and Free Will: An Essay on the Immediate Data of Consciousness* (Montana: Kessinger, 2000), p. 100.
519 Bergson, *Time and Free Will*, p. 101
520 Bergson, *Time and Free Will*, p. 101
521 Breeur, 'Bergson's and Sartre's Account of the Self', p. 183

also means creativity, changing and growth, for each new experience introduces a new reorganisation. It creates a new organic whole, and the self undergoes. Now, it should be noted that the self does not intervene the duration. If I stop liking something it is not because I changed my mind, but it is because my will changed (Proust).[522]

According to Bergson it is only through intuition (the realm of *non-ratioid*) that we can have an access to the inner self or transcendental self, and this, for Bergson is the condition of freedom. I am free when 'I completely coincide with that inner duration, when I am thus completely myself and when my act reflects my being, when my act totally emerges out of my real self.' As opposed to this fundamental or deeper self we may say that there is the empirical self or the subject as a defensive construction necessary for survival. We generally perceive this empirical self by refraction though space: 'our conscious states crystallise into words' and 'our living and concrete self thus gets covered with an outer crust of clean-cut psychic states, which are separated from one another and consequently fixed.'[523]

Like Musil, Bergson claims that this sort of knowledge, i.e. to have an access to the inner self, is not impossible, as aesthetic faculty proves us:

> Our eye perceives the features of the living being, merely as assembled, not as mutually organised. The intention of life, the simple movement that runs through the lines, that binds them together and gives them significance, escapes it. This intention is just what the artist tries to regain, in placing himself back within the object by a kind of sympathy, in breaking down, by an effort of intuition, the barrier that space puts up between him and his model.[524]

The difference is that Musil attempts to show what Bergson says.

His protagonist Ulrich, although he discusses it, does not explore essayism in any concrete way, rather drifting through the novel and its loosely connected episodes. However, he then meets his long-forgotten sister Agathe. It is at this point, the beginning of the 'final' third of the book, that he opens himself to an experimental mode of life. He calls this 'the other condition.' This is a notoriously elusive idea and yet a crucial one. When Musil refers to it he is not so much offering a definition of it – if it could be easily defined it would not be worth exploring at such length. He says that: 'The categories of truth and falsity do not apply in 'the other condition' (recall intuition in Bergson), what matters is whether it produces an ascending

---

522 Breeur, 'Bergson's and Sartre's Account of the Self', pp. 183-184
523 Bergson, *Time and Free Will*, p. 167
524 Bergson, *Creative Evolution*, p. 177

or descending feeling.'[525] The world is experienced in its wholeness as a 'unity of all things' that cannot be experienced unless one releases oneself from the fixed identities that are dictated by society. In 'the other condition', openness to new experiences and to the world, all dichotomies like subject and object disappear.

This is rather vague and general, and our interest in Musil lies in the fact that he tries to show rather than say what 'the other condition' might mean. He does so through the depiction of the relationship between Ulrich and his sister Agathe. This relationship cannot be understood without some consideration of Ulrich's relationship with women more generally. As we will see, it is only in his relationship with Agathe that Ulrich gradually becomes less representative of the masculine and patriarchal features of his culture, but also takes us towards new ideas about human relationships as such.

V.iv. Ulrich's Company of Women

The first woman with whom Ulrich is involved is Leona: a cabaret singer and a prostitute. She is described as tall, handsome, full of lust and as a pure beauty, yet a beauty without intellect, who can understand a joke only several days after it has been told. It is Ulrich who gives her the animal name Leona but he also likens her to 'Juno', a supremely feminine being.

Then, Ulrich meets Bonadea – as he calls her – who takes him home while he is in a semi-conscious state as a result of being attacked and robbed in the street. In a way, Bonadea (*Bona Dea* means good goddess) becomes his saviour and the representation of the opposite of human brutality. That is why Ulrich feels something 'maternally sensual' about her. She is the wife of a respected man and the mother of two boys. But she has one fault: she can 'become inordinately aroused at the mere sight of a man.'[526] She is not lustful but sensual: for instance she suffers from sweaty hands or blushes too quickly. Through his caricature-like description of Bonadea, we encounter Musil's first critique of the stereotype of ideal woman: a perfect mother and a wife who models herself on conventional ideals as a result of which she neglects her body and finds herself in a state of constant longing for her self.

---

525 As Paulson writes, for Musil, experience 'is as though one is set in motion by something, but the stimulus cannot be identified with particular external objects, rather it is an amorphous cause, which, seen outside of 'the other condition' is both internal and external to the individual; it is life itself.' Ronald M. Paulson, *Robert Musil and The Ineffable* (Stuttgart: H. –D. Heinz, 1982), p. 16.

526 Musil, *MwQ*, p. 39

In fact, Bonadea is a minor embodiment of sexual drives; Ulrich's cousin Diotima represents a more impressive figure in her relationship with her body. Diotima is the first and only woman to whom Ulrich tells two of his most important ideas: about impersonal love and life lived as literature. Unlike Leona and Bonadea she is a woman of ideas and ideals. She is also the wife of a respected man, Count Tuzzi, and though holding no professional position, a stronger figure than he. In fact, it is Diotima who administers the Parallel Campaign with Count Leinsdorf, a noble man and a conservative, and the real inventor of the Parallel Campaign. In Musil's society of women Diotima has a distinctive position because of her power over the masculine realm of ideas and intellect. However, through the ineffectual Parallel Campaign which becomes a means for Diotima to display her high-mindedness as well as her beauty, Musil shows that she also is doomed to disillusionment. She demands a place in the masculine world; yet, she is also motivated by the image of man's ideal woman, of beauty and of the image of modern intellectual woman. She believes that women should not abandon their sexual desires and should become aware of their body; however, she can find no union between her inner life and the external demands of her social position. In a way, once we move to more intellectual women in the hierarchy of Musil's women, the gap between the inner and the outer worlds of individuals becomes more visible. Ulrich is longing for someone with whom he can realise another participation in the world, yet Diotima cannot be it since for him it is better to lead a formless life than a life with false ideas. In fact a formless life even means a life full of possibilities, a life that can be reformed and reshaped constantly. The only possible partner for Ulrich in his search for complete union – which at the same time means the dissolution of this union – between the inner and the outer, subject and object, would be one with whom he could live free of all inherited predispositions.

A more likely candidate for such a union would seem to be his friend Clarisse. Clarisse and her husband Walter are Ulrich's close friends. Unlike other women in the novel Clarisse is well defined from the interior as well as from the exterior. Like Diotima she is a woman of ideas, but ideas that are inspired by Nietzsche and that result in a desire to break apart conventional ideas and rules, to go beyond good and evil. She is slim and even hermaphroditic. She is less feminine than Leona, Bonadea and Diotima, even at times appearing boylike. Till now, she seems to be the most possible candidate for the longed-for partner with whom Ulrich can explore a different mode of existence. However, her Nietzschean ideals and her belief in her power on men make her too conscious of her subjecthood. Her hermaphrodism does not lead to a formless existence, but on the contrary makes her want to be both man and woman. On the one hand, she represents the dark side of every woman in the novel; on the other hand, she wants to be a mother and a saviour for her husband, whom she regards as a troubled genius. She believes that only by giving up her femininity and taking on the male's strength can she redeem the demons in her husband and awaken the hidden genius in him; at the same time she wants to give birth to Ulrich's child. In fact, her lack of intellectual wisdom and precision, her lack of power to give an order to her ideas plunges her into a state that is half insane. In the end, she becomes another example of the disharmony between the inner and outer life.[527]

Throughout the second book Ulrich gradually becomes more impatient about not being able to find a solution to the duality inherent in him. He cannot find a union between the mathematician and the mystic in him, between precision and soul, between metaphor and truth.[528] The more he comes across people the more he sees this imbalance in them as well as in himself.

The last chapter of the second book is entitled as 'The Turning Point.' At the beginning of this chapter Clarisse visits Ulrich, and criticizes him for his passivity, for not taking action to realize his ideas. In fact, Clarisse merely repeats Ulrich's ideas and even quotes him explicitly while adopting a Nietzschean voice. With Clarisse in this state, Ulrich prepares himself for the journey to his hometown to attend his father's funeral. There it seems that all ideas and grand gestures will lose their meaning with the shattering effect of death.

The movement from the second part of the novel to the third, where Agathe is encountered for the first time, is striking. The title of part three is 'Into the Millennium (The Criminals)'. In fact, the third part of the novel is completely different from the first two parts. It is in this last section in which Musil, by focusing on the extraordinary relationship between the siblings, opens the reader to the possibility of different ways of living, to 'the other condition.'

V.v. 'The Other Condition' and Ethics

Ulrich and Agathe meet each other for the first time in the house they grew up in, as they prepare for their father's funeral. They have not seen one another for many years, and when they do, they realise that they resemble each other very

---

[527] For further discussion of the society of Musil's women see Lisa Appignanesi, *Femininity and Creative Imagination: A Study of Henry James, Robert Musil and Marcel Proust* (Evanston: Northwestern University Press, 2005).

[528] According to Thomas Mann this was Nietzsche's mission as well, 'to bring art and knowledge, science and passion, even nearer to each other, to make truth and beauty mingle together.' See Thomas Mann, 'Schopenhauer' in *Essays of Three Decades* (London: Secker and Warburg, 1947), p. 374.

much; indeed, when Agathe enters the room and Ulrich notices the similarity, he feels that it is he himself who has come in through the door and his sister is a dreamlike altered image of himself. Agathe has the same feeling: 'I had no idea we were twins!'[529] This awareness of similarity registers straight away the idea of dissolving fixed gender positions. But Musil challenges these positions in a particular way. For instance, Ulrich realizes that there is something missing and disturbing in Agathe's face; it lacks expression and gives no clue about her character. This means that the two of them are similar, but this is not because of any definite features or because of their social positions; Ulrich and Agathe have not seen each other for years, and the only things that they know about each other have been learned from their father. In fact, Agathe is similar to Ulrich because she is a 'woman without qualities' just as he is a man without qualities.

In the first part of the novel we do not always know whether Ulrich or Musil is speaking. This is because several of the chapters are like essays, and many of Ulrich's 'own' ideas are only expressed as internal monologues. In the scenes involving Agathe, these thoughts which have not gone far beyond monologues pour into speech, and although there is no more 'action' here than in the early parts, the novel becomes more dynamic and fast-flowing. After the funeral of their father, they spend time in the house, and an extraordinary dialogue takes place between them. The siblings who have become two strangers constantly talk during the long walks and the time they spend at home. Here we learn that Agathe is not only physically but also mentally similar to Ulrich. As the dialogues and sharing continue, Agathe realizes that what she intuitively accepts to be true is transferred into thoughts in Ulrich and her feelings are articulated thanks to their communication.

However, these feelings do not remain mere feelings. In the chapter titled 'A Family of Two' Ulrich discusses family roles, the division between individualism and collectivism, between 'Me' and 'We.' To him, people's 'bond with others or the self's bruised recoil from that bond into the illusion of its uniqueness'[530] are the natural impulses of individuals and 'they are both entangled with the idea of the family'; for him life in a family is not a full life and one cannot feel fully at home within the life of family. Agathe, too, resists conventional rules whether they are rules of individuals in a family life or in marriage, but although she is not happy in her own marriage, until she meets Ulrich again – who helps her to articulate her feelings – her resistance to these determinate institutions is passive. Now, she

---

529 Musil, *MwQ* p. 734
530 Musil, *MwQ*, p. 778

decides – instantly – not to return to her husband Hagauer, to whom she has remained married for many years:

> ...suddenly, she had realized that how carelessly she had always behaved, like the time she had simply thought things would 'somehow' work out with Hagauer, because he was a 'good person'. ......When was it, for example, that Ulrich had said that under certain circumstances it might be possible for him to love a thief but never a person who was honest from habit?...but it had not been Ulrich but she herself who had said it. As a matter of fact, much of what he said she had been thinking herself, only without words; all on her own, the way she used to be, she would never have made such bold assertions.[531]

Musil depicts something transgressive in her attitude, and then explains how this happens in terms that point towards the consequences of the 'dissolution of the subject.'

Agathe decides to leave Hagauer, but then she becomes bolder. Their father, whose body is lying in the library, has stated that he wishes to be buried wearing all of his decorations as a civil servant. In his will he says that these medals are a symbol of his rejection of the individualist theory of the state. The law states that when he dies his heirs should give the medals back to the authorities. He has therefore bought copies of them, but has insisted that they be exchanged for the originals only at the last moment, when the coffin is closed. When Ulrich reads this and explains it to Agathe, she immediately finds the copies and exchanges them for the originals on her dead father's chest, thus defying her father's last will. This breach of trust between the living and the dead is more serious than leaving her husband. It breaks the relationship between father and daughter. The chapter in which it happens is titled: 'They Do Wrong'. Later on, Ulrich and Agathe will not only break with conventional relationships like this. They will start an unconventional relationship of their own.

One interesting point about Musil's representation of Ulrich and Agathe is that although when they meet again they are said to be similar, Musil still depicts them at this stage in terms of an opposition between rationality (Ulrich) and feeling (Agathe). This is especially true when he talks about the way in which their thoughts converge. When Agathe shows a willingness to act, Ulrich is said to appreciate her 'in spite of her lack of principle, with the remarkable feeling that it was his own thoughts that had gone from him to her and were now returning from her to him, poorer in deliberation but with that balsamic scent of freedom about them like a

---

531 Musil, *MwQ*, p. 793

creation of the wild.'[532] This masculine/feminine opposition continues for a while, but as the dialogues between them progress, they become less representatives of 'positions' or 'roles' at all.

In the chapter entitled 'Holy Discourse: Erratic Progress', both Ulrich and Agathe open themselves to the other without any sense of self-preservation and an open and free communication develops. In Ulrich's relation to Agathe, there is no egotism, just pure openness and acceptance. Although Agathe is described as the missing part of Ulrich, Agathe is not like Eve in relation to Adam, not his 'feminine side'; by representing the lawlessness and illogical sides of Ulrich, she is different from him and a real person in her own way. At one point Agathe refers to Plato's *Symposium*.[533] Recall this passage from *Symposium* where Aristophanes distinguishes three different genders:

> Our original nature is not what it is now, but quite different. For one thing there were three sexes, rather than the two (male and female) we have now. The third sex was a combination of these two.....Secondly each human being formed a complete whole, spherical, with back and ribs forming a circle. They had four hands, four legs, and two faces, identical in every way, on a circular neck.[534]

Aristophanes adds that when man's natural form was split into two each half went around in order to find this other half. This is why, Aristophanes, concludes, we have innate love for another. Agathe reminds Ulrich of this passage from Plato, however, by declaring that they are Siamese twins, the siblings attempt to dissolve any kind of differences based on sexuality or gender roles. They experience a sense of different participation in the world which is beyond any cultural and ideological grounds and 'they enter into a relationship of intimacy and trust which is otherwise entirely presuppositionless and open to risk.'[535] This alternative way of living, is what Ulrich calls 'the other condition'.

It would have been easy for Ulrich to reject scientific rationality in the name of some sort of religious alternative, like mysticism or the monastic life. But he sees science and science's opponents as part of the same problem, as two sides of another binary opposition. Ulrich believes that 'even religious people are under the influence of the scientific way of thinking, that they do not trust themselves to look into what is burning in their inmost hearts but are always ready to speak of this ardour in medical terms as a mania, even though officially they take a different

---

532 Musil, *MwQ.*, p. 867
533 Musil, *MwQ*, p. 980
534 Plato, *Symposium* (Berkeley: University of California Press, 1986), line 189d-e.
535 Luft, *Crisis,* p. 250

line.'[536] Bourgeois morality splits into intelligence and mysticism, into 'practical improvements and unknown adventure.'[537] Moreover to him, the existence of a certain alternative has deeper origins than religion, partly because 'civilized communities of religious people have always treated this condition with the kind of mistrust the bureaucrat feels for the spirit of private enterprise.'[538] Christian morality attempts to function through regulated and intelligible morality. Ulrich reads religious books not because he is a religious person but because he is trying to understand the possibility of inner movement and divergence from the ordinary which is characteristic of mysticism. But the way he describes mysticism makes it clear that he does not see it as a solution.

> ...a man has two modes of existence, of consciousness, and of thought, and saves himself from being frightened to death by ghosts-which this prospect would of necessity induce – by regarding one condition as a vacation from the other, an interruption, a rest, or anything else he think he can recognize. Mysticism, on the other hand, would be connected with the intention of going on vacation permanently.[539]

Ulrich considers it as a state of mind which is a possibility that can be realized without being isolated from the outer world. In other words, it is possible to be in 'the other condition' without being a saint:

> There is no need to be a saint to experience something of the kind! You could be sitting on a fallen tree or a bench in the mountains, watching a herd of grazing cows, and experience something amounting to being transported into another life! You lose yourself and at the same time suddenly find yourself. [540]

He wishes to believe that people should be both intelligent and mystics and the existence of one should not exclude the other. Behind his search for the relationship between 'the other condition' and 'normal condition', there is his attempt to bring back the appropriate relationship between precision and soul, intellect and passion as well as between good and evil. The discussion of two sides of people, the outer and inner worlds – thought and feeling – between siblings indicates their attempt not simply to establish a balance between these two worlds – that was a feature of the utopia of exactitude – but to experience both at the same time. In other words, Musil does not present 'the other condition' as something that can and should be realised as an alternative to the normal condition, on the contrary, the other

---

536 Musil, *MwQ*, pp. 833-834
537 Musil, *MwQ*, p. 837
538 Musil, *MwQ*, p. 832
539 Musil, *MwQ*, p. 833
540 Musil, *MwQ*, p. 827

condition is precisely the constitutive other of the normal condition, however, as art disrupts the everyday experience of reality, 'the other condition' for Musil not only disrupts the normal condition, but also transforms the ordinary reality.

Ulrich's most explicit statement of what this means is the passage in which he compares the experience of reality in the other condition with being 'like the ocean':

> ...you must now imagine this ocean as a state of motionlessness and detachment, filled with everlasting, crystal-clear events. In ages past, people tried to imagine such a life on earth. That is the Millennium, formed in our own image and yet like no world we know. That is how we will live now! We shall cast off all self-seeking; we shall collect neither goods, nor knowledge, nor lovers, nor friends, nor principles, nor even ourselves! Our spirit will open up, dissolving boundaries toward man and beast, spreading open in such a way that we can no longer remain 'us' but will maintain our identities only by merging with all the world![541]

In fact, Ulrich is not sure whether or not it is possible to live in such a world without being isolated from the everyday order and from people in this order. On the other hand, the communication that has developed between Agathe and Ulrich in the short time they spent together and isolated from other people, leads them to think that they may experience 'the other condition' together, and so they decide to live together in Ulrich's house, in Vienna. This proves to be a fateful decision.

> For today our lives are divided, and parts are entangled with other people; what we dream has to do with dreaming and also with what other people dream; what we do has sense, but more sense in relation with what others do; and what we believe is tied in with beliefs only a fraction of which are our own. It is therefore quite unrealistic to insist upon acting out of the fullness of one's own personal reality. Especially for a man like himself, who had been imbued all his life with the thought that one's beliefs had to be shared, that one must have the courage to live in the midst of moral contradictions, because that was the price of great achievement.[542]

On the one hand, Ulrich himself is not sure whether he believes in the possibility and significance of another kind of life; on the other hand, he is emotionally drawn to it. Moreover, the attempt to realize the promise of a Millennium he has mentioned once is a 'call for all the delicacy and selflessness he could muster – qualities that had been all too lacking him.'[543] In his own individual and lonely life, there was no thinking, protecting and caring for the other, taking responsibility for

---

541 Musil, *MwQ*, p. 871
542 Musil, *MwQ*, p. 950
543 Musil, *MwQ*, p. 950

the other. Now, he is about to begin a shared life with Agathe who is standing in front of him with all her nakedness and who has opened to him with all her naiveté.

Ulrich and Agathe are similarly 'without qualities', but living in an age where qualities make the person. Their decision to live together is a way of saying that the 'dissolution of the subject' may mean a kind of human freedom. This human freedom cannot be achieved by living alone, as Ulrich has been doing. Nor can it be realized if the relationship they enter into has a definite purpose or a fixed aim or a social function. But a relationship without a 'purpose' is risky.

> Perhaps the content of the Millennium is merely the burgeoning of this energy, which at first shows itself in two people, until it grows into a resounding universal communion,...living for another person must be, must be happiness that could move one to tears, as lovely as the lambent sinking of day into the peace of evening and also, just a little, an impoverishing of spirit and intellect to the point of tears.[544]

Ulrich thinks that what he feels for Agathe is nothing but an imaginary, or 'seraphic love' which is a 'love without a partner' or 'love without sex'.[545] He realizes that Agathe is his self-love which has been embodied in her instead of himself and which he has always lacked.

Their attempt aims to realise 'the other condition', however, this may require a withdrawal from their environment. Ulrich distances himself from his previous environment for a while and just spends time with Agathe and the way they wish to live works out quite well once the company of others leaves them free. They are open 'to live in the *fire*' and at the threshold. The acceptance as he is or she is by the other is the crucial theme for both. The relationship between Agathe and Ulrich can be regarded as the transgression of the law of the family and of the father: it is not a love story but an experiment. Ulrich is aware that their attitude is a 'protest against life':

> 'It is pretty obvious that the two of us are psychologically suspect. Incestuous tendencies, demonstrable in early childhood, together with antisocial dispositions and a rebellious attitude toward life. Possibly even a not sufficiently rooted gender identification, although I –.'
>
> 'Nor I, either!', Agathe broke in, laughing, if possibly somewhat against her will. 'I have no use for women at all!'[546]

Agathe's statement here sounds like that of an early anti-feminist. But that would be a premature conclusion.

---

544 Musil, *MwQ*, pp. 950-951
545 Musil, *MwQ*, p. 952
546 Musil, *MwQ*, p. 1024

In *Difference and Repetition* Deleuze describes the Musilian subject as a 'becoming-child', a 'becoming-woman'.[547] Ulrich refers to 'incestuous tendencies, demonstrable in early childhood', and to a failure of gender identification. He implies that the condition for overcoming gender divisions would be a return to childhood, and that we cannot imagine an adult solution to the problems that gender divisions create. Ulrich and Agathe were last together when they were children, and in a way their dialogue has begun at the point when it left off – in their childhood. There is nothing naïve or innocent about it though because Ulrich is far more of an adult than his age would suggest.

Now, for Deleuze and Guattari, 'there is a becoming-woman, becoming-child, that does not resemble the woman or the child.'[548] On the other hand, even a woman has to become-woman because her becoming, her body, is stolen from her as well as from a child. Rosi Braidotti's 'philosophy of becoming' is similar to that of Deleuze in the sense that for her, becoming is a desire 'not to know who we are', yet, 'what, at last, we want to become.'[549] Similarly, Michel Foucault writes: 'I do not feel that it is necessary to know exactly what I am. The main interest in life and work is to become someone else that you were not in the beginning.'[550,551]

---

547 In *Difference and Repetition* Deleuze refers to Musil as a distinctive figure who achieved Nietzsche's project through his literary works. According to Deleuze, the Musilian 'subject' is impersonal, freed from fixed identities and fixed ideas. See Gilles Deleuze, *Difference and Repetition* trans. Paul Patton (London; New York: Continuum, 2001) chp. 3. In *The Logic of Sense* Deleuze argues that Nietzsche 'explored a world of impersonal and pre-individual singularities, a world he then called Dynosian or of the will to power, a free and unbound energy.' Gilles Deleuze, *The Logic of Sense*, trans. Mark Lester (London: Continuum, 2001), p. 122. Following Nietzsche Deleuze introduces the 'nomadic subject,' which is open to the infinity of singularities through which it passes. The 'nomadic subject' loses its centre, its identity as a concept and as a self. 'Nomadic singularity', in Deleuze's words, is free and anonymous. No form, no shape, and no quality can define the nomadic singularity.
548 Deleuze, Gilles&Guattari, Felix. *A Thousand Plateau*, trans. Brian Massumi (London: Athlone, 1987), p. 275.
549 Rosi Braidotti, *Metamorphoses: Towards a Materialist Theory of Becoming* (Cambridge: Polity Press: 2002), p. 2.
550 Foucault, Michel. 'Technologies of the self', in *Technologies of the Self: A Seminar with Michel Foucault* (London: Tavistock, 1988), pp 16-49.
551 According to Braidotti, 'the Deleuzian becoming is the affirmation of the passivity of difference, meant as a multiple and constant process of transformation. Both teleological order and fixed identities are relinquished in favour of a flux of multiple becoming.' Rosi Braidotti, *Nomadic Subjects: Embodiment and Sexual Difference in Contemporary Feminist Theory* (London: Zed Books, 1994), p. 111. However, he finds

So far so good. However, one question that follows from this is how, if there is no unified identity or a continuous self, we can talk about ethical issues like responsibility and accountability. Judith Butler not only believes that we can, but that the idea of the 'de-centering' or the dissolution of the subject should be regarded as a new beginning for ethics: 'Indeed, to take responsibility for oneself is to avow the limits of any self-understanding and to establish this limit not only as a condition for the subject, but as the predicament of the human community itself.'[552] She claims that even when we speak as an 'I' we must not make the mistake of thinking that we know everything that we are doing since according to her 'my very formation implicates the Other in me…my own foreignness to myself is, paradoxically, the source of my ethical connection with others.'[553]

> I am wounded, and I find that the wound itself testifies to the fact that I am impressionable, given over to the Other in ways that I cannot fully predict or control. I cannot think the question of responsibility alone, in isolation from the Other, or if I do, I have taken myself out of the mode of address that frames the problem of responsibility from the start.[554]

And if the constitution of the self is not to be separated from the relation with the other, any attempt of ours to resist the existing order is also an ethical issue since 'the boundary of the body as well as the distinction between internal and external is established through the ejection and transvaluation of something originally part of identity into a defiling otherness' and 'what constitutes through division the 'inner' and 'outer' worlds of the subject is a border and boundary tenuously maintained for the purposes of social regulation and control.'[555] Then any subversive repetition – i.e. 'the pastiche effect of parodic practices in which the original, the authentic, and the real are themselves constituted as effects'[556] – is also an invitation to the Other to join with us in breaking apart the taken-for-granted social roles and rules with us.

---

this position of Deleuze problematic, even dangerous. Firstly, saying that 'her body, her becoming' is stolen from the woman implies a core identity in the beginning. Moreover, even though the becoming-woman can be regarded as an important step, it is so only as long as woman is the privileged figure of otherness. *Nomadic Subjects*, p. 114.
552 Judith Butler, 'Giving an Account of Oneself', *Diacritics*, Vol. 31, No. 4 (Winter, 2001), p. 37.
553 Butler, 'Giving an Account', p. 37
554 Butler, 'Giving an Account', p. 38
555 Butler, *Gender Trouble: Feminism and the Subversion of Identity* (New York; London: Routledge, 1990), p. 133.
556 Butler, *Gender Trouble*, p. 146

In fact, Butler's writing can be regarded as a performative act since not only the content but also the form emphasizes the impossibility of the conceptualization of subjectivity, identity and selfhood. Nietzsche saw this problem as well. This is why he neither suggests a final message nor maintains a philosophical doctrine. Yet, he attempts to liberate our potentialities for life from the concept of man or human essence which hinders us, and he aims to overcome the fixed oppositions whether they are mind and body, subject and object, 'free will' and determinism etc. which constrain our philosophical thinking.

However, even though Nietzsche devotes considerable space to the problem of the 'subject' and adopts a writing style which is also consistent with the content, i.e. essay and aphorism, I suggest here that literature is able to convey in detail what other disciplines provide only in general terms. This does not quite mean that only through literature can one speak to the plight of particular people living particular lives; it does mean that the 'types of human being' or characters presented in novels allow for a more differentiated and nuanced account of the problems and possibilities of identity, sexuality and gender. My referring to Butler and Braidotti and Foucault is no coincidence. Their attempt to rethink the relationship between the self and the Other or ethics in general has given rise to widespread discussion. Yet seventy years ago, Musil anticipated much of their work, and he did so more performatively, through his mode of writing.

In the 'other condition' sexual definitions of persons dissolve. The importance of the changing role of women lay 'not in the realm of the emancipation of the woman but, rather, in the emancipation of the man from traditional styles of eroticism; and the path sketched by ideology runs from the passive enfranchisement of women to sensuousness and from there to a refined humanity.'[557] The other side of the liberation of men from conventional styles of eroticism was the liberation of both men and women from conventional assumptions about gender.[558] And this would be possible only through 'actively forgetting' or unlearning the conventional styles of life and going back to childhood where these dichotomies were not established. As Ulrich says:

> ...nature provides men with nipples and women with rudimentary male sex organs, which should not lead us to conclude that our ancestors were hermaphrodites. Nor need they have been psychological hybrids either. And so it must have been from outside that they received the double possibility of a giving and a receiving vision,

---

557 Quoted in David Luft, *Eros and Inwardness in* Vienna: *Weininger, Musil, Doderer* (Chicago; London: University of Chicago Press, 2003), p. 112.

558 Luft, *Eros*, p. 112

as a dual aspect of nature, and somehow all this is far older than the difference of gender, on which the sexes later drew to fill out their psychological wardrobe.....[559]

Behind Ulrich's search for the relationship between 'the other condition' and the 'normal condition', there is his attempt to bring back the appropriate relationship between precision and soul, intellect and passion as well as between good and evil. The discussion that takes place between siblings about two sides of people, the outer and inner worlds, – thought and feeling – indicates their attempt not simply to establish a balance between these two worlds but to experience both at the same time. Such an experience also requires the collapse of phallogocentrism precisely by shattering the Same/Other binary. This leads, or may lead, to what McBride calls 'the ineffable promise of unconditional happiness.' 'Ineffable' here means 'destined to remain as a black hole for language and thought.'[560] In other words it resists any sort of conceptualization, which is another way of saying that it may have to be addressed through literature rather than philosophy, as we will see.

However, it should be noted that Ulrich is still masculine enough to appear unable to develop his feminine side without projecting it onto a woman. Even though Ulrich wants to think that Agathe is his missing part, his feminine part in fact, Agathe is herself a hermaphrodite. Thus, it is Agathe, not Ulrich who is too intellectual, who constantly deconstructs taken-for-granted roles. She is extraordinary because she does not attempt to form herself in the image of the male's ideal of femininity or according to society's prescriptions. Unlike other women in the novel, she does not suffer from her desire to prove herself in the male realm. While Ulrich 'always arrives quickly at the moral story his sister is talking about, sums things up in formulas',[561] Agathe acts to change things in her life. As Ernst Fischer writes: 'Everything in her is plastic possibility. What for him is merely the possible, turns in to reality; what for him were merely shadows, takes shape in her; what he thinks, she attempts to live.'[562]

I said earlier that Butler claims that we can break apart binary oppositions through the subversive repetition of already existing roles. In this sense, the practices of repetition are a protest against the idea of the 'continuity of the person through time'; an attempt to deconstruct the notion of the linear time which

---

559 Musil, *MwQ*, p. 748
560 McBride, *The Void*, p. 4
561 Musil, *MwQ*, p. 810
562 Ernst Fischer, Introduction, in the Turkish version of *The Man without Qualities*. Translated by the author from the Turkish from Ernst Fischer, 'Robert Musil', in Robert Musil, *Niteliksiz Adam* (İstanbul: YKY, 1999), p. 67.

has characterized western philosophical thought. However, such an understanding also implies that there is no escape from the existing order; that we can protest against it only through it. Musil's 'the other condition', on the other hand, requires the dissolution of space and time and suggests a totally different participation in the world. By being a pure possibility, or becoming, or hermaphrodite, Agathe in a way has no past, she is creating her present as well as her future. As such, she anticipates a theme to be found in the work of some postmodern feminists who write about a 'subject' in the process of becoming, something that is held to involve the idea that an open future, 'uncontained by the chains of the determinism that constrain the future directly through the past, that is, a future yet to be made, is the very lifeblood of political struggle, the goal of feminist challenge.'[563]

Perhaps this is where the difference between Nietzsche and Musil on the question of life becomes more apparent: their strategies of dissolving the subject for the sake of revealing the 'true' self. Nietzsche suggests a life as a flux of actuality, whereas Musil's 'the other condition' is a withdrawal from life, back to the matrix of potentialities, even though this withdrawal should not be understood as a complete detachment from life, or from a 'normal condition'.

Despite what we have said about Musil's showing what philosopher's have said and perhaps showing more, I end this chapter with an attempt to clarify philosophically the meaning of phrases like 'pure possibility' and 'potentiality'.

Potentiality (*dynamis*) traditionally is understood as the opposite of actuality (*energia*). In Aristotle the distinction between potentiality and actuality is related to his distinction between matter and form, the former being the stuff of a substance that it is composed of; the latter being the way that the stuff is put together. The distinction between matter and form is a synchronic distinction, whereas between potentiality and actuality is a diachronic one, that is to say, Aristotle gives actuality priority over potentiality. Potency is the power to act, yet, a man who is sleeping, for instance, has the potentiality or power of thinking, but he is not actually thinking.

Aristotle distinguishes between priority in *logos*, in time, and in substance.[564] Firstly, actuality is prior in *logos* because when we want to refer to something potential we have to cite the actuality first: 'what has the capacity to see means what can see.'[565] As regards temporal priority, Aristotle says 'an actual being is ahead

---

563 Elizabeth Grosz, 'Histories of a Feminist Future', *Signs*, Vol. 25, No. 4, Feminisms at a Millennium (Summer, 2000), p. 1017.
564 Aristotle, *Metaphysics*, 1049b4-20, p. 192
565 Aristotle, *Metaphysics*, 1049b10-20, p. 192

of another being of the same kind that is only potential.'[566] A particular acorn is temporally prior to the particular oak tree but it is preceded in time by the actual oak tree that produced it. According to Aristotle we must say that before the seed there is a man, – not the man produced from the seed, but another from whom the seed comes.[567]

Coming to the third point, Aristotle argues for the priority in substance of actuality over potentiality in two ways. The first argument is related to his notion of final causality. Things that come to be move toward an end (*telos*), in other words, 'the actuality is the end, and it is thanks to it that a power is possessed; for animals do not see in order that they may have the power of sight, but they have the power of sight in order that they may see ...a matter is potential because it may attain form; it is when it is actual that it is in its form.'[568]

The second argument[569] is related to his notion of 'the unmoved mover'. A potentiality means something that is capable of being is also capable of not being. Anything that can potentially not be is perishable. The eternal substance, for Aristotle, is fully actual. We cannot talk about any potentiality about the eternal substance, the First Mover. The cause of everything is 'something which moves without being moved, being eternal, substance and actuality'[570] and this 'first mover' must exist necessarily (Spinoza).

We see this opposition between potentiality and actuality in many philosophers in one way or another. For Hegel, for instance, Reason is what is capable of actualizing itself, that is to say, Reason unfolds its potentiality into actuality. Overturning Hegel's argument Marx locates the power of actuality not in Reason but in material labour power.

A notable departure from these ideas is found in the work of Giorgio Agamben. Agamben gives a radical account of actuality and potentiality, one in which actuality does not posit an opposition to potentiality and in which the one is not derivable from the other. In 'On Potentiality' Agamben claims that potentiality is not simply non-Being, but rather '*the existence of non-Being*', in other words, the presence of absence. Let us consider this essay.

In Aristotle we know that there are two kinds of potentiality. The first one is *generic* potentiality, that is, one has the potentiality to become something: a child

---

566 Aristotle, *Metaphysics*, 1049b18-19, p. 192
567 Aristotle, *Metaphysics*, 1073a, p. 260
568 Aristotle, *Metaphysics*, 1050a9-17, p. 193
569 Aristotle, *Metaphysics*, 1050b6-1051a2, p. 194-196
570 Aristotle, *Metaphysics*, 1073a4-7, p. 260

has the potential to know, or to become the Head of the State. This potentiality, however, is not what Aristotle is interested in. What interests Aristotle is the potentiality of someone who already has knowledge or ability to do something, that is *existing* potentiality. For instance, an architect has the potentiality to build, a poet to write poems and so on. Only in the latter there is already *existing* knowledge, that is to say, 'the architect is potential insofar as he has the potential to not build, the poet the potential not to write poems.'[571] This is the potentiality 'not to pass into actuality.'[572] But what would this potentiality look like?

Agamben likens it to shadow. This time he turns to Aristotle's *De Anima* where Aristotle is concerned with the problem of vision. Agamben points out that the object of sight, for Aristotle, is colour; darkness, however, is the colour of potentiality. Agamben's crucial point here is that even if we do not see we still are able to distinguish darkness from light, in other words, we are able to see darkness.[573]

---

571 Giorgio Agamben, 'On Potentiality', in *Potentialities: Collected Essays in Philosophy* (Stanford: Stanford University Press, 1999), p. 179.
572 Agamben, 'On Potentiality', p. 180
573 Agamben's treatment of light and darkness can also be read as a problematisation of 'sight' and 'light' within the philosophical tradition from Plato to Enlightenment or even to Husserl and Heidegger. Agamben is not alone in this. Emmanuel Levinas, for instance, problematises the concept/metaphor light and, correspondingly, how vision and seeing always have been privileged over the other human senses. Levinas claims that in western philosophy the relation between conscious act and its object is always accompanied by a third element 'light' which blurs the distinction between me and the object. According to Descartes, something is intelligible if it is 'clearly' and distinctly perceived by the mind, i.e. if there exists a total adequation of consciousness with what is thought. This critique of light as the third element becomes central in Levinas' ethics for according to Levinas, phenomenology hitherto was concerned with the subject qua 'knower' and although Heidegger criticises traditional philosophy for forgetting the question of 'Being,' for Levinas Heidegger, too, rejoins the Platonic tradition of Western philosophy where the relation to particular beings is always understood by way of mediation with a third term: universal form or *eidos* in Plato, Spirit in Hegel, and Being in Heidegger. Levinas' *Totality and Infinity* (1961) concentrates on the relation between *the Same* (or the totality) and *the Other* (or the infinite) throughout the book whose subtitle – an essay on exteriority – indicates that the Other cannot be integrated into any consciousness or other form of interiority. Emmanuel Levinas, *Totality and Infinity* (Boston; London: Kluwer, Dordrecht, 1991). However, in 'Violence and Metaphysics' Jacques Derrida claims that Levinas cannot express his position without using the very concepts he criticises, without using the language of the tradition with which he attempts to break. This critique applies to the language of *Totality and Infinity*. Derrida writes: 'Light is only one example of these

What does it mean? For Agamben, to be able to see darkness is nothing other than the experience of potentiality-in-itself. Agamben says:

> If potentiality were, for instance, only the potentiality for vision and if it existed only as such in the actuality of light, we could never experience darkness (nor hear silence in the case of the potentiality to hear). But human beings can, instead, see shadows (*to skotos*), they can experience darkness: they have the *potential* not to see, the *possibility of privation.*[574]

Here Agamben turns to Aristotle's Book Theta (9) of *Metaphysics*, where Aristotle writes, 'Impotentiality [*adynamia* αδυναμία] is a privation contrary to potentiality. Thus all potentiality is impotentiality of the same and with respect to the same.' This for Agamben is the originary structure of potentiality: all potentiality is impotentiality. This structure is far away from the binary account of potentiality as something not-actual-yet. In Agamben's account there is no teleological movement from one to the other. However, why is this important? It is important because this notion of potentiality is directly related to ethics in Agamben.

Agamben argues that we are the only animals who are capable of their own impotentiality. In Kant, Hegel and Marx human freedom is regarded as the actualisation of a potency of an act; it is the annihilation of impotentiality. Agamben, on the other hand, locates human freedom – ethics – in potentiality, the potential to not-be. In *The Coming Community* he describes this freedom as 'being Bartleby', referring to Melville's scrivener who does not simply cease writing but prefers not to.[575] This is another way of saying there is no human essence, nor is there biological destiny that humans must realise, and precisely because of this ethical experience would be possible. Agamben further adds: 'This does not mean, however, that humans are not, and do not have to be...There is in effect something that

---

"several" fundamental "metaphors," but what an example! Who will ever dominate it, who will ever pronounce its meaning without first being pronounced by it? What language will ever escape it? How, for example, will the metaphysics of the face as the *epiphany* of the other free itself of light? Light, perhaps, has no opposite; if it does, it is certainly not night. ..... "Perhaps universal history is but the history of the diverse intonations of several metaphors.' Jacques Derrida, 'Violence and Metaphysics: An Essay on the Thought of Emmanuel Levinas' in *Writing and Difference* (London: Routledge, 2001), p. 114.
574 Agamben, 'On Potentiality', p. 181
575 Giorgio Agamben, *The Coming Community* (Minneapolis; London: University of Minnesota Press, 1993), p. 36.

humans are and have to be, but this something is not an essence nor properly a thing: *It is the simple fact of one's own existence as possibility or potentiality.*[576]

V.vi. Conclusion: Ulrich Returns to the Parallel Campaign

This chapter has shown how, through the Moosbrugger episodes, Musil problematises ideas of responsibility and selfhood to be found in scientific, legal or other 'universalistic' discourses; for Musil the novelist, the Moosbrugger 'case' is not a 'case' in any of the senses in which these disciplines would understand it. We also saw how essayism was an important device for avoiding these false universalisms, in particular how 'essayism' implies hostility or at least scepticism towards the idea of a conclusion. A shorthand way of summing these two points up is to say that Musil's subject matter is ethics rather than morality. In the final section of the chapter we saw that the exploration of 'the other condition' was Musil's most sustained engagement not only with ethics as a topic but with a positive ethical vision. At its heart lay an idea of potentiality, and we attempted to give some more weight to this in our discussion of Aristotle and Agamben. The title of Agamben's book, *Man without Content* can hardly be a coincidence.

However, the final chapters of *The Man without Qualities* are dedicated to a meeting of the Parallel Campaign. Ulrich has returned to Vienna with Agathe, and renewed his interest in the Parallel Campaign. His self-confident manner, which once makes him detached observer, now makes him a more or less competent member of the campaign. One is tempted to see this as a sign of the failure of Ulrich and Agathe's experiment, but this would be against the idea of a 'trying morality'; moreover in returning to the Parallel Campaign Ulrich is not entering a world of fixed professional identities either, nor is the parallel campaign any more advanced than at the beginning of the novel. The very meaninglessness of it is a kind of freedom, but the sort of empty freedom that throws 'the other condition' into sharper relief.

Perhaps Girard captures this:

> To triumph over self-centeredness is to get away from oneself and make contact with others but in another sense it also implies a greater intimacy with oneself and a withdrawal from others...Victory over self-centeredness allows us to probe deeply into the Self and at the same time yields a better knowledge of Others. At a certain depth

---

576 Agamben, *The Coming Community*, p. 42

there is no difference between our own secret and the secret of Others. Everything is revealed to the novelist when he penetrates this Self, a truer Self than that which each of us plays.[577]

If Agamben's remarks on potentiality help to make sense of Musil, if it is inspired in some way by Musil, the fact remains that Musil is doing something, or trying to, that he thinks philosophy, as metaphysics or philosophical psychology or philosophical ethics, cannot. He is not applying philosophy to the novel but using the novel to explore or reveal matters in which philosophy can seem limited. Essayism is an important part but not the only part of his attempt to do so, and so the next chapter will explore a little further the question of what sort of writing Musil is doing.

---

577 René Girard, *Deceit, Desire, and the Novel: Self and Other in Literary Structure* (Baltimore; London: John Hopkins University Press, 1976), p. 298.

Chapter VI: Intermediate Reflections II: Metaphor, Irony and Simile

In *Speech Genres* Bakthin draws a distinction between *Bildungsroman* and other traditional types of novel (the travel novel, the novel of ordeal, the biographical (autobiographical) novel) that preceded it.[578] The main difference, Bakthin argues, lies in the fact that the hero of the traditional novel does not and cannot develop, because, in Gürle's words: 'he is caught up in a static world model, where space and time adhere to the laws of suspense.'[579] In the *Bildungsroman*, however, the hero is in the process of becoming.

Goethe's *Wilhelm Meister* can be regarded as one of the first – maybe the first – examples of the *Bildungsroman*. In *The Theory of the Novel* Lukács argues that the theme of *Wilhelm Meister* is 'the reconciliation of the problematic individual, guided by his lived experience of the ideal, with concrete social reality.'[580] Though rather difficult, such a reconciliation is possible. The idea of the hero in the process of becoming along with the idea that there is a dialectical relationship between the individual and the society leads Franco Moretti to the conclusion that *Bildungsroman* is, in fact, the narrative equivalent of Hegelian thought.[581]

> it is *biographical*, assuming the existence of a coherent individual identity which constitutes the focal point of the narrative; *dialectical*, defining identity as the result of an interplay between conflicting forces, usually the individual and the society; *historical*, depicting formation as a temporal process which is represented by means of a linear and chronological narrative; and *teleological*, unfolding towards the projected goal of the protagonist's access to self-knowledge, which emerges as a consensus between the individual and the society.[582]

My aim here is not to give a detailed account of the *Bildungsroman*, nor is it to investigate the relationship between it and Hegel's thought. I mention it here

---

578 Mikhail Bakhtin, *Speech Genres and Other Late Essays* (Austin: University of Texas Press, 1986), p. 9.
579 Meltem Gürle, *Oğuz Atay's Dialogue with the Western canon in The Disconnected,* (PhD. Diss., Boğaziçi University, 2008), p. 115.
580 Georg Lukács, *The Theory of the Novel* (Cambridge; Mass.: MIT, 1971), p. 132.
581 Franco Moretti, *The Way of the World: The Bildungsroman in European Culture* (London: Verso, 1987), p. 7.
582 Gürle, *Oğuz Atay's Dialogue*, pp. 117-118

because Musil's novel starts where the *Bildungsroman* ends: Ulrich has already finished his 'one-year' flight from life, and as a thirty-two year old man he is not a representative of the youth which is a key feature of the *Bildungsroman*; as an adolescent nor was Törless; young men like Wilhelm Meister are not the protagonists of Musil's novels. Thus, it may be not an exaggeration to claim that *The Man without Qualities* is, in fact, an anti-*Bildungsroman*, or that some features of it are a parody of a *Bildungsroman*: Ulrich attempts to develop himself before his flight from life, whereas after his journey he is, far from being mature, without qualities; there is not even a home to turn back to. And this idea is conveyed with a rather ingenious analogy: 'Modern man is born in a hospital and dies in a hospital, so he should make his home like a clinic.'[583]

Nor in terms of form does Musil's novel resemble the *Bildungsroman*. At one point Musil criticises the traditional way of relating events:

> The basic law of this life, the law one longs for, is nothing other than that of narrative order, the simple order that enables one to say: 'First this happened and then that happened....' It is the simple sequence of events in which the overwhelmingly manifold nature of things is represented, in an unidimensional order, as a mathematician would say, stringing all that has occurred in space and time on a single thread, which calms us;...Lucky the man who can say 'when,' 'before' and 'after'!... Most people relate to themselves as storyteller...and the impression that their life has a 'course' is somehow their refuge from chaos. It now came to Ulrich that he had lost this elementary, narrative mode of thought to which private life still clings, even though everything in public life has already ceased to be narrative and no longer follows a thread, but instead spreads out as an infinitely interwoven surface.[584]

Musil constructs his novel – and Ulrich his world – in such a way that it might have been constructed in many other ways. At the beginning of the book the narrator adopts a God-like point of view, the God being one who, unlike Leibniz's, 'probably preferred to speak of His world in the subjunctive of possibility, for God creates the world and thinks while He is at it that it could just as well be done differently.'[585] The idea of 'sense of possibility' is quite explicit in Musil's storytelling. For instance before the accident which will be witnessed by the couple, the narrator tells us that 'their names might have been Ermelinda Tuzzi and Arnheim – but then, they couldn't be, because in August Frau Tuzzi was still in Bad Aussee with her husband and Dr. Arnheim was still in Constantinople.'[586] And

---

583 Musil, *MwQ*, p. 15
584 Musil, *MwQ*, pp. 708-709
585 Musil, MwQ, p. 14
586 Musil, *MwQ*, p. 4

a couple of pages later the narrator says: 'Had the distinguished couple followed its course a little longer, they would have come upon a sight that would certainly have pleased them.'[587]

As we have seen, the idea of essayism was one version of how to live; but it was also one way in which Musil could challenge traditional writing styles. In *Soul and Form* Lukács declares that the essay is an art form,[588] an idea that Adorno is critical of for reasons that Musil would have appreciated. According to Adorno:

> instead of accomplishing something scientifically or creating something artistically, its [essay's] efforts reflect the leisure of a childlike person....It starts not with Adam and Eve but with what it wants to talk about; it says what occurs to it in that context and stops when it feels finished rather than when there is nothing to say.[589]

In the same essay Adorno calls Walter Benjamin a master of the essay in this sense. In 'One Way Street' Benjamin writes:

> To great writers, finished works weigh lighter than those fragments on which they work throughout their lives. For only the more feeble and distracted take an inimitable pleasure in conclusions, feeling themselves thereby given back to life. For the genius each caesura, and the heavy blows of fate, fall like gentle sleep itself into his workshop labour. About it he draws a charmed circle of fragments. 'Genius is application.'[590]

Now, such a style is bound to lack the storyteller 'I'. If in his *Essays* Montaigne claims that he never looks at the outer world, and that all he is concerned with is himself, Benjamin adopts the principle of not using the word 'I', except in letters.[591] Probably this is one of the fundamental differences between the modern essay and its earlier versions: Montaigne, the inventor of the literary form of essay, addresses the reader at the beginning of his *Essays* saying that 'I myself am the subject of my book.' Moreover he says: 'Here I want to be seen in my simple, natural, everyday fashion without striving or artifice.'[592] This 'I' is absent from Benjamin's essays, as it is from Musil's writing.

Musil's *The Man without Qualities* is a 'sort of novel' which consists of many chapters, some of them virtually self-contained essays. Even though it is the

---

587 Musil, *MwQ*, p. 56
588 Lukács, *Soul and Form* (London: Merlin Press, 1974), p. 2.
589 Theodor Adorno, *Notes on Literature* (New York: Columbia University Press, 1991), p. 4.
590 Walter Benjamin, *One Way Street and Other Writings* (London: NLB, 1979), pp. 47-48.
591 Nurdan Gürbilek, Introduction, in Walter Benjamin, *Son Bakışta Aşk* (Istanbul: Metis, 2008), p. 29.
592 Michel de Montaigne, *The Complete Essays* (London: Penguin, 2003).

narrator who tells the story, Musil's aim is to give the reader neither a feeling of omnipotence nor of identification with the protagonists. He wants the reader to think, and so it is not an 'easy' novel; one cannot give himself/herself to the flow of the events, for events are constantly interrupted by rather sophisticated philosophical discussions. He even provokes the reader: one of the chapters is entitled 'A chapter that may be skipped by anyone not particularly impressed by thinking as an occupation'.

Lukács argued that the quality fundamental to the essay is irony.[593] Probably the most ironic event in the novel is the Parallel Campaign, for the 'year of peace' chosen for the celebrations is 1918, the 70th anniversary of the Austrian Emperor's accession, but also the 30th anniversary of the accession of the German Kaiser Wilhelm II, and as the reader knows, the year that sealed the fate of both. Ulrich himself is an ironic figure. According to Luft, it is the irony of Musil's essayism which established a distance from both the old bourgeois values and modern mass culture.[594] In fact, Musil himself gives the definition of irony in a chapter in the *Nachlass* of *The Man without Qualities*:

> Irony is: to portray a clerical in such a way that a Bolshevik is captured in the same description. Portray an imbecile so that the author suddenly feels: I am that in part myself. This kind of irony – the constructive irony – is relatively unknown in Germany today. It is the connection of things from which they come forth naked. One takes irony for mockery or ridicule.[595]

In his essay on Musil Blanchot claims that irony is one of the centres of the novel, but that it does not manifest itself on the level of words: 'It lies rather in the very composition of the book; it is in the way certain situations turn on themselves, in the fact that the most serious thoughts, the most authentic impulses of the hero, Ulrich, will then play themselves out a second time in other characters, where they take on a pitiful and comic aspect.'[596] For instance, Blanchot argues, the effort to associate the ideal of exactitude with the void of the soul, or in other words, the proper relationship between precision and soul – one of Ulrich's main concerns – is then caricatured through the beautiful souls Diotima and Arnheim. This 'connection of things' is vital to Musil's 'new irony' and to his writing in general.

As we have seen, Musil does not narrate in terms of a cause-effect pattern, but of functionality. Or in Rüdiger Görner's words: 'with a delicate balancing of

---

593 Lukács, *Soul and Form*, p. 9
594 Luft, *Crisis*, p. 21
595 Quoted in Luft, *Crisis*, p. 233
596 Blanchot, *The Book to Come*, p. 138

the elements of a situation, a character, an event or life, in which each element is inextricably linked with the other and the consequences of any action cannot be anticipated with Newtonian certainty but remain unpredictable.'[597] We saw that the idea that 'each element is linked with the other' was already explicit in *Törless*; in fact, his representation of such a Spinozistic world was not unique in *fin-de-siècle* Vienna. Consider this passage from Hofmannsthal's *The Letter of Lord Chandos*:

> To sum up: in those days, I, in a state of continuous intoxication, conceived the whole of existence as one great unit: the spiritual and physical worlds seemed to form no contrast, as little as did courtly and bestial conduct, art and barbarism, solitude and society:[598]

Or this:

> As soon, however, as this strange enchantment falls from me, I find myself confused; wherein this harmony transcending me and the entire world consisted, and how it made itself known to me, I could present in sensible words as little as I could say anything precise about the inner movements of my intestines and a congestion of my blood.[599]

What makes Musil distinctive is the fact that he explores this mystical self: a task that he started with *Törless*, and continued in his novellas. Here the idea of 'connection of things' reaches its highest point and does so precisely through an experimental approach to the use of language.

The two novellas in *Unions* (*The Temptation of Quiet Veronica* and *The Perfecting of Love*) were published in 1911, and were received with silence even by Alfred Kerr who had helped to make *Törless* a literary success.[600] The stories are not easy, indeed, they are exhausting. In order to enjoy them one needs to accept Musil's invitation to float – or wade – through a complex of images through which the inner and the outer are interwoven. Consider this passage from the very opening page of *The Perfecting of a Love*:

> Outside, looking out upon the street, the dark green shutters were part of a long row of dark green shutters and in no way distinct from the rest. Like a pair of dark eyelids, lowered in indifference, they concealed the glitter of this room, where from

---

[597] Rüdiger Görner, 'Reception without Qualities': Robert Musil's Impact on Austrian and German Writers' in *Companion*, p. 399
[598] Hugo von Hofmannsthal, 'The Letter of Lord Chandos', in *Selected Prose* (New York: Pantheon Books, 1952), p. 132.
[599] Hofmannsthal, *Chandos*, p. 138
[600] Silvia Bonacchi and Philip Payne, 'Musil's "Die Vollendung der Lieber": Experience Analysed and Reconstituted', in *Companion*, p. 175

a satin-silver teapot the tea now flowed, striking the bottom of each cup with a faint tinkle and then remaining poised in mid-air, straw-coloured, a translucent, twisted column of weightless topaz.[601]

Or this passage from *Veronica*:

'Sometimes on dead afternoons' she went on, 'when I went for a walk with Aunt, there was a light like that on everything. I could feel it bodily, as though the very notion of that ghastly, nauseating light were radiating from my stomach.'[602]

This complex, thick language of his novellas raises the question why Musil felt the urge to adopt it. One answer may be that it was a response to the complex reality of the experience of modernity along with the rejection of the conventions of prose realism and the discourse of psychology. However, Musil's task is something more than this. At one point he does give us a clue:

The defect of this book is being a book. That it has binding, backing, pagination. One ought to spread out a few pages of it between glass plates and change them from time to time. Then one would see what it is. – People know only the causal story…This book is nothing of the kind.[603]

'This book is nothing of the kind', and one reason has to do with Musil's use of metaphor and simile, in particular his preference for the latter over the former. Why should simile be more adequate to his purposes than metaphor?

We may suggest, tentatively, one reason. In *Paradigms for a Metaphorology* Blumenberg makes a distinction between relative and absolute metaphor. Relative metaphors are devices or images that we resort to as aids to an investigation whose end result might be expressed in concepts; absolute metaphors are a response to the most basic and yet most unanswerable, ineffable questions of human existence. An example of the first would be 'society is a network' or 'social life is a drama', in which the social scientist tries to find an image in which to distil an idea about social relations, social relations that may be thought about through the conceptual language that is 'proper' to social science. This can lead to some dead ends or traps, however, by virtue of the fact that metaphor takes the form 'A is B', subject and predicate. The identity that is asserted then closes off some imaginative possibilities while opening others.

---

601 Musil, 'The Perfecting of a Love', in *Tonka and Other Stories* (London: Picador, 1965), p. 13
602 Musil, 'The Temptation of Veronica', in *Tonka and Other Stories* (London: Picador, 1965), p. 73.
603 Quoted in Luft, *Crisis*, p. 88

Blumenberg contrasts these relative metaphors, tools that become fetishes, with absolute metaphors, metaphors that seek answers to 'unanswerable' questions, such as 'what is the world?'[604] Many of Blumenberg's books are about the exemplary images through which human beings have sought to convey their relationship to this question, images that have persisted as iconic constants across epochal divides, not as unalterable Jungian archetypes but as objects of continual reinterpretation and variation: the laughter of the maid as Thales of Miletus falls into the well; Prometheus chained to the rock in the Caucasus; Faust; the idea that nature is a book that might be read; the situation of the spectator who, on firm ground, gazes out at a shipwreck, Plato's cave.. Absolute metaphors resist any sort of conceptualisation because they are deployed by human beings as responses to the most unanswerable but at the same time most basic questions of human existence. Blumenberg finds absolute metaphors significant because they survive precisely by being open to a variation that is endless; the task of reinterpreting them never ceases, they do not become the object of dogmatic veneration. They help human beings create a distance towards the world but also symbolise the human being's creativity in doing so.

In 1873, in 'On Truth and Lies in a Nonmoral Sense', Nietzsche had been less sanguine, warning of the dangers of the use of metaphors as such. In a famous passage, he writes that truth is a 'movable host of metaphors, metonymies, and anthropomorphisms: in short, a sum of human relations which have been poetically and rhetorically intensified, transferred, and embellished, and which, after long usage, seem to a people to be fixed, canonical, and binding. Truths are illusions which we have forgotten are illusions.'[605] Of concepts he writes:

> A word becomes a concept insofar as it simultaneously has to fit countless more or less similar cases—which means, purely and simply, cases which are never equal and thus altogether unequal. Every concept arises from the equation of unequal things.[606]

Nietzsche is not against metaphors; on the contrary, our invention of metaphors is an indication of our artistic creativity. However, his point is that we should not forget that it is we who invent concepts (and metaphors) for ease of communication, and that this very ease of communication can be a barrier to cognition as well as an aid to it.

---

604 Hans Blumenberg, *Paradigms for a Metaphorology*, trans. Robert Savage (New York: Signale, 2010). On the distinction between relative and absolute metaphors see also Charles Turner, *Investigating Sociological Theory* (London: Sage, 2010), pp. 79-111.
605 Nietzsche, 'On Truth and Lies…', p. 117
606 Friedrich Nietzsche, 'On Truth and Lies in a Non-moral Sense', in *The Nietzsche Reader* (Oxford: Blackwell, 2006), p. 117.

One way of understanding Musil is to realise how hesitant he is about the use of metaphor and how often he deploys simile, whose form is the much 'weaker', less assertive 'A is like B'. In doing this it may be that Musil wanted to show, rather than say, that is fix, the ineffability of the transformation that his protagonists experience. Luft reports that in *The Perfecting of a Love*, a story of around 50 pages, Musil employs the comparative constructions 'like', and 'as if' (*wie, wie wenn, als ob*) 337 times, that he also cancels adjectives and adverbs with *–un* or *los* 224 times, and negates a whole sentences or phrase 208 times.[607] Luft writes: 'Nearly every line of his novella is negated or relativised in some way, in order to describe emotions by analogy and simile as "not-this but like that, which would be as if."'[608] No adjective, no adverb, or simply no word seems wholly suitable to convey what has to be conveyed. This insistence on what cannot be said adequately but must be said somehow is partly what accounts for the exhausting quality of Musil's novellas, the most intense pieces he wrote. The sense of tension, sometimes nervous tension, in Musil's writing arises from the way he seems to hold together, or rather steer a course between, Wittgenstein's view that what is most important cannot be said, and the idea that the most important things can be said via absolute metaphor.[609]

He makes this point helpfully explicit at the very beginning of *Young Törless* through an excerpt from Maeterlinck:

> In some strange way we devalue things as soon as we give utterance to them. We believe we have dived to the uttermost depths of the abyss, and yet when we return to the surface the drop of water on our pallid fingertips no longer resembles the sea from which it came. We think we have discovered a hoard of wonderful treasure-trove, yet when we emerge again into the light of day we see that all that we have brought back with us is false stones and chips of glass. But for all this, the treasure goes on glimmering in the darkness, unchanged.

Musil the writer did not choose silence, rather, his task was to invent the inner person, to explore the ineffable characteristics of ethical experience along with the ethical and aesthetical link between the two conditions through his world of similes, functions, and unfixed values. His novellas and stories do not allow the reader to pause at one word or sentence: the images move constantly. Yet they cannot be skated over either.

---

607 Luft, *Crisis*, p. 93
608 Luft, *Crisis*, p. 93
609 A comparison with Kafka suggests itself though it cannot be explored here: Musil reworks and multiplies adjectives, while Kafka abandons the use of them. But as Luft suggests, the results achieved by both writers are not so different, in that Musil's multiplication of them is pushed so far as to amount to a suspension.

Musil does not resolve or attempt to resolve the problem of reality, a task that would be in vain. Musil may not be the only one who emphasises this but few have been as true to the idea. In the following chapters we turn to another author, Oğuz Atay, who may be considered a candidate for such a title.

Oğuz Atay's *The Disconnected*, like *The Man without Qualities* and *Törless*, focuses on/problematises the theme of the dissolution of the subject; correspondingly, it is a book about language in its confrontation with the ineffable. Written in 1968 and published in 1971, *The Disconnected* can be regarded as an avant-garde novel that breaks with the realism that was approved by the majority of Turkish critics and authors at that time. The main way in which it achieves this break is that, instead of seeking to enlighten and inform, or even to entertain, people, it handles the inner conflicts of individuals. *The Disconnected* has been described as a novel 'which has turned its back on the realism of the 19th century, with one foot in modernism and the other in post-modernism.'[610] It was stated that '…Atay broke the literary taboos of the 1970s cultural milieu in Turkey, shattered the narrow frames of discussion about the uses of art, and allowed the Turkish language to find the possibilities of expressing the distress of modern existence.'[611]

As in *The Man without Qualities*, the novel deals with the inner states and conflicts of the main characters, and it is difficult to outline its 'external' narrative. There is little 'action'. Like Musil, Atay implies a critique of the modern constitution of the 'self' and the social order of his time. Like Musil, he was a close reader of Nietzsche. But he was a keen reader of Musil as well.[612] On the other hand, if it is correct to say the novel has one foot in modernism and another in postmodernism, then this marks a difference between it and Musil's novel, which, as I said before, has one foot in realism and one in modernism.[613] I said earlier that some of the action and characters in *The Man without Qualities* could have come from a nineteenth century realist novel, albeit that Musil is a modernist concerned with the thought processes of some of the characters and with the mode of the novel's presentation. Because it is devoted to the internal states of people, Atay's

---

610 Berna Moran, *Türk Romanına Eleştirel Bir Bakış* (İstanbul: İletişim Yayınları, 1992), p. 199.
611 Suna Ertuğrul, 'Belated Modernity and Modernity as Belatedness in *Tutunamayanlar*', *The South AtlanticQuarterly,* 102 (2/3), (Spring/Summer 2003), p. 629.
612 Yıldız Ecevit, "*Ben Buradayım…" Oğuz Atay'ın Biyografik ve Kurmaca Dünyası* (Istanbul: Iletisim Yayınları, 2005), p. 175.
613 These distinctions between realism, modernism and postmodernism are never very stable and are only used here as a convenient way of pointing to what is important in the novels.

The Disconnected too might be said to be a modernist novel; but it also contains postmodern elements, in particular in its handling of time, which is sometimes linear and sometimes cyclical, and the fact that Atay's own narrative voice is far less evident, less 'sovereign', than Musil's.

Chapter VII: Atay on History and Authority

VII.i. Introduction

Oğuz Atay (1934-1977) was born in Inebolu, a small town in the Black Sea region of Turkey. His father was a judge and his mother a schoolteacher. He attended school in Ankara until 1951, after which he enrolled at Istanbul Technical University, graduating as a civil engineer in 1957. Shortly after graduation Atay he started an enterprise as a building contractor, which rapidly failed. In 1960 he joined the staff of the Istanbul Academy of Engineering and Architecture, where he taught for many years until diagnosed with a brain tumour in 1976. He went to London for treatment, but never recovered and died in 1977.

Atay's first novel, *The Disconnected* (*Tutunamayanlar*), appeared in 1971-72 in two volumes. It was never reprinted in his lifetime, but a new edition came out in 1984, seven years after he died. A UNESCO survey described it as 'probably the most eminent novel of twentieth-century Turkish literature': 'a work that won high critical acclaim and popular following, *Tutunamayanlar* offers an endless series of tragicomic observations, an expansive and critical panorama of Turkish manners, attitudes and clichés through a profound sense of irony, parody, dark humour and existential questioning.'[614] *The Disconnected* was awarded the prize of the Turkish State Radio and Television Institution, TRT in 1970, before it had been published.

Atay's first publication was not a novel but a 1970 textbook on surveying, *Topography*, submitted in application for promotion to an associate professorship. In 1973, soon after the release of the second volume of *Tutunamayanlar/The Disconnected*, his second novel, *Tehlikeli Oyunlar* (Dangerous Games) appeared; this was followed by a biographical novel: *Bir Bilim Adamının Romanı: Mustafa İnan* (The life of a Scientist: Mustafa İnan) in 1975. In the same year his short stories, *Korkuyu Beklerken* (Waiting for Fear) were published, then his last book, a play called *Oyunlarla Yaşayanlar* (Those who live by Games). His unfinished fiction *Eylembilim* (The Science of Action) was edited and published by his friends. What he had hoped would be his *magnum opus*, *Türkiye'nin Ruhu* (The Spirit of Turkey), also remained unfinished, a series of notes and diary entries.

---

614 http://portal.unesco.org/culture/en/ev.php-URLID=19184&URLDO=DO-TOPIC&URL SECTION=201.html

None of Atay's books was widely read in his life time: 'I am here, my reader, where are you?', he once noted in his diary. On its first publication *The Disconnected* was received with silence, despite its critical descriptions of Turkey in the 1970s – whose roots Atay traces back to the foundation of the Turkish Republic in 1923 – and its problematisation of Turkish modernisation. It seems that, not unlike *The Man Without Qualities*, *The Disconnected's* radical form and style acted as a barrier to the reception of its substantive content. However the reception of the second edition of *The Disconnected* (1984) was totally different from that of the first (1971): it was praised by many leading literary figures of the time, even by those who were very critical of the novel when it was first released.

The biography of Atay shows a similarity to that of Musil. Like Musil he was trained as a civil engineer and then became an academic. He was a keen reader of Nietzsche, but also of Musil himself.[615] Unlike Musil he did not witness the decline and fall of an Empire which had been a major power for centuries; however, he lived in an era in which the effect of the sudden transition from the Ottoman Empire to the modern Turkish State was still palpable.

The Disconnected begins with the main protagonist Turgut receiving the news that his friend Selim has committed suicide and left a letter for him. Selim's death, and his letter, are not only personally distressing, but shatter Turgut's sense of the order of things. In fact, while holding the letter in his hand, Turgut is not only saddened, but also accuses Selim of being weak, of escaping from a life he could not bear; he also questions his own situation and daily life. He begins to direct his anger towards the objects in the room in which he is sitting; these objects become simply indicators of the order of a life that has become meaningless.[616]

---

615 Yıldız Ecevit, *"Ben Buradayim..." Oğuz Atay'ın Biyografik ve Kurmaca Dünyası* (İstanbul: İletişim Yayınları, 2005), p. 175.

616 This technique of problematising social relations by problematising the relations between people and objects is also found in Musil, who sometimes describes objects as not fitting into their proper place or even the walls of rooms expanding and contracting. We encounter the overdescription or absurd description of objects in Alain Robbe-Grillet and Graham Greene as well, though for different reasons. If Greene uses objects to indicate the workings of psyches, Robbe-Grillet attempts to present objects that do not have any function in narration at all. See Richard Creese, 'Objects in Novels and the Fringe of Culture: Graham Greene and Alain Robbe-Grillet,' *Comparative Literature*, Vol. 39, No. 1 (Winter, 1987), pp. 58-73; Roland Barthes, 'Objective Literature', in *Critical Essays*, trans. Richard Howard (Evanston: North-western University Press, 1972).

At first, he does try to continue with his life as it was before Selim's suicide, but the shattering event makes this increasingly difficult, and he begins to question not only the objects that surround him as indicators of 'bourgeois' life, but the actual social relationships in which he is involved, including those with his wife and children. One day, he decides to visit the flat of his dead friend; there he discovers a large number of manuscripts – diaries, plays, short stories, long stories – and begins to read them. This is the start of a journey that takes him away from his existing life in society and into the internal life of Selim. This internal life, however, is not that of Selim alone; the manuscripts in which this internal life is represented contain numerous other people, both real people who Selim knew but Turgut did not, those who both Turgut and Selim knew at university, and characters from fiction and history, including Jesus, Don Quixote, Hamlet, Dostoyevsky and Oblomov. It is clear to Turgut that Selim thinks of these fictional or historical characters as just as much friends and acquaintances as his real ones. Turgut reads these manuscripts throughout the novel, and increasingly identifies with Selim, even visiting some of the friends and acquaintances mentioned in the various manuscripts. In a way, the novel is the story of how Turgut becomes disconnected, not by detaching himself from society and withdrawing into himself, but by becoming Selim.

Here there is an interesting parallel with *The Man without Qualities*. Ulrich's search for 'the other condition' begins as a series of internal monologues that take place while he is meeting other people and participating in the meaningless Parallel Campaign. It takes some time before he realises that 'the other condition' depends on a kind of relationship with another person, his sister Agathe. Ulrich and Agathe seem to 'merge' with one another as a man and a woman who resemble one another; Turgut may be said to merge with Selim, although he does so by absorbing himself in Selim's writings. Throughout the novel the reader follows Turgut's becoming disconnected, how he learns to be in a position of lack and imitation by following the traces of Selim. Here again, then, 'the dissolution of the subject' is an important theme, though one with different ramifications.

We said earlier that as vulnerable creatures human beings seek mechanisms with which to put some distance between themselves and the external world (Blumenberg). Both Nietzsche and Musil experiment with the idea of a defenceless self, though applying different strategies (Participatory self and Transcendental self) which lead to different consequences. In Atay's writings we will see that both Nietzsche's idea of the Participatory self, the self joining the stream of Reality, becoming one with fate, and Musil's notion of the self – the self understood as an existence of possibilities or of plasticity – are problematised. What if, he suggests, this state of becoming-child in a larva period (Musil) brings about a detachment or a state of being *disconnectus erectus* rather than freedom? If Nietzsche is right in saying that what we call the subject is nothing other than the product of conceptual discourses of psychology, philology, and epistemology, what does the person who rejects these discourses and manages to get himself free of layers of identity encounter? Why doesn't the dissolution of the subject also lead to the dissolution of language, and to a state of ineffability, stammering and stuttering?

As a basis for addressing these questions, this chapter is arranged in the following way: the next section (VII.ii) summarises Atay's critique of the 'official' history of Turkey; I then (VII.iii) discuss Atay's critique of language in general and of the language reformation in Turkey,[617] and his critique of authority and bureaucracy (VII.iv); finally, I make a first approach to the relationship between language and the subject (VII.v), a theme that will be pursued in more detail in chapter VIII.

VII.ii. History: 'Yesterday, Today, Tomorrow'

One of the central themes in the novel is the question of history. Atay's questioning of history or of the official history of Turkey reaches its peak point in a mock-autobiographical text called 'Yesterday, Today, Tomorrow', written by Selim and found by Turgut after Selim's death. In this 130 page text Selim applies different speech genres such as songs, plays, encyclopaedic articles, academic analyses etc. Selim parodies official Turkish history through a parody of his own personal history and vice versa.

> The urge to create a consistent philosophy of history resulted in the deliberate concealment of numerous facts. It could not have been otherwise, something had to be done. Nobody had the right of detaching Selim from his past and future. Somebody had to pay the price, and somebody would. Yesterday, today and tomorrow were his, and had to become one and the same with his life [...] This is what the song derives its name from. What exactly had happened yesterday? One had to dig into the past and look for yesterday, because it was the sole ground upon which today and tomorrow rest. This is what Selim did, because only then could he walk around naked in his second coming – as he says in line 237.[618]

---

617 This took place on November 1, 1928, and was carried out by the Language Commission on the initiative of Kemal Atatürk, founder of the Turkish republic. *Ata* means father and ancestor in Turkish. *Ata+türk* means 'The Father of Turks.' In accordance with the new surname law, Turkish Grand National Assembly granted Mustafa Kemal the surname Atatürk on 24 November 1934.

618 Quoted in Gürle, *Oğuz Atay's Dialogue*, p. 49

Here, in a passage in which one of the central characters – who is dead – writes about himself in the third person, Atay problematises the concept of history; in other passages, as we shall see, he problematises the process of the foundation of Turkish republic as an ideal state, a state which based its ideological discourses on a rejection of the past – that of the Ottoman Empire – and which took the West – or a version of the West – as its model. Of course, it is more complicated than this, and here I shall not give a detailed political account of the early republican period and its relationship with the European west; yet I shall follow Atay's lines, who while problematising these issues does not appear to take sides. We saw that Kundera strongly opposes the idea that his novels are political, suggesting that if they are it is only by virtue of their being unpolitical. Atay's position is similar.

'Yesterday, Today, Tomorrow' problematises the official history of Turkey, a history which seeks to forget a past which, however, and unavoidably so, appears and reappears like a phantom: in language, in manners, in politics, in short, in every social realm. Selim, by revisiting and reinterpreting his own personal history, in other words, by digging into the past in order to see what happened yesterday with eyes freed from social roles and ideology, and making use of a variety of genres, believes that he can also reveal what was obscured in the official historical record, in the version of history that is transmitted to us and becomes part of our personal lives.[619] In other words, Selim suggests a productive interpretation of history, but an interpretation which requires before anything honesty: 'History is nothing but a misrepresentation. History is a dream that stretches from the past into the future, and that we are having today. Like all dreams it can be interpreted, but not while you are living it.'[620]

It has been suggested that the provisions of the republican revolution incorporated the idea of progress as a constitutional principle.[621] The doctrine of progress was employed by the Kemalist regime (referring to Mustafa Kemal Atatürk – the founder of Turkish Republic) which, roughly speaking, equated modernity with Westernization. Turkish modernisation has been described as 'grounded in the bourgeois idea of modernity, which is characterised by a doctrine of progress based on the cult of reason, an ideal of freedom defined within the framework

---

619 By the official history I mean the general knowledge about the history of modern Turkey. This knowledge is mostly based on the textbooks that are introduced by the Education Ministry and that Turkish students read at school.
620 Quoted in Gürle, *Oğuz Atay's Dialogue*, p. 51
621 Camilla Nereid, 'Kemalism On the Catwalk: The Turkish Hat Law of 1925,' *Journal of Social History*, Spring, 2011, pp. 708-728.

of an abstract humanism, an orientation towards pragmatism.'[622] The republican revolution aimed to diminish the conventional and/or religious practices and regulations applied by the Ottoman Empire. The adoption of the Swiss Civil Code, the Italian Penal Code, the Gregorian calendar, the Latin alphabet, and Sunday as the weekly holiday are all examples of this sudden but at the same time belated reformation. The passage of the Hat Law which banned the fez can be seen as the absurd extension of this logic.[623]

The idea of progress, which can be linked to the Enlightenment even though it is an older idea, is based on the idea that the development of science and reason will result in an improvement in social, economical and political life. In *Meaning in History*, Löwith focuses on the philosophers of history from Voltaire, Turgot, and Condorcet to Hegel, Marx, and Comte; all of them subscribe to an idea of progress in which different periods are to be understood as necessary stages. As opposed to the Greek and Roman mythologies according to which history shows a repetitive, periodic pattern, moving within a circle as a result of which the past is regarded as an everlasting foundation, for the advocates of the idea of progress, Löwith argues, the past is related to the future as a promise and a preparation.[624]

---

622 Gürle, *Oğuz Atay's Dialogue*, p. 1.
623 Nereid, 'Kemalism,' p. 708. In the early years of the republic it was the fez which was perceived as the symbol of conservatism. In fact in 1829 it had been the fez that replaced the 'traditional' turban. See Reşat Kasaba, 'Kemalist Certainties and Modern Ambiguities,' in *Rethinking Modernity and National Identity in Turkey*, ed. Sibel Bozdoğan and Reşat Kasaba (Seattle: University of Washington Press, 1997), pp. 24-25.
624 Karl Löwith, *Meaning in History* (Chicago; London: The University of Chicago Press, 1949), p. 6. Löwith is as skeptical about these ideas of progress as many other twentieth century thinkers are; but he is also skeptical about 'the possibility of interpreting their ideas as naïve projections of contemporary scientific and technical progress, economic growth and "bourgeois-democratic" revolutions onto the screen of the history of the human race as a whole.' Instead he thinks that modern philosophies of history are nothing but the secularization of the eschatological pattern that Christianity and Judaism introduced. See Robert M. Wallace, introduction in *The Legitimacy of the Modern Age* by Hans Blumenberg (Cambridge; Massachusetts; London: MIT Press, 1983), p. xv. On the idea of progress see also John B. Bury, *The Idea of Progress: an Inquiry into its Origin and Growth* (London: Macmillan, 1920); Robert Nisbet, *The The History of the Idea of Progress* (New York: Basic Books, 1980); Henryk Skolimowski, 'The Scientific World View and the Illusions of Progress', *Social Research*, 41:1 (1974:Spring) pp. 52-82; Hans Blumenberg, 'On a Lineage of the Idea of Progress,' *Social Research*, 41:1 (1974:Spring) pp. 5-27.

'Progress' for the Kemalist regime, however, meant a break – political, social, cultural – with the past. This idea of progress seems to be quite different from that of the one that Löwith attributes to Marx and Hegel. However, I still use the word 'progress' because even though the Kemalist regime aims to start from a 'zero-time' the idea of advancement in science, technology, and the quality of human life, is fundamental to this understanding. Consider this passage from Kemal Atatürk's speech in 1925 in which he addressed the question of dress for the first time:

> ... But I say to you, as your twin brother, your friend and father, when the Turkish people say that they are civilized, they are obliged to prove and display that they actually are civilized in their opinions and mentality. The one who claims to be civilized must show it in his family life and his lifestyle. Briefly, the one who claims to be civilized is obliged to manifest that he actually is so, even in his outward appearance, from top to toe. I want to make my last words completely clear and understood by the whole world. Therefore I ask: Is our attire national attire? Is our attire civilized and international? Is there any sense in smearing a valuable ore with mud and then showing it off to the world? If someone does not understand that inside the mud there is something hidden that is very precious, does that serve him? To be able to exhibit the ore, the mud must be removed. To protect something valuable [the ore] must not the protection itself be constructed of valuable materials?[625]

'True civilisation' is equated with 'western' and true Turkishness with being civilised, from which it follows that the civilised Turk dresses in a civilised manner.[626] But this civilisation – True Turkishness – has been covered by mud and it should and must be cleansed so that it can be revealed in every realm of social life: 'Through this new interpretation of history, Kemal invites his audience to adopt the new "we," a pre-Ottoman "we" that has been "buried under mud" during the Ottoman era, but that is now allowed to blossom again.'[627] In other words, the period of the Ottoman Empire was not a necessary and a contributing stage for the modern Turkish Republic. The ore must be revealed but then very quickly we should turn our faces to the future:[628]

---

625 Quoted in Nereid, 'Kemalism,' p. 712
626 This attitude also reminds us of post-revolutionary Russia where the peasants were the 80% of the population in 1917. See Richard Pipes, *Russia under the Old Regime* (London: Penguin, 1995); *Russia under the Bolshevik Regime* 1919-1924 (London: Harvill, 1997). See also Oleg Kharkhordin, *The Collective and the Individual in Russia: a study of practices* (California, University of California Press, 1999).
627 Nereid, 'Kemalism', p. 713
628 One doubts whether Ataturk read Walter Benjamin, but the idea of extracting an 'ore' reminds one of Benjamin's 'Theses on the Philosophy of History'. There, Benjamin

...Gentlemen, for centuries the Turkish people *[millet]* have suffered bitter experiences and memories, the people's destiny must no longer be attached to ideas belonging to the seventh and eighth centuries. The only valid aspect of its destiny is the future *[istikbal]*, the future alone. Civilization *[medeniyet]* and nothing but civilization.[629]

In Robert Nisbet's words, the idea of progress is the idea that 'mankind has slowly, gradually, and continuously advanced from an original condition of cultural deprivation, ignorance, and insecurity to constantly higher levels of civilisation, and that such advancement will, with only occasional setbacks, continue through present into the future.'[630] However, in the Turkish case it is a future which requires a total forgetting and unlearning – the Ottoman Empire was an 'occasional setback'; it must be quickly forgotten in order to create a future cut off from the past. In this respect there were of course similarities to the French Revolution, although, as Rudolph Vierhaus reminds us, at the level of political institutions at least, that cutting off of the past only gave rise to a series of reactions, so that 'progress' was a protracted and often unstable struggle.

> the Revolution which in France was followed by the military dictatorship of Napoleon and the restoration of the monarchy, bequeathed not only the idea of a better political system and a more just social order but also the counterexperience of *dérapage* once it attempted to accelerate progress in a revolutionary manner.[631]

---

attributes the faith in the idea of progress to historicism. Historicism, he says 'contents itself with establishing a causal connection between various moments in history' (Theses A). Historicism 'gives the "eternal" Image of the past' (Thesis XVI). Its method is additive, that is to say, it 'musters a mass of data to fill the homogenous, empty time' (Thesis XVII). In opposed to all this, the historical materialist sees history not only as the flow of thoughts but their arrest as well (Thesis XVII). The historical materialist strives to establish a messianic relation with the past. In other words, the historical materialist 'establishes a conception of the present as the "time of the now" *[Jetztzeit]* in which the present and past are drawn into a messianic relation (Thesis A). Where the historicist perceives a 'chain of events,' the historical materialist sees a past in need of salvation (Thesis IX). Above all, the fundamental difference between the materialist historiography and historicism is that the latter is based on the idea of progress (Theses VIII-XIII). Walter Benjamin, 'Theses on the Philosophy of History,' in *Illuminations* (London: Fontana, 1992).

629 Quoted in Nereid, 'Kemalism', p. 715
630 Robert Nisbet, *History of the Idea of Progress* (New York: Basic Books, 1980), p. 10.
631 Rudolph Vierhaus, 'Progress: Ideas, Skepticism, and Critique –The Heritage of the Enlightenment', in *What is Enlightenment?: Eighteenth-Century Answers and Twentieth-Century Questions,* ed. James Schmidt (London: University of California, 1996), p. 332.

An adequate comparison between the French Revolution and the Revolution in Turkey is beyond the scope of this book. However, the ideals of the revolution in Turkey, in a way, adopted an understanding of the past that was inspired by the French Revolution: a new beginning full of promises. The French hearkened to what Lynn Hunt calls a 'mythic present', that is to say, 'the instant of creation of the new community, the moment of the new consensus.'[632] Hunt contrasts this understanding of 'newness' with that of the new community of American radicals, which was an outgrowth of a living tradition: the Americans inhabited a new world geographically, but drew upon an existing tradition to identify the corruption of English politics.[633]

There are two crucial differences between the French and the Turkish cases: in the Turkish case, there was no counter-revolutionary or legitimist restoration of the Ottoman Sultanate; and Turkey lacked the intellectual continuities that in France nevertheless persisted across the initial break in political institutions.

The reforms in Turkey, such as the abolition of the Sultanate and the Caliphate, the proclamation of the Turkish republic, and the unification of the education system and abolition of the religious schools, had to be realised very quickly.[634] People had to adapt themselves to these reforms very quickly as well, a rapid and a 'belated' modernisation. Part of the interest of Atay's writing is the way it seeks to show how this task proved too much for the Turkish people; rapid modernisation, rather than bringing about rational or enlightened thought, produced a number of impressive external achievements, but at the psychic level produced a 'nation of children', who despite their superficial capacity for adaptation to new circumstances continue to believe in non-rational phenomena such as miracles:

> ...we remain a nation of children and we still seriously interpret events, the world in terms of miracles, 'myths.' So deadly seriously that a wise Westerner would respond by laughing...we are so unfinished that our drama and our tragedy are incomprehensible. Moreover we are unaware of the fact that we are in a tragedy. We think our life is beautiful.[635]

The tragedy that we are living in is partly because of the problematical, even traumatic relationship with the past. Recall here Nietzsche's 'On the Uses and Disadvantages of History for Life'. At the beginning of the essay he writes: 'We need it, [history] that is to say, for the sake of life and action, not so as to turn

---

632 Lynn Hunt, 'The Rhetoric of Revolution in France', *History Workshop*, No. 15 (Spring, 1983), p. 82.
633 Hunt, 'The Rhetoric of Revolution', pp. 81-82.
634 Nereid, 'Kemalism', p. 712
635 Oğuz Atay, *Günlük* (Diaries) (İstanbul: İletişim, 1992), p. 26.

comfortably away from life and action.....We want to serve history only to the extent that history serves life...'[636] As we have seen, instead of focusing on past events, Nietzsche proposes an interpretation of history which will redeem the past in order to be open to the future; this requires us to be partially 'unhistorical', when necessary to partially forget. However, Nietzsche also says 'When the past speaks it always speaks as an oracle: only if you are an architect of the future and know the present will you understand it.'[637] Every nation requires a certain kind of knowledge of the past, but this knowledge is worthwhile only as long as it is in the service of life. But we should be careful here: Nietzsche is not suggesting a total forgetting or covering over of the past; his genealogical method is concerned with that 'which can be documented, which can actually be confirmed and has actually existed, in short, the whole, long, hard-to-decipher hieroglyphic script of man's moral past!'[638] It is a method which seeks for the various reasons of an event and relations of power rather than focusing on a cause-effect formula. Nietzsche introduces the concept of 'force' which is the basic element in the dynamics of any process. In every event there are successions of forces, which coexist and struggle. The existence of a force depends on the features of other forces with which it struggles. Nietzsche's theory of forces provides us with a framework for uncovering the constitution of a thing within its own historical process. His genealogical analysis of the constitution of something does not mean that we should simply go back to a natural, fixed origin and trace the line of descent. Instead, 'his emphasis is on fundamental transformations, on disruptions, and on psychological innovations and moral inventions that emerge in specific material and cultural context.'[639] Nietzsche's lesson is clear: if we cover up things that we don't want to face our present itself becomes full of apparitions. As Otto Rank once said, the need 'to detach ourselves from our past while we are still living on its spiritual value creates all the human problems and social difficulties which the humanistic cannot solve.'[640] Atay, too, while planning the themes of his unwritten book *Türkiye'nin Ruhu* (The Spirit of Turkey) may be said to adopt the attitude of a genealogist:

> The development of the theme will start with a systematic investigation. The documents to be analysed will be classified for the same approaches. In this

---

636 Nietzsche, *UM* II, p. 59
637 Nietzsche, *UM* II, p. 94
638 Nietzsche, *GM*, preface 7, p. 8.
639 Kieth Ansell-Pearson, Introduction, in *On the Genealogy of Morality*, p. xx.
640 Otto Rank, 'The Double as Immortal Self', in *Beyond Psychology* (New York: Diver Publications, 1941), p. 63.

way, even the same document will be handled several times from different angles and each time a different side of it will be noted...It is like making cross-references between different entries of an encyclopaedia – because a theme cannot be separated from another with a clear line.[641]

And a couple of pages later Atay writes:

> While important historical events are approaching, the individuals and peoples who have influence in shaping these events continue to develop by travelling in different directions. In other words, the spirit of a people does not disappear with that people; as in a relay race ideas and sensibilities are transferred from one generation to another: it is a kind of collective consciousness. If it was possible to trace back our contemporary human being with all its richness, it would be possible to find its root in the past. During this process success may pass through many hands. For instance, it might be possible that some individuals or peoples who are harmed by a revolution can later on develop and obtain sovereign power at some future turning point...Today our country has been impoverished and has lost its power. However, despite all this if it is still standing, the positive reasons for this should be the consequence of positive past behaviour. Of course, here one should avoid the exaggerated one-sided interpretations. Yet again in investigating the real links with the past, it is equally dangerous to consider the past as a chain of negative events and intentions. [642]

Atay's genealogical attitude is quite different from that of the idea of starting from a new beginning, a task to which foundation myths are crucial. We saw that Blumenberg sees myths as a compensation mechanism that reduce the anxiety of the helpless ego and transforms it into a more bearable fear. However, it should be noted that the myths that interest Blumenberg are those that transcend nations: Prometheus chained to the rock, Faust, Plato's cave, not narrowly national myths, then, but ones that are 'not only a "model of" but also a "model for" reality' as a result of which are 'laden with authority in a given society.'[643]

Atatürk's *Nutuk* [The Speech] which was delivered over six days for a duration thirty-six hours and thirty-one minutes, and which 'described the heroic accounts of the Independence Struggle of Turkey against the Allies (1919-1922), particularly the military leadership of Mustafa Kemal [Atatürk] during the struggle'[644]

---

641 Atay, *Günlük*, p. 238
642 Atay, *Günlük*, p. 241-42
643 Hülya Adak, 'National Myths and Self Narrations: Mustafa Kemal's *Nutuk* and Halide Edib's *Memoirs* and *Turkish Ordeal*', *The South Atlantic Quarterly*, 102:2/3, Spring/Summer 2003, Duke University, p. 513.
644 Adak, 'National Myths', p. 513

mythicises the Turkish Independence War.[645] Comparing Atatürk's *Nutuk* to that of an eighteenth century *Bildungsroman* according to which 'human reality is seen to be profoundly historical'[646] and history is associated with a story of progress, Adak emphasises that *Nutuk* also presents a linear and progressive accounts of historical events, however, the events begin in May 19, 1919, the day Kemal Atatürk went to the Anatolian soil, Samsun, to start his national cause.[647] This date is the beginning of the rebirth of the Turkish Nation. This myth of rebirth is based on a narrative of discontinuity which distances the new Turkish Nation from the Ottoman Empire on many levels.[648]

Modern Turkish history then starts with the Independence War. As Reşat Kasaba observes 'the core policy makers and ideologues who gathered around Kemal Atatürk after the purges of 1925' were convinced that 'anything that was newly attained, acquired, adopted, or built was naturally desirable and superior to everything that was inherited from the past and hence "old."'[649] Consider this passage from Atay's last novel, which depicts the 'Alphabet Reform' as a battle between the old and the new:

> Every day everything was changing. First the alphabet changed, a totally new script appeared. Of course, the old script did not disappear at once. The old and the new, in every case, were living together; the opposite opinions were trying to destroy each other. The intellectuals were reading the books which were published in the new script and noting down their opinions in the old script. Then the words changed.

---

645 George Schöpflin defines myth as: 'a particular set of ideas with a moral content told as a narrative by a community about itself. In this sense, myth may or may not be perceived as related to historical experience, although those who rely on the narrative generally believe that it is. At most myth is a way of organising the past in such a way as to make sense of it for that particular community.' George Schöpflin, *The Dilemmas of Identity* (Tallinn: TLU Press, 2010), p. 73. On myth and nationalism see also Bruce Lincoln, *Discourse and the Construction of society: Comparative Studies of Myth, Rituals, and Classification* (New York: Oxford University Press, 1989); George Schöpflin, 'The Functions of Myth and Taxonomy of Myths', in *Myths and Nationhood,* ed. Geoffrey Hosking and George Schöpflin (New York: Routledge, 1997).
646 Adak, 'National Myths', p. 515
647 Adak, 'National Myths', pp. 515-516. Adak claims that the narrative of the self, namely Ataturk, in *Nutuk* differs from the one in the *Bildungsroman* by being cyclical and repetitive. The self of *Nutuk* is a prophetlike figure, in other words, he has a knowledge of future events. He knows how the war will end and how the 'self' will establish the Turkish Republic.
648 Adak, 'National Myths', p. 516
649 Reşat Kasaba, 'Kemalist Certainties and Modern Ambiguities', pp. 15-16

Every day hundreds of words were coined, hundreds of words that had been coined one day before were deleted. Meanwhile, the old words were wounded as well, were abolished. Both sides were suffering damage...It was difficult...to say that..this war would end with success like the Turkish Independence War...Is it necessary to fight on so many fronts? Does the enemy have that many front lines? Or was a war too declared against some friends who were taken as enemies?[650]

Even though Atay problematises this attitude and the official history record of Turkey it does not follow from this that he was anti-reformist or anti-Kemalist or Kemalist or anti-Ottoman or pro-Ottoman. In fact, the author of *Bir Bilim Adamının Romanı* (The life of a Scientist: Mustafa İnan), Atay's last novel, cannot dismiss or ignore the promises of Kemalism in the early Republic period, even though now, in the 1970s, all these promises had become little more than mottos or slogans that had to be repeated at national festivals.[651] Atay's novels transcend all these anti's or pro's by questioning every position from every side. For instance the writer of *The Disconnected* is rather suspicious about the promises of enlightened tomorrows, not because he does not appreciate the promises of modernity with its values like freedom, democracy and the praise of science, but because of the manner in which these values have been adopted by a society which 'belatedly modernized' and has come to accept its insufficiency before a modern one presuming to be superior, and by a culture that has adopted an infantile role when confronted by foreign modern ideals.'[652] At one point in *Bir Bilim Adamının Romanı* the question of why Turkey did not produce a figure like Gauss in the 1930s is answered as following:

> Tradition and especially what is called 'system' were forgotten. It was forgotten that there was such a thing as the unsystematicness of the East. It was forgotten how to reconcile the tradition of the East with the tradition of science...It was assumed that by bringing Gauss' German fellow citizens to the country many Gausses would flower.[653]

It is a system of thought which is torn between finding its authentic identity (the ore) and imitating the superior West, a recurring theme in the novel. Selim's

---

650 Oğuz Atay, *Bir Bilim Adamının Romanı: Mustafa İnan* (İstanbul: İletişim, 2007), pp. 74-75.
651 See also Nurdan Gürbilek, 'Kemalizmin Delisi Oğuz Atay', in *Oğuz Atay'a Armağan*, ed. Handan İnci (İstanbul: İletişim, 2008).
652 Nurdan Gürbilek, 'Dandies and Originals: Authenticity, Belatedness and Turkish Novel', *The South Atlantic Quarterly*, Volume 102, Number 2/3, Spring/Summer, 2003, Duke University Press, pp. 599-600.
653 Atay, *Bilim Adamının Romanı*, pp. 68-69. Johann Carl Friedrich Gauss (1777-1855) was a German mathematician and scientist.

autobiographical 'Yesterday, Today, Tomorrow' problematises this all the way through the text. It begins with a four line poem which consists of sentences or phrases from English, French and Turkish:

> *When I was a little child*
> Bir yokluktu Ankara [Ankara was poverty]
> *Apres moi dull and wild*
> Town ne oldu [what was], *que sera*

At another place, Selim asks:

> Cranium fibula radius
> Sacrum patella carpus
> How am I going to learn by heart
> The Latin names of the bones
> Of a man who prays in Arabic to his God?[654]

How can we become 'western and remain national at the same time?'[655] Emphasising the way in which the Turkish elite thought they could be more 'modern' and sophisticated if they could utter a few French words, Selim, referring to his provincial father who also follows this trend, writes:

> As for the issue of French, the whole country was made up of *francophones* those days. Languages like Armenian or Greek spoken by the provincial minorities or taught at *mekteps* – before the Republic – were no more considered as foreign languages. Even Numan Bey, who had a vague acquaintance with the languages of minorities, would scold his wife in French when he thought there was not enough salt in his supper (he always found some fault with supper). '*Donmez-moi un peu de sel*!' he would say. (Numan Bey thought politeness was waste of time, and hence he would not add '*Si'l vous plait.*')[656]

---

654 Quoted in Gürle, *Oğuz Atay's Dialogue*, p. 50
655 Gürle, *Oğuz Atay's Dialogue*, p. 50
656 Quoted in Gürle, *Oğuz Atay's Dialogue*, p. 50. French was the language of the minorities, especially the Greek and the Jewish minorities, in Istanbul. See Philip Mansel, *Levant* (London: John Murray, 2010). Mansel claims that the relationship between France and the Ottoman Empire goes back as early as the sixteenth century. The modern Levant, he argues, in fact, was born from one of the most successful alliances in history: between the French and the Ottoman Empires: 'The Levant was defined not only by geography, diplomacy and the capitulations, but by also language: first by lingua franca…after 1850 by French' (p. 14). Moreover, he says: 'By 1912 the enormous total of 108,112 pupils were receiving an education in French establishments in the Ottoman Empire' (p. 145). French was also the language of Russian nobility. It was first Peter the Great (1672-1725) who encouraged the learning of foreign languages,

The use of these French sentences or phrases even by those who do not know the language itself shows nothing but 'the illusion that the country is on its way towards a more western and modern state.'[657] This sort of 'illusion' along with the tension between those who hold onto the old-order, i.e. pre-Republic period and the reformists are reflected in language.

> The disputes between my father and my teacher constituted the loveliest memories of my first encounters with what is called 'culture.' I remember deriving a secret pleasure from the communication between these two parties, who were talking through me, and did not even know that they were arguing. The first day of school, I remember rushing back home and informing my father about my first discovery: 'Father, you were wrong. I am not going to *mektep*, but to school.[658] My father lifted his face from the newspaper he had been reading and gazed at me with tired and indifferent eyes: 'Let things stand for now', he said. As I later found out, this phrase was the summary of my father's personality. 'Let things stand for now' he would say, and having said this he would not only make himself stop, but also bring a halt to everything...[659]
>
> 'How come dad?' I said. 'When you sent me to the teacher didn't you tell me to listen to him very carefully?' I said. As though not hearing me: 'School means ekol', he said. Adapted from the French. You don't understand.' He said. You see, in this they were in an agreement: 'You don't understand.'[660]

It was in language that the clash between the 'conservatives' and the reformists might be grasped, as we shall see.

VII.iii. 'Words, words, words': Excess of Words

One of the issues that Atay problematises in *The Disconnected* is language in general, and the language reformation in particular, in other words, the implementation of 'pure Turkish' and abolition of many foreign words, mostly Arabic and Persian, that were introduced into Ottoman-Turkish. Atay mocks both highly

---

   especially French which was the political and intellectual language of Europe at the time, and remained an integral part of Russian aristocratic culture. See Leo Tolstoy, *War and Peace* (London: Penguin, 1982).
657 Gürle, *Oğuz Atay's Dialogue*, p. 50
658 *Mektep* means school in Ottoman-Turkish and in Arabic. In fact, the Turkish word *okul* sounds like the French word école which emphasises the contradiction between the father and the 'Enlightened' teacher. See Gürle, *Oğuz Atay's Dialogue*, p. 75.
659 Quoted in Gürle, *Oğuz Atay's Dialogue*, p. 75; Translation corrected.
660 Oğuz Atay, *Tutunamayanlar* (İstanbul: İletişim, 1992), p. 77. Hereafter *Disconnected*.

stylised Ottoman-Turkish and efforts to create a pure Turkish. He can write in both, often following a passage in the so-called pure Turkish with one in Ottoman-Turkish. In an interview he says: 'There is a part in the novel written completely in pure Turkish, and another part that is written in Ottoman Turkish. If you read, you will see that I can write in both languages with equal ease. And, of course, I also have my own language.'[661]

The fake autobiography we mentioned in the previous section, namely 'Yesterday, Today, Tomorrow' consists of two parts: a 600 line song/poem and a commentary. The commentary part takes one line or a couple of lines from the poem and explains it, but not in a straightforward way: while Musil wrote in a fairly uniform, essayistic style, and Nietzsche experimented with different styles but in different works – essays, aphorisms, poems – the commentary part of 'Yesterday, Today, Tomorrow' combines parodies of several speech genres in a single text. In fact the whole novel is full of parodies about the language reformation, about different discourses, as well as about the way in which an unscientific official history was written or created with the aid of this 'pure Turkish'. Consider this passage from the commentary part of 'Yesterday, Today, Tomorrow':

> Before they migrated from Central Asia to the motherland, the life of the Turks was entirely tribal. The social order in the Turkic tribes rested on the needs of a tent civilisation. We can prove how far we have moved from that tribal life by taking a look at some words, which were completely unknown and alien to the language of those tribes (namely pure Turkish), but which we cannot do without in today's daily life, such as glass, straw, necktie, rent, cherry, lighthearted, table, plate, coffin, music, education, bed frame, word and sentence. The fact that these words did not exist in pure Turkish, which is an archaic branch of modern Turkish, might give us an idea about the lives of these tribal people:
>
> > Turks did not look out of window.
> > Turks did not sit on straw mats, and did not shovel issues under
> > the straw. This habit started with the Ottomans.
> > Turks did not wear neckties.
> > Turks did not like lightheartedness. They were sober people.
> > Turks did not pay rents. The habit of paying rents started when
> > Turks moved from the period of primitive communism to that of the landed
> > bourgeoisie.
> > Turks did not eat cherries at all.
> > Turks did not have supper at table, and did not use any plates
> > whatsoever. They ate from the pot in the middle.

---

661 Quoted in Gürle, *Oğuz Atay's Dialogue*, p. 41

> When Turks died they were not put into coffins and buried. The old Turks did not have such customs.
> Turks did not listen to music.
> Turks did not go to school.
> Turks did not express themselves with linguistic devices like words and sentences.[662]

In the commentary part Atay constantly introduces new characters: heroes, reformists, philosophers etc. For instance we encounter the great reformist Ziya Özdevrimsel – meaning 'true revolutionary' – who was a devoted follower of the revolution to such an extent that after the Hat Reform no one has seen him without a hat, after the Apparel Reform without a suit and after the Alphabet Reform reading texts written in the old script.[663] Not only is he a follower of the reforms but also thanks to his trips to Europe and America he himself attempts to introduce new reforms one of which is the 'Baby Swaddling Reform'. In a hospital in Childharoldshire[664] where he is taken after an accident which occurs as a result of his not knowing what traffic lights are, he sees the western way of wrapping babies. He recovers from his injuries quickly and immediately after he comes back to Turkey he introduces the 'Baby Swaddling Reform' along with the 'Traffic Lights Reform'.

Several pages later there is a commentary on the following two lines: 'Let us, Selim, tell about Hegel, Fichte a bit/Let us eat bread in philosophy.'[665] The commentary on this introduces us to the butcher/philosopher Gustav Willibald Franz Hegel. Hegel was born in 1774 in Stadthamburg, but not well educated. Thanks, however, to his Slovakian Jewish mother – a more cultivated person than his father

---

662 Quoted in Gürle, *Oğuz Atay's Dialogue*, pp. 41-42; *Disconnected*, p. 141. Translation corrected.
663 Atay, *Disconnected*, p. 166
664 Here Atay might be referring to Lord Byron's *Childe Harold's Pilgrimage*, a lengthy poem which describes the travels of a young man in Europe during the Napoleonic Wars. In the preface Byron says that the poem should not be regarded as autobiographical, however, the first two cantos (the third and fourth cantos were added and published later) were written during his travels to Europe (1809-1811) and it is clear that the poem reflects Byron's political views, for instance his support for Greek independence from Turkey. Perhaps Atay had in mind not only the traveller Byron/Childe Harold but also Byron the swimmer who swam across the Hellespont separating Europe from Asia. Byron swam the Hellespont in honour of the mythological character Leander who swam across the Hellespont every night to see his beloved Hero who lived in Sestos, on the European side of the Dardanelles.
665 Atay, *Disconnected*, p. 119

– Hegel has learned how to read and write properly. The commentary tells the story of how Hegel the butcher, the son of a butcher, becomes a philosopher.

One day while Hegel is checking his accounts, Josef Georg Fichte, president of the Stadthamburg Butchers and Tripe Merchants' Association and editor of the monthly journal of Meat and Animal Husbandry, enters the shop. Fichte looks rather worried: a poor writer, he has been asked to produce an article critical of recent government measures. Hegel, whose mother taught him grammar, volunteers to write the article himself:

> ...In our society in which we see that everything changes, we feel more than at any other time that the old German customs are gradually decaying and a determinate order is lacking. The absence of productive developments and the fact that all progressive movements lose their momentum after a while, and cede their place to other movements which hold the opposite understanding, is extremely upsetting especially to those of us who handle one of the country's most vital resources...I am ending my letter with an excerpt from *Bible* which I would like to be our constant guide.
>
> 'Hereby, if my brother is hurt because I am eating meat, I will never eat meat again. Just so that my brother is not hurt.'
>
> Let God's absolute
Mercy be on us
Your brother G. W. F. Hegel[666]

The story gets more complicated after this: one year later, Professor Heinemann, a friend of the great philosopher Georg Wilhelm Friedrich Hegel and the head of the History Department in Göttingen University, comes to Stadthamburg to spend some time in the library archive. In the library he comes across Hegel the butcher's article entitled 'An Essay on the Insensitivity of the State towards the Slaughter of Animals' signed by G. W. F. Hegel. Heinemann cannot help being surprised at this coincidence and when he is back in Göttingen tells this to his friend Hegel the philosopher. It amuses them, but two months later, in an article critical of the great philosopher Hegel's ideas about the absolute function of the state, Heinemann cites Hegel the butcher: 'In this matter even the butcher Hegel in Stadthamburg would say more consistent things than you.'[667] This reference makes Hegel the butcher famous in his town and they start to call him 'Hegel the philosopher.' Hegel the butcher takes this seriously and in a letter that he writes to Heinemann he says that he does not want to be a butcher anymore, and wants to devote himself

---

666 Atay, *Disconnected*, p. 182
667 Atay, *Disconnected*, p. 183

full time to philosophy. He is invited to Göttingen by Heinemann where he starts to study, and after working day and night manages to become a professor nine years after his graduation. However, some months after becoming a professor, he starts to suffer from terrible headaches which make him question the reason for his being in Göttingen: 'What am I doing? Where am I?' he says constantly. The only thing that he can think about is Stadthamburg: he cannot eat, he cannot sleep. Then one day while he is trying to read Kant in bed he suffocates and cannot carry on; he cannot face opening a book at all, and decides to go back to his little shop in Stadthamburg where he sees out his last years in peace.

The commentary part of 'Yesterday, Today, Tomorrow' is full of stories like this. Each story can be treated individually and with each Atay clearly wishes to communicate something, although largely as straightforward satire. However, the question why we are told all these different stories in an allegedly autobiographical text which mocks different speech genres is still to be answered. We said that throughout the text, Atay is both mocking reductionist and unscientific history writing and the language reformation. However, there is more to it.

Selim's mock autobiography reminds us of Laurence Sterne's *Tristram Shandy*. The events of the Tristram's life and the Shandy history are constantly interrupted in order to tell a different story which may lead to other stories which themselves may cause the narrator to tell other stories. Sometimes even a word causes the narrator to jump from one event to the other, which distorts the linearity and the order of the story. Even though the book is supposed to be about the life of Tristram, he cannot tell us events in a simple plot and in linear time. In fact, he opens so many parentheses and embarks on digressions constantly that we do not come to his birth until volume III.[668] This constant interruption draws attention to the question of narration itself, which also a question that Atay occupies himself with. In fact, in his *Diaries* he tells us why he prefers a non-linear narration:

> *The problem of form*: there are two possibilities – either the themes will be given in the classical order, by juxtaposing them, or by emancipating the associations (connotations) an organic and spiritual development can be realised since the events and factors are intertwined.[669]

Like *Tristram Shandy*, though not at that extreme level, Selim's autobiography turns out to be full of stories about history, language, modernity, Europe etc. It seems that for Selim – and later Turgut – there is either too much to say or nothing

---

[668] Laurence Sterne, *The Life and Opinions of Tristram Shandy, Gentleman* (New York: Signet, 1962), Vol. III, Chp. XXIII.
[669] Atay, *Günlük*, pp. 238-39

to say. Neither way – neither silence nor noise – helps them to exist in language. According to Nurdan Gürbilek there is always an excess of words in Atay's novels: 'The noise that soars from Atay's novels stems from the commingling and clashing of all these discourses...It sounds like the noise that little kids make when they change roles while playing a game. It is a noise that sounds like gibberish to an outsider.'[670]

We said that 'Yesterday, Today, Tomorrow' is supposed to be a mock-autobiography of Selim, however, far from being an autobiography (self-documentation) or an account of Selim's life, it does not tell the reader much about Selim, does not reveal anything; in the act of attracting the reader's attention to the words it distracts attention from Selim. In the commentary part of the autobiography this tactic reaches its peak point: we read about all sorts of characters – fictional or real – except Selim. It is more like a defence mechanism: the more he says the more we hear about other people rather than Selim himself. In Musil's 'the other condition' all dichotomies like subject and object disappear, a new participation in the world as well as one's self become possible. The moments of 'mystical' illumination cannot be translated into the language of ordinary life. Selim, however, does not seem to know any other world apart from the world of words. And the question is, is language here another defence mechanism that keeps the world at a distance by ordering it, that acts as a flood barrier, or is it the flood itself? Perhaps a line in 'Yesterday, Today, Tomorrow' *Kelime ve Yalnızlık* ('Word and Loneliness') which is then explained in the commentary part gives us a clue:

> 'In the beginning was the Word', so begins *Bible* according to the Gospel of John. Before the Word there was Loneliness. And after the Word, Loneliness carried on existing....It started where the Word ended; it started before the Word could be uttered. The Words made Loneliness be forgotten and Loneliness lived on in humans along with the Words. The Words told of Loneliness and melted and disappeared in Loneliness. Only Words quietened the pain of Loneliness and once Words came to the mind of the individual, Loneliness increased, it became unbearable.[671]

---

670 Quoted in Gürle, *Oğuz Atay's Dialogue*, p. 44. See Nurdan Gürbilek, *Ev Ödevi* (İstanbul: Metis Yayınları, 1998), p. 13.
671 Atay, *Disconnected*, p. 154. The first verse in the Gospel According to St John reads '*In the beginning was the Word, and the Word was with God, and the Word was God.*' The phrase 'the Word' is a translation of the Greek word *Logos* which is mostly interpreted as referring to Jesus. The word *Logos*, meaning 'word', 'an opinion', 'a ground', 'speech', 'account', 'reason' was an important term for Heraclitus, Stoics, Plato, Aristotle. Later on Philo introduced the word into Jewish philosophy. St. Justin Martyr and Philosopher is the first one, in *Dialogue with Trypho*, who made a summary

Selim is tired of 'words, words, words':[672]

> Then suddenly Selim jumped out of bed; he smashed all the words and lives under his feet. He approached the sun light. After some time the sun light hurt his eyes, and he closed the curtains and returned to the darkness of the Words. Some Words forgave him; they allowed him to live among them again. Allied with one another, he and the words attacked other Words mercilessly – those Words that humiliated him, trampled him, and granted him no respite. He won, he lost, in the end he lost out to these Words in the war which he had declared on them. Loneliness was always there.[673]

Selim's leaving his bed and running to the sun light reminds us of Plato's cave allegory, which is no coincidence, for according to Clement of Alexandria Plato equated *Logos* – the word – with Truth, a fundamental property of all ideas,[674] while Selim, by telling us of this contest between the word and loneliness, equates it with Loneliness, a tragic truth of the human condition. In the cave allegory, a group of people has lived chained in the cave and gazing at the shadows on the wall; one day one of them frees himself from his chains and goes out, only then realising that what they all had been looking at so far were only the shadows of the real objects in real life. He is the philosopher. Atay reverses Plato's allegory: The 'real' world Selim finds himself in is full of apparitions, repetitions and imitations.

We saw that according to Musil's Ulrich repetition underlies all rationalisation. Science is possible only where situations repeat themselves. Saying this Ulrich is not critical of the idea that repetition is the ultimate principle not only in the realm of scientific knowledge but also in the realm of morality. There is also the realm of *non-ratio*, that is to say, a realm where events are unique and non repeatable. But we also saw that Musil does not present 'the other condition' or the realm of *non-ratio* as something that can be realised as an alternative to the normal condition, on the contrary, the other condition is precisely the constitutive other of the normal condition. Selim, by contrast, may be said to be striving to live in the other condition all the time. It is a task that will defeat him, and defeat him more radically than it defeated Ulrich.

> of the *Logos* names: Praise the Lord, the Son, Wisdom, Messenger, God, Lord, Word. See St. Justin Martyr, 'Dialogue with Trypho,' in *The Fathers of the Church*, trans. Thomas B. Falls (Washington: The Catholic University of America Press, 1948), Chp. 61, p. 244. On the word *Logos* see Mihai D. Vasile, 'Logos' Life from Plato to the Teachings of Early Christian Doctrine,' http: //cogito.ucdc.ro/nr_2v2/LOGOS/pdf

672 William Shakespeare, *Hamlet* (Oxford: Oxford University Press, 1998), Act 2.2, p. 214.
673 Atay, *Disconnected*, p. 155
674 Vasile, 'Logos'

Having too much to say and yet not being able to say it, the lack and at the same time the excess of words makes Selim, eventually, talk to himself alone. Rejecting the repetitive patterns of daily language, seeking to live without any sort of imitation of others, without habits, manners, traditions of speech, he comes to believe that if only he could change the meanings of the words he might express himself appropriately. But to whom?

There is a parallelism here, not so much between Selim and Ulrich as between Selim and Törless. As we have seen, Musil's subject matter is adolescence. Törless is neither a child, nor an adult; he is 'wordless' and 'worldless'. He is at the threshold between two realms, and yet longs to attain another realm. Törless cannot articulate his thoughts in the rational realm, cannot talk at all. Selim, on the other hand, ends up with repetitions, excesses of words and parodies. Where Törless stutters, Selim/Turgut talks too much, albeit in a voice which only he himself can hear. In the voice that others can hear he could talk only in repetition, imitation, parody:

> Days passed. Monday came, then it was Sunday, and then Monday again, then Sunday came again. It was impossible to catch up with, overtake; then it was Sunday again. They woke up late. Breakfast, a large breakfast was eaten late. The Sunday papers were read, crossword puzzles were solved; the same crossword puzzles solved the previous week. Dinner was served at home, they went to others for dinner. Dinner was eaten at homes that did not resemble your homes at first sight, but that actually did. Did we give the last dinner, or did we go to Kaya's? Or was it Mehmet's? What difference does it make? We eat at the same house, with the same excitement, the same preparations, I wore the same tie, all my white shirts look the same. My trousers are creased in the same place. Did I spill the dinner on Kaya, or was it Kaya who spilled it on me? I am Kaya. And Kaya is Mehmet. As long as Turgut, Kaya, Mehmet are together... it is something like an image reflected in three mirrors.[675]

Although this might be a standard description of daily life, *The Disconnected* goes further by accompanying Selim and Turgut in their struggle against life. For example, there is not only the predictable and repetitious character of Sundays in general; there is also a predictability to the details of everyday interaction. In one episode, Turgut goes to Ankara for a business trip and considers visiting his wife's relatives. But he visualizes in his mind the conversation that might occur and when he does this he feels like he has already gone and that there is no point to the visit.[676]

---

675 Atay, *Disconnected*, p. 335
676 As Sibel Irzık has indicated 'other people seem to have talked as well, but they only speak the words that Turgut expects from them and that render his cynical responses possible.' See Sibel Irzık, *'Tutunamayanlar'*da Çokseslilik" ve Sınırları', *Varlık Dergisi*, Ekim (1995), p. 46.

> I did not encounter any difficulties in finding your new house. Your son has grown very much. I hope you will grow to be an engineer like your Uncle Turgut. Let him be worse. How is Nermin doing? She is fine, she sends her regards and love. I hope I can bring her the next time. Tell me, are you studying your lessons? He frowned. Uncles sometimes frown: you can't trust them. You will remember Süheyla: my aunt's daughter-in-law. Nice to meet you. The dinner was delicious. The location of your house is very nice as well. You look younger. I have some work to do at the hotel tonight. The next time, come with Nermin. I said we would, why delay? Don't think of going to a hotel. Fine: We will directly land here and collapse the building.[677]

It seems that even 'spontaneous' speech, everyday conversation, is endlessly repeated, that what has happened once will happen again and again. The existing order is nothing other than a play and Turgut, according to Selim, is also involved in this play called life; he got married and benefited from the boons of existing order, something which Selim saw as a betrayal. For Turgut, the existing order, to which he has adapted through his silence, becomes a problem only after Selim's death. Turgut attempts to 'defend himself against Selim and against what he represents for Turgut: an impossible existence that, by going against every norm and order (and doing this without grounding itself in any other determinate order), perished in the end.'[678] Yet, as his reflections on his trip to Ankara demonstrate, he learns to view those norms even more cruelly, in his internal monologues.

The location for this trip, Ankara, is no coincidence. It is where Atay's critique of bureaucracy – one of his major themes – reaches its peak point. Turgut's visit involves going to an official bureau where nothing seems to happen according to any rational ground, where the 'rule of office' seems to have no rules. Atay's account of it stands in the tradition of Max Weber, Kafka...and Musil.

VII.iv. Fathers and Sons: Authority and Bureaucracy

In 'Hamlet Kuşağı' ('The Hamlet Generation') Bülent Somay warns us against the danger of allegories which 'can destroy an individual's, indeed a whole generation's life.'

---

677 Atay, *Disconnected*, p. 250
678 Suna Ertuğrul, 'Belated Modernity and Modernity as Belatedness in Tutunamayanlar', *The South Atlantic Quarterly,* 102 (2/3), (Spring/Summer 2003), p. 633.

I was only fourteen when I encountered the allegory which turned upside down my life and that of my generation. They were staging Beklan Algan's *Hamlet 70* in Bakırköy Halkevi...And right at the very beginning of the play, in the Ghost scene the allegory appeared. Who do you think is Hamlet's father's ghost? None other than the ghost/soul of Mustafa Kemal [Atatürk]! Moreover, Algan gave the line 'Something is rotten in the state of Denmark', which belongs to the guard Marcellius, to the ghost as well. Thereby, Hamlet learns from the mouth of the dead father that the mother is being raped by the wicked uncle, and is called to take revenge...In this allegory Hamlet was us, youth. The ghost of the father was Mustafa Kemal [Atatürk] and the ghost warns us about the fact that the state, the Mother-Republic, is being usurped and raped by the Right wing/Americanophile politicians; maybe by Demirel himself.[679]

Nine years before Somay, Jale Parla claims that the novels of the Reformation period in the Ottoman Empire (*Tanzimat*)[680] were distinctive in that the authors employed a totalising attitude towards the text and the characters. The first Ottoman-Turkish novelists, writing between 1870-1890, believed that the fundamental principles of the Ottoman-reformation had to be based on Eastern moral and cultural values and that the sultan had to be the guardian of these values at the national level, as had the father in the household and the novelist at the literary realm. They also thought that in such a period, during which the authority of the sultan is endangered, the novelist had to take on the role of the father, normally performed by the sultan.[681]

> What determines Reformation thought is not the desire to kill the father, but rather the effort to resurrect the dying father. [...] The father-son relationship in the Reformation is not that of a confrontation but one that is based on continuity. Our first novelists are the offspring of this conservative relationship and they are all authoritarian children who had to become their own fathers in search of the long lost fathers of their own.[682]

---

679 Bülent Somay, 'Hamlet Kuşağı', *Defter*, Yaz 1999, p. 50. Süleyman Demirel was the prime minister of the time.
680 The *Tanzimât* means *reorganization* of the Ottoman Empire. It was a period of reformation that began in 1839 and ended with the First constitution Era in 1876. The reforms, heavily influenced by European ideas, were intended to effectuate a fundamental change of the empire from the old system based on theocratic principles to that of a modern state. See Walter F. Weiker, 'The Ottoman Bureaucracy: Modernization and Reform', *Administrative Science Quarterly*, Vol. 13, No. 3, Special Issue on Organizations and Social Development (Dec., 1968), pp. 451-470.
681 Jale Parla, *Babalar ve Oğullar: Tanzimat Romanının Epistemolojik Temelleri* (İstanbul: İletişim, 2010), p. 19.
682 Quoted in Gürle, *Oğuz Atay's Dialogue*, p 89

Gürle, applying Parla's allegory of 'fatherless son' to the political environment of 70s Turkey, claims that the problem was no longer that of not having a 'father' but, on the contrary, having a father that was rather 'too much'.

> The fatherless sons of the Ottoman Empire became very rigid fathers themselves in order to create a nation out of the remains of the dying monarchy. The Turkish Republic was, in fact, established by the 'fathers of the text' who have always expressed a firm belief in an absolute truth and never suspected that it might be their own fabrication.[683]

The metaphor according to Gürle, 'takes the form of an authoritarian father representing the modernist state.'[684] Perhaps a closer look at the political atmosphere of the late 60s will be helpful. Gürle writes:

> In the 1970s the enemy is still the West, but it is no longer portrayed as a *mademoiselle* seducing the shy Ottoman gentleman, but rather as a wicked old man pointing his bony finger at you in the posters of Uncle Sam – or, more vividly, as the solid presence of American battleships on the Bosphorus.[685]

As in much of Europe, 1968 was a crucial year in Turkey: students went to the streets, the state's reaction was rather repressive, even brutal, and in the end there was a military coup in 1971: the students were imprisoned, tortured and three of them were hung. What is interesting about the objective of the Turkish left of this era, Gürle argues, is that this Turkish youth did not see any contradiction between their search for freedom and equality on the one hand and the authoritative Kemalist ideology and the totalising attitude of the state on the other.[686] In other words, following the ghost of their father's (Kemal Atatürk) call, the left wing youth of the 60s wanted to save the Republic.

It was not until the 70s that this authority itself was questioned. Atay was one of the first to question it. Once again we shall look at 'Yesterday, Today, Tomorrow'. Consider the commentary on another single line, which runs *The year nineteen-hundred and forty-nine*:

> The year nineteen-hundred and forty-nine...We got out of the war which we had entered without entering...A word called democracy appeared...Everyone asks questions like how much more these American cars will be developed, what sort of novelty they will introduce to the design...Something called a drainage system is constructed. Everyone is learning English to be able to speak to Americans. Some

---

683 Gürle, *Oğuz Atay's Dialogue*, p. 90
684 Gürle, *Oğuz Atay's Dialogue*, p. 90
685 Gürle, *Oğuz Atay's Dialogue*, p. 90
686 Gürle, *Oğuz Atay's Dialogue*, p. 91

youngsters passed by in front of Selim's house while carrying a man on their shoulders. Apparently he was a racist. Selim followed them to the Youth Park. There, the fire brigade turned its hoses on them....Fridges appeared in some houses. Writers who supported the Germans during the war are now talking about the indispensable character of democracy...Mr. Numan said that those who followed illegal orders during the one-party period are not guilty...They want permission to publish the suicide news in the newspapers. Selim was set an essay on the United Nations and Human Rights.[687]

Here, as opposed to the excess of words and the mock speech genres that Atay adopts throughout the novel, the sentences are short and sharp. However, these fragmentary sentences capture the dramatic atmosphere of this one year, and anticipate the coming years. Perhaps it is no coincidence that Atay gives us a dark, dirty and gloomy description of Ankara, the capital city, in the following section: 'Ankara, especially at that time, was very dirty. According to the story, for this city which was founded on marshland, a suitable place had not been found.'[688]

The authority of the modern state is mocked and dramatised. On a business trip to Ankara Turgut goes to an official state bureau (*daire*). His observations of the bureau reflect not only the routine character of this official institute but also its hierarchical structure: 'The bureau, that oversized mass, was stirring and stretching. Section heads were waiting for the bus, managers were at home having breakfast, managing directors were still asleep.'[689] While Turgut is waiting for the director an engineer, Musta Bey, who is also waiting, begins to tell him how he became an engineer and how he regrets it, how he could have continued his father's business as a modest shopkeeper in a small town. Instead of this he is a civil engineer charged with the duty of constructing a base for the gendarmerie on a mountain site somewhere in the Eastern part of Turkey. In a nearby town Musta Bey has found a truck driver to deliver the stones, along with some workers who either have nothing to do or are crazy enough to go to the construction area where the only living creatures are mosquitoes. These 'village idiots', Musta Bey tells Turgut, almost caused the death of the engineer: in order to decrease the cost of the construction they took the gravestones from the nearest village cemetery and brought them to the site so that they could be used for the construction; why spend money on stone? The engineer thinks he definitely will be killed by the villagers. He goes to

---

[687] Atay, *Disconnected*, p. 229-31
[688] Atay, *Disconnected*, p. 231
[689] Atay, *Disconnected*, p. 295

the gendarmerie in the town and tells the story to the prosecuting attorney, who taking two gendarmes with him, accompanies our engineer to the village, where they find the angry villagers gathered around the square. Thanks to this authority figure, matters are resolved rather easily:

> The prosecutor got off his horse. He took a translator with him. After all he is the government. The agha[690] could not not get off his horse and approach them. The agha says…'This foreigner did not leave one single stone in our cemeteries. What will happen now? We will mix up our dead. We won't be able to pray two lines. Let us punish him.' The prosecutor listened to him coolly; though carrying out a regular job. Then 'There is nothing to be angry about in this', he says. 'The order of the Government.' I stood open mouthed. 'The order of the Government?' 'Yes, the order of the Government. You ignorant men, don't you know that the new Alphabet was introduced? Haven't all identity cards been renewed? Don't you all have the new script? An order came from Ankara. All the grave stones will be replaced with new ones because they have the old script on them.[691]

Musta Bey finishes his story and is about to begin another one – for as long as the state is there these stories never finish – when the director appears. Not that he will sign Turgut's document so readily:

> When all the clerks have arranged your documents (papers) as you wanted, when the only thing that remains is the signature of the director, a mere formality, when sensing the first flush of victory you persuade the usher (office boy) and take the documents from him, and when you open the door slowly which hides terrifying surprises behind it and when you dare to enter into this silent temple, to contravene the intimacy of it…suddenly the whole world collapses. He doesn't sign it, efendim, he does not sign it…The more you insist the more he doesn't sign. Ten times, a hundred times, a thousand times he does not sign it. If you don't insist, even before your shadow disappears at the threshold of the room he forgets you. You are temporary, he is permanent…He is not a human being, he is the state, the authority. He is an abstract concept. He himself knows that he is an abstract concept…Then…then they say that he has signed it. How come? While you are not there, in a moment when you were not paying attention…It is like a dream of someone else…you are floundering: how did he sign it? What did he say? How was his face? They didn't pay attention, they missed it.[692]

---

690 Agha, also Aga (from Turkish *ağa* 'chief, master, lord'), is a title for a civil or military officer in the Ottoman Empire. It is also a title given to the tribal chieftains or to village heads in Kurdistan. In the villages in Turkey the word is still used in the latter sense.
691 Atay, *Disconnected*, p. 306
692 Atay, *Disconnected*, p. 307-308

If in Kafka's world one can neither be outside the system nor position oneself in opposition to it, in Atay's world the disconnected can mock the system, though at the price of not only being outside the system but being excluded by it. By satirising the absurdity of bureaucracy and authority, by making this abstract State something material, in other words, precisely by fixing this abstract 'thing' called State on to the world, by materialising it, Atay gives the disconnected something of a voice. One might say that this is a fight against the system, though one that, because of Atay's language, has much of the conventional drama taken out of it.

VII.v. Comedy, Irony and the Subject

In the next chapter we will examine in more detail the relationship between Atay's writing strategy and the things he wishes to say about the self. It will be a difficult one because what he wants to say will be more complicated than a familiar story about individual freedom and state bureaucracy, or about the shaping of subjects by modern institutional practices. As we will see, the account of the dissolution of the subject will owe much to his use of intertextuality. But even when the themes are the familiar ones about history and bureaucracy and national identity that we have discussed in this chapter, the question of the relationship between literary devices and the status of the self can be asked.

Gürbilek reminds us of a characteristic, even a function of comedy:[693] to forget. Some people write comedy in order to familiarise what has been unfamiliar (*unheimlich*) and fearful so far, to break a spell, to suspend the authority which is the source of this fear, in order to create some freedom.[694] In this respect comedy can be therapeutic. According to Richard Rorty, Proust is the master of comedy in this respect: 'Proust temporalised and finitised the authority figures he had met' precisely 'by seeing them as creatures of contingent circumstance.' Proust manages this not by showing us what these authority figures really are, but just watching them becoming other than what they are or they seem to be when they are redescribed by other authority figures.[695] Gürbilek suggests that Atay's

---

693 The word comedy derives from the Greek word *komodios* (singer in the revels), from *komos* (revel, carousel) + *oidos* (singer, poet). Atay's calling Selim's mock autobiographical text 'Yesterday, Today, Tomorrow' a song may not be a coincidence.
694 Gürbilek, 'Kemalizmin Delisi Oğuz', p. 241
695 Richard Rorty, *Contingency, Irony, and Solidarity* (Cambridge: Cambridge University Press, 1989), p. 103.

mock-discourse, parody, imitation and digressions, as well as his irony, do not allow us to forget and therefore it does not create this sense of freedom. However, the extent to which Atay's technique is one of irony may be questioned.[696] Ali Akay, for instance, claims that the distinctive feature of Atay's novels was not irony but simply his sense of humour. For Akay such a distinction is vital because if we go back to the origins of irony we see that irony (*eirōneia*) in Greek philosophy was employed to reveal the truth.

In Aristophanes, for instance, irony is employed to tell important truths about social problems. Irony as it was used by Plato in *Socratic Dialogues,* attempts to shed light on a particular truth by stating its opposite. 'Socratic irony' is defined by *The Oxford Dictionary of Philosophy* as 'Socrates' irritating tendency to praise his hearers while undermining them, or to disparage his own superior abilities while manifesting them.'[697]

A popular definition of irony might be that ironic speech conveys something that is not said, or means the opposite of what is said. However, this was not the way the playwright Aristophanes understood it: in fact, the purpose of Aristophanic *eirōn* is to conceal what is not said. In *Symposium* and *Gorgias* Plato uses the word *eirōn* in its former sense – to convey what is not said, but in some texts he uses it in Aristophanic sense. According to Cicero Socratic irony is serious play and its playful purpose is tied to its transparency to the audience. In other words, once it is said, no one is excluded from what is meant;[698] however, following Aristotle, Leo Strauss says the opposite: irony is the noble dissimulation of one's superiority: 'the magnanimous man – the man who regards himself as worthy of great things while in fact being worthy of them – is truthful and frank because he is in the habit of looking down and yet he is ironical in his intercourse with the many. Irony is then the noble dissimulation of one's worth, of one's superiority.' In Strauss' account irony's audience is limited to the philosophical few: 'If irony is essentially related to the fact that there is a natural order of rank among men, it follows that irony consists in speaking differently to different kinds of people.'[699]

---

696 Ali Akay, 'Oğuz Atay'da Kimliksizleşme ve *Sense of Humour*', in *Oğuz Atay'a Armağan,* ed. Handan İnci, (İstanbul: İletişim, 2008), pp. 314-323.
697 Simon Blackburn , *The Oxford Dictionary of Philosophy* (Oxford University Press, 2005), p. 344.
698 Melissa Lane, 'Reconsidering Socratic Irony', *The Cambridge Companion to Socrates,* ed. Donald R. Morrison (Cambridge: Cambridge University Press, 2011), pp. 237-260.
699 Leo Strauss, *The City and Man* (Chicago: Chicago University Press, 1978), p. 51. Strauss' account of irony is similar to that of Aristotle. In fact, in this quoted passage

For Alexander Nehamas the purpose of irony, including Socratic irony, is mysterious, conferring a superiority on the ironist. It does not necessarily entail the opposite of what is said, nor does it necessarily convey the meaning. However, it implies that the ironist believes something other than what he says. The ironist can be or chooses to be mysterious.[700] As the extracts quoted above should make clear, Atay's attitude, however ambivalent, is not mysterious in Nehamas' sense.

We said that Musil the ironist describes how the characters in the novel gather around the Parallel Campaign, an attempt to give a purpose to a country that lacks a central will power, and sets the campaign in the 'peace year' of 1913, a 'peace year' that responds to the German celebrations of the one hundredth anniversary of the defeat of Napoleon at the battle of Leipzig. Ulrich the ironist knows the truth that the parallel campaign is a sham, while the reader is given a position superior to that of Ulrich: we know that 1913 was followed by 1914.

In *The Magic Mountain* Thomas Mann, like Musil, gives the reader a superior position to that of the characters. The reader of *The Man without Qualities* knows that Ulrich has a very strong sense of reality, that he is clever but not quite clever enough to foresee the coming war. In *The Magic Mountain*, even though there is a war on the horizon, the reader's knowledge of this coming war does not have any effect on his/her feeling superior to Hans Castorp, the main protagonist. Castorp is a young man who is about to start his career as an engineer. Before doing so he decides to visit his tubercular cousin, Joachim Ziemssen, who is being cured in a sanatorium in the Swiss Alps. Having intended to stay for three weeks, Hans too is diagnosed as having tuberculosis and ends up staying for seven years. In the earlier chapters he is there as a visitor, an observer who is not bound by its obligations. Soon, the reader realises that there is something wrong with Hans, something that he refuses to face and that constantly delays his departure. Very early in the book we learn that both Hans' father and grandfather died from the sort of lung illness from which Joachim suffers, and so Hans has a lot of evidence for the presence of the illness, yet he constantly finds an alternative explanation for his ailments.

The genius of Mann's irony lies in the way he plays with the reader. At first, the reader and Hans have the same evidence for the presence of the illness, but while Hans deceives himself constantly for understandable reasons, the reader, from the

---

he is referring to Aristotle's 'portrait of the magnanimous man' and his being ironic. See Aristotle, *Nicomachean Ethics* (London: Penguin, 2005), 1124b29-31, pp. 96-97; on irony see also 1127a20-26, p. 105.

700 Alexandar Nehamas, *Yaşama Sanatı Felsefesi: Platon'dan Foucault'ya Sokratik Düşünümler* (İstanbul: Ayrıntı, 2002), p. 161.

beginning, knows the truth, having no reason to deny it. In other words, the same evidence that Hans has makes the reader come to the obvious conclusion: Hans is ill and like all the others in the sanatorium will die eventually. Feeling clever, thinking that Hans is deceiving himself constantly, the reader then forgets that he/she is doing the same, that his/her cleverness is only a gift granted by the author.[701]

Atay's treatment of his reader differs in this respect from both Musil and Mann. In Musil, one character, Ulrich, is superior to the others, but sometimes Musil gives that position to the reader. In Mann, the reader is always superior to the character Hans, the truth about whose illness is for a long time unstated but without being a mystery that will be suddenly revealed. In Atay, there is no character that is superior in the sense with which we meet it in Musil or Mann, not Turgut, not Selim, not Atay, not even the reader. Once Turgut receives the letter from Selim there is no going back: we are all part of this game called life: the reader, the writer, the narrator, and the characters. It is funny but at the same time painful for Turkish readers to be reminded of how they had to learn and remember the ridiculous details of the foundation myths of Turkic culture, how *Bozkurtlar* (Steppenwolves) flew all the way from China to Tanca,[702] how they had to learn lines like 'Kelkevser, fesalli lirabbike....'[703]; the stories told by their parents or grandparents about how their birth certificates were given to them some three or four years after they were born, with the standard birth date of 1st January.

Atay is not an ironist.[704] As we have seen, whether in an Aristophanic or Aristotelian or Straussian sense, the function of irony is to reveal the Truth to

---

701 On irony and Thomas Mann see Erich Heller, *Thomas Mann: the Ironic German* (Cambridge: The Cambridge University Press, 1981).
702 Atay, *Disconnected*, p. 121. Tanca is a region of central Asia to which the 'original' Turks are said to have migrated from China.
703 Atay, *Disconnected*, p. 133. These words appear in an Arabic prayer. The words are known by many Turkish people, their meanings by few of them.
704 Rorty has a totally different understanding of irony. The ironist is someone who fulfils three conditions: a – 'she has radical and continuous doubts about the final vocabulary she currently uses'; b – 'she realises that argument phrased in her present vocabulary can neither underwrite nor dissolve these doubts'; c – insofar as she philosophises about her situation, she does not think that her vocabulary is closer to reality than others, that it is in touch with a power not herself.' The ironists never take themselves seriously because they know that the terms that they are using are subject to change, they are aware of the contingency of their final vocabularies – the words which they use to tell the story of their lives – and accordingly their selves. The opposite of the ironist is the person with common sense. People with common sense use the final vocabulary to which they are habituated. Rorty, *Contingency*, pp. 73-75. Now, if we

the audience or to the philosophical few, but the assumption is that there is a Truth. In *Apology*, for instance, Socrates says that his aim in cross-examining is to show that the person who thinks that he is wise is not wiser than Socrates, who does not think that he knows what he does not know.[705] When he does this Socrates is not an ironist, he really thinks that he does not know anything which, of course, proves the Delphic oracle to be right: he is the wisest of men. However, Socrates is an ironist when he is cross-examining people: he may not know what the Truth is but he knows that there is Truth and he wants to attain it.

Atay does not try to reveal the Truth, simply because there is no such thing, no truth about Turkish history, no truth about the self (we saw in the last chapter that such a faith in some version of selfhood lay behind Musil's irony). He problematises every position by revealing the absurdity of it. And yet, yet he is not nihilist or cynical either. The objective of the disconnected is a struggle against authority. However, I agree with Gürbilek that Atay's mockery or sense of humour, by familiarising what is unfamiliar, fearful and magical, functions as a therapy, not in the sense that we forget things once we reveal them, on the contrary, we remember them even more, and we are reminded that we cannot forget them or uncover them, and thanks to this sense of humour or mock-discourse we can face them, we can even struggle against them. Everything becomes a game in the hands of the disconnected; they write constantly, writing means remembering, and remembering means more writing.

How then should Atay's task as a writer be formulated? I suggest that it be described as an aesthetics of anxiety. What does this mean? Otto Jentsch once argued that the uncanny derives from intellectual uncertainty;[706] Atay shows that the uncanny can arise from an illusionary certainty. In the games/plays of the disconnected every certainty is shattered, but is not to be replaced by another certainty. The uncanny, the unfamiliar – the fear of tradition, authority, even the fear of the self – is revealed. In fact, the fear of the self – as being the most uncanny and yet the most familiar – is at the heart of *The Disconnected*. What is this fear of the self? What is it that is uncanny about the self, self being the most familiar

---

        take the meaning of ironist in Rorty's sense then Atay as well as Turgut are ironists: Atay the author, like Proust, re-describes everything around him, accordingly, finitises it; Turgut gives up the final vocabulary to which he was habituated and, following the steps of Selim, re-describes things and people around him.
705 Plato, *The Last Days of Socrates* (London: Penguin, 1976), p. 50.
706 Sigmund Freud, *The Uncanny* (London: Penguin, 2003), p. 125.

'thing'? These are the questions that Turgut occupies himself with after the shattering effect of loss, that is to say death.[707]

VII.vi. Conclusion

Throughout the novel Atay criticises the ideals of the modern Turkish state which equated modernisation with Westernisation, which meant a total break with the past. His critique of the modern Turkish state goes hand in hand with his critique of authority and bureaucracy. However, in doing this he neither adopts a superior position nor does he take a side and try to impose his own position on us. On the contrary, he attempts to show the inefficient or even sometimes ridiculous sides of different views or ideologies.

Atay does not give any privileged position to the languages of the sciences which is simply one more of our languages nor does he consider the language of history writing as taken-for granted. In other words, he problematises the position which sees language as a medium of representation, a medium which reveals the self what is out there. He also problematises the position that considers language as a medium of expression.

Richard Rorty said that 'Truth cannot be out there – cannot exist independently of the human mind – because sentences cannot so exist, or be out there. The world

---

[707] Freud's etymological analysis of the word uncanny is noteworthy. The references in Freud's essay range from Shakespeare to Schnitzler, but the main texts in focus are the German Dictionary and Hoffmann's *The Sand Man*. In the first section Freud gives us different meanings of the word *unheimlich* as it appears in German dictionary along with various meanings of the translation of *unheimlich* in various European languages. The nearest semantic equivalents of the word *unheimlich* in English, Freud says, are 'uncanny' and 'eerie' which etymologically corresponds to 'unhomely'. The uncanny, 'is that species of the frightening that goes back to what was once well known and had long been familiar' (124). However, it is more complicated than this: Freud shows that among various meanings of the word *heimlich* there is one in which it emerges with its formal antonym, *unheimlich*. The word *heimlich* is associated with two distinct though not mutually contradictory ideas. While one meaning is to do with what is familiar and comfortable, the other concerns what is concealed and kept hidden. In that sense, *unheimlich* is the antonym of *heimlich* only in the first sense of *heimlich*. And this means the semantics of this word come to a full circle: the uncanny is the revelation of what is hidden. The self as the most uncanny and yet at the same time the most familiar 'thing' can be seen in this light.

is out there, but descriptions of the world are not.'[708] Rorty means that no language is privileged over any other, that language is neither a pure medium of expression – 'of articulating what lies deep within self' – nor of representation – 'showing the self what lies outside it.'[709] Rorty's conclusion is that it is precisely out of this contingency of language with respect to the subjective and objective worlds that a common, communal or social world can be created and maintained. The contingency of language is consistent with the contingency of the community in which we routinely live. The contingency of language is not the inadequacy of language; the contingency of community is not the impossibility of community; and the contingency of selfhood is not the lack of coherent personality. So the sort of yearning represented by both Torless and Ulrich is misplaced. So is the questioning of Selim and then Turgut.

In a sense both Musil and Atay take the idea of contingency and push it much further than Rorty, to the point where language can appear to dissolve or fail to grasp anything, to the point where any mode of social or political membership appears absurd, or to the point where the self as subject dissolves. But neither of them does this in the name of cynicism or nihilism or anarchy. On the contrary, hovering over the work of both is the idea of a different mode of relatedness to the world, to other people and to the self, a different ethics. Musil's 'other condition' was to be an account of this different ethic, but we saw how Ulrich and Agathe ultimately retreated from it.

In Atay's writing the prospects for such an alternative ethics or ideal of selfhood seem more remote. Ulrich and Agathe's relationship may dissolve the distinction between brother and sister, man and woman, but hermaphrodism and incest are not entirely unknown phenomena even if they are not direct 'models' for the other condition. And Musil's transcendental selfhood draws on a tradition of sorts. But what of Atay?

This will be the focus of next chapter.

---

708   Rorty, *Contingency*, p. 5
709   Rorty, *Contingency*, p. 11

Chapter VIII: Atay on the Self

VIII.i. Introduction

In this chapter I discuss Atay's problematisation to the self (VIII.ii) through the substantive theme of the double (VIII.iii), and the formal device of self-conscious intertextuality (VIII.iv), which raises questions of literary originality (VIII.v.), and the role played in it by the act of reading (VIII.vi.). I suggest that intertextuality plays as important a role for Atay as 'essayism' does for Musil, helping him create a character such as Selim whose identity is not so much contingent as radically unstable.

VIII.ii. The Self

As we have seen, *The Disconnected* begins with the main protagonist Turgut receiving the news that his friend Selim has committed suicide and left a letter for him. The letter for Turgut, which shatters his sense of reality, functions as a 'call': once it is heard there is no going back. It is a call which, according to Ertuğrul, 'fissures the illusionary unity of the "I" and leads one to undergo an experience of absolute responsibility for the other.'[710] At first Turgut wishes to ignore the 'call' but realising that it is impossible, he decides to visit Selim's flat where he discovers a large number of manuscripts – diaries, plays, short stories, long stories – and begins to read them. The manuscripts contain numerous other people, both real people who Selim knew but Turgut did not, those who both of them knew, but also characters from fiction and history, including Jesus, Don Quixote, Hamlet, Dostoyevsky and Oblomov. Turgut reads these manuscripts throughout the novel, and increasingly identifies with Selim.[711]

What does Turgut discover in Selim's manuscripts? He discovers a man who has withdrawn from society, become disconnected, and has tried to discover himself. This disconnection was not a voluntary act, but a gradual process of drifting

---

710 Ertuğrul, 'Belated Modernity', p. 634
711 In a way the plot in *The Disconnected* is similar to that of Nabokov's *The Real Life of Sebastian Knight* in which the main character is writing a biography of his brother by reading the texts that the brother left behind.

apart from society. It begins when Selim is a child – when he starts to compose the manuscripts – and continues to the point where the manuscripts stop and he finally commits suicide. Selim's withdrawal is not a withdrawal from the conventions of bourgeois society because his it begins before he can become a competent adult member of it. Turgut, by contrast, is an adult whose own withdrawal begins as a voluntary act of reading; he then becomes absorbed into the world Selim has created and taken along by Selim's person. This procedure is not exactly what Nietzsche means in *Thus Spoke Zarathustra* by becoming a child, because this decentering of his adult subjecthood, takes place through his reading of Selim's manuscripts. These are devoted to the study of and dialogue with numerous characters, real and fictional. By inhabiting their various worlds, Turgut will discover multiple selves for himself.

Even as a child, Selim was in a kind of non-position; he did not associate with others easily, a fact that he recalls in a diary entry written shortly before his death: 'They taught me ordinary ways they showed to others. They should have treated me with another kind of attention.'[712]

> Abnormal. This child is abnormal. This child is not normal. I was abnormal as I read without stopping – I didn't use to read a lot as far as I remember – and I didn't go next to the guests- this 'going next to' phrase made me shiver and made me dizzy- and as I couldn't find the proper words – they also used to call me stupid because of that. I was eager to make them feel ashamed by being normal when I grew up. I think they were right. How did they know? As I know that they were fools, insensitive and ignorant, I am furious that they are right with my entire heart and mind. I should have been right. It didn't happen that way. Damn the ones who caused this, I uttered a word that is disconnected once. Now I find this word insufficient.[713]

When Selim writes about how he was misunderstood as a child, he compares his experience with that of Nietzsche, who came long before his proper time 'also died this way',[714] in loneliness. In fact, what Turgut will discover in Selim's manuscripts is a man who has become disconnected from society at an early age and whose disconnectedness has been deepened to the point of suicide by entering into the alternative world of literature and history. Selim has embarked on a quest to find himself by finding himself in figures from the past and by writing plays about his acquaintances. The interesting point here is that these figures of the past include characters that were disconnected themselves: Jesus, Hamlet, and also Don Quixote.

---

712 Atay, *Disconnected*, p. 620
713 Atay, *Disconnected*, pp. 618-619
714 Atay, *Disconnected*, p. 619

> For me, all plays, novels, stories have different meanings from other people's perceptions. All of life, all of humanity was told and consumed in these books. Living a new experience is like reading a new book to me. I live with the novels and their writers. I live with the forewords. The writers do not astonish me because I know their lives very well. On the other hand, in the real world as we call it, it is impossible to guess people's intentions. They astonish me everyday. It is much easier to live with my writers. He was born in 1886, in N. His/her father, mother, environment, his pains which no one knows while he/she was alive, the real reason concerning the quarrels with his friends were all told between the lines. In the first pages of the book I wonder about his/her unknown aspects but I know I will learn everything.[715]

This quotation is an important clue to what Selim is searching for in his reading and writing. Despite the variety of authors, 'it is easier to live with my writers' than to live with people. His way of living with people is not simply to ignore or avoid them, but to construct interactions with him in his mind, in which he is their voice as well as his own. In this way, they will always give him the responses he desires from them. Perhaps this is the main difference between the relationship between text/reader and all forms of social interaction, i.e. lack of face-to-face interaction in the former.[716] The vital exception to this is his lover, Günseli. In many ways he is as closed to her as to everyone else; the difference is that he loves her. Only he cannot love her actively, in his outward behaviour, because that involves sharing, clarity, responsibility and care. Whereas lovers may experience this as something that makes relationships with others easier and lighter, for Selim it only reminds him of his disconnectedness with others, except his mother, with whom his relationship can have this lightness, but only because he is a child:

> [Günseli] wants to help me, but she tires me. She cares, that means she expects care. At least she expects that her care is noticed. My mother is not like this. She knows how to be with me without involving herself.[717]

In a way Selim is seeking a stable world to which he can belong, and the kind of stable personal identity – or subjectivity – that the order of everyday life provides for its members and that was denied to him since childhood. But the private, disconnected manner in which he does it only confirms to him that his personal identity is opposed to the identity of society.

---

715 Atay, *Disconnected*, p. 375
716 On this see Wolfgang Iser, *The Act of Reading* (Baltimore; London: The Johns Hopkins University Press, 1994), pp. 163-180.
717 Atay, *Disconnected*, p. 623

This process of identifying oneself with others is taken to another level when Turgut discovers Selim's manuscripts, reads them and challenges the fixed character of his own 'self'. He reads Selim's accounts of his acquaintances, and then seeks them out himself, as though he were Selim's ghost. All of them turn out to be themselves disconnected in various ways. One of them, Esat, the only one who had a place in Selim's life during his high school years, confirms the statement about living in the world of writers, and then describes how Selim was regarded by others as both an 'abnormal' and a 'wonderful' child.

> He consented to their considering him a wonderful child. 'I am getting spoilt and then I utter such a stupid word that we all regret. But I never want to make a mistake. I wish to be a wonderful child who is one hundred percent pure because what is one hundred percent pure is nothing but itself. I want to be my own self.'[718]

It is significant that Atay conveys the mystical and mythical side of Selim by giving him the surname, 'Işık' (light), recalling the description of Jesus Christ as light in the Bible; the word 'light' also points to the way in which Turgut is able to follow in the footsteps of Selim. As Yıldız Ecevit puts it:

> The parallelism that is intended between Selim Işık, who is equipped with the abstract features of *the disconnected* and the leader of them as pure and clean as a child, and Jesus Christ is emphasized in his surname…The other story characters always yearn for Selim who is rich with mystical/mythical traits. He is like Jesus whose second coming is awaited. Every step of Turgut in the way of becoming a person – thereby a writer – is taken under the light of Selim. Being Selim is the point where Turgut struggles to reach on his way to live himself purely.[719]

Selim is a pure person who 'easily believes in people, never becomes suspicious about what they say.'[720] But as Atay points out, the purity is mixed with the lack and loss and disconnection that helped to nurture it:

> He was neither selected for the football team nor became the class president. Somehow he managed to remain naïve/clean in one respect – maybe in all respects.
>
> Yet he experienced a fear mixed with suspicion/doubt;
> Lived with the fear of something bad happening in the end, he, Selim Işık.
>
> Every event. An old wound tingled, every time he approached,
> People. Always wished to live as a child and fearless,
> When he is born again/reincarnates.

---

718 Atay, *Disconnected*, p. 365
719 Ecevit, *"Ben Buradayım…"*, p. 295.
720 Atay, *Disconnected*, p. 337

> Growing is required only for those connected.
> In his second coming he will walk around stark naked.
> In the strictest sense of the word stark naked.[721]

In *The Disconnected* Selim does not return but is replaced by Turgut, who, having read his manuscripts and diaries, seeks out Selim's friends and relatives. Some of them are mutual friends, but some of them were known only to Selim: Selim's girlfriend Günseli, his friend from military service Süleyman Kargı, his mother. In a sense, Turgut may be said to be the very opposite of open and 'innocent', because he already knows the people he is encountering for the first time; he shares no past with them – and no present, for they never discover where he lives – except the past that he has read about in Selim's account of them. But this knowledge of their pasts means that he can be whoever he wants to be. Moreover, his voice can be anybody's voice. This is illustrated in the meeting with Günseli, Selim's one-time lover.

We understand from Selim's diary that he never opened up to her. When Turgut and Günseli meet, they talk about her and Selim. After some time, in fact after many pages without punctuation and where it becomes impossible to say who the narrator is, Turgut seems to visualize the relationship between Selim, Günseli and Turgut. He does so in a way that makes it difficult to know which one is being imagined:[722]

> ... I am not talking Günseli there are hundreds of people everybody knows them but I am not talking I am judging I I despise them I do not crawl like them I I I you are tired Günseli let us take a break...[723]

Although Turgut is the ghost of Selim, he is fully aware of the differences between himself and his dead friend. Atay conveys this difference through Turgut's surname: Özben (in Turkish, '*öz*' means essence, '*ben*' means 'I', so that Özben could mean 'the essential I' or 'the genuine self'[724]). Yet, even Turgut himself does not know how to define what he is searching for and calls it simply 'thing':

---

721 Atay, *Disconnected*, p. 124
722 With respect to the theme 'Unity of multiple voices in *The Disconnected*' see Irzık, '*Tutunamayanlar*'da Çokseslilik ve Sınırları', p. 46.
723 Atay, *Disconnected*, p. 486
724 Most of Turkish names and surnames have meanings. Names of the objects and things can become names of people. Some common Turkish names are, for instance, spring, river, summer, rose, rain, free, revolution, evolution etc. Also people can combine different words and make up names such as black+cloud. In that sense the Turkish name '*Özben*' (essence+I) does not sound as strange or didactic as it might do in English.

Shall I embark on the adventure with all my power? Shall I not be able to, shall I fail to protect it? It, that 'thing'? A part no one knows, hard to describe, yet the 'thing' is completely aware of its existence/presence. Shall he jeopardize/endanger it as well? He had never surrendered the whole Turgut. Never. He had kept it for himself. A 'thing' only Turgut appreciated…I know what I am saying. It is me, the self of Turgut Özben.[725]

'A part no one knows' says Turgut and immediately after this the 'I's are replaced by the third person 'he', as if this 'thing' is an alien 'thing' within oneself.

One is tempted to read this passage from Atay through the lenses of one familiar philosophy or another, such as Kant's distinction between two selves as two descriptions of ourselves: empirical self-consciousness and transcendental self-consciousness. The former, being the self as an object of perception, an object of knowledge, and subject to the categories, takes the form of a subject-object relationship. It is the individual self which has a history, and personality. The latter, the synthetic original unity of apperception, on the other hand, is the condition that guarantees the unity of my experiences since one cannot think without presupposing a subject. The transcendental unity of apperception is neither conceptual nor empirical in nature. Or we might appeal to Bergson who, critical of the Kant's notion of the transcendental self which is outside of time and space, argues that it is possible to have an access to the 'deeper' self, and that it is pure duration which is the interiority of self. And only through intuition we can have access 'to the very inwardness of life', as well as to the 'deeper' self.

However, Atay's use of language seems to be partly designed to resist such direct readings. The apparently arbitrary and random shift between the first and the third person modes of address is perhaps the clearest indication of this. This 'thing' like quality is conveyed in an episode that Turgut recalls from his years at university, where one day he and Selim had sat down together to write an essay which they called 'The Co-ordinates of Life'. In this essay Selim criticised Turgut for being overly rationalist. It begins with an unnecessarily 'accurate' description of the location of Turgut's house: 'a house in the northeast of the city, between forty one degrees, zero minutes and one second latitude, and twenty nine degrees, twelve minutes and one second longitude.'[726] This sort of precision, which, in fact, does not mean anything in the outer world, involves a supposedly objectivist attitude to the outside world, but at the same time a distance to oneself. In so far as Turgut absorbs himself in Selim's manuscripts, becomes Selim, he moves radically away from this attitude. He finds it increasingly difficult to maintain the external appearance of everyday order and engages in a series of internal monologues that reflect on his own situation, and in internal dialogues with

---

725 Atay, *Disconnected*, p. 327
726 Atay, *Disconnected*, pp. 27-28

others and with his dead friend. The character of Turgut is represented by Atay – as the character of Ulrich is represented by Musil in the first two parts of *The Man without Qualities* – through these internal monologues and dialogues.

Eventually, although he has tried to find Selim's friends and has held internal dialogues with many others, Turgut speaks only with Selim. By this stage he can neither return to daily life nor can he transform his internal monologues and dialogues into an active rejection of it, nor yet anticipate a different mode of daily life.

The novel ends with Turgut's going on a journey with no fixed destination. He begins to live in train compartments, liminal spaces between destinations. He has Selim's diaries, a copy of *Don Quixote*, and writing paper with him. At one point on this journey he meets a journalist and hands him a manuscript with the title *The Disconnected*. The reader is left with an ambiguity: is this the original manuscript of Selim's, Turgut's account of his own encounters with Selim, or the novel that we are reading? Is there actually a Selim and/or a Turgut? Did Turgut really give up his 'self' and emerge with Selim? Did he become Selim's double?

The double is a common enough theme in literature, but generally the double is a sinister figure who appears from nowhere and threatens the unity of the self. Turgut and Selim's relationship is different in that Turgut voluntarily merges with Selim[727], and also in that the Selim he merges with is himself someone who is engaged in a constant process of becoming someone else. This raises more questions about identity and subjectivity.

---

[727] In fact, Turgut's eventual merging with Selim reminds us of the relationship between Ulrich and Agathe. They don't merge with each other in the sense that Turgut did with Selim or Selim with literary and historical characters; however, there is an interesting scene at the siblings' first meeting. When Ulrich and Agathe meet each other for the first time after their father's death they are in Pierrot costumes. Agathe enters the room and Ulrich notices the similarity, he feels that it is he himself who has come in through the door and his sister is a dreamlike repetition and alteration of himself. Agathe has the same feeling: 'I had no idea we were twins!' The theme double is doubled here through the Pierrot costumes. Now, the figure Pierrot is a character of pantomime and commedia dell'arte, an Italian genre which was introduced on the French stage in the seventeenth century. Many artists and writers were attracted by the figure Pierrot who assumes the identity of an angel or a monster who would reveal the meaning of life if he had not been mute. In fact, this silence is where the half of Pierrot's secret lies. He refuses the production of any meaning which enables him to become anything. The other half of his secret is his mask which again means a refusal of an identity. In fact, the defining character of Pierrot is his naiveté, however, according to Jonsson, it is his lack of identity that attracted many modernist writers and artists. Stefan Jonsson, *Subject without Nation, Robert Musil and the History of Modern Identity* (London: Duke University Press, 2000), pp. 175-177.

VIII.iii. The Double

In 'The Double as Immortal Self' Otto Rank traces the theme of the double back to peoples in whom the concept of the soul appears as a duality: the self and its shadow, the living and the dead person. In its most primitive form, Rank argues, this concept of the soul as a duality is encountered from Northern Melanesia to aboriginal Australia, from Fiji to Greenland. Rank shows that some even used the same word for shadow and soul.[728] The question of how man saw the soul in his shadow is answered by Rank through the assumption that first man saw his own image in his shadow, inseparable from himself. The fact that the shadow changes its form and disappears at night leads Rank to conclude: 'this observation of the human shadow disappearing with the fertilising sun to reappear with its return made it a perfect symbol for the idea of an immortal soul.'[729] It is regarded as the most vital element of human being for it protects the self even in the deepest sleep. We encounter the dualistic nature of man in Homer as well, the one being the visible appearance, the other in his invisible image which becomes free only after his death. In Plato we have the world of images and the world of appearances. But of course in Plato's cave allegory, the relationship between the shadow and the self is reversed: what we see in the world of appearances, in the world of material of change, is nothing but the shadows of things, whereas it is only the world of Forms that can constitute real knowledge.

The presentation of the second self as shadow or reflection is a common theme in Romantic literature as well, though as Rank suggests, with a decisive twist: 'Originally conceived of as a guardian angel, assuring immortal survival to the self, the double eventually appears as precisely the opposite, a reminder of the individual's immortality, indeed the announcer of death itself.'[730] This change was due to the Christian interpretation of immortality as interpreted by the church: the promise of immortality to those good ones, and the denial of it to evil ones. The Devil as it appears in the Middle Ages is nothing other than the personification of the moralised soul. In Goethe's *Faust* the soulless Devil seduces a good man to do evil things by promising the immortality of his soul.[731]

Whether there is a link between good/evil in Christianity and the disturbing, even terrifying characteristics of the other self as it appears in modern novels – the

---

728 Rank, 'The Double as Immortal Self', p. 73
729 Rank, 'The Double as Immortal Self', p. 74
730 Rank, 'The Double as Immortal Self', pp. 75-76
731 Rank, 'The Double as Immortal Self', p. 76

shadow, or the reflection in the mirror or a rival – is not something that we can pursue here. Yet the other selves we encounter in Dostoyevsky's *The Double*, or Oscar Wilde's *The Picture of Dorian Gray*, or Goethe's *Faust*, or E.T.A.Hoffman's *The Sand Man* have a common feature: they are figures full of friendly intentions at first, who become the enemy or rival of the hero. This is rather explicit in Dostoyevsky's *The Double* in which the horror and the nightmare of everyone, that is to say meeting his/her double, is depicted in the most disturbing, but at the same time, as Otto Rank puts it, 'the most moving and psychologically the most profound' way.[732]

The hero, Mr. Golyadkin, a government clerk, paranoically claims that he is surrounded by enemies, enemies who wear masks that conceal their real faces. Even though he has a sense of being excluded from society as well as from the world of officialdom, he cannot recognise the symptoms in himself that, in fact, have led to this exclusion. He makes a fool of himself when he appears at a party to which, to his astonishment, he has not been invited, and from which he is roughly ejected. After such humiliation Golyadkin looks 'as if he was trying to hide from himself, as if he wanted to run away from himself.' Even more says the narrator: 'Mr. Golyadkin wanted not only to run away from himself but even to annihilate himself, to cease to be, to return to the dust.'[733] Wanting 'to annihilate' themselves and 'to cease to be' seem to be a common wish among the anti-heroes of such novels.

Dostoyevsky then multiplies Golyadkin's humiliation and loss of dignity by making him encounter someone who looks exactly the same as him. This 'double' first approaches Golyadkin in the friendliest manner, disarming our hero who then reveals important secrets about his foes; yet later on he becomes an enemy, a rival. Golyadkin junior, the double, attempts to destroy Golyadkin senior's good name in society, even more, he claims his position in the office. Golyadkin junior secures and empowers his position in the world of bureaucracy and hierarchy while Golyadkin senior loses it gradually. The more Golyadkin senior 'annihilates' himself and 'ceases to be', the more the rival, Golyadkin junior, comes into being.

In this short novella Dostoyevsky both questions the 'realities' of nineteenth century Russia with its aristocratic and bureaucratic establishments, and addresses a universal topic: the question of the original and the copy or the question of the unity of the self. The fact that the word 'mask' appears in the novella many times is no coincidence: everyone wears a mask, says our hero, everyone but him, for he

---

[732] Otto Rank, *The Double*, trans. Jr. Harry Ducker (Capel Hill: University of North Carolina Press, 1971), p. 27.
[733] Fyodor Dostoyevsky, *The Double* (London: Penguin, 1985), p. 166.

wears it only at balls. Since everyone wears masks they do not even notice this miraculous similarity between his and his double. Anton Antonovich, another clerk, notices it only after he is told about it by Golyadkin: 'the resemblance is positively miraculous, it is fantastic as people say, I mean he's exactly like you...yes, I own I didn't pay attention at first. Miraculous, really miraculous!'[734] The problem for Golyadkin senior is a two-fold one: the fact that they don't even notice the resemblance shows that he is not even recognised by the members of the society to which he longs to belong; not being recognised equals non-existence in this hierarchical and bureaucratic social order. But once the resemblance is pointed out to them, he faces another question: who is the original Golyadkin, and who is the copy? Not only Golyadkin himself, but we, as the readers, face the same question: is there actually a second person? Dostoyevsky articulates this tension in the most ingenious way: once we are about to be convinced that there is no second Golyadkin, and that everything happens in our hero's mind, we have evidence for his existence, a third eye from the outer world: sometimes it is the servant Petrushka, sometimes someone from the government department like above mentioned Anton Antonovich. This is also what makes the story brutal: the reader is in this dark hole, the truth escapes us, it is not revealed.

A similar technique is applied by Atay. A book with the title *The Disconnected* is given to a journalist by Turgut to be published, in the novel's first chapter, entitled 'The Beginning of The End.' Thus in a way, the course of the novel is that of time folding back on itself. But this does not mean that the novel makes clear something that appears obscure at its beginning. The reader is constantly left with an ambiguity: is *The Disconnected* that we have in our hand the story of Turgut's merging with his dead friend Selim, following the course of his life and thoughts and then setting them down in a manuscript of his own, or are Selim and his manuscripts and his suicide all the product of Turgut's imagination? Does Turgut inhabit Selim's mind or does Selim inhabit Turgut's? Either way one thing is certain: by merging with his dead friend who himself merged with fictional and historical characters constantly, and who, at one particular period in his life always lived with his double – be it Hamlet, Nietzsche, Jesus etc., the merging becomes a constant movement through identities. And of course it is no coincidence that Selim's last 'double' is Jesus Christ: doubling becomes infinite for Christ, in a way, is meant to stand for the whole of humanity, timeless and spaceless.

---

[734] Dostoyevsky, *The Double*, p. 180

In an interview Atay once said that those who read *The Disconnected* are not wrong to link him with Kafka and Dostoyevsky.[735] At one point the narrator of the novel addresses Selim as the captain of the underground men and of the devils.[736] Yıldız Ecevit claims that Selim is none other than Prince Myshkin.[737] In fact, Selim is more like an underground man. Not only as the anti-hero of *Notes From the Underground* but also as a concept: all of Dostoyevsky's characters are underground men in one way or another.[738] The underground man shows himself in the name of Prince Myshkin, or Golyadkin senior or Raskolnikov or Karamazov. What is it to be an underground man?

The underground man, lacking anything distinctive about him, is characterless, is treated 'like an insect'.[739] It might be true that the Russian title of the *Notes From Underground*, Zapiski iz podpolya, 'suggests (pod, 'under'; pol, 'floor') vermin spawning and wriggling under floorboards, gnawing at the foundations of a house and peering out with bloodshot eyes through grimy cracks, brooding over destruction and chaos with a rat-like intensity, perverseness, and resentment against the forces that keep them imprisoned.'[740] However, it is also true that the underground man's motive is 'simple': he longs for originality, for his 'self'. This is why the hero of the *Underground* goes to the park every day in order to be noticed by an officer. This is why Raskolnikov talks about the authenticity of the article he published and of his being an extraordinary man. Unlike the other underground men, however, Raskolnikov chooses evil freely, transgresses the law and gets closer to originality or to freedom: as he mentions in his article there are three features of the extraordinary or original man: transgression of the law, acting for the benefit of humanity, and feeling no pangs of conscience about one's transgressive actions. Raskolnikov believes that the murder of the old woman is his test. He will break the law, do something for the good of humanity by getting rid of a universally despised person, and not regret it. However, precisely the planned murder of a defenseless old woman who everyone despises may be said to be no test at all. It is too easy to justify. In fact, it is the unplanned and spontaneous murder of the innocent and harmless daughter that will become the true test of Raskolnikov's

---

735 Ecevit, *"Ben Buradayım..."*, p. 203
736 Ecevit, *"Ben Buradayım..."*, p. 207
737 Ecevit, *"Ben Buradayım..."*, p. 207
738 Monroe C. Beardsley, 'Dostoyevsky's Metaphor of the 'Underground,' *The Journal of the History of Ideas*, Vol. 3, No. 3 (Jun., 1942).
739 Dostoyevsky, *Notes from the Underground* (London: Penguin, 1985), p. 52.
740 Beardsley, 'Dostoyevsky's Metaphor', p. 266.

extraordinariness. Raskolnikov fails this test, suffering the pangs of conscience that the extraordinary man is not supposed to feel.

Through the theme or the concept of the underground man Dostoyevsky problematises the question of originality and authenticity. Atay's description of the disconnected recalls Dostoyevsky's underground men:

> From the Encyclopaedia of Bizarre Animals: The Disconnectus Erectus: they are clumsy and cowardly animals...At first sight they even look like humans. But their claws are very weak. They can't climb hills. When they have to descend, they let themselves slide down (they fall frequently). They don't have much body hair. Although their eyes are big, their sight is not well-developed, this is why they can't detect danger from afar. Their males cry in sad tones when they are left alone. They call for mating in the same sad tones. Usually they live in other animals' shelters as long as the host can bear the situation....They don't have any family order. After birth, mother, father, and children go their separate ways....When they live with others, they eat what the others bring in. When they are left alone, they forget to eat. Since all their behaviour depends on imitation, if they don't see the others eating, they don't understand they are hungry...And again because of their imitative nature, they constantly enter into fights because they see other animals doing it.[741]

Atay goes one step further by introducing the idea of 'multiple personalities'. In this context, Ecevit draws our attention to the similarities, not only between Selim and Don Quixote but also between Selim and Hermann Hesse's literary character Harry Haller in *Steppenwolf*. At first Haller is both a wolf and a human being; each wants to destroy the other ceaselessly. Harry 'finds himself a "human being", that is to say, a world of thoughts and feelings, of culture and tamed or sublimated nature, and besides this he finds within himself also a "wolf", that is to say a dark world of instinct, of savagery and cruelty.'[742] He is isolated, alone and struggling with conflicts. Then, Harry who is in the process of becoming realizes that his 'self' is not simply divided but it includes countless singularities. And he learns the 'art of living' by playing with these singularities as a chess player might.[743]

> Harry consists of a hundred or a thousand selves, not of two. His life oscillates, as everyone's does, not merely between two poles, such as the body and spirit, the saint and the sinner, but between thousands, between innumerable poles.[744]

---

741 Quoted in Gürle, *Oğuz Atay's Dialogue*, p. 31
742 Hermann Hesse, *Steppenwolf*, trans. Basil Creighton (Harmondsworth, Penguin Books, 1965), p. 70.
743 Ecevit, *"Ben Buradayım..."*, p. 178
744 Hesse, *Steppenwolf*, p. 70

Similarly, Selim is described as someone who 'wishes to live too many things all together. Whichever one he hangs on to, wrong done to the other one. How many parts could he break into?'[745] Moreover, Selim says: 'as a matter of fact I fall for anyone I see. In no time I am prepared to be like him, to submit my whole self to him and to absorb his whole existence into myself.'[746]

Ecevit draws our attention to the same inner conflicts and the theme the 'self as a multiplicity' in Atay's other novels. In *Tehlikeli Oyunlar*, Atay increases the number of the divisions of inner conflicts: from the main character Hikmet he creates an army of Hikmets: bourgeois Hikmet, Hikmet under the pressure of the instincts, child Hikmet, and marginal Hikmet. In this novel Atay goes one step further by building his literary character Hikmet as someone whose organs are taken from different people. Not only this, the organs are taken from people who lived at different times:[747] 'By all accounts these pieces are not taken from people of the same century; they even differed in race, language and religion.'[748]

VIII.iv. Intertextuality and the 'Dissolution of the Subject'

We saw in the discussion of Musil that 'essayism' refers not only to one style of writing among others, but is also a condition for creating a literary character such as the man without qualities; ultimately essayism was presented as an idea of living as well as writing. For Atay, intertextuality plays a similar role, creating a literary character such as Selim who lacks any fixed identity.

The term 'Intertextuality' was introduced by Julia Kristeva. In 'Word, Dialogue and Novel' she says that a text cannot exist as a self-sufficient whole, cannot function as a closed system. There are two reasons for this: firstly, the writer himself/ herself is a reader as well, secondly a text is only available through some process of reading.[749] Kristeva's theory of intertextuality has its roots in the Bakhtinian idea of 'dialogism' as an open-ended play between the text of the subject and the

---

745 Atay, *Disconnected*, p. 406
746 Atay, *Disconnected*, p. 633
747 Ecevit, *"Ben Buradayım..."*, p. 178
748 Oğuz Atay, *Tehlikeli Oyunlar* (İstanbul: İletişim Yayınevi, 1973), p. 336.
749 Judith Still and Michael Worton, 'Introduction,' in *Intertextuality: Theories and Practices*, ed. Judith Still and Michael Worton (Manchester: Manchester University Press, 1991), p. 1. See also *The Kristeva Reader*, ed. Toril Moi (Oxford: Blackwell, 1995), p. 34.

text of the addressee. In *The Dialogic Imagination* Bakhtin contrasts novels which are monologic to that of those that are in a constant dialogue with other texts as well as other authors.[750] Bakhtin locates in Plato's Socratic dialogues one of the earliest forms of dialogism. In *The Republic* Plato describes the poet as an imitator, who always copies an earlier text, which itself is already a copy. Plato sees poetry as partial and deceptive reality, whereas philosophy is truth-seeking via a plurality of voices in a narrative context. Bakthin follows Plato, degrading poetry's monologism, but celebrating not philosophy but the dialogic novel.[751] To what extent does *The Disconnected* meet these criteria of the dialogic and the intertextual?

Selim does not live in isolation, but reads about and writes about many other literary characters, and identifies with many of them. This process of identifying with characters from the past already has a model of course, *Don Quixote*. Turgut carries a copy of *Don Quixote* on the train when he goes on his long journey. Selim's relationship with his books and manuscripts is a little like that of *Don Quixote* with his books and manuscripts. And like *Don Quixote*, it makes Selim a not very competent member of society.[752]

But Selim is different: while Don Quixote becomes one type of character – a knight from an age that has passed – and forges a sort of identity out of it, Selim constantly changes the character with which he identifies. It is a peculiar art, or act, of reading. 'Reading' Wolfgang Iser tells us 'is not a direct "internalisation," because it is not a one-way process' rather it is 'a dynamic *interaction* between text and reader.'[753] Saying this Iser does not argue that the relationship between the reader and the text is a symmetrical one, on the contrary, unlike all forms of social interaction it lacks ascertainability for the reader cannot question the text to find out to what extent his views about it are accurate. This very lack of ascertainability brings about reader-text interaction. This indeterminacy, Iser concludes, 'increases the variety of communication possible.'[754] In Selim's case, however, the reader seems to be missing in the act of reading. Once he starts to read he immediately becomes the character or the author. The result of this is that one day he will be Hamlet, one day Nietzsche, another Marx, another Oblomov, and so on. None of these identifications provide him with stability. The worlds of Nietzsche, Marx,

---

750 Mikhail Mikhailovich Bakhtin, *The Dialogic Imagination* (Texas: University of Texas Press, 2004).
751 Judith Still and Michael Worton, 'Introduction', in *Intertextuality*, p. 3.
752 For further discussion see Ecevit, *"Ben Buradayim...",* pp. 245-250
753 Iser, *Reading*, p. 107
754 Iser, *Reading*, p. 167

Hamlet and so on are different worlds, and so there is no continuity to Selim's subjecthood, no firm basis for it and no continuity of social relationships. This does not mean that he does not want such continuity. One day, Turgut learns from Esat that Selim once said: 'In *My Universities,* there is someone who is trying to reconcile Nietzsche and Marx.[755] Isn't that strange? He died before even having the opportunity to realize this. What could he have done if he had lived? Such unfinished works give me pain.'[756] In a way, his whole life is one unfinished work, an endless attempt to reconcile irreconcilable influences. Then, one day, he 'becomes' Jesus.

Selim sees Jesus not as a prophet, but as the archetype and 'greatest supporter' of the disconnected, thinking thoughts that were contrary to his era and his attitude of not resisting evil.[757] Selim's attitude to Jesus is different from his attitude to the other people with whom he identifies; these lose their attraction and others replace them, whereas Jesus Christ is described as a successful disconnected because he has truly sacrificed himself. Selim talks about Jesus as a friend whose value was underestimated when he was alive.

> They flew together; they sat together in a high place. They talked about things as the beauty of the soul. They talked about the miseries they have experienced due to people, they couldn't understand how the time passed. While it was getting dark, Jesus asked for permission and he left: his father was waiting above.[758]

Moreover, he writes a humorous letter to Jesus: 'I've been thinking about you for days. I can't put your book down…On Wednesday, my mother won't be home. We can talk freely, if you come.'[759] However, while Jesus is addressed in a humorous way in Selim's fictions, the diary entries shortly before his death display a more melancholic language: 'I haven't shaved my beard for fifteen days. My hair is also long.'[760]

---

755 We active readers can read even this as a quotation. After a debate with Oswald Spengler, Max Weber said: 'The honesty of a contemporary scholar and above all, of a contemporary philosopher, is to be decided on the basis of his attitude to Nietzsche and Marx. Those who do not acknowledge that they could not carry out considerable parts of their work without the work done by these two, are cheating themselves and others. The world in which we ourselves exist intellectually is a world largely molded by Marx and Nietzsche.' See Eduard Baumgarten, *Max Weber: Werk und Person* (Tübingen: J. C. B. Mohr, 1964), pp. 554-555.
756 Atay, *Disconnected,* p. 374.
757 Ecevit, *"Ben Buradayım…",* p. 294
758 Atay, *Disconnected,* p. 156
759 Atay, *Disconnected,* p. 157
760 Atay, *Disconnected,* p. 607

Jesus Christ also says one cannot be a prophet in his own country. They also come to us. The ones who don't come are worse. Oh, were I not born in an underdeveloped country, were I not finished myself with my severe rage, I would show you! Your end has come: Jesus Christ is going to show you all, Jesus Christ has come to us.[761]

Selim dies and his diaries and manuscripts live on, not as Jesus' teachings did but through the efforts of Turgut. Turgut, however, is not a disciple of Selim; after starting to follow the trace of Selim, Turgut who learns how to be Selim, in other words, the disconnected, by imitating Selim, also identifies with the literary characters he and Selim read: 'I, Turgut Özben, am the son of the King of Denmark.'[762] Like Hamlet Turgut loses his sanity...or pretends to.

However, thanks to an imaginary friend, Turgut still has some connection with the external world. The name of this friend is thick with resoances: Olric. Berna Moran sees a parallel with Orlick in Charles Dickens' *Great Expectations* and with Yorick in *Hamlet;* Orhan Pamuk says: 'Olric is very similar to Yorick in *Tristram Shandy.*'[763] Or perhaps Atay meant Yorick not in *Tristram Shandy* but in *A Sentimental Journey.*[764] But since Atay was a close reader of Musil, one cannot avoid the conclusion that he intended a connection between Olric and Musil's Ulrich.

Olric first appears during a traumatic visit that Turgut makes to a brothel, accompanied by Metin, a mutual friend from university. He appears in the form of Turgut's internal interlocutor, and from then on Olric accompanies Turgut both in his internal monologues and dialogues, and in his external dealings with society. Olric functions for Turgut as an advisor who is present in the room with him but of which others are unaware. The most dramatic scene in which this relationship is depicted takes place during the collapse of his relationship with his wife:

> As a person who wanted to keep his thoughts to himself, he was scared of the uneasiness that could be brought by closeness in bed, so he was prolonging the conversation... He was standing by the bed without moving. He was waiting without moving, without getting undressed. Nermin [his wife] moved closer, undid his tie. A bad beginning. I don't want to be touched Olric...Tonight I don't want her to see me getting undressed. I am in strangely shy Olric. They used to say that you were like that in the land of ice. You did not have anybody near you when you were getting undressed.[765]

---

761 Atay, *Disconnected*, p. 667
762 Atay, *Disconnected*, p. 236
763 Ecevit, *"Ben Buradayım..."*, p. 250. In *Tristram Shandy* Parson Yorick is a close of Shandy family.
764 The narrator of *A Sentimental Journey* is called Reverend Mr. Yorick. Laurence Sterne, *A Sentimental Journey through France and Italy* (Harmondsworth: Penguin, 1986).
765 Atay, *Disconnected*, pp. 569-571

Eventually Turgut, who feels suffocated in the ambiguity of words and noise just like Selim did, can only set himself free from the boredom of daily life and fixed patterns of behaviours if he goes on a journey – with Olric, his imaginary companion:

> I should let go of myself, he murmured. I should give up resisting. I must live and see. I should not be afraid of travelling to a country I do not know. I should enter the world of these indistinct people. Selim's trip was interrupted; his mind as well... let yourself go: what is better than living in a dream? You can take with you whomever you like, such as the clerk at the office who wants to be an engineer. Live your adventure...You won't have any bitterness inside. [766]

I said that Turgut realises that towards the end of his life Selim identifies himself with Jesus and stops reading anything other than *The Bible*. While Selim becomes Jesus gradually and eventually, Turgut becomes Hamlet, and in doing so he is convinced more and more that Selim did not commit suicide but was killed and that his task is to find the murderers, or the traitors:

> You killed him once. I am not going to let you do it again. I will clean him up from his first death and open the way for his Second Coming. I wish it weren't me. I wish it were somebody else to fulfil this task. Someone more able than I am. Can a coward and a weakling like me handle such a difficult situation?[767]

I said that Turgut becomes more like Hamlet. This parallelism can be seen in the re-enactment of the murder of Hamlet's father. Towards the end of Act II of Shakespeare's play, Hamlet is told that there are some players coming to the city, and sees this as an opportunity to reveal the murder of his father. They will perform *The Murder of Gonzago*,[768] but he will insert some extra lines. Of course this play is the re-enactment of the murder of his father by his uncle Claudius, who soon afterwards married his mother. Hamlet wants Horatio to keep an eye on the king during the poisoning scene as he thinks he can catch the king's guilty eyes: 'I prithee, when thou seest that act afoot/Even with the very comment of thy soul/ Observe my uncle. If his occulted guilt/Do not itself unkennel in one speech/It is damned ghost that we have seen.'[769] The truth will be revealed. The brothel scene in *The Disconnected* echoes this re-enactment scene of the murder in *Hamlet*.

At one point, halfway through the novel, Turgut goes to Ankara. This is supposed to be a business visit; however, his main aim turns out to be meeting some friends of Selim he has learned about from Selim's writings. His purpose is to

---

766 Atay, *Disconnected*, pp. 324-325
767 Quoted in Gürle, *Oğuz Atay's Dialogue*, p. 95
768 Shakespeare, *Hamlet*, Act 2.2, p. 232
769 Shakespeare, *Hamlet*, Act 3.2, p. 252

learn more about Selim's suicide. In Ankara Turgut meets Metin, a friend of Selim's, and is immediately repelled by him, wondering how Selim could possibly have been a friend to him: Selim being the innocent, Metin the devil – or a representative of petit bourgeois life – must have poisoned him. Turgut prepares himself for Metin as if they will perform a play; he dresses very smartly. They meet in the hotel where Turgut stays and go to a pub. After going from one pub to the other they end up in a brothel:

> 'We are going to the origin of things, Metin!' 'What do you mean origin of things? Where are we...' Turgut stood up. He was swinging bravely. 'We are going to the bottom of everything. To the origin of things.' He leaned on the table. He grinded his teeth. 'We are going to the *lombelico del mondo*, to the bellybutton of life, Metin.' But where?' 'TO THE WHOREHOUSE!' Everybody stopped talking. Turgut shouted, 'Bill. Overcoat. Car.' He rushed to the door. He yelled at the driver. 'Go!' 'Where to?' 'TO THE WHOREHOUSE!'[770]

Of course this is all planned by Turgut, who in the brothel behaves like a madman or a Hamlet. By acting as a jester Turgut wishes to reveal the truth: the reason that lies behind Selim's death. It must be people like Metin who once took innocent Selim to a brothel and humiliated him. Like Horatio and Hamlet, Turgut should watch Metin carefully during their visit.

According to Gürle the brothel is a direct reference to Hamlet's telling Ophelia to go to a nunnery. In England at the time, nunnery meant a convent and a brothel.[771] The brothel's being in Ankara is no coincidence:

> When saying 'nunnery' Hamlet might have meant a convent, but obviously Atay takes the metaphor seriously, and sends his Hamlet to a brothel....The ambivalence of the carnivalesque enters the picture also in *The Disconnected*, but the equivalence of ladies and whores in *Hamlet* is approached from the other way round. As opposed to Hamlet, who is disgusted by the behaviour of his mother, and takes his hostility out on innocent Ophelia calling her a whore several times in the play, Turgut treats the prostitutes like ladies and calls the proprietor of the house 'Mother.'[772]

Gürle argues that the brothel scene challenges all forms of authority. In fact, their entering the brothel is quite a scene. Turgut says:

> 'Grand Mama, tell me: is this a substantive (self-governing, freestanding) country? With which laws are you governed?' With the laws of sanitation. 'Are you the ruler of

---

770 Quoted in Gürle, *Oğuz Atay's Dialogue*, p. 104
771 Gürle, *Oğuz Atay's Dialogue*, p. 104 f
772 Gürle, *Oğuz Atay's Dialogue*, p. 104. The treating of prostitutes as ladies also recalls *Don Quixote*.

here? Yes, you are: don't be modest.' Suddenly, he jumped toward the middle of the room. The veins in his neck had swelled, his face had reddened: 'I am becoming your subject. I am Turgut Özben, the son of the King of Denmark', heir to the Ottoman land, I am addressing you from the pulpit of history.[773]

Later on Turgut declares Metin the grand vizier and says: 'All the world is a whorehouse'[774] echoing Shakespeare's 'All the world is a stage.'[775] Here Gürle asks: 'Is Ankara, the heart of Anatolia and the embodiment of the sacred ideals of the Republic depicted as a whore-house?'[776] It may well be, however, this is not the only reason for Turgut's declaring himself Hamlet. Like Jesus, we encounter Hamlet not only in the brothel scene but throughout the whole book. Why is this so?

Eric Levy draws our attention to the urgent interrogation in *Hamlet*. It is a questioning of the meaning and purpose of human life: 'Who is there?' (1.1.1), the first line of the play, 'What is man?' (4.4.33), 'To be or not to be' (3.1.57). According to Levy, the interrogation is so fundamental that merely giving answers would not be enough for its resolution; it requires the 'reformulation of the conceptual context in which the questions themselves are posed.'[777] Levy suggests that, as opposed to the Aristotelian-Thomist paradigm which answers the question 'what is man' by giving priority to reason, Hamlet or *Hamlet* puts emphasis on the perplexity of reason, on the limitations of thought. Hamlet is never mad; his so-called madness is the result of his absolute self-consciousness as well as of knowing the truth. The ghost tells him the truth, but, how can a sane man believe that ghosts exist? Hamlet does believe and he has to behave like an insane man for two reasons: to protect his sanity, and to reveal the truth at the right time. Turgut's alienation from 'real' life is also the result of his absolute self-consciousness. In order to protect his sanity he has to create Olric, who, rather than being Yorick or Osric, is more like Sancho Panza to Don Quixote. Like Hamlet Turgut is longing for truth: why did Selim commit suicide? There must be a reason for this. On the other hand, this is not the main motive behind Turgut's detective-like following of Selim through his manuscripts and friends. Turgut knows the truth: Selim longed for his genuine self; he even became nostalgic about his self, as if he had lost it. It is a search which, as he merges himself with Selim, eventually will become Turgut's search

---

773 Atay, *Disconnected*, p. 269; see also Gürle *Oğuz Atay's Dialogue*, p. 106
774 Atay, *Disconnected*, p. 270
775 Gürle, *Oğuz Atay's Dialogue,* p. 107
776 Gürle, *Oğuz Atay's Dialogue,* p. 107
777 Eric C. Levy, *Hamlet and the Rethinking of Man* (Cranbury: Associated University Presses, 2008), p. 54.

as well. However, Turgut discovers another truth, like Selim did: there is no such thing as an 'original' self.

Atay's interrogation too is so fundamental that merely giving answers would not be enough for its resolution; it requires a new language in order to be able to ask new questions. In other words, Atay problematises not only the fixed Cartesian self, but also Musil's idea of the modern subject as an existence of possibilities or of plasticity or of experimental life that will bring freedom. What if this state of becoming-child in a larval period brings about a detachment or a state of being *disconnectus erectus* rather than one of freedom? I said that according to Nietzsche what we call the subject was nothing other than the product of conceptual discourses of psychology, philology, and epistemology, however, the question that Atay asks is that what does the person who rejects these discourses and manages to get himself free of layers of her identity encounter? Does the dissolution of the subject also lead to the dissolution of the language, and to a state of ineffability or stammering and stuttering?

Once Socrates said that the unexamined life is not worth living.[778] George Eliot's belated response to Socrates was: 'The unexamined life may not be worth living, but the life too closely examined may not be lived at all.'[779] Perhaps I should add to this that too much of an examined life leads or may lead to death. If Levy is right in claiming that the urgent interrogation in *Hamlet* is a questioning of the meaning and purpose of human life, then Hamlet had to die, for Hamlet looks through things, he sees the essence of things, he is like the old blind prophet of Thebes, Teiresias who sees 'things clearly'[780] and who 'sees the truth.' Or even Cassandra of *The Women of Troy*, the daughter of King Priam and Queen Hecuba,

---

778 Plato, *The Apology of Socrates*, in *The Last Days of Socrates* (London: Penguin, 1976), p. 72
779 Melvyn Bragg, *In Our Time*, http://www.bbc.co.uk/programme/p00548dx
780 Euripides, *The Bacchae and Other Plays* (London: Penguin, 1972), p. 197. The blind prophet Teiresias or Tiresias appears in several epic stories and Greek tragedies concerning the legendary history of Thebes. In *The Bacchae*, by Euripides, Teiresias appears with Cadmus, the founder and first king of Thebes, to warn the king Pentheus against denouncing Dionysus as a god. In Sophocles' *Oedipus the King*, Oedipus calls upon Teiresias and wants him to help to uncover the murderers of the previous king Laius. Tiresias knows the truth from the beginning, and is reluctant to tell it to Oedipus. He appears in Sophocles' *Antigone* in which the gods through Teiresias express their disapproval of Creon's decision not to allow Polynices to be buried. See Sophocles, *The Three Theban Plays* (London: Penguin, 1984). Teiresias also appears in *Odysseus* Book XI. Odysseus goes to Hades to consult the soul of Teiresias who unlike the other souls can recognise Odysseus without drinking the black blood. Even

who foresees the destruction of Troy though no one believes her.[781] Her insanity enables her to see the essence of things; she sees things in the totality of time: she witnesses past and future events, and yet she cannot act, nor can Hamlet. Nietzsche thinks that Hamlet resembles the Dionysiac man:

> ...both have truly seen to the essence of things, they have understood, and action repels them; for their action can change nothing in the eternal nature of things, they consider it ridiculous or shameful that they should be expected to restore order to the chaotic world. Understanding kills action, action depends on a veil of illusion: this is what Hamlet teaches us, not the stock interpretation of Hamlet as a John-a-dreams who, from too much reflection, from an excess of possibilities, so to speak, fails to act. Not reflection, not that! True understanding, insight into the horrible truth, outweighs any motive for action, for Hamlet and Dionysiac man alike.[782]

'The horrible truth' makes Hamlet unable to act, but this inactivity is not a failure, rather it is the inevitable consequence of insight into the essence of things; acting is not so much impossible or difficult as pointless. A state of affairs in which acting is pointless, in which nothing is in fact done, bears a close resemblance to death, indeed, it may be part of the definition of death. Cassandra had to die, so did Hamlet. Now, I would not go as far as claiming that Selim also died because he, like Hamlet, or Cassandra, saw the essence of things. However, there is a reason for Atay's referring to Hamlet several times in the novel, a novel whose central character commits suicide. Like Hamlet or Cassandra, Selim is one of those characters who combine deep understanding and powerlessness, the condition of the tragic human being.

As we have seen, Selim's search is a search for his genuine self, a search to which he devotes his whole life. The path that Selim takes in this search is reading and writing which eventually leads him to live through plays/games, plays other than life. Turgut's journey, that is to say his longing for the forgotten self in the midst of the rules and repetitions of routine life, on the other hand, starts with the reading of Selim's manuscripts. His journey requires a complete unlearning.

Odysseus' mother recognises him after taking a draught of black blood. See Homer, *Odysseus* (London: Penguin, 1964).
781 See Euripides, 'The Women of Troy', in *The Bacchae and Other Plays* (London: Penguin, 1972). Cassandra appears in Aeschylus' *Agamemnon* as well. When Agamemnon, King of Argos, returns from Troy, he brings with him Cassandra, the enslaved daughter of Priam, King of Troy, as his mistress. This exasperates Clytemnestra, Agamemnon's wife, who then kills both. Cassandra foresees Agamemnon's death as well as her own. See Aeschylus, 'Agamemnon', in *The Oresteian Trilogy* (London: Penguin, 1964).
782 Friedrich Nietzsche, *The Birth of Tragedy* (London: Penguin, 1993), p. 39.

One of the texts that Turgut finds among Selim's manuscripts is an essay entitled 'What is to be done?' in which he discusses what to do in order to be a genuine individual who wants to change the way things are and who wishes a revolutionary action, rather than imitating the behaviour and attitudes of the people around him in a lazy and indifferent way. The title was made famous by Lenin, but Selim is less interested in revolutionary collective political action than in the question of how something can be done by individuals. To realize an action which can change society, first of all an individual must be able to govern and discipline him/herself. To him, a person who cannot understand himself/herself cannot solve the problems of the society.

> What is to be done? If a prompt answer is requested to this question, of course, only through pure reason, or, with the combination of one or two ideas compiled from here and there, certain temporary solutions may be put forward. A person may believe that these temporary solutions are his/her own inventions. Yet, for example, the slight inspection of the concept regarded as pure reason will demonstrate that this is mostly clichés achieved through the influence of the society... There you are! Even in these basic behaviours, which are thought to be found by the pure reason, supposedly in order to develop and improve social action, and which are put forward as inevitable principles for all sorts of actions, you will look for the secret powers of the demand to obliviously protect the being of the individual and the society, which they do not want to change![783]

Selim suggests re-evaluating the respected values:

> In the process of understanding yourself, we can use the skepticism Descartes applied to science. We must start by not recognizing all of our values. We should never forget that the things we assume as personal values may be nothing but fake qualities acquired by the pressure of the society. For instance, let's take abstract concepts of moral values. There are concepts such as virtue, ethics, etc. We have learnt that these concepts are valid in every society and have also learnt to comply with these rules in every society....They, on the other hand, try to hypnotize us by these abstract concepts to survive the society no matter what the circumstances are. I don't only respect the man appraising himself to have virtues but if that person hasn't spent effort to take the society to a better place with the people who have virtues and if he hasn't tried to resist the wrong ways around him, then that person has no virtues to my opinion. Don't people even steal for a virtue when necessary?...However, let's not value such fake values which exist to maintain order.[784]

---

783 Atay, *Disconnected*, pp. 95-96
784 Atay, *Disconnected*, p. 99

Hamlet pretends to be insane in a world where seeing the 'horrible truth' could mean insanity; Turgut pretends to be 'normal' in a world whose rules are ready-made and are based on repetition.

Thus, intertextuality in *The Disconnected* becomes a tool for Selim/Turgut in their search for a genuine or an 'original' self. Intertextuality for Atay the author, on the other hand, becomes a tool for creating a character which lacks any fixed identity. The dialogue between the writer and his characters is a paradoxical, perhaps impossible chase, resembling a dog with its tail. Selim fails in his search for a genuine self, simply because there is no such thing, or perhaps it is not something to be revealed and intertextuality as his tool reveals this impossible longing, whereas Atay the author writes an 'original' novel partly thanks to his ingenious application of intertextuality. One may conclude that in the end Atay the author wins, for Selim commits suicide; however, this conclusion might be a hasty one for, by the end of the novel, Turgut has, through the act of chasing Selim, replaced Selim. Another Selim, the same one – but not the same one – has appeared and we are back at the beginning. The course of the novel, then, is that of time folding back on itself, a time whose movement is cyclical, and infinite, like the relationship between originality and intertextuality 'themselves.'

VIII.v. The Originality Paradox

> The scholar who actually does little else than wallow in a sea of books – the average philologist may handle two hundred a day – finally loses completely the ability to think for himself. He cannot think unless he has a book in his hands. When he thinks he responds to a stimulus (a thought he has read) and finally all he does is react. The scholar devotes all his energy to affirming or denying or criticising matter which has already been thought out – he no longer thinks himself....To read a book early in the morning, at day break, in the vigour and dawn of one's strength – that I call viciousness.[785]
>
> Nietzsche

When *The Disconnected* was published in 1971 Atay was criticised by many literary leading figures of the time for mixing different styles and genres as well as for giving the reader unnecessary details, for not being able to construct a meaningful

---

[785] Quoted in Thomas McFarland, 'The Originality Paradox', *New Literary History*, Vol. 5, No. 3, History and Criticism: I (Spring, 1974), p. 463.

whole.[786] Mehmet Seyda summarises this attitude: 'Can a novel appear by someone's writing everything that comes to his mind?'[787] In his obituary of Atay, some six years after the novel's appearance, Güven Turan says: *'The Disconnected... cannot be more than an interesting novel which is an attempt of someone who likes to read a lot.'*[788] Berna Moran, otherwise sympathetic, calls the book overloaded.[789] It is true that the novel consists of manuscripts, letters, and diary entries, as well as references to many historical figures or literary characters, sometimes whole sentences or phrases. However, as Murat Belge points out 'This seemingly disorganised material is brought together as a result of careful elimination, and is interwoven into the plotline not randomly, but in such a way that it constitutes a meaningful whole.'[790] Atay himself, in response to Seyda's statements, claims that the uniqueness of the novel lies in the details which are connected to a well-thought fundamental plan.[791]

This multi-layered structure led Gürle to describe *The Disconnected* as an example of the encyclopaedic narrative, a term introduced by Edward Mendelson:

> Each major national culture in the west, as it becomes aware of itself as a separate identity, produces an encyclopaedic author, one whose work attends to the whole social and linguistic range of his nation, who makes use of all the literary styles and conventions known to his countrymen, whose dialect often becomes established as the national language, who takes his place as national poet or national classic, and who becomes the focus of a large and persistent exegetic and textual industry comparable to the industry founded upon Bible [...] For the most part, encyclopaedic authors set out to imitate epics, but, unlike epic poets, they write about the ordinary present-day around them instead of the heroic past.[792]

It is true that Atay adopts and experiments with different styles and genres. He adopts mock-scientific discourse which as Gürle reminds us, is 'the most common manifestation of the encyclopaedic narrative',[793] to raise the questions about the rationality of the Enlightenment project or about the analytic

---

786 Ecevit, *"Ben Buradayım..."*, pp. 319-321
787 Ecevit, *"Ben Buradayım..."*, p. 312
788 Güven Turan, 'Oğuz Atay'ın Ardından', in *Oğuz Atay'a Armağan*, p. 25
789 Berna Moran, *Türk Romanına Eleştirel Bir Bakış* (İstanbul: İletişim Yayınları, 1992), p. 289.
790 Quoted in Gürle, *Oğuz Atay's Dialogue*, p. 28
791 Atay says this to Mehmet Seyda in an interview conducted by Seyda in May, 1972. See *Oğuz Atay'a Armağan*, p. 396
792 Quoted in Gürle, *Oğuz Atay's Dialogue*, p. 27
793 Gürle, *Oğuz Atay's Dialogue*, p. 32

mind 'that the third world borrowed from the west;'[794] he also adopts a mock-old-Turkish or Ottoman-Turkish discourse to raise questions about history and national identity. Let us consider, for instance, the following passage as an illustration of the former:

> According to the bulletin of the institute of healthy amorous advances, in the course of one year there have been registered cases of twelve-thousand-seven-hundred-sixteen dates at pastry shops, seven-thousand-eight at bus stops (one-thousand-eight-hundred-twenty-five of which never really took place), one-thousand-four-hundred-sixty-two in the open air (parks, fields, in the island etc.) and only six-hundred-twelve in the movie theatres. One should also add secret love affairs to these numbers (since there was no sign of Selim's name on the list, we assume his case belongs to this category). The rules of probability tell us that the number of secret love affairs should amount up to four-thousand-six-hundred. According to these records of the police department, there have been approximately one-hundred-twenty-six-thousand cases of looking and sighing, forty-four-thousand slightly touching on the bus, four-thousand-two-hundred aimlessly stalking, eight-hundred-fifty following the girl until she gets home, and fifteen-thousand-seven-hundred intense infatuation with no possibility of being loved back. The number of hopelessly platonic lovers (and this number is precise) is eight-hundred-fourteen.[795]

The similarity between to the opening passage of *The Man without Qualities* is striking: 'A barometric low hung over the Atlantic. It moved eastward toward a high-pressure area over Russia without as yet showing any inclination to bypass this high in a northerly direction... The water vapour in the air was at its maximal state of tension, while the humidity was minimal. In a word that characterizes the facts fairly accurately, even if it is a bit old-fashioned: It was a fine day in August 1913.' Musil's point, we said, is that the scientific and the everyday descriptions seem equally valid; the one is not superior to the other. In other words, neither the language of science nor inadequate conventions of realism can capture the 'Machean flux of sensations in which everything – the people, their 'bourgeois identities, the name of the city – has become subjective and unreal.'[796] Atay's point is similar: by adopting this mock-scientific discourse he shows that 'the analytical mind...borrowed from the west can never capture the world as it is.'[797] However, it does not follow from this that any other language or discourse can.

---

794 Gürle, *Oğuz Atay's Dialogue*, p. 34
795 Quoted in Gürle, *Oğuz Atay's Dialogue*, p. 34
796 Malcolm Spencer, *In the Shadow of Empire: Austrian Experiences of Modernity in the writings of Musil, Roth and Bachmann* (Rochester, N.Y.: Camden House, 2008), p. 16.
797 Gürle, *Oğuz Atay's Dialogue*, p. 34

Atay goes further than adopting different speech genres. Probably these sort of direct and indirect references to many texts made some critics of the time perceive the novel as no more than an interesting attempt of an enthusiastic reader, and the question of the originality of the novel was raised. Perhaps the author himself foresaw such reactions; after a traumatic visit to another friend's of Selim's, Burhan, Turgut says:

> My end came Olric. I would like to write a new foreword for myself. I would like to create a new language. A language that will explain me to myself. They tried many times, your Excellency. Thank God I don't know what they tried, Olric. I am not an heir of any tradition. They say impossible. I insist. Apparently a less-developed country has a poor cultural legacy. I reject this legacy, Olric.[798]

Being tired of repeating the same behaviour and words, Turgut longs for an original language, one only he can speak and understand. Olric, a mixture of different characters from different canonical European novels, tells him that such a thing is impossible. However, Atay writes an avant-garde and an 'original' novel while parodying several speech genres and referring to many texts. Atay not only responds to the possible doubts about the originality of the book but also opens the question about the relationship between tradition and originality, that is to say, the originality paradox. Perhaps Turgut's shouting 'I am not an heir of any tradition' was regarded only as evidence of the great influence of the other texts on the author, of the denial of its being unoriginal. Perhaps not only the readers but also many critics of the 1970s were still not ready to understand the dialogic structure of the novel through which along with other issues the concept of originality is problematised. A discussion which has occupied many thinkers: how can a novel which consists of so many different genres and references to many texts be original? Isn't it just a combination of imitation, though a good one, of other canonical texts like Selim's being a pure imitation of literary or historical characters rather than being an individual in his own way? That discussion goes back to Plato.

In *The Oxford English Dictionary* tradition as a noun is described as following: 'that which is thus handed down; a statement, belief, or practice transmitted from one generation to the other; a long-established and generally accepted custom or method of procedure, having almost the force of law; an immemorial usage; the body of the experiences and usages of any branch or school of art or literature, handed down by predecessors and generally followed.'[799] The word original as an adjective is described as 'present or existing from the beginning; first

---

798 Atay, *Disconnected*, p. 550
799 *The Oxford English Dictionary* (London: Oxford University Press, 1961), Vol. XI, p. 226.

or earliest'; 'created personally by a particular artist, writer, musician, etc.; not a copy; not dependent on other people's ideas'; (noun) 'the earliest form of something, from which copies may be made.'[800] The time dimension is important: something traditional has its origins in the past and is still maintained in the present, something original, whereas, does not have any reference to something already existing. This is where the originality paradox lies: in order to call something new or original a recognition is necessary, such a recognition can come only from already existing knowledge, namely tradition. The discussion is more complicated than this and requires a closer look.

We saw that in *The Republic* Plato declares that poets are merely imitators and that their products, along with the painters', are thrice removed from reality. But does Plato really mean what he says? How can he dismiss the great poet Homer, and is Plato himself not a great poet? These and similar questions are what we should be careful about, Havelock warns us, for first of all the poetry that Plato is talking about cannot be the same as poetry today. It might be the case that our poetry and the poetry of Plato's era have much in common; however, what must have changed is the environment in which poetry is practiced.[801] In other words, if we want to solve the problem of Plato's attack we should understand the nature of poetry that he is against first along with the environment in which they were produced. According to Havelock,

> It was of the essence of Homeric poetry that it represented in its epoch the sole vehicle of important and significant communication. It therefore was called upon to memorialise and preserve the social apparatus, the governing mechanism, and the education for the leadership and social management.[802]

Havelock's point is that the poetry Plato is talking about was a social phenomenon rather than a mode of individual imagination. 'Artistic creation' Havelock says 'as we understand the term is a much simpler thing than the epic performance and it is one which implies the separation of the artist from the political and social action.'[803] Now, this is where McFarland thinks that the origin of the originality paradox lies. According to him the attraction/rejection tension between Plato and Homer is the counterpart of the individual/tradition tension which constitutes the originality paradox.[804] It may well be. But we still did not investigate why Plato

---

800 *The Oxford English Dictionary*, Vol. VII, p. 202
801 Eric A. Havelock, *Preface to Plato* (London: Belknap, 1982), p. 10.
802 Havelock, *Preface*, p. 93
803 Havelock, *Preface*, pp. 90-91
804 McFarland, 'The Originality Paradox,' p. 468

labels the poets as imitators. A closer inquiry is necessary. To do this we should turn to the *Republic* itself.

The word *mimesis* appears in the Book III of the *Republic*. Socrates makes a distinction between the simple narrative and the narrative expressed through imitation,[805] a distinction that is quite familiar to the modern reader. In order to demonstrate the latter Socrates turns to the beginning of *Iliad* where the poet says that the priest asks Agamemnon to let his daughter go. Here Homer is the narrator, however, then he becomes the priest himself, he talks like an old man; he does everything to convince us that it is the priest who is talking, not Homer the poet. This type of storytelling, i.e. tragedy and comedy, Socrates labels as imitative, while in the simple narrative the storyteller tells his own story without becoming anyone else. In the epic poetry we find both, says Socrates. Why is Socrates against this? At this point Socrates turns to the education of the guardians. He asks Adeimantus: 'have you never noticed how imitation, if long continued from an early age, turns into habits and dispositions – of body, speech and mind?'[806] 'Our men' Socrates continues 'do not have a dual or manifold nature, since each of them performs only one task.'[807] The poets, on the other hand, can become anyone through imitation; this means they are only deceivers. Saying this Socrates/Plato does not reject the poets totally. His point is that a poet who is able to imitate anything is not desirable in the education of the guardians, that only the poets who can imitate only the good and just men should be appreciated:

> For our own good we would content ourselves with a simpler, if less enjoyable, poet and storyteller, who can imitate the decent man's way of speaking, and model his stories on those patterns which we laid down at the beginning of our attempt to provide an education for our soldiers.[808]

Homeric epics were a sort of tribal encyclopaedia in a culture of oral communication. In that sense their primary purpose was educational, and precisely because of this they are dangerous. Then Plato puts aside the discussion of the poet and moves onto the discussion of the melody and rhythm. Such a move seems to be odd at first, but, later it becomes clear why Plato suddenly talks about melody and harmony: the young guardian 'has to be an effective guardian of himself and of the music he has been learning, presenting himself rhythmically well-organised

---

805   Plato, *The Republic* (Cambridge: Cambridge University Press, 2000), Book III, 392d, p. 80.
806   Plato, *Republic*, 395d, p. 84
807   Plato, *Republic*, 397e, p. 85
808   Plato, *Republic*, 398, p. 87

and harmonised.'[809] Plato is almost talking about a stable self, but, not yet, he postpones this to Book IV, where he discusses the three principles of the soul: one ruling principle of reason and two subject ones of spirit and desire. And a temperate person is the one who has these three elements in friendly harmony, and in whom reason ought to rule. This is the self-mastery, or the unity of the *psyche*. This is Havelock's main argument: Plato's rejection of poetry, especially Homeric epic, is in fact related to his understanding of individuality.

> At some time towards the end of the fifth century before Christ, it became possible for a few Greeks to talk about their 'souls' as though they had selves or personalities which were autonomous and not fragments of the atmosphere nor of a cosmic life force, but what we might call entities or real substances.....Before the end of the fourth century the conception was becoming part of the Greek language and one of the common assumptions of Greek culture....Scholarship has tended to connect this discovery with the life and teaching of Socrates and to identify it with a radical change which he introduced into the meaning of the Greek word *psyche*.[810]

We have to wait till the last book, Book X, in order to hear more about the unity of the self and, in relation to *mimesis*, why the poets, especially Homer, are to be rejected in a harmonious society. Behind Plato's rejection of the Homeric oral tradition lies this new conception of the self, of the autonomous *psyche* which can think, reflect and criticise. In *Iliad* we encounter Achilles as a man who has a strong character but it is also true to say that 'his acts are responses to his situation, and are governed by remembered examples of previous strong men.'[811] In Homeric epic there is no 'I' that can stand apart the tradition and be critical about it. As opposed to a drama student today, a Greek student, Havelock says,

> had to mobilise the psychic resources necessary to memorise Homer and the poets, or enough of them to achieve the necessary educational effect. To identify with the performance as an actor does with his lines was the only way it could be done. You threw yourself into the situation of Achilles, you identified with his grief or his anger. You yourself became Achilles and so did the recite to whom you listened. Thirty years later you could automatically quote what Achilles had said or what the poet had said about him....Plato's target was indeed an educational procedure and a whole way of life.[812]

---

809 Plato, *Republic*, 398d, p. 88
810 Havelock, *Preface*, pp. 197-98
811 Havelock, *Preface*, p. 199
812 Havelock, *Preface*, p. 45

In other words, this new notion of the self, the Platonic self, had to stop identifying itself with the polymorphic narration in which the self moves from one motion to the other easily, is split up into many selves. This point is more explicit at the last Book where Plato once again comes back to his attack on *mimesis*:

> The law would say that to be patient under suffering is best, and that we should not give way to impatience, as there is no knowing whether such things are good or evil; and nothing is gained by impatience; also, because no human thing is of serious importance, and grief stands in the way of that which at the moment is most required.

In Plato's world Selim/Turgut would perhaps be a case study to show his pupils how one should not be. Not only is Selim completely imitating others, he is emotionally affected by things that he sees and hears, and moreover reads; like the citer of *Iliad* and *Odysseus*, he identifies himself with the character, the writer, even with all potential readers. Plato would also despise Atay the author who in order to be able to write a novel like *The Disconnected* had to identify with all the characters, fictional and historical, that we encounter in it.

Perhaps Plato is not talking about imitation in the context of originality, nor does he see imitation as opposed to originality. As we have seen, Plato is against imitation for educational purposes. Plato would not disagree with Cicero who claims that 'one of the chief steps in Roman education, at least in the training of the orator, was the study and imitation of eminent models'[813] as long as these models would be good and just state men. Like Cicero, Quintilian emphasises 'the effectiveness of imitation in acquiring a fluent mastery of style and especially cites imitation of literary models as the most helpful method.'[814] Like Cicero there is still appreciation of imitation in Quintilian, but this time not even only imitation of the state man but also of the literary models is praised. Now, whether it is the state man or the literary models, neither Cicero nor Quintilian, felt no unease about submerging their individualities in the works of famous predecessors. However, like Plato both Cicero and Quintilian are still talking about the imitation not in the context of artistic ideals, but of education. The discussion of originality in the context of artistic ideals is a familiar one for the modern reader, perhaps a legacy of the Romantic period. However, it is more complicated than a simple opposition between originality and imitation. What makes it complicated is partly because the meaning of the word original is not clear, that it has been defined differently

---

813 Casper J. Kraemer Jr., 'On Imitation and Originality', *The Classical Weekly*, Vol. 20, No. 17 (Mar. 7, 1927), p. 13.
814 Kraemer Jr., 'On Imitation and Originality', p. 135

by different thinkers. George Steiner's distinction between two different species of originality will shed some light on the debate.

In *Grammars of Creation* Steiner distinguishes between two concepts of originality: creation and invention; the former is causing something coming into being out of nothing, *ex nihilo*, which Steiner says is cardinal in theology, in philosophy as well as in our comprehending of literature and art. There is no religion, Steiner adds, which lacks a creation-myth.[815] We don't say for instance 'God invented the universe' but 'God created the universe.'[816] In philosophy as well the investigation of the 'origin' has been a vital issue. Pre-Socratics attempt to explain the element of the universe through one of the four elements water, air, fire or earth, while Plato claims that something changing cannot be the element of the universe since it belongs to the sensual world, so that there must be an unchanging Being or Cause of the universe. Leibniz's theory of the principle of sufficient reason, we have seen, claims that all beings are absolutely determined by the will of God, meaning that, there are only singularities and that there cannot be two entities alike, that everything in the universe is original. Bergson occupies himself with the élan of creativity. No less than theology and philosophy the concept of creation is an important phenomenon in literature and art. Especially Romantics who occupied themselves more than any other era with originality, yet, originality as creation, were hostile to repetitive modes of writing; they were merely imitations. The speech genres like pastiche, parody were strongly devalued. The reason for such an obsession, scholars agree,[817] lies in the historical context, i.e. it can be regarded as a response to growing mass industrialisation through Europe. With the rise of mechanical reproduction the preservation of art and creativity became vital; imitations were given little value. In relation to this there emerges the idea that human soul must struggle in a world full of machinery. Thus Romantic poetry becomes a tool for self-discovery. Moreover, there is an awareness of the rise of mass-culture, of the tradition thanks to the inventions of paper and press. There emerges, Thomas McFarland writes, 'an intellectual fear of inundation by masses of books.'[818]

---

815 George Steiner, *Grammars of Creation* (London: Faber and Faber, 2001), p. 14.
816 Steiner, *Grammars*, p. 13
817 See Jessica Millen, 'Romantic Creativity and the Ideal of Originality: A Contextual Analysis,' *Cross-sections*, Volume VI 2010, pp. 91-104; Thomas McFarland, 'The Originality Paradox,' *New Literary History*, Vol. 5, No. 3, History and Criticism: I (Spring, 1974), pp. 447-476.
818 McFarland, 'Originality Paradox', p. 453

At the other end of the spectrum we have the theories of originality based on invention or recombination. These theories reject the possibility of writing something out of nothing, of being uninfluenced by any other work (intertextuality). According to these theories an original writer or artist is someone who merely rearranges things which are already there, though rearranges in a rather ingenious way. Invention is nothing to do with inspiration but with 'the hard work and skill that are required to shape influencing factors' into art.[819]

In his famous article 'Tradition and the Individual Talent'[820] it seems that T. S. Eliot holds on to an idea of originality but is swinging towards the theory of originality based on invention. He claims that when we praise a poet we have a tendency to look for a kind of individuality and originality, the difference from his predecessors, especially his immediate predecessors. However, Eliot adds 'if we approach a poet without this prejudice we shall often find that not only the best, but the most individual parts of his work may be those in which the dead poets, his ancestors, assert their immortality most vigorously.'[821]

> No poet, no artist of any art, has his complete meaning alone. His significance, his appreciation is the appreciation of his relation to the dead poets and artists. You cannot value him alone; you must set him, for contrast and comparison, among the dead. I mean this as a principle of aesthetic, not merely historical, criticism. The necessity that he shall conform, that he shall cohere, is not one-sided; what happens when a new work of art is created is something that happens simultaneously to all the works of art which preceded it. The existing monuments form an ideal order among themselves, which is modified by the introduction of the new (the really new) work of art among them. The existing order is complete before the new work arrives; for order to persist after the supervention of novelty, the *whole* existing order must be, if ever so slightly, altered; and so the relations, proportions, values of each work of art toward the whole are readjusted; and this is conformity between the old and the new.[822]

In other words, Eliot is pointing out the originality paradox. That is to say, in order to call something new or original a recognition is necessary, such a recognition can come only from already existing knowledge, namely tradition. According to McFarland any attempt to solve this paradox is in vain, it leads to nothingness.[823]

---

819 Millen, 'Romantic Creativity', p. 99
820 T. S. Eliot, 'Tradition and the Individual Talent', *Perspecta*, Vol. 19, MIT, 1982, pp. 36-42.
821 Eliot, 'Tradition and the Individual', p. 37
822 Eliot, 'Tradition and the Individual', p. 37
823 McFarland, 'Originality Paradox', p. 448

In *Anxiety of Influence* Bloom argues that poetry as a literary expression is nothing other than an anxiety concerning the difficulty of originality. 'A poem', he asserts, 'is not an overcoming of anxiety but is that anxiety.' In other words, poetry 'is the anxiety of influence, is misprision, is a discipline perverseness.'[824] Bloom's analysis introduces another dimension: the relationship between the poet and his precursors is similar to that of between the father and the son. Bloom sees the poetic misprision as Freudian defence mechanism. We have seen that Gürle claims that the early Republic novelists, that is to say, 'the fatherless sons of the Ottoman Empire' became 'very rigid fathers themselves in order to create a nation out of the remains of the dying monarchy.'[825] Probably Bloom would see this as a healthy state; after all, it is good to be able to kill the father. However, in Bloom's analysis the son/the poet can achieve originality precisely by learning to protect himself, i.e. by misreading her predecessors.

Now, we should be careful here for as Agata Bielik-Robson warns us, any identification of Bloom's analysis of the son/poet with the Oedipal conflict would miss the point. Bielik-Robson argues that for Bloom:

> the Oedipal struggle is merely a figure for a more fundamental, agonistic attitude that can hardly be grasped in its literal state: a troped, indirect expression of the most elemental fantasy-wish 'to become distinct', to be singular beyond the levelling context of endless repetition, and not to be conflated with anybody else, not to be a copy or replica.[826]

This struggle is a distinctive feature of the romantic consciousness. As Bielik-Robson emphasises Bloom is not, in fact, the first who conducts a psychoanalysis of romantic consciousness, however, he is the first critic who 'saw a perverse unity in the romantic soul.'[827] Already in *Deceit, Desire and, the Novel* (1961) Girard introduces the idea of the romantic lie which is central in Bloom's *The Anxiety of Influence* (1973), however, the two authors' difference is too vital to be ignored: 'Girard acts as a structuralist defender of truth, while Bloom, already showing his Nietzschean penchant for emphasising the mendacity of literature, takes the

---

824 Harold Bloom, *The Anxiety of Influence* (Oxford: Oxford University Press, 1997), pp. 94-95.
825 Gürle, *Oğuz Atay's Dialogue*, p. 90
826 Agata Bielik-Robson, *The Saving Lie: Harold Bloom and Deconstruction* (Illinois: Northwestern University Press, 2011), p. 84.
827 Bielik-Robson, *The Saving Lie*, p. 62

romantic lie at its face value and puts it in the centre of his theory of poetic revision.'[828] What is a romantic lie?

Girard 'accuses the romantics of creating a fiction of an autonomous self whose sole function consists in concealing the truth of their real dependence on others.'[829] As opposed to this, says Girard, we have 'literary truth' which is more honest for it does not conceal or attempt to conceal the condition of modern man whose wishes are never original but the copies or desires of other people: 'Unlike the romantics and neo romantics a Cervantes, a Stendhal, and a Flaubert reveal the truth of desire in their novels. But this truth remains hidden at the heart of its revelation.'[830] Girard says: 'A vaniteux will desire any object so long as he is convinced that it is already desired by another whom he admires. The mediator here is a rival.'[831] Among in others like Dostoyevsky, Flaubert and Cervantes, we encounter one of the finest examples of 'literary truth' in Proust: '"recapturing the past" is to welcome a truth which most men spend their lives trying to escape, to recognize that one has always copied Others in order to seem original in their eyes and in one's own.'[832] The hero wants to become the other, and, yet, still be himself.

Bloom transforms this Girardian static scheme into a dialectical mechanism, in other words, in this revised or 'corrected' version of Girardian analysis we have a more dynamic structure where truth and lie coexist.[833] In 'The Breaking of Form' Bloom argues that there is such a phenomenon as anxiety, it is universal, and it becomes more acute in modern times in which the notion of the independent individuals becomes vital. This is where, as Bielik-Robson shows, the crucial difference between Girard and Bloom lies: 'Bloom's argument…combines a universalistic, anthropological approach with a typically modern feel for historical change.'[834]

> Modernity brings two such dramatic changes. It promotes Cartesian individualism which is ontologically hostile to any idea of influence. Second, it unleashes a process of secularisation and disenchantment which deprives influence of its former transcendental aura and turns it into a shameful malaise: a pathological Particular which cannot fully assert its single status, for it is always engendered by omnipresent reduction.[835]

---

828 Bielik-Robson, *The Saving Lie*, p. 63
829 Bielik-Robson, *The Saving Lie*, p. 63
830 Girard, *Deceit, Desire*, p. 15
831 Girard, *Deceit, Desire*, p. 7
832 Girard, *Deceit, Desire*, p. 38
833 Bielik-Robson, *The Saving Lie*, p. 64
834 Bielik-Robson, *The Saving Lie*, p. 65
835 Bielik-Robson, *The Saving Lie*, p. 65

In modern times the anxiety of influence becomes an irremediable pathology, however, precisely because of this it needs to be concealed from the public eye. It is repressed 'into the dark regions of unconscious', as a result of this repression we see literary tradition taking on morbid forms including incest and sadomasochistic parody.[836]

However, Bielik-Robson's argument is that Bloom, by introducing repression, also achieves something else: instead of Nietzsche's modern man who is stuck between memory and forgetting, we have one concept, repression, which comprises these two, that is to say, Bloom's repression functions more like Nietzsche's active forgetting, it is both remembering and forgetting: 'By substituting the dynamic repression for the static aporia, which since Nietzsche up to de Man determined the condition of modern creativity, Bloom engages in a highly original project we may call psychoanalysis of the writing subject.'[837] The writing subject' here is to be understood as poet 'whose only pain comes from his "condition of belatedness" and the resultant complex dialectic of remembering and forgetting.'[838] In other words, the romantic 'I', far from the sovereign self, or from the 'I' that 'thinks', 'has gone through a "creatively destructive" process of psychoanalysis'[839] and now the romantic consciousness is '"the romantic lie" whose role consists in *repressing* the uneasy truth of belatedness and the anxiety of influence threatening the position of the autonomous I.'[840] Another way of saying this is that the romantic self wants to stay in the cave rather than strive upwards to the light[841] as Selim wanted to remain in the darkness, alone with his words…or some of them (VII.iii).

In the last chapter we saw that for Gürbilek, a function of comedy is to enable forgetting, to familiarise what had been unfamiliar (*unheimlich*) and create a sense of freedom. She claimed that Atay's mockery did not allow for such therapy, that his parody, imitation, digression, and irony arise from and foster an inability to forget. Perhaps Girard would replace the word irony with 'literary truth', adding Atay to his list of examples of novels which don't conceal the condition of modern man whose wishes are never original but the copies or desires of other people.

However, Selim and/or Turgut don't imitate the others or the Other, they become the Other. It is a constant movement from one Other to another.

---

836 Bielik-Robson, *The Saving Lie*, p. 66
837 Bielik-Robson, *The Saving Lie*, p. 66
838 Bielik-Robson, *The Saving Lie*, p. 66
839 Bielik-Robson, *The Saving Lie*, p. 62
840 Bielik-Robson, *The Saving Lie*, p. 62
841 Bielik-Robson, *The Saving Lie*, p. 95

I suggested that Atay was not an ironist because his sense of humour is not at the service of any truth; if he does familiarise what is unfamiliar, fearful and magical, and if this is a kind of therapy, it is not a therapy of forgetting, on the contrary, we remember even more, and through such remembering may struggle against them. The disconnected write constantly, for writing means remembering, and remembering means forgetting. What they write, however, is an aesthetics of anxiety.

Thus, against the *Ich denke* of Kant and Hegel or *Cogito ergo sum* of Descartes which give a too general account of human consciousness, the disconnected, like the romantic self, struggle for distinctness, for *Ich bin*. The romantic self reinterprets Freud's 'where id was, the ego should emerge' in favour of the 'I am', not of the ego: 'The Freudian ego merely wants *to be and to be accepted* in its attempt to survive in the unwelcoming world of universal *Unbehagen* (discomfort)' whereas the romantic '"I" wants...to be recognised as a separate entity that seizes its own chance of being in a unique way.'[842] The difference between Freudian self and the romantic self is 'between acceptance and recognition..., between sublimation and agon.'[843] And the stage for this agon is the text, however, not the writer of the text, but the text itself for 'this late and revised romantic subject is not some fantastic entity, accessible through immediate self-experience, but a "contaminated" subject, simultaneous and synonymous with its anxiety, "achieved" only in the world of texts.'[844]

I said earlier that we had to be careful about Bloom's use of Freudian language. As Bielik-Robson says Hamlet's spirit of revenge cannot be reduced to the desire for his mother, not can be it read as deriving from an erotic rivalry with the father, rather, Hamlet's spirit of revenge derives 'from a conviction that the prince, as an avenger, can restore the power of the wronged name and appropriate it for himself, and thus become the one and only, truly memorable Hamlet.' The only way to do this is 'to turn himself into a poet, his life into a "poem unlimited," and everybody else into personages in his poem, speaking his own "words, words, words."'[845] Turgut says: 'I, Turgut Özben [real 'I'], am the son of the King of Denmark.' Turgut does not want to be Hamlet-the-son or Selim or anyone else. Selim commits suicide, withdraws from life completely, whereas Turgut writes *The Disconnected*. By writing he becomes other than Selim.

---

842 Bielik-Robson, *The Saving Lie*, p. 85
843 Bielik-Robson, *The Saving Lie*, p. 85
844 Bielik-Robson, *The Saving Lie*, p. 88
845 Bielik-Robson, *The Saving Lie*, p. 88

I said that Atay's subjects *perhaps* might be called the romantic self, as we encounter both the theme belatedness and the desire to become someone unique; however, Atay's language resists against any interpretation, as such any interpretation becomes only partial. This is why at the beginning I called Atay's position one of ambivalence, infinite ambivalence.

VIII.vi. Originality: The Act of Reading

For the novelists of the early Turkish Republic, fatherless sons of the Ottoman-Empire, the task was to forget the tradition and to create something out of nothing. If despite their differences Eliot, Girard and Bloom all saw an unavoidable continuity between the individual and tradition, for Atay tradition with its political, cultural, social and historical dimensions, is something that one cannot dismiss of forget, a necessary burden. His solution to the difficulty this presented in Turkey was to draw upon the tradition of the novel itself, one that transcends national differences. According to Milan Kundera this tradition is not a world-wide or universal tradition, it is a European one. Different nations took the initiative at different phases of its development, France with Rabelais, Spain with Cervantes, England in the eighteenth century, Germany with Goethe, then the twentieth century: Kafka, Musil, Broch, and Gombrowicz.[846]

Gürbilek claims that literary criticism in Turkey is mostly directed at what Turkish literature lacks. The criticism of lack, Gürbilek argues, is torn between two extremes: 'The first one assumes that what is original is elsewhere ("outside," namely in the West) while the second insists that we do have an authentic literature and a genuine native thought but in order to appreciate it we have to leave aside all those lifeless imitations and snobbish efforts related with the West.'[847] According to her, while the first assumption reduces its object to an import, the second assumption 'takes sides with a true self that was almost crushed by the foreign ideal, waiting for the right moment when the oppressed tradition, the repressed past, or the autonomous inner world will speak with a language completely its own.'[848] Atay, being critical of both assumptions, questions not only the idea of the 'true self' but also of the 'original' Turkish novel. Echoing Kundera, Atay says there is no such thing as an 'original' Turkish novel nor is there an original self, or

---

846 Kundera, *Testaments*, pp. 28-29
847 Gürbilek, 'Dandies and Originals,' p. 600
848 Gurbilek, 'Dandies and Originals,' p. 601

'thing' or substance. In other words, unlike some novelists of the early Republic who searched for an original Turkish literature,[849] which implies that creating an original literature must be rooted in an original national self, Atay places his novel in the tradition of modern novel. The subject matter is a common one or even a universal one: the self, or the modern self. We have seen that according to Moran *The Disconnected* is a novel 'which has turned its back on the realism of the 19th century, with one foot in modernism and the other in post-modernism.'[850] Atay's adoption of cyclical time can be considered as a feature of the post-modernist novel, whereas the subject matter, the modern man, is a concern of the modern novel. Even its turning its back to the realism of the nineteenth century cannot be seen as a rejection of the tradition. It is the rejection of the tradition of the realist novel, but this novel itself is part of a bigger tradition, the tradition of the novel. Thus, rejection in this context still implies a sort of relationship with the past.

I want to emphasise here that Atay's *The Disconnected* is an 'original' novel where originality is understood as recombination. Far from being no more than an interesting attempt of an enthusiastic reader, I believe that *The Disconnected* is a product of careful elimination and systematic thought which were inserted into the plot in a way that constitutes a meaningful whole. As we have seen, Atay's use of intertextuality made some critics come to the conclusion that the novel was not original at all, however, as I tried to show, precisely because of his use of intertextuality, Atay could create a character which lacks any fixed identity, the same tool which led the dissolution of Selim's subjectivity. Perhaps this is the main difference between Selim and Turgut: while Selim, having seen the impossibility of finding an original self, decided to perish, Turgut, more like a man without qualities, welcomes the idea of the dissolution of the subject and carries on his life, a life which means a constant movement between different individualities. Turgut's choice adds to the infinite movement of the novel. As we have seen, the chase between the writer and his characters is a paradoxical, perhaps impossible one. The paradox – maybe the game – is completed with the cyclical time of the novel.

So far I discussed what makes Atay's novel an original text: among other things the relationship between the writer and his characters. However, I should also say something about the relationship between the author, the characters and the reader. As I said before, Atay's novel does not spare anyone, not even the reader.

In the previous section I focused on the literature about the relationship between originality and tradition, the question being whether a text – or an individual – can

---

849 Gürbilek, 'Dandies and Originals', p. 602
850 Moran, *Türk Romanı*, p. 199

be original. Eliot, as we have seen, argues that it can, but an original text cannot be detached from a tradition, indeed precisely because of coming from a tradition it can be original. In 'Signature, Event, Context' Derrida goes one step further by pointing out the relationship between the Latin word *iterare* ('to repeat') and the Sanksrit word *itara* ('other') and notes that repetition involves alteration,[851] an idea that Borges examines in his short story *Pierre Menard, Author of the Don Quixote*.

According to the story Pierre Menard, a French writer, wants to write another *Don Quixote*. However, 'he did not want to compose another *Quixote* – which is easy – but *the Quixote itself*.'[852] Borges' question seems to be straightforward at first glance: what is originality? Does it lie in the composition of the words in a given language? Once Voltaire famously said that '*originality* is nothing but judicious imitation. The most original writers borrowed one from another.' According to this there is no such thing as originality at all and whatever is written is nothing other than borrowing from pre-existing texts. But this is Borges' point: Menard's originality lies in its unoriginality. A closer look at the story is necessary.

At the beginning we are given a catalogue of Menard's work in chronological order. The catalogue consists of monographs, articles, manuscripts, sonnets, translations etc. Then the reader learns that there is also a *magnum opus* of Menard. This work which the narrator describes as 'perhaps the most significant of our time' consists of the ninth and the thirty-eighth chapters of *Don Quixote* and a fragment of chapter twenty-two. Obviously, we are told, Menard 'never contemplated a mechanical transcription of the original; he did not propose to copy it, his admirable intention was to produce a few pages which would coincide – word for word and line for line – with those of Miguel de Cervantes.'[853] Even though the narrator does not tell us how, he insists that Menard manages to write an original text without falling into plagiarism, a text which consists of the same combinations of words. In order to demonstrate this, the narrator quotes two sentences from Cervantes and Menard which, in fact, are exactly the same; however, he insists that they are different in tone and style. Rene de Costa claims that Borges, the real author, by distancing himself from the narrator of the story who seems to be a scholar – and the story is, in fact, in the form of an essay – creates the irony. The narrator gives us several footnotes, in one of which we learn that the narrator, in fact, knew Menard. This adds to the joke, in such a way that when it was first

---

851 Jacques Derrida, 'Signature, Event, Context', in *A Derrida Reader* (London; New York: Harvester Wheatsheaf, 1991), p. 90.
852 Jorge Luis Borges, *Labyrinths* (London: Penguin, 1983), p. 65.
853 Borges, *Labyrinths*, pp. 65-66

published in the form of article in the literary journal *Sur*, even rather sophisticated readers of Borges thought that it was an article rather than a short story.[854] In other words, on the one hand Borges suspends the authorship of the real author, i.e. himself; on the other hand, precisely because of this suspension he gives even more authority to the fictional narrator, who is none other than Borges, or at least this seems to be the case till the last paragraph where Borges the author intervenes. Even a careful reader who is rather familiar with Borges' traps cannot stop being suspicious about the real author, and in relation to this, about whether there was actually a Menard.

A similar technique is applied by Atay. As we have seen the book with the title *The Disconnected* was given to a journalist by Turgut to be published. Actually, this happens in the first chapter of the novel, entitled 'The Beginning of The End'. Thus in a way, the course of the novel is that of time folding back on itself. But this does not mean that the novel makes clear something that is obscure at its beginning. The reader is constantly left with an ambiguity: is *The Disconnected* that we have in our hand the story of Turgut's merging with his dead friend Selim, following the course of his life and thoughts and then setting them down in a manuscript of his own, or are Selim and his manuscripts and his suicide all the product of Turgut's imagination? Who is the narrator? After all it is not a first person narration, there is a narrator, but Turgut or the journalist? Like Borges, only at the very end does Turgut intervene; in 'The Letter of Özben', he talks directly; though whether to the reader or to the journalist is not clear:

> I don't think that these notes will be published. As you know, I brought this work forth as a result of a lot of compilation... If, at the end of the book, you add this short section which I could not place among the notes for fear of spoiling the integrity of them – they look messy at first glance but for me there is an integrity to them – then some readers, if they want, can read it, while others don't since the book finished anyway. You will free many readers from a burden who don't like things written at the beginning and end of books.[855]

However, there is more to it, as well as there is more to Borges' point. Now, we might conclude that Borges takes the question of authorship and through it the relationship between tradition and originality to its limits but there is a third dimension of this, a dimension which cannot be separated from the position of the narrator, i.e., the readership.

---

854 Rene de Costa, *Humour in Borges* (Michigan: Wayne University Press, 2000), pp. 50-51.
855 Atay, *Disconnected*, p. 729

Borges' point might be that the originality does not only essentially or maybe necessarily lie in the text itself but also in the readership, or the relationship between the narrator/author and the reader both of whom see things from a tradition. The two writers might have written the same text word by word, line by line, however, the reader may perceive them differently. Borges makes this point clear in the last paragraph in which the voice of the real author Borges is more audible than the essayist or the narrator of the essay or the story:

> Menard (perhaps without wanting to) has enriched, by means of a new technique, the halting and rudimentary act of reading: this new technique is that of the deliberate anachronism and the erroneous attribution. This technique, whose applications are infinite, prompts us to go through the *Odyssey* as if it were posterior to the *Aeneid* and the book of *Le jardin du Centaure* of Madame Henri Bachelier as if it were by Madame Henri Bachelier.[856]

Borges' point is that the relationship between the past and the present is not only a linear relationship, but it is also cyclical. In Atay there is no Menard who attempts to write an original text by merely rewriting. However, *The Disconnected* is full of all sorts of speech genres from letters, essays, and scientific scripts to articles, biographies and autobiographies. According to Jale Parla[857] there is no dialogue in the novel, there is no variety because no one is listening to the other, everyone is talking at the same time, however, I argue that precisely because of this excess there is a dialogue between the author and the reader,[858] or at least Atay invites the reader to such a dialogue. Like Borges Atay philosophises the relationship between reader/narrator/author while at the same time questioning the originality paradox.

In *A Map of Misreading*, Bloom says: 'Reading…is a belated and all-but-impossible act, and if strong is always a misreading.'[859] Influence, means 'there are *no* texts, but only relationships *between* texts…The influence-relation governs reading as it governs writing, and reading is therefore a miswriting just as writing is a misreading.'[860]

VIII.vii. Conclusion

I said earlier that when *The Disconnected* was published it was a shock for many leading literary figures of the time for it was an avant-garde novel that breaks with

---

856 Borges, *Labyrinth*, p. 69
857 Parla, *Don Kişot'tan…*, p. 213
858 Gürle, *Oğuz Atay's Dialogue*, p. 38
859 Harold Bloom, *A Map of Misreading* (New York: Oxford University Press, 1975), p. 3.
860 Bloom, *A Map of Misreading*, p. 3

the realism that was approved and preferred by the majority of Turkish critics and authors at that time. Suna Ertuğrul tells us Atay broke the literary taboos of the 1970s cultural milieu in Turkey not only by shattering the narrow discussions about the uses of art but also by raising the questions about the modern subjectivity.[861] In that sense, it is perhaps ironic, or merely comic, that such an avant-garde novel was perceived by some critics as unoriginal.

Conclusion

According to Martin Heidegger, the modern age 'is defined by the fact that man becomes the measure and centre of being.'[862] It began when Descartes posited the cogito as the foundation of being, and ended with Nietzsche's critique of it. It is this end, and its consequences, that were our concern. I explored Nietzsche's, Musil's and Atay's critique/problematisation of the Cartesian 'self' in which the 'I' is posited as the knower of the known (subject-object separation). Descartes starts with the Augustinian method of radical reflexivity, i.e. with introspection, however, only to move from the first person experience into an objectified, impersonal stand-point. We have to objectify the world and our bodies in order to stand back from them so that we can have a clear and distinct idea about the objects in the outer world. The 'dissolution of the subject' may be seen simply as a loss of faith in the Cartesian account of the self, in the idea of disengaged reason. However, it is a not a faith that is easy to lose; and the prefix dis- does not give a negative meaning to dissolution, rather it may be consistent with a new beginning. Nietzsche, Musil and Atay are significant in that they all experiment with, and explore, the idea of a defenceless and fearless self. Such defencelessness can take several forms.

Nietzsche's ideal self can be called the Participatory Self, meaning joining the stream of reality-nature, becoming one with fate. Becoming one with fate here is not only to be understood cosmologically, but involves 'accepting oneself as if fated, not wishing oneself "different."'[863] This is also an ethical gesture, for Nietzsche celebrates an ethics which does not primarily rest on our relation with the others, but on our relation with ourselves, on the art of self-mastery and

---

861 Ertuğrul, 'Belated Modernity', p. 629
862 Martin Heidegger, *Nietzsche,* trans. David Farrell Krell (San Fransisco: Harper and Row, 1991), p. 28.
863 Nietzsche, 'Why I am so wise,' *Ecce Homo*, 6

self-governance. This is what 'become what you are' means: being engaged in a constantly continuing process of affirmation of one's own self. The 'self' is creation and interpretation, which involves the ability and willingness to accept responsibility for everything we have done, since what we have done constitutes us. As opposed to the Cartesian or Kantian or Spinozistic self which locates reason in the centre, we encounter a new centre of organisation of the self in Nietzsche: the sovereign centre of the will intensified in the vision of eternal return. In this vision the sovereign individual – be it Zarathustra or Übermensch or just the modern man – is the one who can say 'But thus I will it! Thus, I shall will it!' instead of 'it was'. Active forgetting is one of the characteristics that Nietzsche attributes to the sovereign individual who has power over himself and his fate. He knows that he does not have power over 'it was': but active forgetting means the absence of guilt and bad conscience. In other words, active forgetting does not mean covering things, or 'forgetting' them literally, instead, it is, almost in a therapeutic way, remembering even more, remembering to forget. This is what 'active' is about. Active forgetting means to be able to take responsibility, not to let the past be a burden to our future. This is freedom for Nietzsche.

Nietzsche often refers to literary and artistic models to understand the world. For instance in *The Birth of Tragedy*, he saw Dionysus reborn in the person of Wagner through his art.[864] In a way, Wagner, became 'the poet of his life'. However, we should note that when Nietzsche refers to these models he does not simply want us to imitate them. Directly imitating any other person, even Nietzsche himself, would miss his point. That is why Zarathustra, who can be regarded as an exemplary creator of his own self, refuses to be followed and imitated: "Now I bid you lose me and find yourselves; and only when you have all denied me will I return to you.'[865] The reason that Nietzsche does not give any description of the ideal person is the idea that no one can be a best model for me. The 'self' is not something that must be discovered but created. This activity in Nietzsche's terms is the 'art of living', an idea that we encounter in Greek philosophy, particularly in Stoicism.

The idea of the 'art of living' is related to the idea of the 'care of the self' which was a vital activity for the Stoics. The precept of 'care of the self' was a positive principle which was the matrix for strict moralities. This notion reappears transposed in Christian morality or in a 'modern' non-Christian morality, yet, within

---

864 Friedrich Nietzsche, *The Birth of Tragedy*, trans. Douglas Smith (Oxford: Oxford University Press, 2000), 19.
865 Nietzsche, *Zarathustra*, I:22, 'On the Bestowing Virtue'

a context of a general ethic of non-egoism taking the form either of a Christian obligation of self-renunciation or of a 'modern' obligation towards others.[866]

One thing, however, we did not emphasise is that for the Stoics the 'care of the self' is a social activity. Foucault argues that around the care of the self 'there developed an entire activity of speaking and writing in which the work of oneself on oneself and communication with others were linked together,' in this sense, 'it is not an exercise in solitude but a true social practice.'[867] Nietzsche's ethics, however, seems to require an absolute solitude. We see Zarathustra abandoning his home and the lake of his home to go to the mountains where he lives for ten years. Zarathustra says 'Flee, my friend, into your solitude'[868] one of the characteristics of the new thinkers of the future, of 'free spirits' is solitude (*BGE* 44). Not to mention Nietzsche's own life. Horst sees this as Nietzsche's method:

> Temporary retreats into solitude are the main part of the deconstructive aspect of self-shaping in which one could begin to dissolve one's own entrapment in a 'slavish' identity. Withdrawals into solitude would make free spirits realize how they are caught in resentment and the desire for revenge that inform the institutions and interaction rituals of modern societies. Solitude would permit someone to avoid being continually re-infected by these strong negative emotions. It would open an individual's deeply rooted line of fate and would show the means by which a 'slavish' self could be dissolved.[869]

This might be Nietzsche's method, and he might have chosen this intentionally or he might have been driven to it. In any case it is not an easy method, as our discussion implied. However, our discussion also addressed the difficulty connected with Nietzsche's style of presentation of his ideas, and we suggested that even the most exploratory and literary modes of presentation may take us to the limits of what philosophy can offer in this area. It was for that reason that two thirds of this book are devoted to the work of two novelists. We did this, not in order to say that literature can say what philosophy cannot, because it is a distinctive feature of their work that they explore the limits of literature, or at least the novel. Each of our writers, then, problematises the self by problematising the modes of presentation of that problematisation.

---

866 Michel Foucault, *The Hermeneutics of the Subject*, (New York: Palgrave Macmillan, 2005), pp. 8-10.
867 Michel Foucault, *The Care of the Self, History of Sexuality*, Vol 3, New York: Vintage Books, 1986, 'The Cultivation of the Self', p. 51.
868 Nietzsche, *Zarathustra*, I:12, 'On the Flies of the Market Place'
869 Horst Hutter, *Shaping the Future: Nietzsche's New Regime of the Soul and Its Ascetic Practices*, (New York; Oxford: Lexington Books, 2006), p. 5

Like Nietzsche, Musil regarded the idea of the dissolution of the subject as an opening of a new discussion of the 'self.' We called this simply the Transcendental Self, rooted, if that is the word, in a tradition of thinking that is Augustinian, Kantian, Bergsonian rather than Cartesian. But we also saw that Musil drew equally on his scientific training and interests, so that his work is an engagement not only with *Lebensphilosophie* but also with epistemology. Hence his insistence that 'precision' and 'soul' do not refer to antagonistic ideas. I said earlier that Nietzschean ethics rested primarily on a 'relationship with oneself', but Musil's art enables him to explore ethical experiences that involve the Other. The first two parts of *The Man without Qualities* may be read partly as a discussion and problematisation of Nietzschean ethics, while part three is an exploration of different modes of participation with the world, and with others: an experiment that Ulrich attempts to realise with his sister Agathe. This difference between the first two and the final third is paralleled by a difference between a monologic and dialogic presentation of the main characters.

Musil attempts to show Ulrich's understanding of a 'trying morality' which is open to new experiences and to the world via his description of the relationship between Ulrich and Agathe. They try to reconcile feeling and intellect, the rational and the irrational, masculinity and femininity. However, their attempt to realize 'the other condition' can also be read as a critique of Nietzsche, since although the siblings can live 'in the fire' while they are isolated, they cannot continue to live like that in the midst of urban society. In a way, 'the other condition' demands the absence of others; or at least, the absence of others with established patterns of institutional roles. Nietzsche would say, only certain types of individual, 'free spirits', can realize it.

As we have seen, Musil's 'the other condition' requires a totally different participation in the world. Each of Ulrich's attempts to become something, i.e. a mathematician, a soldier and an engineer, is an attempt by 'a man of possibility' to become 'a man of reality.' Just as he fails to commit himself to any profession, so he fails to become a passionate supporter of any particular idea. Precisely because of his failure to become something he can exist differently as a matrix of potentialities. However, by being a pure possibility, or becoming, or hermaphrodite, Agathe, more than Ulrich, in a way has no past which might be a burden to her, she is creating her present as well as her future. As such, she is a pure possibility. Or as Ernst Fischer puts it, 'Everything in her is plastic possibility.' This is where Agamben locates human freedom: the potential to not-be. The negative prefix 'not' is not to be understood as nothingness, on the contrary, there is something humans are and have to be, but this something is not an essence nor properly a thing: '*It is the simple fact of one's own existence as possibility or potentiality.*'[870]

When discussing the work of Oğuz Atay we were confronted with a number of problems that make it difficult to find labels for any positive vision that his work contains. We suggested a link with the romantic self (as understood, for instance, in Bloom's account of Plato's cave metaphor) but the suggestion here was a more hesitant one. Atay proved more difficult to place within a recognisable philosophical/literary tradition, partly because his own tradition offered little in the way of models, partly because he wilfully disrupts or plays with those ways of writing that he does adopt or 'import'.

We said that Musil stands with one foot in realism and the other in modernism, and that this is reflected in the fact that one can, with effort, read *The Man without Qualities* as a nineteenth century novel with 'characters', but also in the fact that many chapters read like stand-along essays. We saw too that the idea of essayism was not only a writing style but could also be read as a way of living. Finally, the relationship between Ulrich and Agathe offered a vision of 'the other condition' that is recognisable if marginal.

We said too that Atay stands with one foot in modernism and the other in postmodernism. Although such labels are inadequate, this distinction perhaps points to the difficulty that Atay presents to the reader, for Atay's account of the dissolution of the subject through intertextuality is a less stable affair than Musil's account through essayism. If both cases involve an exploration of possibility, Musil's ends – though it does not end – with Ulrich and Agathe's retreat from their experiment, while Selim's experiment, his dissolution through becoming others and finally Jesus, ends in suicide; this in turn gives birth to Turgut's quest that is not a quest, as a result of which Turgut becomes a novelist, not a novelist with a vocation or profession, but a disconnected novelist living in railway carriages on trains that connect people – other people – with places endlessly.

How should one finish a book that has been partly about dissolution, potentiality, unfinishedness? The first chapter of *The Disconnected* is called 'The Beginning of the End', but several hundred pages later there is a sense that we are no closer to it, with Turgut in the railway carriage. Musil's novel was famously unfinished at his death, and maybe he did not intend to finish it; the fact that after their period of experimentation with 'the other condition' Ulrich returns to Vienna and becomes involved again in the parallel campaign, and in a less detached way, does not suggest any sort of resolution.

---

870 Agamben, *The Coming Community*, p. 42

The essay, even the essay 'as form', refuses ossification, just as intertextuality is endless, and it was out of these that Musil and Atay fashioned characters without qualities, disconnected from the conditions that might makes them 'finished' subjects. One condition of their being able to do this in the novel was that Nietzsche had hinted at it in philosophy.

Bibliography

Adak, Hülya. 'National Myths and Self Narrations: Mustafa Kemal's *Nutuk* and Halide Edib's *Memoirs* and *Turkish Ordeal.*' *The South Atlantic Quarterly*, 102:2/3, Spring/Summer, Duke University (2003): 509-27.

Adorno, Theodor. *Notes on Literature*. New York: Columbia University Press, 1991.

Aeschylus. 'Agamemnon.' In *The Oresteian Trilogy*. London: Penguin, 1964.

Agamben, Giorgio. 'On Potentiality.' In *Potentialities: Collected Essays in Philosophy.* Edited by Daniel Heller-Roazen, 177-185. Stanford: Stanford University Press, 1999.

–, *The Coming Community*. Minneapolis: University of Minnesota Press, 1993

Akay, Ali. 'Oğuz Atay'da Kimliksizleşme ve *Sense of Humour.*' In *Oğuz Atay's Armağan*. Edited by Handan Inci. İstanbul: İletişim, 2007.

Alexander, Jeffrey. 'The Dialectic of Individuation and Domination: Weber's Rationalization Theory and Beyond.' In *Max Weber, Rationality and Modernity.* Edited by Sam Whimster, Scott Lash, 185-206. London: Allen and Unwin, 1987.

Amann, Klaus. 'Robert Musil: Literature and Politics.' In *A Companion to the Works of Robert Musil*. Edited by Philip Payne, Graham Bartram, Galin Tihanov, 53-86. New York: Camden House, 2007.

Ansell-Pearson, Keith. 'Beyond Compassion: On Nietzsche's Moral Therapy in *Dawn.'Continental Philosophy Review*, (2011): 179-204.

–, *How to Read Nietzsche*. London: Granta, 2005.

–, *Viroid Life: Perspectives on Nietzsche and the Transhuman Condition*. London; New York: Routledge, 1997.

Ansell-Pearson, Keith, and Duncan Large, ed. *The Nietzsche Reader*. Oxford: Blackwell, 2006.

Appignanesi, Lisa. *Femininity and Creative Imagination: A Study of Henry James, Robert Musil and Marcel Proust*. Evanston: Northwestern University Press, 2005.

Aristotle. *Metaphysics*. New York: Columbia University Press, 1952.

–, *Nicomachean Ethics*. London: Penguin, 2005.

Aschheim, Steven E. *The Nietzsche Legacy in Germany 1890 – 1990*. Berkeley; London: University of California Press, 1994.

Atay, Oğuz. *Bir Bilim Adamının Romanı: Mustafa İnan*. İstanbul: İletişim, 2007.

–, *Günlük*. İstanbul: İletişim, 1992.
–, *Tehlikeli Oyunlar*. İstanbul: İletişim Yayınevi, 1973.
–, *Tutunamayanlar.* İstanbul: İletişim, 1992.
Bailey, Thomas. '"The Animal that may Promise": Nietzsche on the Will, Naturalism, and Duty.' *Pli,* Coventry: Warwick University Press, 11 (2001): 103-21.
Bakhtin, Mikhail. *Speech Genres and Other Late Essays*, Austin: University of Texas Press, 1986.
–, *The Dialogic Imagination*. Texas: University of Texas Press, 2004.
Barnouw, Dagmar. 'Skepticism as a Literary Mode: David Hume and Robert Musil,' *Comparative Literature*, Vol. 93, No. 5, December (1978): 852-70.
Barthes, Roland. 'Objective Literature.' In *Critical Essays*. Translated by Richard Howard, 13-25. Evanston: Northwestern University Press, 1972.
Baumgarten, Eduard. *Max Weber: Werk und Person*. Tübingen: J. C. B. Mohr, 1964. Bauman, Zygmunt. *Legislators and Interpreters: On Modernity, Postmodernity and Intellectuals*. Cambridge: Polity Press, 1987.
Beardsley, Monroe C. 'Dostoyevsky's Metaphor of the 'Underground.' *The Journal of the History of Ideas*, Vol. 3, No. 3 (1942): 265-290.
Beiser, Frederick. *The Early Political Writings of the German Romantics*. Cambridge: Cambridge University Press, 1996.
–, *The Fate of Reason: German Philosophy from Kant to Fichte*. Cambridge; Mass.: Harvard University Press, 1987.
Benjamin, Walter. *Charles Baudelaire: A Lyric Poet in the Era of High Capitalism*. Translated by Harry Zohn. London: Verso, 1983.
–, *One Way Street and Other Writings*. Translated by Edmund Jephcott and Kingsley Shorter. London: NLB, 1979.
–, *Son Bakışta Aşk*. İstanbul: Metis, 2008.
–, 'Theses on the Philosophy of History,' in *Illuminations*. London: Fontana, 1992.
Bennett, Jonathan. *A Study of Spinoza's Ethics*. Cambridge: Cambridge University Press, 1984.
Bergson, Henri. *Creative Evolution*. Translated by Arthur Mitchell. Lanham: University Press of America, 1983.
–, *The Creative Mind: An Introduction to Metaphysics*. New York: Citadel, 1946.
–, *The Two Sources of Morality and Religion*. Translated by R. Ashley Audra and Cloudesley Brereton, Indiana: University of Notre Dame Press, 2006.
–, *Time and Free Will: An Essay on the Immediate Data of Consciousness*. Montana: Kessinger, 2000.
Berkowitz, Peter. *Ethics of an Immoralist*. Cambridge; London: Harvard University Press, 1995.

Bielik-Robson, Agata. *The Saving Lie: Harold Bloom and Deconstruction*. Illinois: Northwestern University Press, 2011.

Blackburn, Simon. *The Oxford Dictionary of Philosophy*. Oxford University Press, 2005.

Blanchot, Maurice. *The Book to Come*. Translated by Charlotte Mandell. Stanford: Stanford University Press, 2003.

Bloom, Harold. *A Map of Misreading*. New York: Oxford University Press, 1975.

–, *The Anxiety of Influence*. Oxford: Oxford University Press, 1997.

Blumenberg, Hans. 'On a Lineage of the Idea of Progress,' *Social Research*, 41:1 Spring (1974): 5-27.

–, *Paradigms for a Metaphorology*. Translated by Robert Savage. New York: Signale, 2010.

–, *The Legitimacy of the Modern Age*. Translated by Robert Wallace. Cambridge; Massachusetts; London: MIT Press, 1983.

–, *Work on Myth*. Transletd by Robert M. Wallace. Cambridge; London: MIT Press, 1985.

Bonacchi, Silvia and Philip Payne. 'Musil's „Die Vollendung der Lieber": Experience Analysed and Reconstituted.' In *A Companion to the Works of Robert Musil*. Edited by Philip Payne, Graham Bartram, Galin Tihanov, 175-99. New York: Camden House, 2007.

Borges, Jorge Luis *Labyrinths*. London: Penguin, 1983.

Bragg, Melvyn. *In Our Times*, http://www.bbc.co.uk/programme/p00548dx

Braidotti, Rosi. *Metamorphoses: Towards a Materialist Theory of Becoming*. Cambridge: Polity Press: 2002.

–, *Nomadic Subjects: Embodiment and Sexual Difference in Contemporary Feminist Theory*. London: Zed Books, 1994.

Braun, Wilhelm. 'The temptation of Ulrich: the problem of true and false unity in Musil's *Der Mann ohne Eigenschaften*.' *The German Quarterly* 29, No. 1 January (1956): 29-37.

Breeur, Roland. 'Bergson's and Sartre's Account of the Self in Relation to the Transcendental Ego.' *International Journal of Philosophical Studies*, 9:2 (2001): 177-198

Bury, John B. *The Idea of Progress: An Inquiry into its Origin and Growth*. London: Macmillan, 1920.

Butler, Judith. *Gender Trouble: Feminism and the Subversion of Identity*. New York; London: Routledge, 1990.

–, 'Giving an Account of Oneself.' *Diacritics*. Vol. 31, No. 4 Winter (2001): 22-40.

Camilla Nereid, 'Kemalism On the Catwalk: The Turkish Hat Law of 1925.' *Journal of Social History*, Spring (2011): 708-28.

Carr, David. *The Paradox of Subjectivity: the Self in the tRanscendental Tradition.* Oxford: Oxford University Press, 1999.

Cartwright, David E. *Historical Dictionary of Schopenhauer's Philosophy.* Oxford: Scarecrow Press, 2005.

Coble, Kelly. 'Positivism and Inwardness: Schopenhauer's Legacy in Robert Musil's *The Man without Qualities.'The European Legacy,* 11:2 (2006): 139-53.

Congdon, Lee. 'Nietzsche, Heidegger, and History.' *Journal of European Studies* 3 (1973): 211-17.

Corino, Karl. *Robert Musil, Eine Biographie.* Reinbek: Rowohlt, 2003.

Costa, Rene de. *Humour in Borges.* Michigan: Wayne University Press, 2000.

Creese, Richard. 'Objects in Novels and the Fringe of Culture: Graham Greene and Alain Robbe-Grillet.' *Comparative Literature*, Vol. 39, No. 1, Winter (1987): 58-73 Canetti, Elias. *Auto da fé.* London: Picador, 1978.

Crooke, William. *Mysticism as Modernity: Nationalism and The Irrational in Hermann Hesse, Robert Musil, and Max Frisch.* Oxford; New York: Peter Lang, 2008.

Curley, Edwin. *Behind the Geometrical Method: A Reading of Spinoza's Ethics.* Princeton, NJ: Princeton University Press, 1988.

Deleuze, Gilles. *Difference and Repetition.* Translated by Paul Patton. London; New York: Continuum, 2001.

–, *Expressionism in Philosophy: Spinoza.* Translated by Martin Joughin. New York: Zone Books, 1990.

–, *Nietzsche and Philosophy.* Translated by Hugh Tomlinson. London: Athlone Press, 1983.

–, *Proust and Signs.* Translated by Richard Howard. Minnesota: University of Minnesota Press, 2000.

–, *Spinoza: Practical Philosophy.* Translated by Robert Hurley. San Francisco: City Lights Books, 1988.

–, *The Logic of Sense.* Translated by Mark Lester. London: Continuum, 2001.

Deleuze, Gilles and Felix Guattari. *A Thousand Plateau.* Translated by Brian Massumi. London: Athlone, 1987.

Derrida, Jacques. 'Signature, Event, Context.' In *A Derrida Reader.* Edited by Peggy Kamuf, 81-111. London; New York: Harvester Wheatsheaf, 1991.

–, *Writing and Difference.* London: Routledge, 2001.

Descartes, Rene. *Meditations on the First Philosophy.* Translated by John Cottingham. Cambridge: Cambridge University Press, 1986.

Dostoyevsky, Fyodor. *Notes from the Underground.* London: Penguin, 1985.

–, *The Double.* London: Penguin, 1985.

Durkheim, Emile. *Suicide*. London: Routledge, 2002.
Ecevit, Yıldız. *"Ben Buradayım...."*: *Oğuz Atay'ın Biyografik ve Kurmaca Dünyası*. İstanbul: İletişim Yayınları, 2005.
Eliade, Mircea. *The myth of the Eternal Return, or, Cosmos and History*. Translated by Willard R. Trask. Princeton: Princeton University Press, 1971.
Eliot, T. S. 'Tradition and the Individual Talent.' *Perspecta*, Vol. 19, MIT (1982): 36-42.
Elveton, R. O. 'Nietzsche's Stoicism: The Depts are Inside.' In *Nietzsche and Antiquity*. Edited by Paul Bishop. Rochester, NY; Woodbridge, Suffolk: Camden House, 2004.
Ertuğrul, Suna. "Belated Modernity and Modernity as Belatedness in *Tutunamayanlar*," *The South Atlantic Quarterly* 102, No. 2/3, Spring/Summer (2003): 629-45.
Euripides. *The Bacchae and Other Plays*. Translated by Philip Vellacott. London: Penguin, 1973.
Foucault, Michel. *A History of Sexuality: The Uses of Pleasure*. New York: Pantheon, 1986.
–, 'Nietzsche, Genealogy, History.' In *Aesthetics*, Vol. II. Edited by James D. Faubion, 369-93. London: Penguin, 2000.
–, *The Hermeneutics of the Subject*. New York: Palgrave Macmillan, 2005.
–, 'The Cultivation of the Self.' In *History of Sexuality*, Vol 3, 39-68. New York: Vintage Books, 1986.
–, 'Technologies of the self.' In *Technologies of the Self: A Seminar with Michel Foucault*. Edited by Luther H. Martin, Huck Gutman, Patrick H. Hutton, 16-50. London: Tavistock, 1988.
–, 'Technologies of the Self.' In *Ethics, Subjectivity and Truth*. Edited by Paul Rabinow, 223-251. New York: The New Press, 1997.
–, 'What is Enlightenment?' In *The Foucault Reader*. Edited by Paul Rabinow, 32-50. London: Penguin, 1991.
Freud, Sigmund. *The Uncanny*. London: Penguin, 2003.
Frisch, Max. *I'm not Stiller*. Translated by Michael Bullock. London: Penguin, 1982.
Gilman, Sander L. *Nietzschean Parody: an Introduction to Reading Nietzsche*. Aurora, Colo.: Davies Group, 2001.
Girard, René. *Deceit, Desire, and the Novel: Self and Other in Literary Structure*. Translated By Yvonne Freccero. Baltimore; London: John Hopkins University Press, 1976.
Goldman, Harvey. *Max Weber and Thomas Mann: Calling and the Shaping of the Self*. Berkeley; Los Angeles; London: University of California Press, 1988.

Görner, Rüdiger. 'Reception without Qualities': Robert Musil's Impact on Austrian and German Writers.' In *A Companion to the Works of Robert Musil*. Edited by Philip Payne, Graham Bartram, Galin Tihanov, 395-408. New York: Camden House, 2007.

Grosz, Elizabeth. 'Histories of a Feminist Future.' *Signs*. Vol. 25, No. 4, Feminisms at a Millennium Summer (2000): 1017-21.

Gürbilek, Nurdan. 'Dandies and Originals: Authenticity, Belatedness and Turkish Novel,' *The South Atlantic Quarterly*, Volume 102, Number 2/3, Spring/Summer, Duke University Press (2003): 599-628.

–, *Ev Ödevi*. İstanbul: Metis Yayınları, 1998.

–, 'Kemalizmin Delisi Oğuz Atay.' In *Oğuz Atay'a Armağan*. Edited by Handan İnci, 241-55. İstanbul: İletişim, 2008.

Gürle, Meltem. *Oğuz Atay's Dialogue with the Western Canon*. PhD. diss., Boğaziçi University, 2008.

Hacking, Ian. *The Emergence of Probability*. Cambridge: Cambridge University Press, 2007.

Hatab, Lawrence.J. 'Breaking the Contract Theory: The Individual and the Law in Nietzsche's *Genealogy.*' In *Nietzsche, Power and Politics*. Edited by Hermann W. Siemens and Vasti Roodt, 169-90. Berlin; New York. 2008.

Havelock, Eric A. *Preface to Plato*. London: Belknap, 1982.

Hegel, Georg Wilhelm Friedrich. *Phenomenology of Spirit*. Translated by A.V. Miller. Oxford: Oxford University Press, 1977.

Heidegger, Martin. *Nietzsche*. Translated by David Farrell Krell. San Fransisco: Harper and Row, 1991.

Heller, Erich. *Thomas Mann: the Ironic German*. Cambridge: The Cambridge University Press, 1981.

Herf, Jeffrey. *Reactionary Modernism*. Cambridge: Cambridge University Press, 1984.

Herity, Emer. 'Robert Musil and Nietzsche.' *The Modern Language Review*, Vol. 86, No. 4 October (1991): 911-923.

Hesse, Hermann. *Steppen Wolf*, trans. by Basil Creighton. Harmondswort, Penguin Books, 1965.

Hofmannsthal, Hugo von. 'The Letter of Lord Chandos.' In *Selected Prose*, New York: Pantheon Books, 1952.

Homer. *The Odyssey*. London: Penguin, 1964.

Hume, David. *A Treatise of Human Nature*. Oxford: Clarendon, 1978.

Hunt, Lynn. 'The Rhetoric of Revolution in France.' *History Workshop*, No. 15, Spring (1983): 78-94.

Hutter, Horst. *Shaping the Future: Nietzsche's New Regime of the Soul and Its Ascetic Practices*. New York; Oxford: Lexington Books, 2006.

Irzık, Sibel. 'Tutunamayanlar"da Çokseslilik" ve Sınırları.' *Varlık Dergisi*, Ekim (1995): 44-48

Iser, Wolfgang. *The Act of Reading*. Baltimore; London: The Johns Hopkins University Press, 1994.

James, Ian. *Pierre Klossowski: Persistence of a Name*. Oxford: European Humanities Research Centre, 2000.

Janik, Alan and Stephen Toulman. *Wittgenstein's Vienna*. New York: Simon and-Schuster, 1973.

Jonsson, Stefan. *Subject without Nation: Robert Musil and the History of Modern Identity*. London: Duke University Press, 2000.

Kahrkhordin, Oleg. *The Collective and the Individual in Russia: a study of practices*. California, University of California Press, 1999.

Kant, Immanuel. 'An Answer to the Question: What is Enlightenment?' In *What is Enlightenment?* Edited by James Schmidt, 58-65. Berkeley; Los Angeles; London: University of California Press.

–, *Groundwork of the Metaphysics of Morals*. Cambridge: Cambridge University Press, 1998.

–, *The Critique of Pure Reason*. Translated by Paul Guyer and Allen W. Wood. Cambridge: Cambridge University Press, 1998.

Karlsson, Mikael. 'Reason, Passion and the Influencing Motives of the Will.' In *The Blackwell Guide to Hume's Treatise*. Edited by Saul Traiger, 235-56. Oxford: Blackwell, 2006.

Kasaba, Reşat. 'Kemalist Certainties and Modern Ambiguities,' in *Rethinking Modernity and National Identity in Turkey*. Edited by Sibel Bozdoğan and Reşat Kasaba, 16-36. Seattle: University of Washington Press, 1997.

Kiremidjian, G. D. 'The Aesthetics of Parody,' *The Journal of Aesthetics and Art Criticism*, Vol. 28, No. 2, Winter (1969): 231-242.

Kleist, Heinrich von. *The Marquis of O—: and Other Stories*. Translated by David Luke and Nigel Reeves. London: Penguin, 1978.

Klossowski, Pierre. *Nietzsche and the Vicious Circle*. Translated by Daniel W. Smith. University of Chicago, 1997.

Kohnke, Klaus Christian. *The Rise of Neo-Kantianism: German Academic Philosophy between Idealism and Positivism*. Cambridge: Cambridge University Press, 1991.

Kołakowski, Leszek. *Positivist Philosophy*. Harmondsworth: Penguin, 1972.

Korsgaard, Christine M. *Self-Constitution: Agency, Identity and Integrity*. Cambridge: Cambridge University Press, 2009.

Kraemer, Casper J. Jr. 'On Imitation and Originality.' *The Classical Weekly*, Vol. 20, No. 17 (1927): 135-36.

Kundera, Milan. *Testaments Betrayed*. Translated by Linda Asher. London: Faber and Faber, 1995.

Lampert, Jay. *Deleuze and Guattari's Philosophy of History*. London: Continuum, 2006.

Lane, Melissa. 'Reconsidering Socratic Irony.' In *The Cambridge Companion to Socrates*. Edited by Donald R. Morrison, 237-260. Cambridge: Cambridge University Press, 2011.

Lash, Scott. 'Life (Vitalism).' *Theory, Culture & Society*. 23: 323 (2006): 323-329.

Lebovic, Nitzan, 'The Beauty and Terror of Lebensphilosophie: Ludwig Klages, Walter Benjamin, and Alfred Baeumler.' *South Central Review*, Vol. 23, No.1, Spring (2006): 23-39.

Leibniz, Gottfried Wilhelm. *Discourse on Metaphysics and Related Writings*. Manchester: Manchester University Press, 1988.

Lenin, Vladimir Ilyich. *What is to be done?* London: Penguin, 1988.

Levinas, Emmanuel. *Totality and Infinity*. Boston; London: Kluwer, Dordrecht, 1991.

Levy, Eric C. *Hamlet and the Rethinking of Man*. Cranbury: Associated University Presses, 2008.

Lincoln, Bruce. *Discourse and the Construction of society: Comparative Studies of Myth, Rituals, and Classification*. New York: Oxford University Press, 1989.

Lloyd, Genevieve. *Routledge Philosophy Guidebook to Spinoza and Ethics*. London; New York: Routledge, 1996.

Loeb, Paul S. 'Finding the Übermensch in Nietzsche's *Genealogy of Morality*.' In *Nietzsche's On the Genealogy of Morals*. Edited by Christa D. Acampora, 163-77 Oxford: Rowman Littlefield, 2006.

Löwith, Karl. *Meaning in History*. Chicago; London: The University of Chicago Press, 1949.

Luft, David. *Eros and Inwardness in* Vienna: *Weininger, Musil, Doderer*. Chicago; London: University of Chicago Press, 2003.

–, *Robert Musil and the Crisis of European Culture 1880-1942*. Berkeley; Los Angeles; London: University of California Press, 1984.

Lukács, Georg. *Soul and Form*. Translated by Anna Bostock. London: Merlin Press, 1974.

–, *The Theory of the Novel*. Translated by Anna Bostock. Cambridge; Mass.: MIT, 1971.

MacIntyre, Alasdair. *After Virtue: A Study in Moral Theory*. London: Duckworth, 1981.

Mann, Thomas. *Essays of Three Decades*. London: Secker and Warburg, 1947.
Mannheim, Karl. *Ideology and Utopia: An Introduction to the Sociology of Knowledge*. London: Routledge and Kegan Paul, 1966.
Mansel, Philip. *Levant*. London: John Murray, 2010.
Marin, Lou. 'Can we save true dialogue in an Age of Mistrust? The encounter of Dag Hammarskjöld and Martin Buber.' *Critical Currents*, 8 January (2010): 45-47.
Martyr, St. Justin. 'Dialogue with Trypho.' In *The Fathers of the Church*. Translated by Thomas B. Falls, 147-369. Washington: The Catholic University of America Press, 1948.
McBride, Patrizia. 'On the Utility of Art for Politics: Musil's "Armed Truce of Ideas."' *The German Quarterly*. Vol. 73, No. 4, Autumn (2000): 366-86.
–, *The Void of Ethics: Robert Musil and the Experience of Modernity*. Illinois: Northwestern University Press, 2006.
McDonald, Fritz J. 'Chris M. Korsgaard, *The Constitution of Agency*.' *Ethical Theory and Moral Practice*, 13 (2010): 235-36.
McFarland, Thomas. 'The Originality Paradox.' *New Literary History*, Vol. 5, No. 3, History and Criticism: I, Spring (1974): 447-76.
Mehigan, Tim. *The Critical Response to Robert Musil's The Man without Qualities*. New York: Camden House, 2003.
Millen, Jessica. 'Romantic Creativity and the Ideal of Originality: A Contextual Analysis.' *Cross-sections*, Volume VI (2010): 91-104.
Moi, Toril, ed. *The Kristeva Reader*. Oxford: Blackwell, 1995.
Montag, Warren. *Bodies, Masses, Power*. London; New York: Verso, 2000.
Montaigne, Michel de. *The Complete Essays*. Translated by M. A. Screech. London: Penguin, 2003.
Moran, Berna. *Türk Romanına Eleştirel Bir Bakış*. İstanbul: İletişim Yayınları, 1992.
Moretti, Franco. *The Way of the World: The Bildungsroman in European Culture*, London: Verso, 1987.
Morley, Neville '"Unhistorical Greeks": Myth, History, and the Uses of Antiquity.' In *Nietzsche and Antiquity*. Edited by Paul Bishop, 8-27. New York: Camden House, 2004.
Musil, Robert. *Diaries*. Translated by Philip Payne. New York: Basic Books, 1998.
–, *Niteliksiz Adam*. İstanbul: YKY, 1999.
–, *On Mach's Theories*. Washington: The Catholic University of America Press, 1982.
–, *Precision and Soul*. Translated and edited by Burton Pike and David S. Luft, Chicago; London: The University of Chicago Press, 1990.

–, *The Man without Qualities*. Translated by Ernst Kaiser and Eithne Wilkins. London: Picador, 1982.
–, *The Man without Qualities*. Translated by Sophie Wilkins and Burton Pike. London: Picador, 1995.
–, 'The Perfecting of a Love'. In *Tonka and Other Stories*, London: Picador, 1965.
–, 'The Temptation of Veronica.' In *Tonka and Other Stories*, London: Picador, 1965.
–, *Young Törless*. Translated by Eithne Wilkins and Ernst Kaiser. New York: Pantheon, 1964.
Nehamas, Alexandar. *Yaşama Sanatı Felsefesi: Platon'dan Foucault'ya Sokratik Düşünümler*. İstanbul: Ayrıntı, 2002.
Friedrich, Nietzsche. *Beyond Good and Evil*. Translated by Walter Kaufmann. New York: Vintage, 1966.
–, *Daybreak: Thoughts on the Prejudices of Morality*. Translated by R. J. Hollingdale. Cambridge: Cambridge University Press, 1997.
–, *Ecce Homo*. Translated by R. J. Hollingdale, London: Penguin, 1979.
–, *Human, all too Human*. Translated by Hollingdale. Cambridge: Cambridge University Press, 1986.
–, 'Notes from 1881.' in *The Nietzsche Reader*. Edited by Keith Ansell-Pearson and Duncan Large. Oxford: Blackwell, 2006.
–, *On the Genealogy of Morality*. Edited by Keith Ansell-Pearson. Cambridge: Cambridge University Press, 2002.
–, 'On Truth and Lies in a Non-moral Sense'. In *The Nietzsche Reader*. Edited by Keith Ansell-Pearson and Duncan Large, 114-24. Oxford: Blackwell, 2006.
–, *The Anti-Christ*. Translated by R. J. Hollingdale. London: Penguin, 1968.
–, *The Birth of Tragedy*. Translated by Shaun Whiteside. London: Penguin, 1993.
–, *The Gay Science*. Translated by Walter Kaufmann. New York: Vintage, 1974.
–, *The Will to Power*. Edited by Walter Kaufmann. New York: Vintage, 1968.
–, *Thus Spoke Zarathustra*. Translated by Walter Kaufmann. London: Chatto and Windus, 1971.
–, *Twilight of the Idols*, in *The Portable Nietzsche* Translated by Walter Kaufmann. London: Chatto&Windus, 1971.
–, *Untimely Meditations*. Cambridge: Cambridge University Press, 1986.
Nisbet, Robert. *The History of the Idea of Progress*. New York: Basic Books, 1980.
Nussbaum, Martha. 'Pity and Mercy: Nietzsche's Stoicism.' In *Nietzsche, Genealogy and Morality: Essays on Nietzsche's Genealogy of Morals*. Edited by Richard Schacht, 139-167. Berkeley; London: University of California Press, 1994.

Owen, David. 'Autonomy, Self-Respect and Self-Love: Nietzsche on Ethical Agency.' In *Nietzsche on Freedom and Autonomy*. Edited by Ken Gemes and Simon May, 197-223. Oxford: Oxford University Press, 2009.
Parla, Jale. *Babalar ve Oğullar: Tanzimat Romanının Epistemolojik Temelleri*. İstanbul: İletişim, 2010.
–, *Don Kişot'tan Bugüne Roman*. İstanbul: İletişim, 2000.
Paulson, Ronald M. *Robert Musil and The Ineffable*. Stuttgart: H. –D. Heinz, 1982.
Payne, Philip. 'Introduction: The Symbiosis of Robert Musil's Life and Works.' In*A Companion to the Works of Robert Musil*. Edited by Philip Payne, Graham Bartram, Galin Tihanov, 1-52. New York: Camden House, 2007.
Pipes, Richard. *Russia under the Old Regime*. London: Penguin, 1995.
–, *Russia under the Bolshevik Regime* 1919-1924. London: Harvill, 1997.
Pippin, Robert B. 'Agent and Deed in Nietzsche's Genealogy of Morals.' In *A companion to Nietzsche*. Edited by Keith Ansell-Pearson, 371-387. Oxford: Blackwell, 2006.
–, 'Lightning and Flash, Agent and Deed,' in *Nietzsche's On the Genealogy of Morals*. Edited by Christa D. Acampora, 131-145. Oxford: Rowman Littlefield, 2006.
Plato, *Symposium*. Berkeley: University of California Press, 1986.
–, *The Republic*. Cambridge: Cambridge University Press, 2000.
–, *The Last Days of Socrates*. London: Penguin, 1976.
–, *Timaeus, and Critias*, Harmondsworth: Penguin, 1971.
Polanyi, Karl. 'The Essence of Fascism.' In *Christianity and the Social Revolution*. Edited by John Lewis, and Donald K. Kitchin. New York: Charles Scribner's Sons, 1936.
Rank, Otto 'The Double as Immortal Self.' In *Beyond Psychology*, 62-102. New York: Dover Publications, 1958.
–, *The Double*. Translated by Jr. Harry Ducker. Capel Hill: University of North Carolina Press, 1971.
Remes, Pauliine, and Juha Sihvola. 'Introduction.' In *Ancient Philosophy of the Self*. Edited by Pauliina Remes, Juha Sihvola, 1-13. London: Springer, 2008.
Rorty, Richard. *Contingency, Irony, and Solidarity*. Cambridge: Cambridge University Press, 1989.
Roth, Joseph. *The Radetzky March*. London: Allen Lane, 1974.
Rosenberg, Adolf. *Der Mythus des 20. Jahrhunderts: Eine Wertung der Seelich-geistigen Gestaltenkämpfe Unserer Zeit*. München: Hoheneichenverlag, 1934.
Schöpflin, George *The Dilemmas of Identity*. Tallinn: TLU Press, 2010.

–, 'The Functions of Myth and Taxonomy of Myths.' In *Myths and Nationhood*. Edited by Geoffrey Hosking and George Schöpflin, 19-35. New York: Routledge, 1997.

Schlegel, Friedrich von. *Dialogue on Poetry and Literary Aphorisms.* Translated by E. Behler and R. Struc. Pennsylvania: Pennsylvania University Press, 1968.

Schluchter, Wolfgang. 'Psychophysics and Culture.' In *The Cambridge Companion to Weber*. Edited by Stephen P. Turner, 59-82. Cambridge: Cambridge University Press, 2000.

Schneewind, Jerome B. *The Invention of Morality: a History of Modern Moral Philosophy.* Cambridge: Cambridge University Press, 1997.

Schopenhauer, Arthur. *On the Basis of Morality*. Translated by E.F.J. Payne. Oxford: Berghahn, 1995.

–, *On the Fourfold Root of the Principle of Sufficient Reason*. New York: Cosimo, 2007.

–, *The World as Will and Representation*. New York: Dover Publications, 1969.

Schorske, Carl E. *Fin-de-Siècle Vienna: Politics and Culture*, Cambridge: Cambridge University Press, 1985.

Schroeder, Ralph. 'Personality and 'Inner Distance': The Conception of the Individual in Max Weber's Sociology.' *History of the Human Sciences* 4 (1991): 61-78.

Sebastian, Thomas. *The intersection of Science and Literature in Musil's The Man without Qualities*. New York: Camden House, 2005.

Sellars, John. 'An Ethics of the Event.' *Angelaki: Journal of the Theoretical Humanities*, 11:3 (2007): 157-171.

Shakespeare, William. *Hamlet*. Oxford: Oxford University Press, 1998.

Simmel, Georg. 'The Metropolis and Mental Life.' In *On Individuality and Social Forms*. Edited by Donald N. Levine, 324-340. Chicago and London: The University of Chicago Press, 1971.

Skolimowski, Henryk. 'The Scientific World View and the Illusions of Progress.' *Social Research*, 41:1, Spring (1974): 52-82.

Skorupski, John.'Morality as Self-Governance: Has it a Future?' *Utilitas*, Vol. 16, No: 2, (2004): 133-45.

Somay, Bülent. 'Hamlet Kuşağı.' *Defter*, Yaz (1999): 50-67.

Sophocles. *The Three Theban Plays*. Translated by Robert Fagles. London: Penguin, 1984.

Sorabji, Richard. *Self: Ancient and Modern Insights about Individuality, Life, and Death*. Oxford: Clarendon, 2006.

–, 'Greaco-Roman Varieties of Self.' In *Ancient Philosophy of the Self*. Edited by Pauliine Remes and Juha Sihvola, 13-35. London: Springer, 2008.

Spencer, Malcolm. *In the Shadow of Empire: Austrian Experiences of Modernity in the writings of Musil, Roth and Bachmann.* Rochester, N.Y.: Camden House, 2008.

Spinoza, Baruch. *Ethics.* Translated by Edwin Curley. London: Penguin 1996.

–, *Tractatus Politicus.* Translated by R. H. M. Elwes. New York: Dover Publications, 1951.

Steiner, George. *Grammars of Creation.* London: Faber and Faber, 2001.

Sterne, Laurence. *A Sentimental Journey through France and Italy.* Harmondsworth: Penguin, 1986.

–, *The Life and Opinions of Tristram Shandy, Gentleman.* New York: Signet, 1962.

Still, Judith and Michael Worton. 'Introduction.' In *Intertextuality: Theories and Practices.* Edited by Judith Still and Michael Worton. Manchester: Manchester University Press, 1991.

Strauss, Leo. *The City and Man.* Chicago: Chicago University Press, 1978.

Taylor, Charles. *Sources of the Self: The Making of the Modern Identity.* Cambridge: Athenaeum Press, 1994.

The Bible. Oxford: Oxford University Press, 1998.

The Oxford English Dictionary. London: Oxford University Press, 1961.

Thiher, Allen. *Understanding Robert Musil.* Columbia: South Carolina Press, 2009.

Thomas, Robert. 'Milan Kundera and the Struggle of the Individual.' *Libertarian Alliance*, Cultural Notes, No.23, London (1991).

Thompson, David L. 'Body as the Unity of Action,' 2011. http://www.ucs.mun.ca/~davidt/bodyunityaction.pdf

Thorpe, Lucas. 'The Point of Studying Ethics According to Kant.' *The Journal of Value Inquiry*, 40 (2006): 461-474.

Tihanov, Galin. 'Robert Musil in the Garden of Conservatism.' In *A Companion to the Works of Robert Musil.* Edited by Philip Payne, Graham Bartram, Galin Tihanov, 117-50. New York: Camden House, 2007.

Tolstoy, Leo. *War and Peace.* London: Penguin, 1982.

Turan, Güven. 'Oğuz Atay'ın Ardından.' In *Oğuz Atay'a Armağan*, Edited by Handan İnci, 25-26. Istanbul: İletişim, 2008.

Turner, Bryan S. 'Periodization and Politics in the Postmodern. In *Theories of Modernity and Postmodernity.* Edited by Bryan S. Turner, 1-14. London; Newbury Park; New Delhi: Sage, 1990.

Turner, Charles. *Investigating Sociological Theory.* London: Sage, 2010.

UNESCO http://portal.unesco.org/culture/en/ev.php-URLID=19184&URL DO=DO TOPIC&URLSECTION=201.html

Ure, Michael. 'Nietzsche's Free Spirit Trilogy and Stoic Therapy,' *Journal of Nietzsche Studies,* 38, Autumn, (2009): 60-84.

Vasile, Mihai D. 'Logos' Life from Plato to the Teachings of Early Christian Doctrine.' http: // cogito.ucdc.ro/nr_2v2/LOGOS/pdf

Vattimo, Gianni. *Dialogue with Nietzsche.* Translated by William McCuaig. New York: Columbia University Press, 2006

Vierhaus, Rudolph. 'Progress: Ideas, Skepticism, and Critique–The Heritage of the Enlightenment.' In *What is Enlightenment?: Eighteenth-Century Answers and Twentieth-Century Questions.* Edited by James Schmidt, 330-43. London: University of California, 1996.

Wallace, Robert M. 'Introduction.' In *The Legitimacy of the Modern Age* by Hans Blumenberg, xi-xxxi. Cambridge; Massachusetts; London: MIT Press, 1983.

Weber, Max. 'Science as a Vocation.' In *Max Weber's 'Science as a Vocation.'* Edited by Peter Lassman, Irving Velody and Herminio Martins, 3-33. London: Unwin Hyman, 1989.

Weiker, Walter F. 'The Ottoman Bureaucracy: Modernization and Reform.' *Administrative Science Quarterly,* Vol. 13, No. 3, Special Issue on Organizations and Social Development, December (1968): 451-70.

Weston, Michael. *Philosophy, Literature and the Human Good.* London; New York: Routledge, 2001.

Williams, Bernard. *Ethics and the Limits of Philosophy.* London: Fontana, 1985.

Wolf, Susan. *Freedom within Reason.* New York; Oxford: Oxford University Press, 1990.

Wołkowicz, Anna. *Mystiker der Revolution: der utopische Diskurs um die Jahrhundertwende Gustav Landauer, Frederik van Eeden, Erich Gutkind, Florens Christian Rang, Georg Lukâcs, Ernst Bloch.* Warszawa: Wydawnictwa Uniwersytetu Waszawskiego, 2007.

Yovel, Yirmiyahu. *Spinoza and Other Heretics.* Oxford: Princeton University Press, 1992.

Index

active/reactive forces 40
actuality 130, 164-167
Adorno, Theodor 173
affect 26, 39, 45, 59, 100
affection 50, 62, 85
Agamben, Giorgio 97, 165-169, 259
amor fati 32, 45, 48, 61, 68-70, 77-79, 81,
Ansell-Pearson, Keith 51, 64, 66, 78,
art of living 61, 72, 132, 226, 257,
Aristophanes 156, 209
Aristotle 9, 11, 13, 69, 107 fn., 109, 164-168, 209, 210 fn.
attribute (Spinoza) 30, 48, 102, 103, 108-110
Aurelius, Marcus 66, 77
autonomy 26, 32, 33, 37, 38, 59, 64, 103, 112, 119, 136

Bakhtin, Mikhail 228
Bataille, Georges 16
Baudelaire, Charles 131
Benjamin, Walter 116, 173, 187 fn., 188 fn.
Bergson, Henri 97, 98, 145, 149, 150, 220, 245
Bertram, Ernst 96
Blanchot, Maurice 16, 120, 174
Blumenberg, Hans 18, 67, 76, 80, 176, 177, 183, 191
becoming 15, 15 fn., 16, 17, 21, 75, 77, 78, 82, 97, 97 fn., 98, 101, 147, 160, 160 fn., 161 fn., 164, 171, 183, 216,

218, 221, 226, 233, 234, 242, 259, 260
Becoming what one is 19, 59, 79
being 9, 14, 15, 19, 27, 55, 56 fn., 67, 69, 74, 77, 97, 97 fn., 98, 101, 102, 107 fn., 108, 109, 136, 165, 166 fn., 245, 256
rational (human) being 12, 20, 30, 37, 57
Benn, Gottfried 95
Bielik-Robson, Agata 247-250
Bildungsroman 171, 172, 192, 192 fn.
Bloom, Harold 247-251, 255, 260
body 9, 39, 40, 43, 44, 48-51, 55, 56, 63, 64, 96, 99, 100, 102, 106, 133, 144, 161, 161 fn., 162, 226, 242
lived body 43
Borges, Jorge Luis 253-255
bourgeois-Christian culture 19, 23, 57
Braidotti, Rosi 160, 160 fn., 161
Bronnen, Arnolt 95
Butler, Judith 161-163

Canetti, Elias 132, 140
Cartesianism 109, 110
Cato 11, 12
causality 28-31, 35, 37, 42, 99, 103, 105, 106, 138, 165
cause-effect 23, 28, 70, 102, 114, 138, 143, 144, 174, 190
Cicero 12, 209, 244
comedy 208, 242, 249
compassion 25, 26, 59, 61, 62, 66

277

conatus 54
conscience 17, 53, 64, 65, 71, 78, 225, 226
   bad conscience 31, 43, 53, 66, 74, 78, 257;
   intellectual conscience 64, 65
   good conscience 66
Cynics 9

Deleuze, Gilles 68, 82, 83, 97, 98, 109, 160, 160 fn., 161 fn.
   Deleuze and Guattari 160
Derrida, Jacques 16, 166 fn., 167 fn., 253
Descartes, René 13, 14, 18, 28, 48, 49, 98, 99, 102, 103, 108, 109, 166 fn., 236, 250, 256
Dilthey, Wilhelm 97
determinism 45, 48, 54, 56, 58, 98, 135, 137, 162, 164
Don Quixote 183, 215, 216, 221, 226, 228, 233, 253
Dostoyevsky 183, 215, 223-226, 248
duration 90, 149, 150, 191, 220
Durkheim, Emile 115 fn.

Eckhart, Meister 123, 124, 135
Eliot, George 234
Eliot, T.S. 246, 251, 253
empathy 26, 62
Empedocles 69
Enlightenment 34-36, 112, 125, 131, 166 fn., 186, 238
Epictetus 62, 63, 66-68, 77, 79
Epicureans 9
essayism 23, 88, 92, 129, 133, 139, 142, 144, 150, 168, 169, 173, 174, 215, 227, 260

essence 25, 55, 109, 110, 124, 131, 168, 219, 234, 235, 260
   human essence 17, 20, 23, 162, 167
eternal return 27, 61, 68, 69, 74, 77-79, 81-84, 88, 131 fn., 257
ethics 11, 13, 14, 16, 17, 19, 23, 25, 25 fn., 26, 27, 32, 43, 51, 53, 54, 59, 62, 64, 77, 92, 99, 106, 118, 129, 132, 133, 137, 138, 144-147, 161, 162, 167-169, 214, 236, 256, 258
   Levinas' ethics 166 fn.
   Musilian ethics 108
   Nietzschean/Nietzsche's ethics 17, 43, 147, 258, 259
   Spinoza's ethics 52, 54, 56 fn.
   Stoic ethics 61, 62, 68
Eudemos 69
evil 27, 42, 43, 45, 59, 66, 81, 146, 222, 225, 229
   good/evil 30, 137, 141, 143, 145, 152, 157, 163, 222, 244

Fechner, Gustav Theodor 99, 100, 100 fn.
Foucault, Michel 9, 14, 62, 63, 70 fn., 97, 98, 131, 160, 162, 258
free will 30, 37, 38, 40, 43, 46, 47, 53, 71, 79, 81, 133-136, 162
freedom 16, 19-21, 23, 24, 30, 32, 37, 45-47, 49, 51, 55-57, 59, 66, 67, 70 fn., 71, 79, 95, 111, 112 fn., 115, 118, 145, 150, 159, 167, 168, 184, 185, 193, 205, 208, 209, 229, 234, 249, 257, 259
   freedom of the will 20, 27, 30, 37, 39, 45, 46, 48, 57, 59
   transcendental freedom 33, 34

Freud, Sigmund 213 fn., 250
Frisch, Max 88, 89
forgetting 52, 54, 57, 73-75, 166 fn., 188, 190, 249, 250, 257
  active forgetting 54, 74, 78, 83, 162, 249, 257

George, Stefan 95, 96, 98
Girard, Rene 83, 168, 247-249, 251
Goethe, Johann Wolfgang von 22, 57, 84, 87, 110, 140, 171, 222, 223, 251
groundlessness 17, 22, 23, 82, 125, 129
guilt 17, 31, 54, 74, 133, 231, 257
Gundolf, Friedrich 95, 96

Hamann, Johann Georg 35, 112
Hamlet/*Hamlet* 183, 203, 204, 215, 216, 224, 228-235, 237, 250
Hegel, Georg Wilhelm Friedrich 31, 66, 76, 145, 165, 166 fn., 167, 186, 187, 250
Heidegger, Martin 97, 166 fn., 256
Heraclitus 69, 97, 97 fn., 200 fn.
Hesse, Hermann 226
Hobbes, Thomas 84
Hofmannsthal, Hugo von 175
Homer 10, 76, 222, 241-243
Hume, David 34, 35, 100, 101, 103
Husserl, Edmund 99, 166 fn.

identity 9, 17, 19, 23, 50, 51, 97 fn., 110, 124, 131, 136, 160 fn., 161, 161 fn., 162, 171, 176, 184, 193, 207, 215, 217, 221, 221 fn., 227, 228, 234, 237, 238, 252, 258
  national identity 131, 208, 239
individualism 22, 36, 96, 118, 154, 248

intellect 9, 45, 46, 55, 64, 65, 98, 99, 111, 140, 143, 144, 146, 147, 151, 152, 157, 159, 163, 259
intellectualism 44, 124
intertextuality 208, 215, 227, 237, 246, 252, 260, 261
irony 171, 174, 181, 208-211, 211 fn., 212, 249, 253

Jacobi, Friedrich Heinrich 35 fn., 97, 112,
intuition 104, 145, 50, 220

Kafka, Franz 21 fn., 178 fn., 203, 208, 225, 251
Kant 12, 12 fn., 14, 15, 20, 23, 26, 27, 32-38, 43, 44, 59, 64, 65, 84, 101-106, 112, 145, 145 fn., 147-149, 167, 199, 220, 250
Kantorowicz, Ernst 95, 96
Kaufmann, Walter 86,
Kemalism 193
Kemalist regime 185, 187
Klages, Ludwig 95-98
Kleist, Heinrich von 21 fn.
Klossowski, Pierre 83, 84, 88, 89
Korsgaard, Christine 32
Kristeva, Julia 227
Kundera, Milan 92, 119, 120, 120 fn., 185, 251

Laertius, Diogenes 68
Landauer, Gustav 124, 128 fn.
Lash, Scott 98, 112 fn.
Lebensphilosophie 94, 95, 97, 98, 259
Leibniz 107-110, 172, 245
Levinas, Emmanuel 166 fn.
Lipsius 66

279

Löwith, Karl 69 fn., 78, 186, 186 fn., 187
Lukács, Georg 97, 118 fn., 171, 173, 174

Mach, Ernst 99-103, 136, 137, 149
MacIntyre, Alasdair 35, 36, 40, 41
Mann, Thomas 153 fn., 210, 211
Mannheim, Karl 126
Marx, Karl 120, 165, 167, 186, 187, 228, 229, 229 fn.
memory 13, 17, 50-52, 54, 74, 78, 82, 83, 98, 101, 249
Merleau-Ponty, Maurice 43, 44
metaphor 18, 63, 67, 73, 80, 153, 166 fn., 167 fn., 171, 176-178, 205, 232, 260
Mill, John Stuart 26, 62
mimesis 14, 242-244
mind 39, 44, 46-51, 54-56, 63, 64, 67, 68, 96, 99, 101, 102, 105, 111, 117, 119, 133, 140, 144, 148, 162, 166 fn., 213, 242
modernity 115 fn., 116, 120, 125-127, 129, 131, 140, 176, 185, 193, 199, 248
morality 10, 13, 20, 21, 23, 25-27, 30, 32-38, 42, 43, 61, 62, 66, 70, 71, 78, 92, 94, 107, 111, 130-133, 137-139, 141, 146, 157, 168, 201
    Christian morality 25-27, 30, 31, 41, 62, 70, 70 fn., 157, 257
    Kantian morality 26, 32, 59
    slave morality 25, 27, 31, 42, 43, 70
    trying morality 21, 92, 131, 141, 143, 168, 259
Montag, Warren 56
Montaigne, Michel de 173
Murdoch, Iris 16

Negri, Antonio 98
Nisbet, Robert 186 fn., 188
Novalis 97, 112
Nussbaum, Martha 16

originality 87, 215, 225, 226, 237, 240, 241, 244-247, 251-255
other condition, the 150, 151, 151 fn., 153, 156-159, 162-164, 168, 183, 200, 201, 214, 259, 260

Panaetius 12
Parmenides 97, 97 fn.
parody 84-89, 172, 181, 184, 202, 209, 245, 249
personae 11, 12
Philips, D.Z. 16
Pinthus, Kurt 95
Pippin, Robert 31, 32, 40
pity 25, 26, 61, 62
Plato 9-11, 13-15, 69, 87, 107 fn., 156, 166 fn., 177, 191, 200 fn., 201, 201 fn., 209, 222, 228, 240-245, 260
Plotinus 13
Polanyi, Karl 96
possibilities of life 21
potentiality 11, 164-169, 260
probability 106, 114, 115, 117, 118, 239
progress 16, 69 fn., 73, 82, 87, 112, 116, 139, 143, 144, 156, 185, 186, 186 fn., 187, 188, 188 fn., 192
promising 17, 52, 57, 73, 79, 222
Proust, Marcel 17, 52, 57, 73, 79, 222
psyche 182, 243

Quintilian 244

Rank, Otto 190, 222, 223
Ranke, Leopold von 76
Rathenau, Walter 122, 128 fn., 140
reality, absolutism of 18, 66-68, 79, 139
reason 9, 11, 14, 15, 26, 27, 30, 33-35, 37, 39, 40, 43, 44, 51, 54-56, 58, 59, 62, 64, 65, 79, 81, 90, 97, 98, 107-109, 110 fn., 111, 112, 112 fn., 113, 113 fn., 125, 136, 148, 165, 185, 186, 200 fn., 236, 243, 257
　disengaged reason 14, 17, 256
　principle of sufficient reason 98, 107, 110 fn., 113, 245
Ree, Paul 23, 25
redemption 74, 77
ressentiment 42, 43
responsibility 17, 19, 44, 52, 57, 59, 79, 89, 132, 133, 135, 136, 147, 158, 161, 168, 215, 217, 257
Romantics 15 fn., 96, 97, 112, 112 fn., 245, 248
Rorty, Richard 208, 211 fn., 212 fn., 213, 214
Rosenberg, Alfred 124
Roth, Joseph 127
Rousseau, Jean-Jacques 34

Schiller, Friedrich 84, 85
Schlegel, Friedrich 15 fn., 97, 112,
Schneewind, Jerry 32, 33
Schopenhauer, Arthur 23, 25, 26, 59, 62, 84, 105, 106, 108, 110 fn., 153
Schuler, Alfred 96, 98
self
　self-affirmation 25, 27, 30, 41, 43
　self-commanding 61, 62
　self-constitution 32
　self-cultivation 25, 66, 97

　self-discovery 245
　self-governance 19, 25, 26, 26 fn., 27, 32-35, 38, 59, 62, 64, 70, 70 fn., 257
　self-knowledge 13, 64, 65, 71, 171
　self-love 37, 43, 159
　self-mastery 14, 19, 25, 27, 59, 61, 62, 64, 72, 141, 243, 256,
　self-overcoming 58, 71, 72
　self-preservation 18, 29, 30, 49, 54, 56, 56 fn., 57, 137, 156
　agential self 20, 30, 57
　care of the self 9, 61, 63, 257, 258
　empirical self 104, 105, 150, 220
　Freudian self 250
　participatory self 18, 79, 106, 183, 256
　rational self 13, 14
　Romantic self 249-251, 260
　transcendental self 18, 103-106, 149, 150, 183, 220, 259
Seneca 66-68
Simmel, Georg 98, 107, 113, 116
Skorupski, John 33, 34
Socrates 9, 87, 209, 212, 234, 242, 243
Sombart, Werner 122
Sorabji, Richard 9, 11, 12
soul 9, 11, 13, 14, 39, 48, 63, 64, 71, 83, 88, 90, 91, 96, 99, 122, 124, 137, 140, 143, 144, 148, 153, 157, 163, 174, 204, 222, 229, 231, 234 fn., 243, 245, 247, 259
sovereign individual 31, 54, 61, 70, 71, 72, 72 fn., 73, 74, 78, 91, 130, 257
sovereignty 38, 70-73
Spinoza 23, 27, 45-59, 61, 67, 68, 99, 109, 165
St. Augustine 13, 14, 69 fn.

Steiner, George 245
Sterne, Laurence 199
Strauss, Leo 209
Stoic/Stoics 9, 11, 41, 61-64, 66-69, 77-79, 200 fn., 257, 258
  Stoicism 61, 64, 66-69, 257, 258
  Stoic therapy 61, 68, 69
Stumpf, Carl 99
subjectivity 14, 19, 20, 123, 133, 135, 142, 162, 217, 221, 252, 256
subjecthood 17, 152, 216, 229
substance 9, 17-19, 28, 30, 48, 49, 53, 95, 100, 102, 103, 109, 110, 164, 165, 243, 252
sympathy 26, 62, 145, 150

Tarde, Gabriel 98
Taylor, Charles 13

transcendental deduction 103
transcendental unity of apperception 104, 105, 220

unheimlich 208, 213 fn., 249
Übermensch/overman/overhuman 19, 20, 54, 70-73, 96, 131 fn., 257

Vattimo, Gianni 21, 22
vitalism 96-98, 142

Weber, Max 100 fn., 110 fn., 112 fn., 113 fn., 145 fn., 203, 229 fn.
Wittgenstein, Ludwig 80, 178
Wolf, Susan 135, 136

Zweig, Stefan 127, 127 fn.

Studies in Social Sciences, Philosophy and History of Ideas

Edited by Andrzej Rychard

Vol. 1   Józef Niżnik: Twentieth Century Wars in European Memory. 2013.
Vol. 2   Szymon Wróbel: Deferring the Self. 2013.
Vol. 3   Cain Elliott: Fire Backstage. Philip Rieff and the Monastery of Culture. 2013.
Vol. 4   Seweryn Blandzi: Platon und das Problem der Letztbegründung der Metaphysik. Eine historische Einführung. 2014.
Vol. 5   Maria Gołębiewska/Andrzej Leder/Paul Zawadzki (éds.): L'homme démocratique. Perspectives de recherche. 2014.
Vol. 6   Zeynep Talay-Turner: Philosophy, Literature, and the Dissolution of the Subject. Nietzsche, Musil, Atay. 2014.

www.peterlang.com